Structural Equation Modeling
with EQS and EQS/Windows

To Alex
and
to Mom and Dad

Structural Equation Modeling with EQS and EQS/Windows

Basic Concepts, Applications, and Programming

BARBARA M. BYRNE

SAGE Publications
International Educational and Professional Publisher
Thousand Oaks   London   New Delhi

For information address:

 SAGE Publications, Inc.
2455 Teller Road
Thousand Oaks, California 91320

SAGE Publications Ltd.
6 Bonhill Street
London EC2A 4PU
United Kingdom

SAGE Publications India Pvt. Ltd.
M-32 Market
Greater Kailash I
New Delhi 110 048 India

Printed in the United States of America

Library of Congress Cataloging-in-Publication Data

Byrne, Barbara M.
    Structural equation modeling with EQS and EQS/Windows: basic
concepts, applications, and programming / Barbara M. Byrne.
        p.   cm.
    Includes bibliographical references and index.
    ISBN 0-8039-5091-8. — ISBN 0-8039-5092-6 (pbk.)
    1. EQS (Computer file) 2. EQS/Windows. 3. Factor analysis—Data
processing. 4. Social sciences—Statistical methods—Data
processing. I. Title.
QA278.5.B97   1994
519.5′354′02855369—dc20   93-38513

    95 96 97 10 9   8   7   6   5   4   3   2

Sage Production Editor: Diane S. Foster

Contents

Part Overview:
The Full Latent Variable Model

Part 3:   Multiple-Group Analyses

Part Overview:
Confirmatory Factor Analytic Models

Part Overview:
The Full Latent Variable Model

Part 4:   Window Treatments:
A Look at EQS/Windows (Version 4)

Foreword

Structural equation modeling has a very long history, going back to the invention of factor analysis almost a century ago, path analysis about three quarters of a century ago, and simultaneous equation models about half a century ago. In my view, it first appeared as a unified discipline that joined models and methods from econometrics, psychometrics, sociometrics, and multivariate statistics about two decades ago, when Ward Keesling and David Wiley, and subsequently Karl Jöreskog, joined the factor analytic and simultaneous equations models. Karl Jöreskog and Dag Sörbom deserve a lot of credit for making this work practically available for research in their generations of the LISREL program.

In spite of this long history, even today there are no comprehensive texts that cover the mathematical and statistical theories involved, and also provide a thorough discussion of concrete illustrations with real data to cover the range of models and applications that a researcher typically will encounter. Certainly my *EQS Program Manual* was not able to achieve this integration, and perhaps no single author can cover both ends of the technical and practical spectrum. Barbara Byrne's wonderful book does not try to do everything. It concentrates on the practical issues, using many illustrations from the real world, but also introduces just enough of the technical material—as well as some new perspectives that she has originated—to provide an appropriate context. All of this is exquisitely done, as Dr. Byrne is a gifted writer. Her cheer and enthusiasm are clearly conveyed in her writing, leading one to like the author as well as the material.

In view of the historical importance of LISREL, it may not be surprising to note that Dr. Byrne wrote a superb book on it some years ago. I am flattered that she also chose to write about modeling from the point of view of the EQS program. Computer programs are integral to this methodology, because the estimation and testing process cannot be accomplished by hand compu-tations. Of course, a book of applications and illustrations could be program-neutral, but then it would be difficult to learn how to actually carry out the complex decision sequences that are integral to the modeling process. By tying descriptions to a program implementation, the choice points become clearer, and the consequences of decisions become highlighted, especially if the reader also implements models as discussed in the text on their own computer.

Why, then, EQS? If the joining of psychometric and econometric tradi-tions into a single model was historically pivotal, why not stay with this historical tradition? The reason is that history can blind as well as guide. While it is valuable to think about the measurement model and the structural model, as Dr. Byrne reminds us in Chapter 1, this may not be the most comprehensive way nor even the simplest way to think about every model. David Weeks and I decided that an equally general but more systematic and coherent way to think about a model was as a set of linear equations. Virtually all researchers are acquainted with the single equation regression model, in which a dependent variable has an equation that expresses its dependence on its predictor variables. The jump to a model that consists of a set of such equations for a set of dependent variables is not only natural, but, I believe, inevitable. Every dependent variable needs its own equation, and there are as many equations in a model as dependent variables. Variables that do not have equations are independent variables. Of course some of the equations can reflect the factor analytic model, and others the simultaneous equation model, but it is not necessary to think so rigidly. The variables in any equation can be measured or latent, or mixed in any way desired. There is no reason to restrict one's creativity.

EQS implements the Bentler-Weeks model in a particularly friendly way. To set up any model, no matter how complicated, an equation is generated for each dependent variable. Then the main new concept needed to specify a model involves the variances of the independent variables, and possibly, their covariances or correlations. Believe it or not, it's that simple!

Of course, there is more to modeling than this basic idea. As Dr. Byrne clarifies: There are classic designs that are worth knowing about because they work in many different contexts; parts of models may create frustrating problems because they are not identified; many statistical estimation meth-ods exist, and each has its own good and bad features; even one's best model may turn out to be not quite good enough, and it will be necessary to use special tools to find out how to improve it; and so on. As Barbara Byrne leads one through real data analysis, she systematically describes the many options in EQS that enable one to deal with standard as well as special modeling circumstances. This superb book will help you master the tools needed to be able to creatively and reliably apply this wonderful methodology in your own research.

—PETER M. BENTLER
University of California, Los Angeles

Preface

In the early 1980s, applications of structural equation modeling (SEM) in the social and physical science literatures were uncommon. This phenomenon can probably be linked to the mathematically sophisticated nature of the existing computer programs, which were not readily understood by researchers who lacked a mathematical background. Early recognition of this fact prompted Bentler to develop the computer program EQS, which over the past decade set itself apart from other SEM programs by offering a user-friendly approach to SEM applications long before this became fashionable. Thanks to the pioneering work of Bentler (1989, 1992a) and more recently Bentler and Wu (1993) in their development of EQS/Windows, there is now a movement to make SEM programming more accessible to the applied researcher.

The intent of the present book is to illustrate the ease with which various features of the EQS program can be implemented in addressing research questions that lend themselves to SEM. Specifically, the purpose is threefold: (a) to present a nonmathematical introduction to basic concepts associated with SEM, (b) to demonstrate basic applications of SEM using the EQS and EQS/Windows programs, and (c) to highlight particular features of EQS that address important caveats related to SEM analyses.

The present book is intended neither as a text on the topic of SEM nor as a comprehensive review of the many statistical functions available in the EQS program. Rather, it is intended to provide a practical guide to SEM using the EQS approach. Consequently, the reader is "walked through" a variety of SEM/EQS applications that include both factor analytic and full latent variable models. Ideally, this volume serves best as a companion book to the EQS manual (Bentler, 1989, 1992a) and *EQS/Windows User's Guide* (Bentler & Wu, 1993), as well as to any statistics textbook dealing with the topic of SEM.

The book is divided into four major sections. In Part 1, Chapter 1, I introduce you to basic concepts associated with SEM in general and the EQS program in particular. In Part 1, Chapter 2, which focuses solely on the EQS program, I detail the key elements required in the building of an EQS file.

Part 2 focuses on applications involving single-group analyses: these include three first-order confirmatory factor analytic (CFA) models, one second-order CFA model, and one full latent variable model. The first-order CFA applications demonstrate testing for the validity of the theoretical structure of a construct (Chapter 3), the factorial structure of a measuring instrument (Chapter 4), and multiple traits assessed by multiple methods within the framework of a multitrait-multimethod design (Chapter 6); the second-order CFA model bears on the factorial structure of a measuring instrument (Chapter 5). The final single-group application tests for the validity of an hypothesized causal structure (Chapter 7).

In Part 3, I present applications related to multigroup analyses. Specifically, I show you how to test for measurement and structural invariance related to a theoretical construct (Chapter 8), a measuring instrument (Chapter 9) and a causal structure (Chapter 11). Finally, in Chapter 10, I outline basic concepts associated with latent mean structures and demonstrate testing for their invariance across groups.

Part 4 is devoted to the new Windows version of EQS. Here I first acquaint you with the basic elements of working with EQS within the Microsoft Windows environment (Chapter 12) and then illustrate many of the graphical and statistical features available in EQS/Windows (Chapter 13). Finally, in Chapter 14, I walk you through one final SEM application and use the unique BUILD EQS option in addressing a longitudinal data problem. Readers who have the Windows version of EQS may wish to scan Chapters 12 and 13 first and then skip back to Chapter 1.

In writing a book of this sort, it was critical for me to have access to a number of different data sets that lent themselves to various applications. To facilitate this need, I have drawn all examples from my own research; related journal references are cited for readers who may be interested in a more detailed discussion of theoretical frameworks, aspects of the methodology, or substantive issues and findings. In summary, each application in the book is accompanied by the following:

- Statement of the hypothesis to be tested
- Schematic representation of the model under study
- Explanation bearing on related EQS input file(s)
- Explanation and interpretation related to selected portions of EQS output file(s)
- Published reference from which the application was drawn

It is important to emphasize that although all applications are based on data that are of a social/psychological nature, they could just as easily have been based on data representative of the health sciences, law, business, or a multitude of other disciplines; my data, then, serve only as one example of each application. Indeed, I urge you to seek out and examine similar examples as they relate to other subject areas. To assist you in this endeavor, I have provided a few references at the end of each application chapter (Chapters 3-11, 14). Finally, if you are interested in testing structural equation models related to medical or marketing research, I suggest that you read the excellent review articles by Bentler and Stein (1992) and Bagozzi (1991), respectively.

Acknowledgments

I wish to express my thanks and appreciation to those people who were instrumental in my writing this book. I am most grateful to Bill Sanders, BMDP Sales Director, for planting the idea in my head. When Bill first made the suggestion, my immediate thought was to say "thanks, but no thanks." This reaction was triggered by vivid recall of the seemingly endless months involved in my first such book (Byrne, 1989). Nonetheless, he encouraged me to think about it—and I did. Thank you, Bill, for a great idea! And thanks also for suggesting ways in which I could improve the clarity of my EQS/ Windows figures.

I am truly indebted to Peter Bentler (UCLA) on several counts—for his enthusiastic encouragement to write this book and his continued support throughout the project; for his very thorough reading and editing of the manuscript, accompanied by a wealth of valuable comments and suggestions bearing on its improvement; for his promptness in replying to my E-mail cries for help in explaining particular SEM phenomena and in checking out certain operations related to the EQS program; for providing me with the opportunity to spend my 1992 sabbatical working with "The Bentler Group," and for answering my daily list of questions in simple, nonmathematical language; and finally, for the plethora of wonderfully clear application-type SEM papers that he and his colleagues have written. Although my copies are now well tattered and torn from extensive use over the years, they remain important sources of inspiration in my own application work.

I wish to express my gratitude to Eric Wu and Shinn Wu (UCLA) for initiating me into the world of EQS and for helping me to resolve diverse computer difficulties during my tenure at UCLA; to Dwayne Schindler (University of Ottawa) for showing me how to capture the EQS/Window figures, and for his endless patience in explaining the many "how to's" of microcomputing; to Monica Brown (University of Ottawa) for her speedy production of my SEM figures (after I discovered to my dismay that working with "Draw" programs is not as easy as it looks!), and to Kathryn Lewis, Technical Support Manager at BMDP, for keeping me up-to-date with the most recent releases of the DOS and Windows versions of EQS. Thanks are due also to Judith Stein, Maia Berkane, and Michael Newcomb (UCLA) for taking the time to answer my many questions related to EQS applications, and to Leona Aiken and Stephen West (Arizona State University) for their many welcome "pep" talks, sound advice on innumerable issues related to publishing, and for introducing me to C. Deborah Laughton, my editor at Sage. Needless to say, I owe a huge thank you to THE one and only C. Deborah for her encouragement and support of this project from start to finish!

Finally, I wish to thank my husband, Alex, for his continued patience, understanding, and support—and for not giving up on me even though he knows (deep down) that my impulsiveness is likely to lead me into yet another project of a similar sort! And, last but not least, I am happy to have had the company of my yellow Lab, Amy, a constant companion throughout the writing of this book. I am certain that her demands for a run from time to time helped me to maintain at least some modicum of sanity.

—BARBARA M. BYRNE
University of Ottawa
Ottawa, Ontario

PART ONE

Introduction

CHAPTER 1: STRUCTURAL EQUATION MODELS

CHAPTER 2: USING THE EQS PROGRAM

1

Structural Equation Models

S tructural equation modeling (SEM) is a statistical methodology that takes a hypothesis-testing (i.e., confirmatory) approach to the multivariate analysis of a structural theory bearing on some phenomenon. Typically, this theory represents "causal" processes that generate observations on multiple variables (Bentler, 1988). The term **structural equation modeling** conveys two important aspects of the procedure: (a) that the causal processes under study are represented by a series of structural (i.e., regression) equations, and (b) that these structural relations can be modeled pictorially to enable a clearer conceptualization of the theory under study. The hypothesized model can then be tested statistically in a simultaneous analysis of the entire system of variables to determine the extent to which it is consistent with the data. If goodness of fit is adequate, the model argues for the plausibility of postulated relations among variables; if it is inadequate, the tenability of such relations is rejected.

Several aspects of SEM set it apart from the older generation of multivariate procedures (see Fornell, 1982). First, it takes a confirmatory rather than an exploratory approach to the data analysis (although aspects of the latter can be addressed). Furthermore, by demanding that the pattern of intervariable relations be specified a priori, SEM lends itself well to the analysis of data for inferential purposes. By contrast, most other multivariate procedures are essentially descriptive in nature (e.g., exploratory factor analysis), so that hypothesis testing is difficult, if not impossible. Second, whereas traditional multivariate procedures are incapable of either assessing or correcting for measurement error, SEM provides explicit estimates of these parameters. Finally, whereas data analyses using the former methods are based on observed measurements only, those using SEM procedures can incorporate both unobserved (i.e., latent) and observed variables.

Given these highly desirable characteristics, SEM has become a popular methodology for nonexperimental research, where methods for testing theories are not well developed and ethical considerations make experimental design unfeasible (Bentler, 1980). Structural equation modeling can be utilized very effectively to address numerous research problems involving nonexperimental research; in this book, I illustrate the most common applications (e.g., Chapters 3, 4, 7, 8, 9), as well as some that are less frequently found in the substantive literatures (e.g., Chapters 5, 6, 10, 11, 14). Before showing you how to use the EQS program (Bentler, 1989, 1992a) in the application of various SEM models, however, it is essential that I first review key concepts associated with the methodology. I turn now to their brief explanation.

BASIC CONCEPTS

Latent Versus Observed Variables

Latent variables are those representing theoretical constructs (i.e., abstract concepts) that cannot be observed directly and are rather presumed to underlie particular observed measures. Regarded more commonly as **factors,** such variables traditionally have been of greatest interest to researchers in the social and behavioral sciences. Examples of latent variables in psychology are self-concept and depression; in sociology, anomie and social class; in education, school climate and teacher expectancy; in economics, capitalism and economic conservatism.

Because latent variables are unobservable, their measurement must be obtained indirectly. The researcher accomplishes this by linking the unobserved variable to one that is observable. Thus the latent variable of interest is operationally defined in terms of some behavior believed to represent it. Assessment of this behavior then constitutes the direct measurement of an observed variable as well as the indirect measurement of an unobserved variable (i.e., the underlying construct). It is important to note that the term **behavior** is used here in the broadest sense to include scores on a particular measuring instrument. Thus observation may include self-report responses to an attitudinal scale, scores on an achievement test, in vivo observation scores representing some physical task or activity, coded responses to interview questions, and the like. These measured scores (i.e., measurements) are termed **observed** or **manifest** variables; within the context of SEM methodology, they serve as **indicators** of the underlying construct that they are presumed to represent. Given this important linkage between latent and unobserved variables, it should now be clear why methodologists caution researchers to be cirumspect in their selection of measuring instruments. Although the choice of psychometrically sound instruments has an important effect on the credibility of all study findings, such selection becomes even more critical when the observed measure is presumed to represent an underlying latent construct.[1]

The Factor Analytic Model

The oldest and best known statistical procedure for investigating linkages between sets of observed and latent variables is that of **factor analysis.** In using this technique, the researcher examines the covariation among a set of observed variables in order to gather information on their underlying latent constructs (i.e., factors). There are two basic types of factor analyses: exploratory factor analysis (EFA) and confirmatory factor analysis (CFA). We turn now to a brief explanation of each.

EFA is designed for the situation where links between the observed and latent variables are unknown or uncertain. The analysis proceeds in an exploratory mode to determine how the observed variables are linked to their underlying factors. Typically, the researcher wishes to identify the minimal number of factors that underlie (i.e., account for covariation among) the observed variables. For example, suppose a researcher develops a new instrument designed to measure multiple facets of academic self-concept (e.g., mathematics self-concept, science self-concept, language skills self-concept). Following the formulation of questionnaire items designed to measure these three underlying constructs, he or she would then conduct an EFA to determine how the item measurements (the observed variables) related to the underlying latent constructs. In factor analysis, these relations are represented as **factor loadings**. The researcher would hope that items designed to measure science self-concept, for example, exhibited high loadings on that factor, though low or negligible loadings on the other two factors. This factor analytic approach is considered to be exploratory in the sense that the researcher has no prior knowledge that the items do indeed measure the intended factors. (For an extensive discussion of EFA, see, e.g., Comrey, 1992; Gorsuch, 1983; Mulaik, 1972.)

In contrast to the EFA approach, **CFA** addresses the situation where the researcher wishes to test the hypothesis that a particular linkage between the observed variables and their underlying factors does in fact exist. Drawing on knowledge of the theory, empirical research, or both, he or she postulates the linkage pattern a priori and then tests this hypothesis statistically. For example, if we go back to the previous illustration, the researcher would argue for the loading of items designed to measure science self-concept onto that factor, and not onto the mathematics and language skills self-concept factors. Accordingly, a priori specification of the CFA model would allow all science self-concept items to be free to load on that factor, but restricted to have zero loadings on the remaining factors. The model would then be evaluated by statistical means to determine the adequacy of its goodness of fit to the sample data. (For a more extensive discussion of CFA, see, e.g., Bollen, 1989; Hayduk, 1987; Long, 1983a.)

In sum, the factor analytic model (EFA or CFA) focuses solely on how the observed variables are linked to their underlying latent factors. More specifically, it is concerned with the extent to which the observed variables are generated by the underlying latent constructs, and thus the strength of the regression paths from the factors to the observed variables is of primary interest. Although correlational structure among the factors is also of interest, any regression structure among them is not considered. Given its sole interest in the link between factors and their measured variables, the CFA model, within the context of SEM, is considered to represent the **measurement model**. Only applications of the CFA model are demonstrated in the present book.[2]

The Full Latent Variable Model

In contrast to the factor analytic model, the full latent variable model allows for the specification of regression structure among the latent variables. That is to say, the researcher can hypothesize the impact of one latent construct on another in the modeling of causal direction. This model is termed **full** (or **complete**) because it comprises both a measurement model **and** a structural model: the **measurement model,** depicting the links between the latent variables and their observed measures (i.e., the CFA model), and the **structural model,** depicting the links among the latent variables themselves.

A full latent variable model that specifies direction of cause from one direction only is termed a **recursive model**; one that allows for reciprocal or feedback effects is termed a **nonrecursive model**. Only applications of recursive models are considered in the present book.

General Purpose and Process
of Statistical Modeling

Statistical models provide an efficient and convenient way of describing the latent structure underlying a set of observed variables. Expressed either diagrammatically or mathematically via a set of equations, such models explain how the observed and latent variables are related to one another.

Typically, a researcher postulates a statistical model based on his or her knowledge of the related theory, on past empirical research in the area of study, or some combination of both. Once the model is specified, the researcher then tests its plausibility based on sample data that comprise all observed variables in the model. The primary task in this model-testing procedure is to determine the goodness of fit between the hypothesized model and the sample data. Accordingly, the researcher imposes the structure of the hypothesized model on the sample data and then tests how well the observed data fit this restricted structure. As might be expected, perfect fit between the observed data and the hypothesized model is highly unlikely; the discrepancy between the two models is termed the **residual**. The model-fitting process can therefore be summarized as follows:

Data = Model + Residual

where

- **Data** represent score measurements related to the observed variables as derived from persons comprising the sample
- **Model** represents the hypothesized structure linking the observed variables to the latent variables; in some models, linking particular latent variables to one another
- **Residual** represents the discrepancy between the hypothesized model and the observed data

Statistical theory related to this model-fitting process can be found in texts devoted to the topic of structural equation modeling (e.g., Bollen, 1989; Hayduk, 1987; Loehlin, 1992; Long, 1983b; Saris & Stronkhorst, 1984), and in methodologically oriented journals such as *Multivariate Behavioral Research, Psychometrika, Sociological Methods & Research, Journal of Educational Statistics, British Journal of Mathematical and Statistical Psychology,* and *Sociological Methodology.*

THE GENERAL EQS MODEL

As with any form of communication, one must first understand the language indigenous to the medium used before being able to interpret the message conveyed. So it is in comprehending the specification of structural equation models. In this regard, the language of EQS is straightforward and easy to understand. The basic lexicon of the EQS program is described below.

EQS Notation

EQS regards all variables as falling into one of two categories: measured (observed) variables and unmeasured (unobserved, latent) variables. All **measured** variables are designated as **V**s and constitute the actual data of a study. All other variables are hypothetical and represent the structural network of the phenomenon under investigation.

Although conceptually unnecessary, it makes sense in practice to differentiate among the **unmeasured** variables. There are three such variables: (a) the latent construct itself (regarded generally as a factor in EQS), which is designated as **F**; (b) a residual associated with the measurement of each observed variable (**V**), designated as **E**; and (c) a residual associated with the prediction of each factor, designated as **D**. Residual terms are indicative of less than perfect measurement of the observed variables, and less than perfect prediction of the unobserved factor; in other words, both represent error. To distinguish error in measurement from error in prediction, the former is referred to as **error,** whereas the latter is termed **disturbance**; hence the designation of Es and Ds in EQS. For simplicity, all Es and Ds are numbered to correspond with the Vs and Fs with which they are associated, respectively.

To comprehend more fully how this numbering system works, and how all variables in a specified model may be linked to one another, let's turn to the pictorial presentation of a simple hypothetical model presented in Figure 1.1 and examine it within the context of the EQS program. Such schematic representations of a model are termed **path diagrams** because they provide a visual portrayal of relations that are assumed to hold among the variables under study.

The EQS Path Diagram

By convention, in the schematic presentation of structural equation models, measured variables are shown in boxes and unmeasured variables in ellipses (or circles). Thus, in reviewing the model depicted in Figure 1.1, we see that there are two latent variables (F1, F2), and five observed variables (V1-V5); the Vs function as **indicators** of their respective underlying latent factors. Associated with each observed variable is an error term (E1-E5), and with the factor being predicted (F2), a disturbance term (D2). Although these residual terms are unobserved variables, typically only the Ds are enclosed in ellipses.

In addition to the above symbols representing variables, certain others are used in path diagrams to denote hypothesized processes involving the entire system of variables. In particular, one-way arrows represent structural regression coefficients and thus indicate the impact of one variable on another. In Figure 1.1, for example, the three unidirectional arrows leading

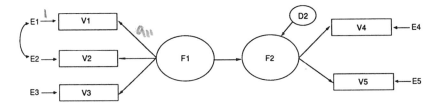

FIGURE 1.1. An EQS Structural Equation Model

from Factor 1 (F1) to each of three observed variables (V1, V2, V3), suggest that scores on the latter are "caused" by F1. Similarly, the unidirectional arrow pointing toward F2 implies that F1 causes F2.[3]

The sourceless one-way arrows pointing from the Es and D2 indicate the impact of random measurement error on the observed Vs and error in the prediction of F2, respectively. Finally, curved two-way arrows represent co-variances or correlations between pairs of variables. Thus the bidirectional arrow linking E1 and E2 as shown in Figure 1.1 implies that measurement error associated with V1 is correlated with that associated with V2. These symbols are summarized in Table 1.1.

The Bentler-Weeks Representation System

The core parameters of concern in structural equation models are the regression coefficients, and the variances and covariances of the independent variables.[4] However, given that sample data comprise observed scores only, there needs to be some internal mechanism whereby the data are transposed into parameters of the model. This task is accomplished via a mathematical model representing the entire system of variables. Such a representation system can and does vary with particular SEM computer programs; in EQS, the mathematical model derives from the work of Bentler and Weeks (1979, 1980). (For a comparative review of the representation systems for EQS and LISREL, for example, see Bentler, 1988.)

The thrust of the Bentler-Weeks model is that **all** variables in a model can be categorized as either **dependent** or **independent** variables. Any variable that has a unidirectional arrow aiming at it represents a **dependent** variable; if there is no unidirectional arrow aiming at it, a variable is considered to be **independent**.

As is customary, dependent variables are explained in terms of other variables in the model, whereas independent variables serve as the explanatory variables. Not so customary, however, is the Bentler-Weeks conceptualization of what constitutes a dependent or independent variable. Indeed, their interpretation of this concept is much broader than is typical. According

TABLE 1.1. Symbols Associated With Structural Equation Models in EQS

Symbol	Representation

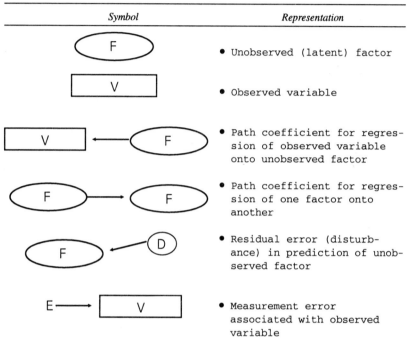

- Unobserved (latent) factor

- Observed variable

- Path coefficient for regression of observed variable onto unobserved factor

- Path coefficient for regression of one factor onto another

- Residual error (disturbance) in prediction of unobserved factor

- Measurement error associated with observed variable

to Bentler and Weeks, any variable that **is not** a dependent variable is considered automatically to be an independent variable, regardless of whether it is an observed score, a factor, or a residual. For example, in Figure 1.1 the **dependent** variables are V1, V2, V3, V4, V5, F2; the **independent** variables are E1, E2, E3, E4, E5, F1, D2.

A dependent variable, then, is any variable that can be expressed as a structural regression function of other variables. Thus, for every dependent variable, this regression function can be summarized in the form of an equation. Turning again to Figure 1.1, we can translate each regression function into an equation as follows:

$$F2 = F1 + D2$$
$$V1 = F1 + E1$$
$$V2 = F1 + E2$$
$$V3 = F1 + E3$$
$$V4 = F2 + E4$$
$$V5 = F2 + E5$$

It will be clear that the one-way arrows linking the factors to the observed variables, and Factor 1 to Factor 2, represent regression coefficients. However, explanation regarding the linkage of residual terms to their associated variables via one-way arrows may be somewhat less obvious. Although these arrows also symbolize regression coefficients, their paths are implicit in the prediction of one variable from another; they are considered to be known and are therefore fixed to 1.0. For example, in the language of simple regression, the prediction of V1 from F1 can be written as $V1 = b_{11}F1 + E1$, where b_{11} represents the unknown beta weight associated with the predictor F1, and E1 represents error in this prediction. Note that there is no beta weight associated with the error term, thereby indicating that it is not to be estimated. By implication, then, the beta weight for E1 is considered to be known and fixed arbitrarily to 1.0.[5] Similarly, the prediction of F2 from F1 can be written as $F2 = b_{12}F1 + D2$, where D2 represents error in the prediction, although this prediction involves the prediction of one **factor** from another, whereas the former prediction equation involved the prediction of an **observed variable** from a factor (hence the distinction between the terms **E** and **D**).

Although in principle there is a one-to-one correspondence between the schematic presentation of a model and its translation into a set of structural equations, it is important to note that neither one of these model representations tells the whole story; some parameters critical to the estimation of the model are not explicitly shown and thus may not be obvious to the novice structural equation modeler. For example, in both the path diagram and the equations above, there is no indication that the variances of the independent variables are parameters in the model; indeed, such parameters are essential to all structural equation models and to the running of EQS in particular. Thus the researcher must be mindful of this inadequacy of path diagrams when specifying his or her model input for EQS.

Considering the flip side of the coin, however, it is equally important to pay attention to the specified nonexistence of certain parameters in the model. For example, in Figure 1.1, the absence of a curved arrow between E4 and E5 suggests the lack of covariance between the error terms associated with V4 and V5. Likewise, there is no hypothesized covariance between F1 and D2; absence of this path addresses the usual and most often necessary assumption that the independent or predictor variable is in no way associated with any error arising from the prediction of the dependent or criterion variable.

Finally, an important corollary of the Bentler-Weeks model is that the variances of dependent variables, or their covariances with other variables, are **never** parameters of the model; rather, they remain to be explained by those parameters. In contrast, the variances and covariances of independent variables are important parameters that need to be estimated.

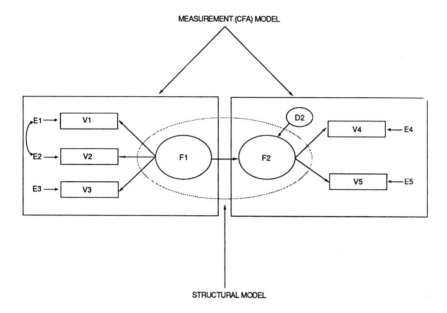

FIGURE 1.2. Measurement and Structural Components of an EQS Structural Equation Model

Source: Adapted by Byrne (1989). Copyright 1989 by Springer-Verlag. Reprinted by permission.

THE EQS CONFIRMATORY FACTOR ANALYTIC MODEL

In the section, Basic Structure, we reviewed the general structure of the CFA model and noted that it focuses solely on relations between the observed variables and their underlying factors. Because of this orientation, the CFA model is considered to represent a measurement model. For sake of didactic purposes in clarifying this important concept, let's examine Figure 1.2, in which the same model presented in Figure 1.1 has been demarcated into measurement and structural components.

Considered separately, the elements modeled within each rectangle in Figure 1.2 represent two CFA models: one related to a factor labeled Factor 1 and the other to a factor labeled Factor 2. The enclosure of the two factors within the ellipse represents a structural model and thus is not of interest in CFA research. In essence, both CFA models described in Figure 1.2 represent first-order factor analytic models. However, second- and higher order CFA models, though less commonly found in the literature (see Kerlinger, 1984) can also be analyzed using EQS. Discussion and application of CFA models in the present book are limited to first- and second-order models only. (For a more comprehensive discussion and explanation of first- and second-order CFA models, see Bentler, 1989, 1992a; Bollen, 1989; Kerlinger, 1984.) We turn now to an explanation of each within the framework of the EQS program.

Although most standard models permit a separation of measurement and structural models, it is indeed possible for a model not to overtly fit this distinction. For example, suppose that in Figure 1.2 we were to add a path from V1 to V4. It would then be inappropriate to consider this path as part of either the measurement or the structural models. Yet such paths may make sense and can be easily implemented in EQS. Models of this type are called **nonstandard** models (see Bentler, 1989, 1992a).

First-Order CFA Model

As demonstrated in the previous section, structural equation models can be depicted both diagrammatically and as a series of equations. Let's now dissect a simple first-order CFA model within the context of both formats. Accordingly, suppose we have a four-factor model of self-concept (SC), with each factor measured by three observed variables; let the four factors represent academic SC (ASC), social SC (SSC), physical SC (PSC), and emotional SC (ESC). The diagrammatic representation of this model is shown in Figure 1.3.

Portrayal of the model in this way makes it easy to conceptualize how its various components relate to one another. The four factors are easily identified within each ellipse, as are each of the observed measurements (their indicators) within boxes. The curved two-headed arrows linking all possible pairs of factors suggest that the factors are intercorrelated. The single-headed arrows leading from the ellipses to the boxes represent the proposed regression of item scores on each factor in accord with beliefs about which variables are valid measurements of the factor in question. Finally, the sourceless single-headed arrows indicate that random measurement error has some bearing on the reliability of the observed variables in their measurement of the underlying factors.

The simplicity of EQS notation makes it very easy to see at a glance exactly which variables and coefficients are explicitly modeled and how many parameters are to be estimated. In Figure 1.3, we can discern 12 observed variables (V1-V12), 4 factors (F1-F4), 6 covariances ($\updownarrow$), and 24 regression coefficients ($\leftarrow$), 12 leading from the Fs to the Vs (these represent first-order factor loadings), and 12 indicating the impact of random measurement error on the Vs. In Bentler and Weeks's terms, then, we have 12 dependent variables and 16 independent variables. Not explicitly modeled are the variances associated with each of the 12 error terms, and each of the four factors. Recall, however, that any variance associated with the dependent variables (the Vs) remains to be explained by the model.

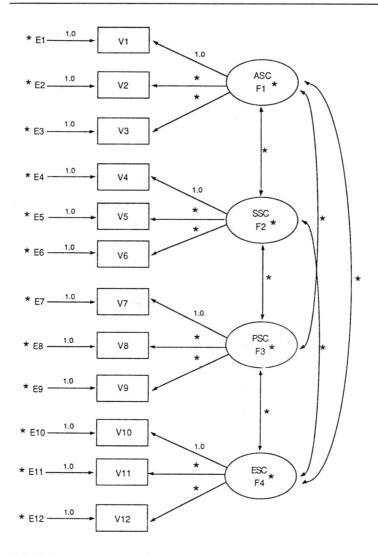

FIGURE 1.3. Hypothesized First-Order CFA Model With EQS Notation

For didactic purposes and for reasons that will become evident when we examine EQS specification rules in Chapter 2, asterisks have been placed beside all model parameters that are to be freely estimated. You will note that no asterisks accompany any of the regression paths for the error terms; as previously pointed out, these parameters are not estimated but rather are fixed arbitrarily to a value of 1.0. You will note also that the first of each set of regression paths associated with the factors is fixed to 1.0. Both of these specifications address the issue of **statistical identification,** a complex topic that is difficult to explain in nontechnical terms. Indeed, a thorough explanation of the identification principle exceeds the scope of the present book and is not critical to the reader's understanding and use of the book. Nonetheless, because some insight into the general concept of identification will undoubtedly help you to better understand why, for example, particular parameters are specified as having certain fixed values, I will attempt to give you a brief, nonmathematical explanation of the basic idea underlying this concept. Essentially, I will address only the so-called *t*-rule, one of several tests associated with identification. Readers are urged to consult the following texts for a more comprehensive treatment of the topic: Bollen, 1989; Hayduk, 1987; Long, 1983a, 1983b; Saris & Stronkhorst, 1984.

In broad terms, the issue of identification focuses on whether there is a unique set of parameters consistent with the data. Within the context of EQS, this question bears directly on the Bentler-Weeks approach to transposing the variance-covariance matrix of a set of observed variables (the data) into the structural parameters of the model under study. If a unique solution for the values of the structural parameters can be found, the model is considered to be identified, and the parameters are therefore estimable and the model testable. If, on the other hand, a model cannot be identified, the parameters are subject to arbitrariness, with the implication that different parameter values define the same model; such being the case, attainment of consistent estimates for all parameters is not possible, and thus the model cannot be evaluated empirically.

Structural models may be just-identified, overidentified, or underidentified. A **just-identified model** is one in which there is a one-to-one correspondence between the data and the structural parameters. That is to say, the number of data variances and covariances equals the number of parameters to be estimated. However, despite the capability of the model to yield a unique solution for all parameters, the just-identified model is not scientifically interesting because it has no degrees of freedom and therefore can never be rejected. An **overidentified model** is one in which the number of estimable parameters is less than the number of data points (i.e., variances, covariances of the observed variables). This situation results in positive degrees of freedom that allow for rejection of the model, thereby rendering it of scientific use. The aim in structural equation modeling, then, is to specify a model such that it meets the criterion of overidentification. Finally, an **underidentified model** is one in which the number of parameters to be estimated exceeds the number of variances and covariances (i.e., data points). As such, the model contains insufficient information (from the input data) for the purpose of attaining a determinate solution of parameter estimation; that is, an infinite number of solutions are possible.

Reviewing the CFA model in Figure 1.3, let's now determine how many data points we have to work with (i.e., how much information we have with respect to our data). As noted above, these constitute the variances and co-variances of the observed variables; with p variables, there are $p(p + 1)/2$ such elements. Because there are 12 observed variables, we have $12(12 + 1)/2 = 78$ data points. Now let's count up how many parameters there are to be estimated by reviewing the number of asterisked parameters in the model. Accordingly, we have 8 regression coefficients, 6 factor covariances, 12 error variances, and 4 factor variances, yielding a total of 30 unknown parameters. Thus, with 78 data points and 30 parameters to be estimated, we have an overidentified model with 48 degrees of freedom.

It is important to point out that the specification of an overidentified model is a necessary but not sufficient condition to resolve the identification problem. The imposition of constraints on particular parameters can sometimes be beneficial in helping the researcher to attain an overidentified model. One rule of thumb with respect to residuals is that one can either constrain the path coefficient to some fixed value (say, 1.0) and allow the variance to be freely estimated **or,** alternatively, fix the variance (to say, 1.0) and estimate the path coefficent. However, the free estimation of both types of parameters is not possible; the result will be an underidentified model. Reviewing the residual terms (the Es and Ds) in our CFA model (Figure 1.3), we see that their paths ($\rightarrow$) are fixed (to 1.0 by implication), while the variances are free to be estimated. If both a variance and the path were fixed, one would have a very restricted model that probably would not fit one's data.

Linked to the issue of identification is the requirement that every latent variable have its scale determined. This is accomplished within the specification of the measurement model by mapping the unmeasured latent variable onto its related measured variable. More specifically, the requisite is satisfied by constraining one of a set of factor loadings to some known value (typically 1.0). In other words, for one of the three regression paths leading from each SC factor to its set of observed indicators, some fixed value should be specified.[6] Alternatively, but pertinent to **independent** variables only, one could fix the factor variance to some known value (say, 1.0) and allow all factor loadings to be freely estimated. For example, one could constrain the variance for each SC factor to 1.0 and estimate all factor loadings. It is important to note, however, that the scale of a **dependent** latent variable cannot be determined in this way because the variances of dependent variables are never parameters of the model. Turning to Figure 1.3 again, we see that in order to establish the scale of the four self-concept factors, the first of each set of indicator regression paths was fixed to 1.0.

From the CFA diagram in Figure 1.3, we can now express the structural regression portion of the model as a series of equations as follows:

$$
\begin{array}{lll}
V1 = F1 + E1 & V2 = {}^*F1 + E2 & V3 = {}^*F1 + E3 \\
V4 = F2 + E4 & V5 = {}^*F2 + E5 & V6 = {}^*F2 + E6 \\
V7 = F3 + E7 & V8 = {}^*F3 + E8 & V9 = {}^*F3 + E9 \\
V10 = F4 + E10 & V11 = {}^*F4 + E11 & V12 = {}^*F4 + E12
\end{array}
$$

where * represents parameters to be estimated.

Second-Order CFA Model

In our previous factor analytic model, we had four factors (ASC, SSC, PSC, ESC) that operated as independent variables; each could be considered to be one level or one unidirectional arrow away from the observed variables. Such factors are termed **first-order factors**. However, the theory may argue for some higher level factor that is considered accountable for the lower order factors. Basically, the number of levels or unidirectional arrows that the higher order factor is removed from the observed variables determines whether a factor model is labeled as second-order, third-order, or some higher order; as noted earlier, only a second-order model will be considered here. Accordingly, let's examine the pictorial representation of this model in Figure 1.4.

This model has essentially the same first-order factor structure as that presented in Figure 1.3. However, in the present example, a higher order general self-concept (GSC) factor is hypothesized as accounting for or explaining all variance and covariance related to the first-order factors. As such, general SC is termed the **second-order factor**. It is important to take particular note that general SC does not have its own set of measured indicators; rather it is linked indirectly to those measuring the lower order factors. Although at first blush this model does not seem too drastically different from the one presented in Figure 1.3, more careful study of its structure reveals several technically distinctive characteristics that demand substantially different specifications for the two models. Let's now take a closer look at the parameters to be estimated for the second-order model.

One of the first things to notice here is that although the first-order factor structure of this model appears basically the same as it did in Figure 1.3, these factors now appear to operate as dependent as well as independent variables; this is not so, however, because variables can only function as one or the other. The fact that the first-order factors operate as dependent variables means that their variances and covariances are no longer estimable

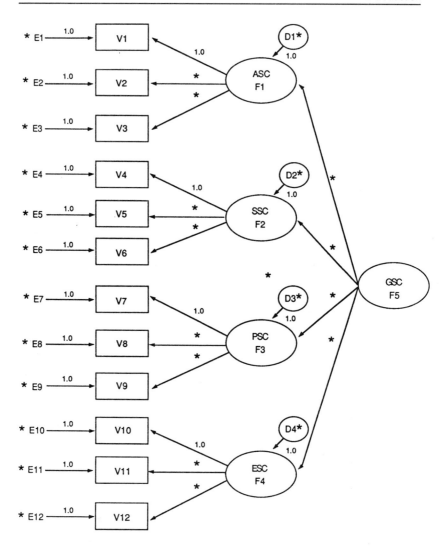

FIGURE 1.4. Hypothesized Second-Order CFA Model With EQS Notation

parameters in the model; such variation and covariation is presumed to be accounted for by the higher order factor. As a reflection of this structure, there are now no two-headed curved arrows linking the factors, and no asterisks printed beside them, thereby indicating that neither their factor covariances nor their variances, respectively, are to be estimated.

A second feature of this model is the presence of single-headed arrows leading from the second-order factor (F5) to each of the first-order factors.

These regression paths represent second-order factor loadings, and all are freely estimated, as indicated by the asterisks. Recall, however, that either one of the regression paths **or** the variance of the independent factor can be estimated, but not both. Because the impact of general SC on each of the lower order SC factors is of primary interest, the variance of the higher order factor is constrained to equal 1.0.

Finally, the prediction of each of the first-order factors from the second-order factor is presumed not to be without error. Thus a residual disturbance term is associated with each of the lower-level factors (D1-D4). In this instance, because only the variances of the Ds are of interest, the regression paths for the Ds are fixed to 1.0.

As a first step in determining whether this second-order model is identified, we now tally up the number of parameters to be estimated; as such we have 8 first-order regression coefficients, 4 second-order regression coefficients, 12 measurement error variances, and 4 residual disturbances, making a total of 28. Given that there are 78 pieces of information in the sample variance-covariance matrix, we conclude that this model is identified with 50 degrees of freedom.

Before leaving this identification issue, however, a word of caution is in order. With complex models in which there may be several levels of latent variable structures, it is wise to visually check each level separately for evidence that identification has been attained. For example, although we know from our initial CFA model that the first-order level is identified, it is quite possible that the second-order level is indeed underidentified. Because the first-order factors function as indicators of (i.e., the input data for) the second-order factor, identification is easy to assess. In the present model, we have four factors, thereby giving us 10 pieces of information from which to formulate the parameters of the higher order structure. According to the model depicted in Figure 1.4, we wish to estimate 8 parameters, thus leaving us with 2 degrees of freedom and an overidentified model. However, suppose that we had only three first-order factors. We would then be left with a just-identified model as a consequence of trying to estimate six parameters from six ($3[3 + 1]$)/2) pieces of information. In order for such a model to be tested, additional constraints would need to be imposed (see Bentler, 1989, 1992a). Finally, let's suppose that there were only two first-order factors; we would then have an underidentified model since there would be only three pieces of information, though four parameters to be estimated. Although it might still be possible to test such a model, given further restrictions on the model (see Bentler, 1989,1992a), the researcher would be better advised to reformulate his or her model in light of this problem (see Rindskopf & Rose, 1988).

Considering the model in Figure 1.4, let's now write the series of regression equations that summarize its configuration. These are as follows:

$$F1 = *F5 + D1 \quad F2 = *F5 + D2 \quad F3 = *F5 + D3 \quad F4 = *F5 + D4$$
$$V1 = F1 + E1 \quad V2 = *F1 + E2 \quad V3 = *F1 + E3$$
$$V4 = F2 + E4 \quad V5 = *F2 + E5 \quad V6 = *F2 + E6$$
$$V7 = F3 + E7 \quad V8 = *F3 + E8 \quad V9 = *F3 + E9$$
$$V10 = F4 + E10 \quad V11 = *F4 + E11 \quad V12 = *F4 + E12$$

where * represents parameters to be estimated.

THE EQS FULL STRUCTURAL EQUATION MODEL

In contrast to a CFA model, which comprises only a measurement component, the typical full structural equation model encompasses both a measurement and a structural model. Accordingly, the full model embodies a system of variables whereby latent factors are regressed on other factors as dictated by theory and observed measures on appropriate factors. In other words, in the full SEM, certain latent variables are connected by one-way arrows, the directionality of which reflects hypotheses bearing on the causal structure of variables in the model. For a clearer conceptualization of this model, let's examine the relatively simple structure presented in Figure 1.5.

The structural component of this model represents the hypothesis that academic achievement (AA) in high school derives from a student's perception of his or her overall academic competence (ASC; academic SC), which in turn derives from his or her self-perception of competence in math (MSC) and science (SCSC). The measurement component of the model shows each of the SC factors to have three indicator measures and the academic achievement factor to have two.

Turning first to the structural part of the model, we can see that there are four factors; the two independent factors (F1, F2) are postulated as being correlated with each other (as indicated by the curved two-way arrow joining them), but they are linked to Factors 3 and 4 by a series of regression paths, as indicated by the unidirectional arrows. Because F3 and F4 have one-way arrows pointing at them, they are easily identified as dependent variables in the model. Residual errors associated with the regression of F3 on both F1 and F2 and the regression of F4 on F3 are captured by the disturbance terms D3 and D4, respectively. (As with the second-order CFA model, paths for the disturbances are fixed to 1.0, thus leaving their variances free to be estimated.) Finally, because one path from each of the two independent factors (F1, F2) to their respective indicator variables is fixed to 1.0, their variances are to be freely estimated; variances of the dependent variables (F3, F4), however, are not parameters in the model.

By now, you probably feel fairly comfortable in interpreting the measurement portion of the model, so substantial elaboration is not necessary here.

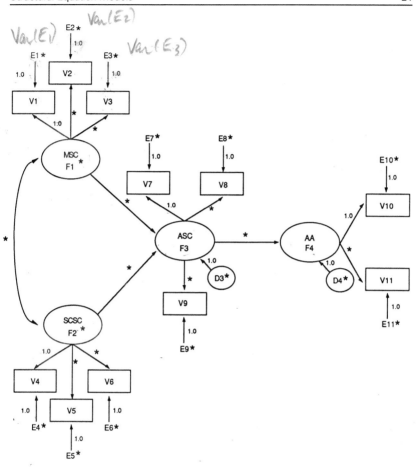

FIGURE 1.5. Hypothesized Full Structural Equation Model With EQS Notation

As usual, associated with each observed measure is an error term, the variance of which is of interest; its regression path to the observed measure is by necessity fixed (say, to 1.0). Because the observed measures are dependent variables in the model, their variances are not estimated. Finally, to establish the scale for each unmeasured factor in the model (and for purposes of identification), the first of each set of regression paths is fixed to 1.0; note again that path selection for the imposition of this constraint was purely arbitrary.

For this, our last example, let's again determine if we have an identified model. Given that we have 11 observed measures, we know that we have 66 (11[11 + 1]/2) pieces of information from which to derive the parameters of the model. Counting up the number of asterisks displayed in the model, we see that we have 24 parameters to be estimated: 7 measurement regression paths (F→V; the factor loadings); 3 structural regression paths (F→F); 11 error variances (Es); 2 disturbance variances (Ds); 1 covariance (F1↔F2). We therefore have 42 (66 − 24) degrees of freedom and, as a consequence, an overidentified model.

Our final task is to translate this full model into a set of equations. These are as follows:

$$
\begin{aligned}
F3 &= *F1 + *F2 + D3 & F4 &= *F3 + D4 \\
V1 &= F1 + E1 & V2 &= *F1 + E2 & V3 &= *F1 + E3; \\
V4 &= F2 + E4 & V5 &= *F2 + E5 & V6 &= *F2 + E6 \\
V7 &= F3 + E7 & V8 &= *F3 + E8 & V9 &= *F3 + E9 \\
V10 &= F4 + E10 & V11 &= *F4 + E11
\end{aligned}
$$

where * represents parameters to be estimated.

Now that you are familiar with the basic concepts underlying structural equation models, and with the related EQS notation, let's turn our attention to the rules of format and syntax associated with use of the EQS program.

Notes

1. Throughout the remainder of the book, the terms **latent, unobserved,** or **unmeasured** variable are used synonymously to represent a hypothetical construct or factor; the terms **observed, manifest,** and **measured** variable are also used interchangeably.

2. With EQS/Windows, however, you can now also conduct an EFA and then import the factor loadings into a CFA file.

3. In this text, a "cause" is a direct effect of a variable on another within the context of a complete model. Its magnitude and direction are given by the partial regression coefficient. If the complete model contains all relevant influences on a given dependent variable, its causal precursors are correctly specified. In practice, however, a model may omit key predictors and may be misspecified, so that it may be inadequate as a "causal model" in the philosophical sense.

4. Other parameters may also include the means and intercepts (see Chapter 10) or the higher order multivariate product-moments of skewness and kurtosis (see Bentler, 1983).

5. If, on the other hand, it were of interest to estimate the regression path, this could certainly be done. However, in this case, the variance of E1 would need to be fixed to 1.0 because the regression coefficient **and** the variance cannot both be estimated simultaneously. This fact is linked to the concept of statistical identification, which will be addressed later in this chapter.

6. Although the decision as to which parameter to constrain is purely arbitrary, the measure having the highest reliability is recommended, if this information is known; the value to which the parameter is constrained is also arbitrary.

2

Using the EQS Program

The purpose of this chapter is to introduce you to the general format of the EQS program. You have already learned the basic EQS notation; now it's time to see (a) how these symbols can be linked together to form admissible program statements and paragraphs used in the building of an SEM input file, and (b) how to run an EQS job so that the model specified in the input file is evaluated. We turn now to each of these EQS operations.

CREATION OF AN INPUT FILE

The **input** file describes the model under study. It is composed of several statements that are clustered within paragraphs or sections according to certain rules. We'll first look at the basic dicta governing the construction of EQS input files, then examine the components of their basic structure, and finally examine input files related to the three example problems presented in Chapter 1.

Basic Rules and Caveats

Keywords

Like most computer programs, EQS uses a system of keywords that are interpreted by the program as basic commands. Primary keywords in EQS are the names used to identify particular paragraphs comprising the input file (e.g., **SPECIFICATIONS** paragraph). Secondary keywords represent each statement within a paragraph; they operate as subcommands in the sense that they refer to only one aspect of the paragraph, allowing the user to choose one of several options pertinent to this component. For example, one aspect of the **SPECIFICATIONS** paragraph involves the method of estimation. Of the available choices, the user may wish to use maximum likelihood estimation. If so, he or she would state **ME=ML,** where **ME** is the abbreviated form of the keyword **METHOD,** a subcommand indicating the method of estimation to be used, and **ML** is the two-letter keyword indicating that maximum likelihood is the estimation method to be used.

Two major rules govern the use of the paragraph keywords: (a) they must always be preceded by a slash (e.g., **/SPECIFICATIONS**), and (b) the line in which the keyword appears must contain no other input information. One optional use of paragraph keywords is that they may be abbreviated to the first three characters (e.g., **/SPE**).

Descriptive Statements

All information describing the model and data must be expressed as specific statements that are written within the appropriate paragraph. Each statement **must** be separated by a semicolon (;). Although it is not necessary, users are advised to construct their file in a way that renders it easy to read. One way to do this is to start paragraph keywords in column 1, with all other statements within the paragraph indented a few characters.[1] Finally, all input statements should be specified in no more than 80 columns per line.

At times, you may wish to insert a reminder comment in your input file regarding some aspect of your data. EQS allows you to include such in-line comments by means of the exclamation mark (!). In particular, the exclamation mark must precede your comment; all material to the right of the punctuation symbol will then be ignored by the program.

File Editors

In order for EQS to run, the input file must be a plain file that contains no hidden control characters. Because some word processors (e.g., WordPerfect) use such symbols in the formulation of text, input files cannot be created by these means; plain text editors (e.g., KEDIT) must be used. One way around this problem, however, is to use a word processing system that permits the stripping of these invisible characters. For example, WordPerfect 5.1 will allow you to save a text in ASCII format, which can be read by EQS.

Data Input

Data in the form of a covariance or correlation matrix can either be embedded within the input file or reside in an external file. Raw data must

always reside in a separate file. Specifics regarding the integration of data files with the EQS input file will be covered in the following section.

Basic Structure

As noted earlier, the basic structure of an EQS input file comprises a series of statements grouped within paragraphs, each of which is introduced by means of a keyword that is preceded by a slash. At this time, we'll discuss the important features of six basic paragraphs; other paragraphs will be examined in subsequent chapters of the book as they bear on particular model applications. We turn now to these important building blocks of the EQS input file.

/TITLE *(Optional)*

Although this paragraph is optional (i.e., not required in order to run an EQS job), I highly recommend that you use it and that you be generous in the amount of information included in the title. Not uncommon to each of us is the situation where what might have seemed obvious when we conducted the initial analysis of a model does not seem quite so obvious several months later when, for whatever reason, we wish to reexamine the data using the same input files. Liberal use of title information is particularly helpful in the case where numerous EQS runs were implemented for a given data set. In this regard, EQS allows you to use as many lines as you wish in establishing your title.

An example /TITLE paragraph is:

```
/TITLE
CFA of BDI - French Version
Initial Model
```

/SPECIFICATIONS *(Required)*

This paragraph defines both the data to be analyzed and the method of analysis to be used. In particular, it details (a) the number of cases and number of input variables, (b) the desired method of estimation, and (c) a variety of other information that may be needed in order to guide the EQS run. A summary of possible specifications, along with defaults and available options, is presented in Bentler (1989, 1992a).

There are three important factors to note with respect to the /SPE paragraph. First, although input information can be placed in any order, each operand must be delineated by a semicolon. Second, information related to sample size and number of variables must **always** be provided. Finally, sub-command keywords can be abbreviated to three- and two-letter format. We'll now take a general look at the various aspects of this paragraph; for more details, see the manual (Bentler, 1989, 1992a).

CASES (CAS). This term defines the number of subjects comprising the sample data. The number should represent **all** cases, regardless of any that may later be deleted. Such deletions, as specified by the user and taken into account by EQS in the analytic procedures, **never** actually alter the original data set; thus the number of cases **always** stays the same. If the input data are in the form of a correlation or covariance matrix, it is critical that the number of cases be correct because EQS has no way of checking on the accuracy of this number; an incorrect number will lead to incorrect statistics. However, if the input data comprise raw scores, this number does not need to be specific; EQS automatically tallies the number of cases in the file, and this number is the one used in all computations.

VARIABLES (VAR). The number that you state here should represent the **total number** of variables in the data set; it does not represent the number of variables to be analyzed in any specific EQS run. The program automatically sorts out which variables to include in the analyses by its subsequent reading of the **/EQUATIONS** and **/VARIANCES** paragraphs.

METHOD (ME). The EQS user can select from seven available methods of estimation: maximum likelihood (ML), least squares (LS), generalized least squares (GLS), elliptical LS (ELS), elliptical GLS (EGLS), elliptical reweighted LS (ERLS), and arbitrary distribution GLS (AGLS). If no method is specified, the program automatically uses ML estimation; in other words, ML represents the **default** method. It is important to note that only the normal theory methods (ML, LS, GLS) can be based unconditionally on the input of either raw or correlational (or covariance) data. The elliptical methods can use the latter if a value of the KAPPA[2] coefficient is provided; otherwise they must be based on raw data. AGLS must **always** be based on raw data.

A special feature of the EQS program, however, is that it also allows for the specification of several estimation methods in a single job submission; a maximum of two methods can be specified when AGLS is included, and a maximum of three methods otherwise. The elliptical and arbitrary distribution methods are **always** automatically preceded by their normal theory counterparts. More specifically, the ELS, EGLS, and ERLS methods are preceded by the normal theory methods of LS, GLS, and ML, respectively; AGLS is preceded by LS. Nonetheless, the user can override these default prior methods by simply specifying another valid method. (For more details regarding both the specification and appropriate use of these methods, see Bentler, 1989, 1992a.)

Finally, in light of the numerous problems associated with analyses of nonnormal data (Bollen, 1989; Wothke, 1993), EQS allows users to request robust statistics associated with any selected method of estimation except AGLS. For example, by specifying **ME=ML,ROBUST,** the output provides a robust chi-square statistic (χ^2) called the Satorra-Bentler scaled statistic (S-Bχ^2; Satorra & Bentler, 1988a, 1988b) and robust standard errors (Bentler & Dijkstra, 1985), both of which have been corrected for nonnormality in large samples. The S-Bχ^2 has been shown to more closely approximate χ^2 than the usual test statistic and to perform as well as or better than the usual asymptotically distribution-free (ADF) methods generally recommended for nonnormal multivariate data (Bentler, 1989, 1992a; Chou, Bentler, & Satorra, 1991; Hu, Bentler, & Kano, 1992).

The availability of these robust statistics is an extremely valuable feature that is unique to the EQS program. However, three important caveats associated with the **ROBUST** command are worthy of note: (a) robust statistics can **only** be computed from raw data, (b) they are not available when analyses are based on a moment matrix, or with multigroup input files, and (c) because they are computationally very demanding, the user is well advised to request them only in the final stages of model fitting.

MATRIX (MA). This keyword describes the form of the input data: that is, whether it is a correlation, covariance, or raw data matrix (default = Covariance). As noted earlier, raw data are always presumed to reside in an external file; the other data matrices can either be included with the input file (i.e., as an internal file), or reside in an external file. If the data reside as an internal file, the matrix is specified within a separate paragraph labeled **/MATRIX**; if they reside in an external file, EQS must be told where to find that file. For interactive systems such as the IBM/PC, this information is specified using the **DATA** keyword; for noninteractive systems such as a mainframe environment, it is specified using the **UNIT** keyword. Once EQS has located the data file, it needs to know how to read it. If the data are **not** in free format, this information is provided by means of a Fortran format statement via the **FORMAT** keyword. Further elaboration of these three keywords now follows.

DATA (DA). Use of this keyword is governed by two conditions: (1) that the data to be analyzed exist in some external file, and (2) that the computing environment involves an interactive system as described above. The statement would read **DATA** (or **DA**) = **'FRBDI.DAT';,** where the letters enclosed in single quotes represent the name of the data file.

As noted earlier, these data can be in raw, correlation, or covariance matrix form.

UNIT (UN). This keyword is used when the user's computing environment is not interactive, as in the case of mainframe systems such as Wylbur or CMS. The unit number is a Fortran logical unit that can be any number less than 99 (except 4, 6, 8, 11, 15, or 20; Bentler, 1989, 1992a). If no value is specified, UN = 8 is assumed when the data represent a covariance matrix; UN = 9 is assumed when the matrix comprises raw scores.

FORMAT (FO). This keyword is followed by a format statement that must be embedded within single quotes ('), followed by the usual semicolon (e.g., **FO='(6F3.0)';**).[3] Other details regarding this keyword can be found in the manual.

ANALYSIS (ANAL). This keyword describes the type of matrix to be analyzed (default = Covariance); EQS then transforms the data into the correct form for the analyses. If the analyses are to be based on the covariance matrix but the data were input as a correlation matrix, the standard deviations must be added to the input. This is accomplished by providing a separate paragraph introduced with the keyword **/STANDARD DEVIATIONS** (or **/STA**) and then listing the standard deviations on the next line, leaving one blank between each. More than one line can be used if necessary. There are three things to remember when using the **/STA** paragraph: (1) there must be exactly the same number of standard deviations as there are variables in the correlation matrix being read, (2) the standard deviations must be in the same order as the variables in the input matrix, and (3) no semicolon is used to end this input section.

Now let's pull all this together and look at three specification paragraphs describing an input data matrix.

(a) The data matrix as an internal file

```
/SPE
 CASE=250; VAR=4; ME=ML; MA=COR;
/MATRIX
 1.00
 .34 1.00
 .55 .27 1.00
 .48 .33 .63 1.00
/STA
 1.09 .59 .98 1.10
```

Note that the input of data **never** requires a semicolon. Thus there are no ;s in the **/MATRIX** and **/STA** paragraphs.

(b) The data matrix as an external file (e.g., IBM/PC)

```
/SPE
  CASE=250; VAR=4; ME=ML,ROBUST; MA=COV;
  DA='FRBDI.DATA'; FO='(4F2.0)';
```

(c) The data matrix as an external file (e.g., mainframe)

```
//JOB
//EXEC
//DATA DD DSN=xxxxxx.FRBDI.DATA,DISP=SHR
/TITLE
  CFA of BDI - French Version
/SPE
  CASE=250; VAR=4; ME=ML; MA=RAW; UN=9; FO='(4F2.0)';
```

where xxxxxx represents computer account number. The JCL commands, as presented here in the first three lines, will vary with particular mainframe systems. Thus you will need to modify this input in accordance with your own particular mainframe environment. This information should be readily available from a consultant at your local computing facility.

In addition to the subcommands of the /SPE paragraph presented here, there are others that are either optional, or are used with particular applications. Because many such applications are described in this book, we'll delay discussion of these until their appearance in later chapters.

/LABELS *(Optional)*

This paragraph can be used to identify the names of observed (Vs) and/or latent (Fs) variables in the model. Labels may be one to eight characters in length, and are assigned only to V- and F-type variables. Observed variables should be numbered according to their position in the data set. Thus the specification that **V5=MATH** indicates that the fifth variable in the data matrix is to be labeled **MATH**. Although the numbering of latent variables is arbitrary, it should be logically sequenced within the context of the model.

Because EQS automatically assigns V1 to the first observed variable, V2 to the second variable and so on, these designations are used as labels if the user does not provide names for the variables; likewise the latent variables are automatically assigned the labels F1, F2, and so forth. If the user provides labels for only some of the variables, these names will override the default labels (e.g., V1).

/EQUATIONS *(Required)*

This keyword signals that the next paragraph provides specification information regarding the model under study. Specifically, the paragraph defines every regression path in the model. By means of a series of equation statements, the **/EQU** paragraph specifies all linkages among the independent and dependent variables, as well as dependent and dependent variables, and identifies those parameters to be constrained (to zero, 1.0, or some other value) and those to be freely estimated.

Before completing this part of your input file, it is critical that you construct a path diagram of your model in which (a) all observed and latent variables are clearly labeled, (b) all structural regression paths are specified, (c) all error and disturbance terms are specified, along with their related regression paths, (d) all hypothesized covariances (among independent variables) are specified, and (e) all parameters to be estimated (including factor variances) are identified by means of an asterisk. Once you have this visual representation of your model, it is then easy to complete all equations in the **/EQU** paragraph by simply reading off the path diagram.

How to Write Equations. The completion of these equations is carried out as follows. For each **dependent** variable (i.e., any variable having an arrow pointing towards it), you write one equation summarizing the direct impact on it from other variables in the model. Thus there will always be as many equations in the **/EQU** paragraph as there are dependent variables in the model being tested. The dependent variable will always be on the left-hand side of the equation, with all independent (or explanatory) variables appearing on the right. (Recall from Chapter 1 that in EQS, the terms **dependent** and **independent** variables are defined within the context of the Bentler-Weeks model.) Finally, once you have formed your equations, be sure to insert asterisks beside all parameters that are to be estimated. EQS will provide estimates for only the asterisked parameters; all others will be regarded as fixed.

How to Use Start Values. Start values refer to the point at which a program begins an iterative process to establish parameter estimates. The user can either allow the program to supply these values (EQS uses default values such as 0.0 for covariances) or provide his or her own values. User-provided start values represent a "best guess" of what the expected value of a particular parameter estimate will be; these "best guess" values are included in the equation, acting as modifiers of the parameters to be estimated.

Although start values are not needed for most EQS jobs, they often facilitate the iterative process when complex models are under study; such models can generate problems of nonconvergence if the start values provided by EQS are inadequate. Nonetheless, because of the multiplicity of models that can be analyzed using the EQS program, it is almost impossible to furnish any firm set of rules governing the formulation of start values. Speaking in general terms, however, I can suggest that a few key factor loadings (Vs) should be fairly high (~.9 in a standardized metric), variances should always be larger than covariances, and residual E variances should be large and close to the variances of their corresponding derived variables. Moreover, if you either know or suspect that some estimates will be negative, it is very helpful to specify this sign, because negative estimates can be problematic to the iterative process (i.e., may lead to nonconvergence). (For a more extensive discussion of start values, see Bollen, 1989.)

Now, let's examine a few **/EQUATIONS** paragraphs.

(a) Equation without start values

```
/EQU
V1 = F1 + E1;
F3 = *F1 + *F2 + D3;
```

(b) Equation with start values

```
/EQU
V1 = .9F1 + E1;
F3 = .6*F1 + -.2*F2 + D3;
```

Note that the paths associated with E1 and D3 are fixed to 1.00 by default because no value is specified (see above).

/VARIANCES *(Required)*

This paragraph specifies the status of variances related to the independent variables. As such, each variance must be identified either as a fixed parameter in the model or as one to be freely estimated. (Recall that **variances for dependent variables are never specified, regardless of whether they are fixed or free**.) As in the /EQU paragraph, variances that are to be estimated are identified with an asterisk. Although further elaboration of this paragraph will be provided in the section, Input File Examples, let's look at a couple of examples of the **/VAR** paragraph.

(a) Variances without start values

```
/VAR
  F1, F2 = *;
  F1 to F3 = *;
```

The term **to** can be used where a sequence of variables is included in the equation; in this case, the variables are F1, F2, and F3.

(b) Variances with start values

```
/VAR
  F1, F2 = *.3;
  F1 to F3 = *.3;
```

/COVARIANCES *(Optional)*

For obvious reasons, this paragraph is necessary only when covariances are specified in the model. As such, it is used to specify both fixed nonzero and free covariances among the independent variables. It is important to note, however, that any variable involved in a covariance must also have its variance specified in the **/VAR** paragraph; consequently, **covariances also cannot be specified for dependent variables.**[4] In specifying a covariance, the pair of variables are stated and separated by a comma. Examples are as follows:

```
/COV
  E1, E3 = *;
  F1 to F3 = *;
```

Use of the **to** convention here indicates that all possible pairs of the variables named are to be estimated (i.e., F1,F2; F1,F3; F2,F3).

The final keyword in all EQS input files must be **/END**. This keyword lets the program know that there is no more information forthcoming.

TABLE 2.1. EQS Input for Hypothesized First-Order CFA Model

```
/TITLE
 1st-Order CFA of 4-Factor Model of Self-Concept
 Initial Model
/SPECIFICATIONS
 CASE=250; VAR=12; ME=ML; MA=RAW;
 DA='CFASC.DAT'; FO='(12F1.0)';
/LABELS
 V1=SDQASC1;      V2=SDQASC2;      V3=SDQASC3;
 V4=SDQSSC1;      V5=SDQSSC2;      V6=SDQSSC3;
 V7=SDQPSC1;      V8=SDQPSC2;      V9=SDQPSC3;
 V10=SDQESC1;     V11=SDQESC2;     V12=SDQESC3;
 F1=ASC;      F2=SSC;       F3=PSC;      F4=ESC;
/EQUATIONS
 V1 = F1 + E1;
 V2 = *F1 + E2;
 V3 = *F1 + E3;
            V4 = F2 + E4;
            V5 = *F2 + E5;
            V6 = *F2 + E6;
                   V7 = F3 + E7;
                   V8 = *F3 + E8;
                   V9 = *F3 + E9;
                        V10 = F4 + E10;
                        V11 = *F4 + E11;
                        V12 = *F4 + E12;
/VARIANCES
 F1 to F4 = *;
 E1 to E12 = *;
/COVARIANCES
 F1 to F4 = *;
/END
```

INPUT FILE EXAMPLES

To give you a more comprehensive view of how the various parts of the EQS input relate to the path diagram of a particular model, let's now apply what we have learned so far to the three models presented in Chapter 1. To derive maximum benefit from this section, you are urged to study each figure as you refer to its respective input statement. Because these examples are intended only to illustrate the basic structure of an EQS input file, start values have not been included.

First, let's look at the input statement for a first-order CFA model (Table 2.1; path diagram in Figure 1.3). Although this input file is fairly straightforward, a couple of items are perhaps worthy of review. First, recall that for purposes of identification as well as for setting the scale for the latent factors, the first measurement indicator for each factor (V1, V4, V7) has been specified as fixed (i.e., there is no asterisk beside these parameters). These parameters are constrained to equal a value of 1.0 because F1 = 1.0 F1. Second, recall also that an independent variable can have either its path or its variance estimated, but not both. Thus in the **/EQUATIONS** paragraph you will see also that all beta weights for the Es have been similarly constrained to equal 1.0 because their variances are specified as free (see /**VARIANCES**). Finally, the **to** convention has been used in both the /**VARIANCES** and /**COVARI-ANCES** paragraphs, thereby indicating that the variances of all the independent variables (F1-F4) are to be freely estimated, and so too their covariances.

Now let's look at the input statement for a second-order CFA model (Table 2.2; path diagram in Figure 1.4). Four points are noteworthy with respect to this input file. First, in contrast to the previous CFA example, the /**EQUATIONS** paragraph illustrates regression specifications bearing on the factors; these involve the impact of F5 (an independent variable) on F1, F2, F3, and F4, all dependent variables. Second, in the /**VARIANCES** paragraph, you will note that the higher order factor F5 has had its variance fixed to 1.0 because its regression paths to each of the lower order factors have been specified as free. In the same paragraph, you will note that the variances of the residuals (Ds) are to be freely estimated; as a result, note that their paths, as indicated in the /**EQUATIONS** paragraph, have been constrained to a value of 1.0. Finally, note the absence of a /**COVARIANCES** paragraph. As pointed out in Chapter 1, in second-order models, any covariance among the first-order factors is presumed to be explained by the higher order factor(s).

Finally, let's look at the input statement for a full structural equation model (Table 2.3; path diagram in Figure 1.5). Reviewing this EQS input for a full model, we see that here again are regression equations involving only factors; these are specified for Factors 3 (F3) and 4 (F4) only, because both are explained by other factors in the model. Note in particular that Factor 3 operates both as a predictor and as a dependent variable.[5] Relatedly, note that because Factors 1 and 2 are the sole independent variables comprising the structural portion of the model, they are the only ones for which variances and a covariance are estimated.

Now that we know how to compose a basic EQS input file, let's proceed to the next section, where we learn how to run an EQS job.

EXECUTION OF EQS JOBS

EQS operates as a stand-alone batch program. Thus, regardless of the computing environment (mainframe, PC, etc.), an EQS job is executed (or run) by simply typing the system's conventional name for the program—typically **EQS**.

Input Files

In order for the job to run, EQS must be provided with an **input file** that contains all information pertinent to the model being tested; related file-

TABLE 2.2. EQS Input for Hypothesized Second-Order CFA Model

```
/TITLE
2nd-Order CFA of 4-Factor Model of Self-Concept
Initial Model
/SPECIFICATIONS
CASE=250; VAR=12; ME=ML; MA=RAW;
DA='CFASC.DAT'; FO='(12F1.0)';
/LABELS
V1=SDQASC1;        V2=SDQASC2;        V3=SDQASC3;
V4=SDQSSC1;        V5=SDQSSC2;        V6=SDQSSC3;
V7=SDQPSC1;        V8=SDQPSC2;        V9=SDQPSC3;
V10=SDQESC1;       V11=SDQESC2;       V12=SDQESC3;
F1=ASC;    F2=SSC;    F3=PSC;    F4=ESC;    F5=GSC;
/EQUATIONS
V1  =   F1 + E1;
V2  =  *F1 + E2;
V3  =  *F1 + E3;
            V4  =   F2 + E4;
            V5  =  *F2 + E5;
            V6  =  *F2 + E6;
                    V7  =   F3 + E7;
                    V8  =  *F3 + E8;
                    V9  =  *F3 + E9;
                            V10 =   F4 + E10;
                            V11 =  *F4 + E11;
                            V12 =  *F4 + E12;
F1  =  *F5 + D1;
   F2  =  *F5 + D2;
      F3  =  *F5 + D3;
         F4  =  *F5 + D4;
/VARIANCES
F5  =  1.0;
D1 to D4  =  *;
E1 to E12  =  *;
/END
```

names must be in accord with the computer's operating conventions. For example, using a mainframe environment (say, WYLBUR or CMS), one might wish to name the file using a dotted extension to identify the statistical package (e.g., **FILENAME.EQS**). Within the PC environment, the dotted extension could be used to identify the input/output status of the file (e.g., **FILENAME.INP**). For purposes of illustration, let's apply this file-naming strategy to the input file in Table 2.3 (related to Figure 1.5). If it is a mainframe file, we may wish to name it **ASCAA.EQS**; if it is a PC file, **ASCAA.INP**.

Output Files

The results of an EQS job are placed automatically in a separate file in accordance with the system being used; the manner by which this is accomplished, however, varies with each system. For example, if you are working within CMS on the mainframe, the file will be identified by a "listing" extension (e.g., **FILENAME.LISTING**); if you are working with WYLBUR,

TABLE 2.3. EQS Input for Hypothesized Full Structural Equation Model

```
/TITLE
 Impact of Self-Concept on Academic Achievement
 Initial Model
/SPECIFICATIONS
 CASE=250; VAR=11; ME=ML; MA=RAW;
 DA='ASCAA.DAT';
 FO='(9F1.0,X,2F2.0)';
/LABELS
 V1=MSCSDQ1;      V2=MSCSDQ2;      V3=MSCSDQ3;
 V4=SCSCSDQ1;     V5=SCSCSDQ2;     V6=SCSCSDQ3;
 V7=ASCSDQ1;      V8=ASCSDQ2;      V9=ASCSDQ3;
 V10=GRADES;      V11=TEST;
 F1=MSC;      F2=SCSC;      F3=ASC;      F4=AA;
/EQUATIONS
 V1 =   F1 + E1;
 V2 = *F1 + E2;
 V3 = *F1 + E3;
 V4 =   F2 + E4;
 V5 = *F2 + E5;
 V6 = *F2 + E6;
             V7 =   F3 + E7;
             V8 = *F3 + E8;
             V9 = *F3 + E9;
                        V10 =   F4 + E10;
                        V11 = *F4 + E11;
 F3 = *F1 + *F2 + D3;
 F4 = *F3 + D4;
/VARIANCES
 F1 = *;
 F2 = *;
 D3 = *;
 D4 = *;
 E1 to E11 = *;
/COVARIANCES
 F1,F2 = *;
/END
```

it will be identified only as a job number. Within the PC environment, prior to the running of the job, EQS will prompt you first for the name of the **input** file and then for the name of the **output** file. You are free to use your own convention in naming the output file. For example, you may wish to keep the stem of both files the same, using the extension to distinguish between input and output files (e.g., **FILENAME.OUT** or, as above, **ASCAA.OUT**). However, should you either forget or not wish to name the output file, EQS will automatically label this file as **FILENAME.LOG** (or as above, **ASCAA.LOG**) to prevent the input file from being written over or replaced by the output file.

ERROR MESSAGES

Errors are inevitable, regardless of how familiar one is with various computer environments and software packages. Typically, error messages produced by a particular program provide some clue as to the location and correction of the error. This task for structural equation modeling packages is substantially more difficult, given the combined complexities associated with both the data and the specified model. Nonetheless, compared with other structural equation modeling software packages, EQS is exceptional in this regard. Specifically, error messages in EQS fall into one of two categories—minor and serious.

Minor Errors

These errors are typically syntactical. A few of the most common syntax errors are as follows:

- Using key words that don't conform to the EQS naming convention
- Forgetting to put a slash before the key word
- Forgetting to put a semicolon after each statement
- Forgetting to enclose parenthesized Fortran statements in single quotes (but see note #3)
- Forgetting to specify a name of the external file to be created by the **RETEST** option and to enclose this filename in single quotes
- Forgetting to include the equal sign (=) and yes (no) following specification of the **LMTEST, WTEST,** and **EFFECTS** options

EQS automatically checks for such syntactical errors and prints a message advising the user that an error in syntax has occurred. The program terminates and the message is printed following the Bentler-Weeks representation of the model.

Another minor error that can occur relates to the number of cases specified. If the actual number of cases differs from the number specified in the input file, EQS will warn the user that this has occurred, and analyses will be based on the number of cases in the data file. Unlike the above problem, in this case the program continues with all computations.

Serious Errors

In the event that the input errors cannot be logically corrected by the program, such errors are considered to be fatal, with the result that the program terminates without completing the computations. These error messages generally relate to such problems as a matrix that is not positive definite, start values that are very bad, or a particular variable that is linearly dependent on other parameters (for excellent reviews of these problems, see Bentler & Chou, 1987; Rindskopf, 1984). Given these types of messages, the user needs to study their content carefully in order to resolve the problem.

In general, however, most EQS problems tend to result from typographical or syntactical errors. I strongly urge you to reexamine your input file with a critical eye for syntax error before running the job. In the long run, it can save you many hours of distress!

OVERVIEW OF REMAINING CHAPTERS

Thus far you have been introduced only to the bricks and mortar of SEM applications. As such, you have learned the basics regarding (a) concepts underlying SEM procedures, (b) components of the CFA and Full models, (c) elements and structure of the EQS program, (d) creation of EQS input files, and (e) execution of EQS jobs. Now it's time to see how these bricks and mortar can be combined to build a variety of structures. The remainder of the book, then, is devoted to an in-depth examination of basic EQS applications involving both the CFA and Full models.

In presenting these examples from the literature, I have tried to address the diverse needs of my readers by including a potpourri of EQS setups. As such, some applications will have the data matrix embedded within the input file, whereas others will draw from an external file; some will include job language exemplary of a mainframe environment, whereas others will apply to a PC environment; some will include data in the form of a correlation matrix, whereas others will involve the input of raw data; some will include start values, whereas others will not. For applications in which the data have been included in the input file (e.g., Chapters 3, 8, 10), I urge you to work through the example on your own computer; as is usually the case, personal experience is the best teacher! Taken together, the applications presented in the next 12 chapters should provide you with a comprehensive understanding of how EQS can be used, not only to analyze a variety of structural equation models based on an assorted array of input data, but also to screen and assess these data in the analysis of covariance and mean structures. Let's move on, then, to our first example.

Notes

1. If you use **EASY BUILD,** the interactive file-building feature of EQS/Windows (Version 4), you can easily accomplish this by editing the file after it has been formulated by the program.

2. When elliptical estimation is requested, Kappa is a parameter that can be specified if the input data are in correlation (or covariance), rather than raw matrix form, which is default.

3. Single quotes are not required in EQS/Windows files.

4. If you wish to have two dependent variables covary, just specify that their associated residuals covary. These residuals are always independent variables in standard models.

5. It is tempting to call F3 an "independent" variable in the equation $F4 = *F3 + D4$, but this would not correspond to the Bentler-Weeks convention. A variable such as F3 that has its own equation is only a dependent variable, having no variances or covariances as parameters, even if it is a predictor variable in other equations.

PART TWO

Single-Group Analyses

Confirmatory Factor Analytic Models

CHAPTER 3: APPLICATION 1
Testing the Factorial Validity of a Theoretical Construct (First-Order CFA Model)

CHAPTER 4: APPLICATION 2
Testing the Factorial Validity of a Measuring Instrument (First-Order CFA Model)

CHAPTER 5: APPLICATION 3
Testing the Factorial Validity of a Measuring Instrument (Second-Order CFA Model)

CHAPTER 6: APPLICATION 4
Testing for Construct Validity: The Multitrait-Multimethod Model

The Full Latent Variable Model

CHAPTER 7: APPLICATION 5
Testing the Validity of a Causal Structure

3

Application 1
Testing the Factorial Validity
of a Theoretical Construct
(First-Order CFA Model)

For our first application, we examine a first-order CFA model designed to test the multidimensionality of a theoretical construct. Specifically, this application tests the hypothesis that adolescent self-concept (SC) is a multidimensional construct composed of four factors: general SC (GSC), academic SC (ASC), English SC (ESC), and mathematics SC (MSC). The theoretical underpinning of this hypothesis derives from the hierarchical model of SC proposed by Shavelson, Hubner, and Stanton (1976). The example is taken from a study by Byrne and Shavelson (1986); for a more extensive discussion of the substantive issues and the related findings, readers should refer to the original study.

THE HYPOTHESIZED MODEL

At issue in this first application is the multidimensional structure of adolescent SC. Although numerous studies have supported the multidimensionality of the construct, others hold to the counterargument that SC is unidimensional. Still others might postulate that SC is a two-factor structure comprising only GSC and ASC. The task presented to us here, then, is to test the original hypothesis that SC is a four-factor structure comprising a general component (GSC), an academic component (ASC), and two subject-specific components (English SC [ESC]; mathematics SC [MSC]), against two alternative hypotheses: (a) that SC is a two-factor structure comprising GSC and ASC, and (b) that SC is a one-factor structure in which there is no distinction between general and academic SCs.

We turn now to an examination and testing of each of these hypotheses.

HYPOTHESIS 1:
SELF-CONCEPT IS A FOUR-FACTOR STRUCTURE

The model presented in Figure 3.1 schematically represents Hypothesis 1 and provides the mechanism by which it can be tested statistically. To facilitate interpretation, the model has been labeled both generically and in terms of EQS notation. However, clarification is needed regarding the labeling of the observed variables (Vs) in the model. First, although the numbering of these variables may seem somewhat odd, it is consistent with the order in which each was entered into the data matrix; a review of Table 3.2 should clarify this point. Second, you will note that V7 is missing. This variable represented the academic SC subscale of the Affective Perception Inventory (API; Soares & Soares, 1979) and was intended as an indicator of ASC. However, a preliminary exploratory factor analysis in the original study revealed this subscale to be problematic; it was therefore deleted as a measure of ASC, leaving only two indicators of the construct.

In order to test Hypothesis 1, a description of the model in Figure 3.1 must be translated into a series of computer statements that can be understood by EQS; these statements comprise the input file as discussed in Chapter 2. Before reviewing the related EQS input, however, let's take a few minutes to first dissect the model, taking note of its component parts:

(a) There are four SC factors (as indicated by the four circles labeled F1-F4).
(b) The four factors are intercorrelated (as indicated by the curved two-headed arrows).
(c) There are 11 observed variables (as indicated by the 11 rectangles labeled V1-V12).
(d) The observed variables load onto the factors in the following pattern: V1, V5, and V6 load onto Factor 1; V2 and V8 load onto Factor 2; V3, V9, and V10 load onto Factor 3; and V4, V11, and V12 load onto Factor 4.
(e) Each observed variable loads on one and only one factor.

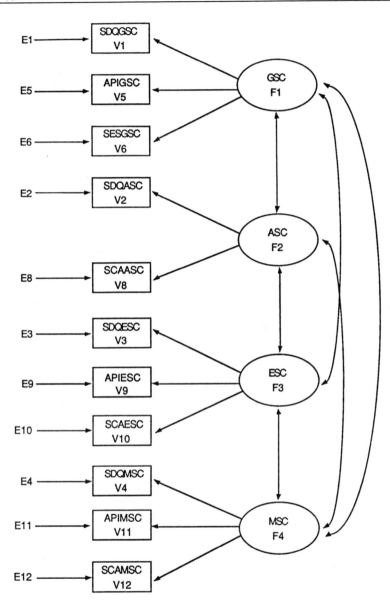

FIGURE 3.1. Initially Hypothesized Four-Factor Model of Self-Concept

Source: Adapted from Byrne (1989). Copyright 1989 by Springer-Verlag. Reprinted by permission,

    (f)   Errors of measurement associated with each observed variable (E1-E6; E8-E12) are uncorrelated.

Recapitulating these observations, let's now present a more formal description of our hypothesized model. Accordingly, we state that the CFA model presented in Figure 3.1 hypothesizes a priori that:

(a) SC responses can be explained by four factors: GSC, ASC, ESC, and MSC.
(b) Each subscale measure has a nonzero loading on the SC factor that it was designed to measure (termed a **target loading**), and zero loadings on all other factors (termed **nontarget loadings**).
(c) The four SC factors, consistent with the theory, are correlated.
(d) Error/uniquenesses[1] associated with each measure are uncorrelated.

Finally, turning to Table 3.1, we see a representation of our model in tabular form. As such, we are better able to visualize the pattern of estimated parameters in both the factor loading matrix and the factor and error variance/covariance matrices. For purposes of identification, you will note that the first of each congeneric set[2] of SC measures is set to 1.0.

The EQS Input File

The data for our first application are in the form of a correlation matrix that is treated as an internal file; in other words, the matrix is incorporated into the input file. Additionally, in this application, no start values have been included. For readers who may be interested in comparing input and output files from both the EQS (Bentler, 1989, 1992a) and LISREL (Jöreskog & Sörbom, 1988, 1993) programs, the present application provides a unique opportunity to do so; although such details are by necessity limited and briefly described in the Byrne and Shavelson (1986) article, they are dealt with more comprehensively in Byrne (1989), where the same analyses presented here were conducted on the same data matrix.

Let's proceed now by examining the link between the four-factor CFA model presented in Figure 3.1 and the translation of its specifications into a file interpretable to EQS. This input file is presented in Table 3.2.

As described by the **/TITLE** paragraph, this file represented the initially hypothesized model. The **/SPECIFICATIONS** paragraph indicates that (a) the sample size is 996, (b) there are 15 observed variables, (c) the method of estimation is maximum likelihood, (d) the data matrix is in correlational form, and (e) the analyses are to be based on a correlation matrix. In light of current knowledge that the analysis of correlational data can be problematic (Cudeck, 1989; Jöreskog & Sörbom, 1988), the latter two specifications require further explanation. First, the specification of **MA=COR** is needed because EQS, by default, assumes that **/MATRIX** represents a covariance

TABLE 3.1. Pattern of Estimated Parameters for Hypothesized Four-Factor Model of Self-Concept

Factor Loading Matrix

Observed Measure	Variable	GSC F_1	ASC F_2	ESC F_3	MSC F_4
SDQGSC	V_1	1.0^a	0.0	0.0	0.0
APIGSC	V_5	$*^b$	0.0	0.0	0.0
SESGSC	V_6	*	0.0	0.0	0.0
SDQASC	V_2	0.0^c	1.0	0.0	0.0
SCAASC	V_8	0.0	*	0.0	0.0
SDQESC	V_3	0.0	0.0	1.0	0.0
APIESC	V_9	0.0	0.0	*	0.0
SCAESC	V_{10}	0.0	0.0	*	0.0
SDQMSC	V_4	0.0	0.0	0.0	1.0
APIMSC	V_{11}	0.0	0.0	0.0	*
SCAMSC	V_{12}	0.0	0.0	0.0	*

Factor Variance/Covariance Matrix

Observed Measure	GSC F_1	ASC F_2	ESC F_3	MSC
GSC	*			
ASC	*	*		
ESC	*	*	*	
MSC	*	*	*	*

Error Variance/Covariance Matrix

	V_1	V_5	V_6	V_2	V_8	V_3	V_9	V_{10}	V_4	V_{11}	V_{12}
V_1	*										
V_5	0.0	*									
V_6	0.0	0.0	*								
V_2	0.0	0.0	0.0	*							
V_8	0.0	0.0	0.0	0.0	*						
V_3	0.0	0.0	0.0	0.0	0.0	*					
V_9	0.0	0.0	0.0	0.0	0.0	0.0	*				
V_{10}	0.0	0.0	0.0	0.0	0.0	0.0	0.0	*			
V_4	0.0	0.0	0.0	0.0	0.0	0.0	0.0	0.0	*		
V_{11}	0.0	0.0	0.0	0.0	0.0	0.0	0.0	0.0	0.0	*	
V_{12}	0.0	0.0	0.0	0.0	0.0	0.0	0.0	0.0	0.0	0.0	*

a. parameter fixed to 1.0.
b. parameter to be estimated.
c. parameter fixed to 0.0

matrix. Second, basing the analyses on the correlation rather than on the covariance matrix serves two useful purposes here: (a) it provides the opportunity to show you the warning message issued by the program when a correlation matrix is to be analyzed, and (b) the analyses will be directly comparable to those of the original study, which was based on the LISREL program. If, on the other hand, we had elected to analyze the data correla-

TABLE 3.2. EQS Input for Initially Hypothesized Four-Factor Model of
Self-Concept

```
/TITLE
 CFA OF 4-FACTOR MODEL OF SELF-CONCEPT
 INITIAL MODEL
/SPECIFICATIONS
 CASE=996; VAR=15; ME=ML; MA=COR; ANAL=COR; FO='(15F4.3)';
/MATRIX
1000
 3011000
 289 3881000
 170 453 0121000
 630 266 227 2001000
 786 306 299 225 6351000
 522 619 389 346 579 5371000
 216 675 343 472 216 283 5451000
 156 442 705 014 190 190 440 3691000
 128 470 543 069 131 174 396 589 6271000
 177 475 066 864 270 257 426 489 142 0961000
 135 424 027 828 188 187 367 577 028 146 8061000
 010 506 162 395 006 063 374 661 147 375 321 4421000
-008 457 219 236-020 039 326 523 261 541 182 241 7941000
-017 349 057 562 001 034 262 489 039 164 477 624 739 5141000
/STANDARD DEVIATIONS
 14.10 12.30 10.00 16.10 9.30 4.90 9.40 5.30 11.30 5.70 11.50
 7.40 10.97 12.76 15.93
/LABELS
V1=SDQGSC;   V2=SDQASC;   V3=SDQESC;   V4=SDQMSC;
V5=APIGSC;   V6=SESGSC;   V7=APIASC;   V8=SCAASC;
V9=APIESC;   V10=SCAESC;  V11=APIMSC;  V12=SCAMSC;
V13=GPA;     V14=ENG;     V15=MATH;
F1=GSC;      F2=ASC;      F3=ESC;      F4=MSC;
/EQUATIONS
V1  =   F1 + E1;
V5  =  *F1 + E5;
V6  =  *F1 + E6;
    V2  =   F2 + E2;
    V8  =  *F2 + E8;
        V3  =   F3 + E3;
        V9  =  *F3 + E9;
        V10 =  *F3 + E10;
            V4  =   F4 + E4;
            V11 =  *F4 + E11;
            V12 =  *F4 + E12;
/VARIANCES
 F1 TO F4 = *;
 E1 TO E6 = *; E8 TO E12 = *;
/COVARIANCES
 F1 TO F4 = *;
/LMTEST
 SET=GVF,PEE;
/END
```

tion matrix as a covariance matrix, we would have easily accomplished this
by simply including a **/STANDARD DEVIATIONS** keyword, followed on
the next line by the standard deviation value for each observed variable.
Although we did not select this option here, these values are included in

Table 3.2 for purposes of illustration (i.e., they are irrelevant to the present analyses because we have opted to analyze the correlation matrix).[3] Because these numbers are presented in free format (i.e., a space between each, and the decimal included), there is no need for a format statement.

In the /SPECIFICATIONS paragraph, you will note also that a format statement has been included. This specification is required because the data are in a fixed format that includes decimals. The FO statement tells EQS that there are 15 rows of data and that the elements within each row are read as four-digit numbers taken to the third decimal place. For example, row 1 is read as 1.000, and row 2 as .301, 1.000. Finally, you will note that there is no need for a DA statement because the data to be analyzed reside within the input file.

Because the data are being treated as an internal file, then, we need to include the /MATRIX keyword, followed on the next and subsequent lines by the actual data matrix (in the form of a correlation matrix).

By now, you will no doubt find the information specified in the next four paragraphs (/LABELS, /EQUATIONS, /VARIANCES, /COVARIANCES) to be fairly straightforward; thus further explanation seems unnecessary. However, the final paragraph, introduced by the keyword /LMTEST, will be new to you and does require some elaboration. This keyword requests that the Lagrange Multiplier (LM) Test be implemented to test hypotheses bearing on the statistical viability of specified restrictions in the model. The basic purpose of this test is to determine whether, in a subsequent EQS run, the specification of certain parameters as free rather than fixed would this lead to a model that better represented the data. Although we're using the LM Test here only to identify which fixed parameters, if set free, would lead to a significantly better fitting model, it is used also to assess the viability of equality constraints.[4] EQS produces univariate and multivariate χ^2 statistics that permit evaluation of the appropriateness of the specified restrictions; it also yields a **parameter change statistic** that represents the value that would be obtained if a particular fixed parameter were freely estimated in a future run.

The LM Test procedure provides for several options, all of which are fully described in the manual (Bentler, 1989, 1992a). One of these options, the SET command, is included in the present input. This command allows the user to limit the LM Test to only a subset of fixed parameters in the model. In our CFA model, for example, the factor loadings and error terms that were fixed to a value of 0.0 are of substantial interest; statistically significant LM χ^2 values would argue for the presence of factor cross-loadings (i.e., a loading on more than one factor) and error covariances (correlated errors), respectively. EQS follows SEM convention in its coding for the SET command. Accordingly, the matrix of which a particular parameter is an element is designated by a Greek letter. However, unlike the LISREL program, in which there are eight such matrices, EQS functions with only three: a variance/covariance matrix of independent factors (PHI), a regression (or coefficient) matrix involving both independent and dependent variables (**GAMMA**), and a regression matrix involving only dependent variables (**BETA**). This minimal set of matrices arises from the EQS requirement that all variables be designated as either independent or dependent variables; only dependent variables can have equations, and only independent variables can have variances and covariances. Coding for the **SET** command comprises three letters; the first represents the matrix (**P, G,** or **B**), and the remaining two represent a submatrix of one of these matrices.[5] For example, the input file in Table 3.2 shows **SET=GVF, PEE**. The letter G represents the **GAMMA** matrix, and the double letters **VF** indicate the regression of the dependent Vs on the independent Fs (i.e., the factor loadings). Likewise, the letter **P** stands for the **PHI** matrix; the double letters **EE** for the covariance between two error terms (i.e., correlated errors).

Before leaving this topic of the LM Test, one vitally important caveat needs to be stressed. Because (a) the LM Test is based solely on statistical criteria, and (b) virtually any fixed parameter (constrained either to zero or some nonzero value) is eligible for testing, it is critical that the researcher pay close heed to the substantive theory before relaxing constraints, as may be suggested by the LM statistics. Model respecification in which certain parameters have been set free **must** be substantiated by sound theoretical rationale; it also demands that attention be paid to the issue of identification.

The EQS Output File

We turn now to the EQS output resulting from the input file shown in Table 3.2. For didactic purposes, the entire output[6] is provided for the initially hypothesized model in Application 1 only; hereafter, selected portions of the output will be displayed. To facilitate the presentation and discussion of results, this material is dealt with in four separate sections. We turn first to Table 3.3, which displays printed output related to model specification.

Model Specification

Recall that for reasons outlined earlier we chose to analyze the correlation matrix. In keeping with recent literature related to this approach, the initial information printed on the output warns that the statistics provided may not be meaningful; this is followed by the correlation matrix to be analyzed, decimals included (cf. EQS input in Table 3.2). Because labels for the observed variables were also specified, they are printed along the rows and columns of the matrix.

TABLE 3.3. EQS Output for Initially Hypothesized Four-Factor Model of Self-Concept: Model Specification

CORRELATION MATRIX TO BE ANALYZED: 11 VARIABLES (SELECTED FROM 15 VARIABLES) BASED ON 996 CASES.

```
*** WARNING *** STATISTICS MAY NOT BE MEANINGFUL
                DUE TO ANALYZING CORRELATION MATRIX
```

		SDQGSC V 1	SDQASC V 2	SDQESC V 3	SDQMSC V 4	APIGSC V 5
SDQGSC	V 1	1.000				
SDQASC	V 2	0.301	1.000			
SDQESC	V 3	0.289	0.388	1.000		
SDQMSC	V 4	0.170	0.453	0.012	1.000	
APIGSC	V 5	0.630	0.266	0.227	0.200	1.000
SESGSC	V 6	0.786	0.306	0.299	0.225	0.635
SCAASC	V 8	0.216	0.675	0.343	0.472	0.216
APIESC	V 9	0.156	0.442	0.705	0.014	0.190
SCAESC	V 10	0.128	0.470	0.543	0.069	0.131
APIMSC	V 11	0.177	0.475	0.066	0.864	0.270
SCAMSC	V 12	0.135	0.424	0.027	0.828	0.188

		SESGSC V 6	SCAASC V 8	APIESC V 9	SCAESC V 10	APIMSC V 11
SESGSC	V 6	1.000				
SCAASC	V 8	0.283	1.000			
APIESC	V 9	0.190	0.369	1.000		
SCAESC	V 10	0.174	0.589	0.627	1.000	
APIMSC	V 11	0.257	0.489	0.142	0.096	1.000
SCAMSC	V 12	0.187	0.577	0.028	0.146	0.806

		SCAMSC V 12
SCAMSC	V 12	1.000

BENTLER-WEEKS STRUCTURAL REPRESENTATION:

```
    NUMBER OF DEPENDENT VARIABLES = 11
        DEPENDENT V'S :        1   2   3   4   5   6   8   9   10   11
        DEPENDENT V'S :       12

    NUMBER OF INDEPENDENT VARIABLES = 15
        INDEPENDENT F'S :      1   2   3   4
        INDEPENDENT E'S :      1   2   3   4   5   6   8   9   10   11
        INDEPENDENT E'S :     12
```

```
3RD STAGE OF COMPUTATION REQUIRED      7337 WORDS OF MEMORY.
PROGRAM ALLOCATE      329728 WORDS

DETERMINANT OF INPUT MATRIX IS   0.52010E-03
MAXIMUM LIKELIHOOD SOLUTION (NORMAL DISTRIBUTION THEORY)
```

PARAMETER ESTIMATES APPEAR IN ORDER,
NO SPECIAL PROBLEMS WERE ENCOUNTERED DURING OPTIMIZATION.

EQS automatically decodes the input file to generate a model specification based on the Bentler-Weeks designation of dependent and independent variables. As shown in Table 3.3, there are 11 dependent variables (note that V7 is missing) and 15 independent variables: 4 factors and 11 error terms.

Following the Bentler-Weeks representation are four summary pieces of information. The first two indicate the amount of memory required to run the job and the numerical value of the matrix determinant value. The third states the estimation method and the distributional theory used in the analysis. We requested maximum likelihood estimation, and this information typically heads each page of the output; to conserve space, however, these additional lines have been excluded from Table 3.3. Finally, EQS prints out a summary statement regarding the technical acceptability of the model parameters; basically, the program checks on the identification status of all parameters. In the ideal case, the message **"PARAMETER ESTIMATES APPEAR IN ORDER, NO SPECIAL PROBLEMS WERE ENCOUNTERED DURING OPTIMIZATION"** will appear, as we see here. It is important to locate this message prior to any interpretation of results; accordingly, we can feel confident that the estimates in the present application are appropriate.

If, on the other hand, the program encounters difficulties in the estimation process, the message locates the problematic parameter and prints out a **Condition Code** that pinpoints the obstacle contributing to its lack of identification. Basically, such problems relate to two situations. First, a parameter is linearly dependent on other parameters in the model, thereby causing the covariance matrix to be singular; the message appears as **"LINEARLY DEPENDENT ON OTHER PARAMETERS"**. This situation occurs either because the parameter is underidentified in the model or because it is **empirically underidentified** as a consequence of the data. (For an extensive explanation of empirical identification [and underidentification], see Bollen, 1989; Hayduk, 1987; Kenny, 1979; Rindskopf, 1984; Wothke, 1993.) The second situation results from the presence of **boundary parameters,** those having values close to the boundary of admissible values; typical examples are correlation estimates that are greater than 1.00 and variance estimates that are zero or some negative value. In contrast to LISREL, which places no constraints on these parameters, EQS forces them to be held to a boundary value (1.00 or zero). Thus the presence of boundary parameters in EQS generates one of two Condition Code messages: (a) **"CONSTRAINED AT UPPER BOUND"** or (b) **"CONSTRAINED AT LOWER BOUND"**. (For greater elaboration on the cause and alternative approaches to addressing these difficulties, see Bentler, 1989, 1992a; Bentler & Chou, 1987; Bollen, 1989; Rindskopf, 1984.)

We turn next to the portion of the output that deals with the various aspects of model fit. These results are presented in Table 3.4.

TABLE 3.4. EQS Output for Initially Hypothesized Four-Factor Model of Self-Concept: Assessment of Fit

RESIDUAL COVARIANCE MATRIX   (S-SIGMA) :

		SDQGSC V 1	SDQASC V 2	SDQESC V 3	SDQMSC V 4	APIGSC V 5
SDQGSC	V 1	0.000				
SDQASC	V 2	0.030	0.000			
SDQESC	V 3	0.089	-0.022	0.000		
SDQMSC	V 4	-0.039	-0.030	-0.049	0.000	
APIGSC	V 5	0.006	0.044	0.063	0.029	0.000
SESGSC	V 6	0.001	0.027	0.093	0.010	-0.008
SCAASC	V 8	-0.062	0.000	-0.078	-0.024	-0.012
APIESC	V 9	-0.059	0.001	0.046	-0.051	0.014
SCAESC	V 10	-0.066	0.071	-0.054	0.010	-0.028
APIMSC	V 11	-0.027	0.004	0.007	0.005	0.103
SCAMSC	V 12	-0.062	-0.031	-0.030	-0.003	0.026

		SESGSC V 6	SCAASC V 8	APIESC V 9	SCAESC V 10	APIMSC V 11
SESGSC	V 6	0.000				
SCAASC	V 8	-0.003	0.000			
APIESC	V 9	-0.031	-0.083	0.000		
SCAESC	V 10	-0.026	0.179	-0.014	0.000	
APIMSC	V 11	0.047	0.006	0.079	0.039	0.000
SCAMSC	V 12	-0.016	0.109	-0.033	0.090	-0.005

		SCAMSC V 12
SCAMSC	V 12	0.000

AVERAGE ABSOLUTE COVARIANCE RESIDUALS	=	0.0330
AVERAGE OFF-DIAGONAL ABSOLUTE COVARIANCE RESIDUALS	=	0.0396

STANDARDIZED RESIDUAL MATRIX:

		SDQGSC V 1	SDQASC V 2	SDQESC V 3	SDQMSC V 4	APIGSC V 5
SDQGSC	V 1	0.000				
SDQASC	V 2	0.030	0.000			
SDQESC	V 3	0.089	-0.022	0.000		
SDQMSC	V 4	-0.039	-0.030	-0.049	0.000	
APIGSC	V 5	0.006	0.044	0.063	0.029	0.000
SESGSC	V 6	0.001	0.027	0.093	0.010	-0.008
SCAASC	V 8	-0.062	0.000	-0.078	-0.024	-0.012
APIESC	V 9	-0.059	0.001	0.046	-0.051	0.014
SCAESC	V 10	-0.066	0.071	-0.054	0.010	-0.028
APIMSC	V 11	-0.027	0.004	0.007	0.005	0.103
SCAMSC	V 12	-0.062	-0.031	-0.030	-0.003	0.026

		SESGSC V 6	SCAASC V 8	APIESC V 9	SCAESC V 10	APIMSC V 11
SESGSC	V 6	0.000				
SCAASC	V 8	-0.003	0.000			
APIESC	V 9	-0.031	-0.083	0.000		
SCAESC	V 10	-0.026	0.179	-0.014	0.000	
APIMSC	V 11	0.047	0.006	0.079	0.039	0.000
SCAMSC	V 12	-0.016	0.109	-0.033	0.090	-0.005

		SCAMSC V 12
SCAMSC	V 12	0.000

AVERAGE ABSOLUTE STANDARDIZED RESIDUALS	=	0.0330
AVERAGE OFF-DIAGONAL ABSOLUTE STANDARDIZED RESIDUALS	=	0.0396

(Continued)

TABLE 3.4. (Continued)

```
LARGEST STANDARDIZED RESIDUALS:
  V 10,V  8    V 12,V  8    V 11,V  5    V  6,V  3    V 12,V 10
    0.179        0.109        0.103        0.093        0.090
  V  3,V  1    V  9,V  8    V 11,V  9    V  8,V  3    V 10,V  2
    0.089       -0.083        0.079       -0.078        0.071
  V 10,V  1    V  5,V  3    V 12,V  1    V  8,V  1    V  9,V  1
   -0.066        0.063       -0.062       -0.062       -0.059
  V 10,V  3    V  9,V  4    V  4,V  3    V 11,V  6    V  9,V  3
   -0.054       -0.051       -0.049        0.047        0.046
```

DISTRIBUTION OF STANDARDIZED RESIDUALS

```
    ----------------------------------
    !                        !
40- !                        -
    !                        !
    !                        !
    !              *         !
    !              *         !          RANGE       FREQ PERCENT
30- !           *  *         -
    !           *  *         !    1  -0.5  -  --       0   0.00%
    !           *  *         !    2  -0.4  - -0.5      0   0.00%
    !           *  *         !    3  -0.3  - -0.4      0   0.00%
    !           *  *         !    4  -0.2  - -0.3      0   0.00%
20- !           *  *         -    5  -0.1  - -0.2      0   0.00%
    !           *  *         !    6   0.0  - -0.1     30  45.45%
    !           *  *         !    7   0.1  -  0.0     33  50.00%
    !           *  *         !    8   0.2  -  0.1      3   4.55%
    !           *  *         !    9   0.3  -  0.2      0   0.00%
10- !           *  *         -    A   0.4  -  0.3      0   0.00%
    !           *  *         !    B   0.5  -  0.4      0   0.00%
    !           *  *         !    C   ++   -  0.5      0   0.00%
    !         *  *  *        !    ----------------------------
    !         *  *  *        !           TOTAL        66 100.00%
    ----------------------------------
      1 2 3 4 5 6 7 8 9 A B C    EACH "*" REPRESENTS 2 RESIDUALS
```

GOODNESS OF FIT SUMMARY

INDEPENDENCE MODEL CHI-SQUARE = 7523.677 ON 55 DEGREES OF FREEDOM

INDEPENDENCE AIC = 7413.67711   INDEPENDENCE CAIC = 7088.97101
       MODEL AIC =   551.57419   MODEL CAIC =   327.23179

CHI-SQUARE =   627.574 BASED ON 38 DEGREES OF FREEDOM
PROBABILITY VALUE FOR THE CHI-SQUARE STATISTIC IS LESS THAN 0.001
THE NORMAL THEORY RLS CHI-SQUARE FOR THIS ML SOLUTION IS   660.041.

```
    BENTLER-BONETT NORMED     FIT INDEX=        0.917
    BENTLER-BONETT NONNORMED FIT INDEX=        0.886
    COMPARATIVE FIT INDEX            =         0.921
```

ITERATIVE SUMMARY

	PARAMETER		
ITERATION	ABS CHANGE	ALPHA	FUNCTION
1	0.387669	1.00000	0.85824
2	0.070388	1.00000	0.75566
3	0.026339	1.00000	0.63471
4	0.008352	1.00000	0.63128
5	0.003084	1.00000	0.63081
6	0.001236	1.00000	0.63074
7	0.000527	1.00000	0.63073

Assessment of Overall Model Fit

The focal point in analyzing structural equation models is the extent to which the hypothesized model "fits," or, in other words, adequately describes the sample data. Given findings of an inadequate goodness of fit, the next logical step is to detect the source of misfit in the model. Assessment of model adequacy involves a number of criteria, some of which bear on the fit of the model as a whole, and others of which bear on the fit of individual parameters. These criteria, as handled in EQS, are now described.

Residual Covariance Matrices. The basic idea in assessing model fit is to determine the degree of similarity between the sample covariance matrix (designated as S), and the restricted (or predicted) covariance matrix (i.e., one on which the structure specified in the hypothesized model has been imposed, designated as $\hat{\Sigma}$). Discrepancy in fit between these matrices is represented by the residual covariance matrix (S-$\hat{\Sigma}$) and its standardized version, which takes standard deviations on the measured variables into account; these appear first on the output as shown in Table 3.4. (Because our analyses here are based on the correlation matrix, the unstandardized and standardized residual matrices will, of course, be identical.) Given that a model describes the data well, these values should be small and evenly distributed; large residuals associated with particular parameters indicate their misspecification in the model, thereby affecting the overall model misfit. For both the residual and standardized residual matrices, EQS computes two averages, one based on all elements of the lower triangular matrix and the other ignoring the diagonal elements; typically, the off-diagonal elements play a more major role in the effect on goodness-of-fit χ^2 statistics (Bentler, 1989, 1992a). Based on an ordering from large to small, the program then lists the 20 largest standardized residuals and designates which pairs of variables are involved. Finally, a frequency distribution of the standardized residuals is presented. Ideally, this distribution should be symmetric and centered on zero.

Turning to the standardized residual information in Table 3.4, we see that the average off-diagonal value is .0396, which reflects a fairly good fit to the data. The largest off-diagonal value is .179, and reflects model misfit associated with variables V10 and V8; both represent the Self-Concept of Ability Scale (SCA) in the measurement of ESC and ASC, respectively. Finally, a review of the frequency distribution reveals that most residual values (95.45%) fall between −.10 and .10; 4.55% fall between .10 and .20 (actually, the upper limit is .179). Taken together, information on the standardized residuals has told us that although global fit of the model is fairly good, there is a small degree of misfit related to at least two variables (V10, V8).

Goodness-of-Fit Summary. Turning to this section of the printout (Table 3.4), we see statistics reported for several goodness-of-fit indices; all relate to the model as a whole. The first of these is the **independence chi-square** statistic ($\chi^2_{(55)} = 7523.677$) reported for the likelihood ratio test of the Bentler and Bonett (1980) null model. This model is one of complete independence of all variables in the model (i.e., in which all correlations among variables are zero). In large samples, the null model serves as a good baseline against which to compare alternative models for purposes of evaluating the gain in improved fit. Given a sound hypothesized model, one would naturally expect the χ^2 value for the null model to be extremely high, thereby indicating excessive malfit; such is the case with the present example ($\chi^2_{(55)} = 7523.677$).

Now skip down three lines to the chi-square value reported for our hypothesized four-factor model; relative to the null model, it represents a substantially better (although still poor) fit to the data ($\chi^2_{(38)} = 627.574$). On the other hand, had the fit of the the four-factor model been close to that of the null model, this would have raised serious questions about the soundness of the hypothesized model. Nonetheless, the probability value of less than .001, printed on the next line, suggests that the hypothesized four-factor model is not entirely adequate either. Interpreted literally, it indicates that the hypothesis bearing on SC relations, as summarized in the model, represents an unlikely event (occurring less than one time in a thousand) and should be rejected. The sensitivity of the χ^2 likelihood ratio test to sample size, however, is well known and is addressed later.

In addition to furnishing χ^2 statistics for the independent (i.e., null) and hypothesized models, EQS provides for the evaluation of both models based on Akaike's (1987) Information Criterion (**AIC**) and Bozdogan's (1987) consistent version of the AIC (**CAIC**). These criteria address the issue of parsimony in the assessment of model fit; thus, that statistical goodness of fit and the number of estimated parameters are taken into account. Although both criteria were developed for ML estimation, they are applied to all estimation methods in EQS. Turning to the output once again, we see that the AIC statistic for both the null and hypothesized models is substantially smaller than the χ^2 statistic. The formula for the AIC is as follows:[7]

$$\text{Independence Model AIC} = \chi^2 - 2d_i$$
$$\text{Hypothesized Model AIC} = \chi^2 - 2d_k$$

where d_i = degrees of freedom for the null model and d_k = degrees of freedom for the hypothesized model.

As noted above, the sensitivity of the χ^2 statistic is now widely known. Consequently, over the past 15 years, numerous alternative indices of fit have been proposed and evaluated (for reviews, see Gerbing & Anderson, 1993; Marsh, Balla, & McDonald, 1988; McDonald & Marsh, 1990; Tanaka, 1993). These criteria, commonly referred to as **subjective, practical,** or **ad hoc** indices of fit, have been used as adjuncts to the χ^2 statistic.

For the better part of a decade, Bentler and Bonett's (1980) **Normed Fit Index (NFI)**[8] has been the practical criterion of choice, as evidenced in large part by the current "classic" status of its original paper (see Bentler, 1992b; Bentler & Bonett, 1987). Addressing evidence that the NFI has shown a tendency to underestimate fit in small samples, Bentler (1990a) revised the NFI to take sample size into account and proposed the **Comparative Fit Index (CFI)**. Although these practical indices of fit are reported in the EQS output, the CFI should be the index of choice (Bentler, 1990b). Values for both the NFI and CFI range from zero to 1.00 and are derived from the comparison of a hypothesized model with the null model, as described above. As such, each provides a measure of complete covariation in the data, a value greater than .90 indicating an acceptable fit to the data (Bentler, 1992b).

As shown in Table 3.4, the NFI (.917) and CFI (.921) were consistent in suggesting that the hypothesized model represented an adequate fit to the data. However, the marginality of adequacy suggests evidence of some misfit in the model. These findings coincide with the standardized residual results and indicate the misspecification of particular parameters in the model, an issue addressed later in this section dealing with the assessment of individual parameter fit.

The formulae for the NFI and CFI are as follows:

$$\text{NFI} = \frac{\chi_0^2 - \chi_k^2}{\chi_0^2}$$

where χ_0^2 = the null model and χ_k^2 = the hypothesized model.

$$\text{CFI} = \left| \frac{(\chi_0^2 - \text{df}_0) - (\chi_k^2 - \text{df}_k)}{(\chi_0^2 - \text{df}_0)} \right|$$

where df_0 = degrees of freedom for the null model, df_k = degrees of freedom for the hypothesized model, and | | indicates trimming to place its value into the 0.0 – 1.0 range.

The last piece of information related to overall model fit appearing on the output is the **iterative summary.** Here we see a synopsis of the number of iterations required for a convergent solution and the mean absolute change in parameter estimates (**PARAMETER ABS CHANGE**) associated with each iteration. The best scenario is a situation where only a few iterations are needed to reach convergence; after the first two or three iterations, the change in parameter estimates stabilizes and remains minimal. As indicated in Table 3.4, this is the case with our CFA model, where only seven iterations were needed to reach convergence. After the first three iterations, the parameter values remained relatively stable.

At the very worst, the number of iterations exceeds the default value of 30, resulting in nonconvergence; if this happens, the iterative process terminates and a message warning the user not to trust the output is issued. If you are presented with this problem, it is unlikely that a simple resubmission of the job with a requested extension in the number of iterations, which you can do with /TECHNICAL, will resolve the dilemma. Rather, you should look for other means of resolution. I have found this situation to be easily solved just by attending to the start values. If start values were not included in the input file, then add them; if they were included, make a few modifications. Given that start values were included, lack of convergence occurs most often due to a wide discrepancy between the start values and actual estimated values related to only a few parameters. A typical example is where the start value is positive but the actual estimate is negative. One quick way to get a handle on more appropriate start values is to review the estimates provided with the failed output; although many of these estimates may be inaccurate, they can often guide you to a more useful start value that better approximates the actual estimated value.

The most efficient approach to achieving more appropriate start values is to use the **RETEST** option provided by EQS. Given the number of basic topics to be covered in this chapter, however, I purposely did not introduce the option here. However, in my judgment, this option is truly worth its weight in gold and I do include it in Chapter 4.

One final point to note in Table 3.4 is the **function**. In general, EQS minimizes a fit function, and when iterations stop, this value should be at the minimum value. Also, (sample size $- 1$) $\times$ Function $= \chi^2$; here, $995 \times .63073 = 627.574$.

Assessment of Parameter Estimates

Thus far in our discussion of model fit assessment, we have concentrated on the model as a whole. Now we turn our attention to the fit of individual parameters in the model. There are two aspects of concern here: (a) the appropriateness of the estimates, and (b) their statistical significance. Parameter estimates and information related to them are presented in Table 3.5.

Feasibility of Parameter Estimates. The first step in assessing the fit of individual parameters is to determine the viability of their estimated values. Any estimates falling outside the admissable range signal a clear indication

TABLE 3.5. EQS Output for Initially Hypothesized 4-Factor Model of
Self-Concept: Parameter Estimates

```
MEASUREMENT EQUATIONS WITH STANDARD ERRORS AND TEST STATISTICS

SDQGSC  =V1  =    1.000 F1    + 1.000 E1

SDQASC  =V2  =    1.000 F2    + 1.000 E2

SDQESC  =V3  =    1.000 F3    + 1.000 E3

SDQMSC  =V4  =    1.000 F4    + 1.000 E4

APIGSC  =V5  =     .819*F1    + 1.000 E5
                   .032
                 25.325

SESGSC  =V6  =    1.030*F1    + 1.000 E6
                   .033
                 31.476

SCAASC  =V8  =    1.027*F2    + 1.000 E8
                   .038
                 26.677

APIESC  =V9  =    1.074*F3    + 1.000 E9
                   .042
                 25.568

SCAESC  =V10 =     .973*F3    + 1.000 E10
                   .041
                 23.665

APIMSC  =V11 =     .975*F4    + 1.000 E11
                   .020
                 49.608

SCAMSC  =V12 =     .944*F4    + 1.000 E12
                   .021
                 45.575

VARIANCES OF INDEPENDENT VARIABLES
----------------------------------
                     V                        F
                     ---                      ---
                             I F1  -  GSC          .762*I
                             I                     .047 I
                             I                   16.226 I
                             I                          I
                             I F2  -  ASC          .657*I
                             I                     .045 I
                             I                   14.472 I
                             I                          I
                             I F3  -  ESC          .614*I
                             I                     .045 I
                             I                   13.766 I
                             I                          I
                             I F4  -  MSC          .881*I
                             I                     .045 I
                             I                   19.410 I
                             I                          I
```

(Continued)

TABLE 3.5. (Continued)

```
                        E                              D
                       ---                            ---
E1   -SDQGSC              .238*I                              I
                          .021 I                              I
                        11.584 I                              I
                               I                              I
E2   -SDQASC              .343*I                              I
                          .023 I                              I
                        14.961 I                              I
                               I                              I
E3   -SDQESC              .386*I                              I
                          .024 I                              I
                        16.093 I                              I
                               I                              I
E4   -SDQMSC              .119*I                              I
                          .010 I                              I
                        11.573 I                              I
                               I                              I
E5   -APIGSC              .489*I                              I
                          .025 I                              I
                        19.424 I                              I
                               I                              I
E6   -SESGSC              .192*I                              I
                          .020 I                              I
                         9.366I                              I
                               I                              I
E8   -SCAASC              .307*I                              I
                          .023 I                              I
                        13.580 I                              I
                               I                              I
E9   -APIESC              .292*I                              I
                          .023 I                              I
                        12.944 I                              I
                               I                              I
E10  -SCAESC              .420*I                              I
                          .025 I                              I
                        16.950 I                              I
                               I                              I
E11  -APIMSC              .162*I                              I
                          .011 I                              I
                        14.502 I                              I
                               I                              I
E12  -SCAMSC              .216*I                              I
                          .013 I                              I
                        17.069 I                              I
                               I                              I
```

COVARIANCES AMONG INDEPENDENT VARIABLES
```
-----------------------------------------
                        V                              F
                       ---                            ---
                          I F2  -  ASC                  .271*I
                          I F1  -  GSC                  .029 I
                          I                            9.423 I
                          I                                  I
                          I F3  -  ESC                  .200*I
                          I F1  -  GSC                  .026 I
                          I                            7.549 I
                          I                                  I
```

TABLE 3.5. (Continued)

```
                              I F4    -   MSC              .209*I
                              I F1    -   GSC              .029 I
                              I                          7.117 I
                              I                                I
                              I F3    -   ESC              .410*I
                              I F2    -   ASC              .031 I
                              I                         13.389 I
                              I                                I
                              I F4    -   MSC              .483*I
                              I F2    -   ASC              .033 I
                              I                         14.442 I
                              I                                I
                              I F4    -   MSC              .061*I
                              I F3    -   ESC              .026 I
                              I                          2.304 I
                              I                                I
```

STANDARDIZED SOLUTION:

```
SDQGSC  =V1  =   .873 F1     + .488 E1
SDQASC  =V2  =   .811 F2     + .585 E2
SDQESC  =V3  =   .783 F3     + .622 E3
SDQMSC  =V4  =   .938 F4     + .345 E4
APIGSC  =V5  =   .715*F1     + .699 E5
SESGSC  =V6  =   .899*F1     + .438 E6
SCAASC  =V8  =   .833*F2     + .554 E8
APIESC  =V9  =   .841*F3     + .540 E9
SCAESC  =V10 =   .762*F3     + .648 E10
APIMSC  =V11 =   .915*F4     + .402 E11
SCAMSC  =V12 =   .886*F4     + .464 E12
```

```
CORRELATIONS AMONG INDEPENDENT VARIABLES
-----------------------------------------
              V                          F
              ---                        ---
                              I F2    -   ASC              .383*I
                              I F1    -   GSC                   I
                              I                                 I
                              I F3    -   ESC              .292*I
                              I F1    -   GSC                   I
                              I                                 I
                              I F4    -   MSC              .255*I
                              I F1    -   GSC                   I
                              I                                 I
                              I F3    -   ESC              .646*I
                              I F2    -   ASC                   I
                              I                                 I
                              I F4    -   MSC              .634*I
                              I F2    -   ASC                   I
                              I                                 I
                              I F4    -   MSC              .082*I
                              I F3    -   ESC                   I
                              I                                 I
-----------------------------------------------------------------
                    E N D   O F   M E T H O D
-----------------------------------------------------------------
```

that either the model is wrong or the input matrix lacks sufficient information. Examples of parameters exhibiting unreasonable estimates are correlations greater than 1.00 and standard errors that are abnormally large or small.[9] A standard error approaching zero usually results from the linear dependence of the related parameter upon some other parameter in the model; such a circumstance renders testing for the statistical significance of the estimate impossible.

Statistical Significance of Parameter Estimates. The test statistic here represents the parameter estimate divided by its standard error; as such, it operates as a z statistic in testing that the estimate is statistically different from zero. Based on an α level of .05, then, the test statistic needs to be greater than ± 1.96 before the hypothesis (that the estimate = 0.0) can be rejected. However, it is important to note that conclusions based on a series of univariate tests, as is the case here, may differ from those based on a multivariate test in which a set of parameters is considered simultaneously. Although this multivariate option is available to EQS users via the Wald Test (Wald, 1943), it is not considered in the present chapter for reasons of parsimony, as noted earlier.

Let's turn now to this part of the printout, as presented in Table 3.5. Scanning the output, you will see that the unstandardized estimates are presented first, followed by the standardized solution; both sets of estimates are presented separately for the measurement equations, the variances, and the covariances.

Let's look more closely at the unstandardized estimates. We see that for the first four variables, (V1-V4), all information appears on one line only; these represent the fixed parameters, and thus no estimated values are presented. For each of the estimated (*) parameters, however, there are three lines of output; the estimated value is presented first, the standard error second, and the test statistic third.

A review of the **unstandardized solution** in Table 3.5 reveals all estimates to be reasonable and statistically significant; all standard errors appear also to be in good order.

In the **standardized solution,** all V, F, E, and D (the latter not being considered in the present example) variables are rescaled to have a variance of 1.0.[10] In contrast to the unstandardized solution, information is summarized on one line. In reviewing the standardized estimates, you will want to verify that particular parameter values are consistent with the literature. For example, within the context of the present application, it is of interest to inspect, in the standardized solution, correlations among the SC factors for their consistency with their previously reported values; in the present example, these estimates are as expected.

Three additional features of the standardized solution are worthy of note. First, in the event that some variances are estimated at negative values, the standardized solution cannot be obtained because the computation requires the square roots of these values. If such is the case, no standardized solution will be printed. Second, you will note that in the standardized solution, parameters that were previously fixed to 1.0 take on new values. Finally, you will note the absence of output for the variances of the independent variables. This is because in standardizing the estimates, the variances automatically take on a value of 1.00.

Assessment of Parameter Misspecification

Determination of malfitting parameters is accomplished in EQS by means of the LM Test. As noted earlier, fixed parameters, as specified in the input file, are assessed both univariately and multivariately to identify parameters that would contribute to a significant drop in χ^2 if they were to be freely estimated in a subsequent EQS run. Results related to the LM Test are presented in Table 3.6.

Univariate Test Statistics. In reviewing these results, we see that the first four parameters, all of which are error covariances, yielded χ^2 values that were substantially larger than those for the remaining parameters. Nonetheless, χ^2 values for the next six parameters, at least, were also highly significant. (In the interest of space, the 82 subsequent parameter values were deleted from the table.) Associated with each of the parameters presented is an estimated parameter change value. Immediately following the univariate test statistics, the program identifies the parameter sets, or submatrices, to be included in the analyses; in this case, the parameters of interest are the error covariances (PEE) and factor loadings (GVF).

Multivariate Test Statistics. Under the univariate LM Test, restrictions in the model are tested independently, and correlations among particular variables are not taken into account. As a result, there are typically more statistically significant LM χ^2s under this test than under the multivariate test. Thus it may be more judicious to base model respecifications on the multivariate LM Test. For example, in examining the **cumulative multivariate statistics,** along with their accompanying **univariate increments,** you will see that there are now only two malfitting parameters (E10,E8; E12,E8), rather than four, that stand distinctly apart from the rest. Interestingly, these are the same two worst fitting parameters that were reported for the ordered univariate statistics; they are also consistent with the two largest standardized

TABLE 3.6. EQS Output for Initially Hypothesized Four-Factor Model of
Self-Concept: Modification Indices

```
      LAGRANGIAN MULTIPLIER TEST REQUIRES      21814 WORDS OF MEMORY.
      PROGRAM ALLOCATES     329728 WORDS.
```

LAGRANGE MULTIPLIER TEST (FOR ADDING PARAMETERS)

ORDERED UNIVARIATE TEST STATISTICS:

NO	CODE		PARAMETER	CHI-SQUARE	PROBABILITY	PARAMETER CHANGE
1	2	6	E10,E8	199.648	0.000	0.227
2	2	6	E12,E8	142.141	0.000	0.133
3	2	6	E9,E3	124.954	0.000	0.308
4	2	6	E11,E9	109.157	0.000	0.106
5	2	6	E9,E8	67.684	0.000	-0.128
6	2	12	V10,F2	63.162	0.000	0.364
7	2	6	E10,E3	59.917	0.000	-0.184
8	2	6	E11,E10	39.360	0.000	-0.069
9	2	12	V3,F1	35.512	0.000	0.181
10	2	6	E12,E2	33.083	0.000	-0.066
.	.	.	.	.	.	.
.	.	.	.	.	.	.
.	.	.	.	.	.	.
.	.	.	.	.	.	.
.	.	.	.	.	.	.
92	2	6	V1,F1	0.000	1.000	0.000

MULTIVARIATE LAGRANGE MULTIPLIER TEST BY SIMULTANEOUS PROCESS IN STAGE   1

PARAMETER SETS (SUBMATRICES) ACTIVE AT THIS STAGE ARE:

PEE GVF

	CUMULATIVE MULTIVARIATE STATISTICS				UNIVARIATE INCREMENT	
STEP	PARAMETER	CHI-SQUARE	D.F.	PROBABILITY	CHI-SQUARE	PROBABILITY
1	E10,E8	199.648	1	0.000	199.648	0.000
2	E12,E8	344.824	2	0.000	145.175	0.000
3	E11,E9	434.797	3	0.000	89.974	0.000
4	E12,E10	472.451	4	0.000	37.653	0.000
5	V3,F1	508.065	5	0.000	35.614	0.000
6	E9,E3	541.378	6	0.000	33.314	0.000
7	E11,E5	565.212	7	0.000	23.833	0.000
8	E2,E1	578.926	8	0.000	13.715	0.000
9	V1,F2	593.431	9	0.000	14.505	0.000
10	E9,E5	603.322	10	0.000	9.891	0.002
11	V11,F3	612.936	11	0.000	9.614	0.002
12	V8,F4	619.514	12	0.000	6.578	0.010
13	V10,F2	625.923	13	0.000	6.409	0.011
14	E3,E1	631.370	14	0.000	5.447	0.020
15	E11,E1	635.651	15	0.000	4.280	0.039
16	V11,F1	640.757	16	0.000	5.106	0.024

```
      Execution begins at 09:43:18.46
      Execution ends   at 09:43:29.78
      Elapsed time =     11.32 seconds
```

residuals noted earlier and with results reported for the original study (Byrne & Shavelson, 1986).

Post Hoc Model Fitting

Provided with this information, a researcher may wish to consider respecifying his or her originally hypothesized model. Should this be the case, however, it is critically important that the researcher be cognizant of both the exploratory nature of, and the dangers associated with, such post hoc model-fitting ventures. (For extensive discussions of the topic see, e.g., Anderson & Gerbing, 1988; Cliff, 1983; Cudeck & Browne, 1983; Jöreskog, 1993; MacCallum, 1986). For our purposes here, we'll now proceed in respecifying the initially hypothesized four-factor model, taking the above misspecification errors into account.

Specification and Analysis of Model 2

Given that all the univariate increments demonstrate significant χ^2 values, you no doubt will wonder how many parameters to respecify. This decision must **always** be based on a judicious combination of both the statistical information provided in the output **and** the researcher's knowledge of his or her substantive area; respecification must make substantive as well as statistical sense. From both of these perspectives, it seems reasonable here that the first two error covariances, involving the ASC subscale of the Self-Concept of Ability Scale and its ESC (E10,E8) and MSC (E12,E8) subscales, should be respecified as freely estimated parameters. Statistically, they yield exceptionally large χ^2 values; substantively, they represent correlated errors among subscales of the same measuring instrument, a common finding with attitude scales in general (e.g., Byrne, 1991, 1992a, 1993; Newcomb, Huba, & Bentler, 1986; Tanaka & Huba, 1984) and with SC instruments in particular (e.g., Byrne, 1988a, 1988b; Byrne & Schneider, 1988). Admittedly, the third parameter (E11,E9) LM χ^2 is also large compared with those remaining. However, in the interest of parsimony, I consider it best to limit respecification in the present case to the first two parameters, reserving judgment concerning the third (and perhaps others) until the results from this respecified model are ascertained.

Specification. One exceptionally important and time-efficient feature of EQS is that modification indices are based on the LM Test, which assesses parameter misfit multivariately. The benefit of this approach is that the respecification of a model can incorporate more than one modified parameter in any single run (cf. the LISREL approach). So let's now respecify our hypothesized four-factor model to include the two error covariances as described above. This is easily accomplished by incorporating two additional statements to the former input file as shown below.

```
/COV
 F1 TO F4 = *;
 E10,E8 = *;  E12,E8 = *;
```

EQS Output. Relevant portions of the output related to the analysis of Model 2 are presented in Table 3.7. These include the goodness-of-fit summary, the unstandardized and standardized estimates for the specified error covariances, and the multivariate χ^2 and univariate increment statistics for the LM Test.

The first important piece of information to note here is the enormous drop in the overall χ^2 value ($\chi^2_{(36)} = 322.656$) for Model 2 compared with the initially hypothesized model. When models are nested[11] as they are here, the difference in χ^2 ($\Delta\chi^2$) between the two models is itself χ^2-distributed with degrees of freedom equal to the difference in degrees of freedom (Δdf), it can be tested statistically, a significant $\Delta\chi^2$ indicating a substantial improvement in model fit. Needless to say, the decrease in χ^2 ($\Delta\chi^2_{(2)} = 304.918$) from Model 1 to Model 2 represents a highly significant improvement in goodness of fit. Consistent with this statistical assessment, the CFI (.962) also reflects a substantial improvement in model fit ($\Delta = .04$). Although these findings provide strong argument for the inclusion of the two error covariances in our CFA four-factor model, we need to examine information bearing on their estimates before arriving at this conclusion.

Of primary interest with respect to the estimates is whether or not the newly specified parameters are statistically significant; indeed, examination of the unstandardized estimates reveal both error covariances to be highly significant (estimate/standard error = 11.011, 9.454). Beyond this fact, the standard errors are reasonable, and the standardized solution reveals correlations among error variables that are moderately high. Taken together, these findings, together with the improvement in overall model fit, provide strong support for a model that includes error covariances among the three subscales of the Self-Concept of Ability Scale.

Finally, we need to examine the LM Test statistics to determine the status of the remaining fixed parameters, and in particular the third error covariance (E11,E9) noted for Model 1. Interestingly, as shown in Table 3.7, this parameter maintained its exceedingly high LM χ^2 and retained its distinctiveness from the remaining fixed parameters; in contrast, the parameter E12,E10 exchanged its position with the factor loading parameter, V3,F1.

TABLE 3.7. Selected EQS Output for Respecified Four-Factor Model of
             Self-Concept: Model 2

GOODNESS OF FIT SUMMARY

INDEPENDENCE MODEL CHI-SQUARE =   7523.677 ON   55 DEGREES OF FREEDOM

INDEPENDENCE AIC =   7413.67711   INDEPENDENCE CAIC =   7088.97101
        MODEL AIC =   250.65613   MODEL CAIC =   38.12123

CHI-SQUARE =   322.656 BASED ON   36 DEGREES OF FREEDOM
PROBABILITY VALUE FOR THE CHI-SQUARE STATISTIC IS LESS THAN 0.001
THE NORMAL THEORY RLS CHI-SQUARE FOR THIS ML SOLUTION IS   310.119.

BENTLER-BONETT NORMED   FIT INDEX=   0.957
BENTLER-BONETT NONNORMED FIT INDEX=   0.941
COMPARATIVE FIT INDEX   =   0.962

COVARIANCES AMONG INDEPENDENT VARIABLES

	E		D	
	---		---	
E10 -SCAESC	.190*I			I
E8 -SCAASC	.017 I			I
	11.011 I			I
	I			I
E12 -SCAMSC	.106*I			I
E8 -SCAASC	.011 I			I
	9.454 I			I

STANDARDIZED SOLUTION:
CORRELATIONS AMONG INDEPENDENT VARIABLES

	E		D	
	---		---	
E10 -SCAESC	.464*I			I
E8 -SCAASC	I			I
	I			I
E12 -SCAMSC	.375*I			I
E8 -SCAASC	I			I

		CUMULATIVE MULTIVARIATE STATISTICS			UNIVARIATE INCREMENT	
STEP	PARAMETER	CHI-SQUARE	D.F.	PROBABILITY	CHI-SQUARE	PROBABILITY
----	---------	----------	----	-----------	----------	-----------
1	E11,E9	90.809	1	0.000	90.809	0.000
2	V3,F1	129.489	2	0.000	38.681	0.000
3	E12,E10	163.224	3	0.000	33.735	0.000
4	E10,E2	195.960	4	0.000	32.736	0.000
5	E11,E5	219.198	5	0.000	23.237	0.000
6	E2,E1	231.365	6	0.000	12.167	0.000
7	V1,F2	245.166	7	0.000	13.801	0.000
8	V11,F2	255.490	8	0.000	10.325	0.001
9	E9,E5	263.681	9	0.000	8.191	0.004
10	E3,E1	269.572	10	0.000	5.891	0.015
11	V10,F2	274.532	11	0.000	4.959	0.026
12	V2,F3	281.566	12	0.000	7.035	0.008
13	E11,E1	286.153	13	0.000	4.587	0.032
14	V11,F1	290.138	14	0.000	3.985	0.046

Execution begins at 10:25:26.74
Execution ends   at 10:25:37.89
Elapsed time =   11.15 seconds

Specification and Analysis of Model 3

On the basis of the above results, I consider it advisable to respecify a third model in which an error covariance between the ESC and MSC subscales of the Affective Perception Inventory (E11,E9) is freely estimated. Let's now examine this model.

Specification. Once again, respecification of the previous model is simply a matter of adding another statement to the **/COVARIANCE** paragraph, which now reads as follows:

```
/COV
 F1 TO F4 = *;
 E10,E8 = *; E12,E8 = *; E11,E9 = *;
```

EQS Output. Model fit and estimated results for Model 3 are presented in Table 3.8.

Turning first to the overall goodness of fit, we see once again a very large and statistically significant drop in the overall χ^2 value ($\Delta\chi^2_{(1)} = 98.646$). In support of this dramatic improvement in model fit is the CFI value of .975. Adding to this, the fact that the newly specified error covariance is statistically significant and reflects a substantially high correlation provides strong argument in favor of retaining this parameter in the model.

Finally, let's review the LM Test statistics. As before, we see at least three fixed parameters that exhibit substantially high LM χ^2s, the largest representing the cross-loading of the ESC subscale of the Self Description Questionnaire (V3) onto the GSC factor. However, in view of the fact that approximately 98% of the covariation in the data has already been explained, as indicated by a CFI = .98, I would fault further post hoc model fitting as an overparameterization of the model. Thus I consider Model 3 to best represent the four-factor model of adolescent SC.[12] A schematic representation of this final model is presented in Figure 3.2.

HYPOTHESIS 2:
SELF-CONCEPT IS A TWO-FACTOR STRUCTURE

The model to be tested here postulates a priori that SC is a two-factor structure consisting of GSC and ASC. As such, it argues against the viability of subject-specific academic SC factors. As with the four-factor model, the three GSC measures load onto the GSC factor; in contrast, all other measures load onto the ASC factor. This hypothesized model is represented schematically in Figure 3.3.

TABLE 3.8. Selected EQS Output for Respecified Four-Factor Model of
Self-Concept: Model 3

GOODNESS OF FIT SUMMARY

INDEPENDENCE MODEL CHI-SQUARE =   7523.677 ON   55 DEGREES OF FREEDOM

INDEPENDENCE AIC = 7413.67711 INDEPENDENCE CAIC = 7088.97101
        MODEL AIC =   154.01021   MODEL CAIC =   -52.62094

CHI-SQUARE =   224.010 BASED ON   35 DEGREES OF FREEDOM
PROBABILITY VALUE FOR THE CHI-SQUARE STATISTIC IS LESS THAN 0.001
THE NORMAL THEORY RLS CHI-SQUARE FOR THIS ML SOLUTION IS   216.846.

BENTLER-BONETT NORMED   FIT INDEX=   0.970
BENTLER-BONETT NONNORMED FIT INDEX=   0.960
COMPARATIVE FIT INDEX   =   0.975

COVARIANCES AMONG INDEPENDENT VARIABLES

	E	D	
	---	---	
E10 -SCAESC	.190*I		I
E8 -SCAASC	.017 I		I
	11.203 I		I
	I		I
E12 -SCAMSC	.103*I		I
E8 -SCAASC	.011 I		I
	9.335 I		I
	I		I
E11 -APIMSC	.095*I		I
E9 -APIESC	.010 I		I
	9.466 I		I

STANDARDIZED SOLUTION:
CORRELATIONS AMONG INDEPENDENT VARIABLES

	E	D	
	---	---	
E10 -SCAESC	.470*I		I
E8 -SCAASC	I		I
	I		I
E12 -SCAMSC	.366*I		I
E8 -SCAASC	I		I
	I		I
E11 -APIMSC	.504*I		I
E9 -APIESC	I		I

		CUMULATIVE MULTIVARIATE STATISTICS			UNIVARIATE INCREMENT	
STEP	PARAMETER	CHI-SQUARE	D.F.	PROBABILITY	CHI-SQUARE	PROBABILITY
----	---------	----------	----	-----------	----------	-----------
1	V3,F1	44.940	1	0.000	44.940	0.000
2	E12,E10	77.477	2	0.000	32.537	0.000
3	E9,E3	109.814	3	0.000	32.338	0.000
4	E11,E5	125.009	4	0.000	15.195	0.000
5	V1,F4	136.519	5	0.000	11.510	0.001
6	E2,E1	147.820	6	0.000	11.301	0.001
7	V11,F2	158.427	7	0.000	10.607	0.001
8	E11,E6	164.648	8	0.000	6.220	0.013
9	E3,E1	170.100	9	0.000	5.452	0.020
10	E6,E5	176.315	10	0.000	6.215	0.013
11	V2,F3	181.917	11	0.000	5.602	0.018
12	V10,F2	187.938	12	0.000	6.021	0.014
13	E6,E3	191.936	13	0.000	3.998	0.046

Execution begins at 10:52:53.52
Execution ends   at 10:53:05.05
Elapsed time =   11.53 seconds

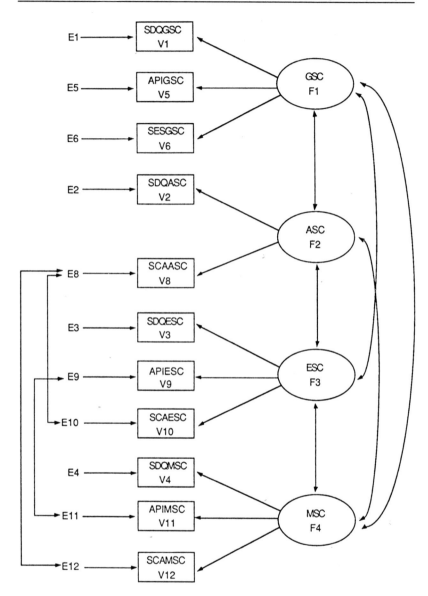

FIGURE 3.2. Final Four-Factor Model of Self-Concept

Source: Adapted from Byrne (1989). Copyright 1989 by Springer-Verlag. Reprinted by permission.

In specifying this two-factor model of SC, only the **/EQUATION,**
/VARIANCE, and **COVARIANCE** paragraphs of the input file require mod-

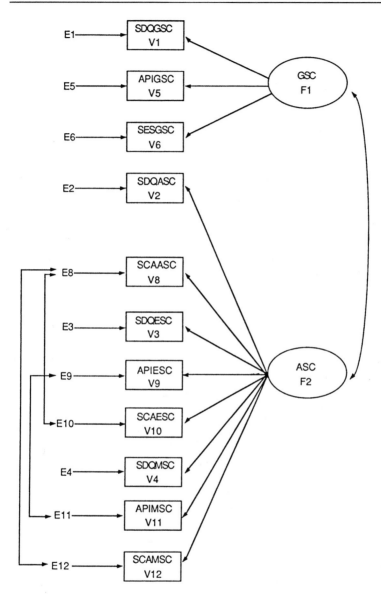

FIGURE 3.3. Two-Factor Model of Self-Concept

Source: Adapted from Byrne (1989). Copyright 1989 by Springer-Verlag. Reprinted with permission.

ification; all previous information remains the same. Thus only this portion of the input file is presented in Table 3.9.

TABLE 3.9. Selected EQS Input for Two-Factor Model of Self-Concept

```
/EQUATIONS
 V1 =   F1 + E1;
 V5 = *F1 + E5;
 V6 = *F1 + E6;
             V2 =   F2 + E2;
             V8 = *F2 + E8;
             V3 = *F2 + E3;
             V9 = *F2 + E9;
             V10 = *F2 + E10;
             V4 = *F2 + E4;
             V11 = *F2 + E11;
             V12 = *F2 + E12;
/VARIANCES
 F1 TO F2 = *;
 E1 TO E6 = *; E8 TO E12 = *;
/COVARIANCES
 F1,F2 = *;
 E10,E8 = *; E12,E8 = *; E11,E9 = *;
/END
```

In reviewing these specifications, a few points are worthy of mention. First, although the pattern of factor loadings remains unchanged for the GSC and ASC measures, it changes for both the ESC and MSC measures in allowing them to load onto the ASC factor. Because only one of these eight factor loadings needs to be fixed to 1.0, the two previously constrained parameters (the loadings for V3 and V4) are now freely estimated. Second, because there are now only two factors in the model, the **/VARIANCES** and **/COVARI-ANCES** paragraphs have been altered accordingly. Third, for comparison purposes, the three error covariances specified in the final four-factor model are similarly specified in the present two-factor model. Finally, because the two-factor model is known to be a poor represention of SC structure (see Byrne & Shavelson, 1986), the LM statistics are not included in the input file. Only the overall goodness-of-fit statistics are relevant to the present application, and these are presented in Table 3.10.

As indicated in the output, the $\chi^2_{(40)}$ value of 2063.507 represents an extremely poor fit to the data and a substantial decrement from the overall fit of the four-factor model ($\Delta\chi^2_{(5)}$ = 1839.50).[13] The gain of five degrees of freedom can be explained by both the reduction (two less factor variances; five less factor covariances), and the addition (two extra factor loadings) of estimated parameters. Finally, as expected, the CFI value of .729 is also indicative of inferior goodness of fit between the hypothesized two-factor model and the sample data.

TABLE 3.10. Selected EQS Output for Two-Factor Model of Self-Concept

```
GOODNESS OF FIT SUMMARY

INDEPENDENCE MODEL CHI-SQUARE =    7523.677 ON    55 DEGREES    OF FREEDOM

INDEPENDENCE AIC =  7413.67711   INDEPENDENCE CAIC =  7088.97101
        MODEL AIC =  1983.50724         MODEL CAIC =  1747.35735

CHI-SQUARE =    2063.507 BASED ON    40 DEGREES OF FREEDOM
PROBABILITY VALUE FOR THE CHI-SQUARE STATISTIC IS LESS THAN 0.001
THE NORMAL THEORY RLS CHI-SQUARE FOR THIS ML SOLUTION IS        2317.334.

BENTLER-BONETT NORMED    FIT INDEX=     0.726
BENTLER-BONETT NONNORMED FIT INDEX=     0.627
COMPARATIVE FIT INDEX             ⛨     0.729
```

HYPOTHESIS 3:
SELF-CONCEPT IS A ONE-FACTOR STRUCTURE

Although it now seems obvious that the structure of adolescent SC is best represented by a multidimensional model, there are still researchers who contend that SC is a unidimensional construct. Thus, for purposes of completeness and to address the issue of unidimensionality, Byrne and Shavelson (1986) proceeded in testing the above hypothesis. More pertinent to our work here, however, is to note that the one-factor model represents a restricted version of the two-factor model. As such, it makes little sense to test this model because it cannot possibly improve upon the goodness of fit.

In summary, it is evident from these analyses that both the two-factor and one-factor models of self-concept represent a misspecification of factorial structure for adolescents. Based on these findings, then, Byrne and Shavelson (1986) concluded that SC is a multidimensional construct, which in their study comprised the four facets of general, academic, English, and mathematics self-concepts.

Applications Related to Other Disciplines

BUSINESS: Nelson, J. E., Duncan, C. P., & Kiecker, P. L. (1993). Toward an understanding of the distraction construct in marketing. *Journal of Business Research, 26,* 201-221.

EDUCATION: Demetriou, A., Platsidou, M., Efklides, A., Metallidou, Y., & Shayer, M. (1991). The development of quantitative-relational abilities from childhood to adolescence: Structure, scaling, and individual differences. *Learning and Instruction, 1,* 19-43.

MEDICINE: Lobel, M., & Dunkel-Schetter, C. (1990). Conceptualizing stress to study effects on health: Environmental, perceptual, and emotional components. *Anxiety Research, 3,* 213-230.

Notes

1. The term **uniqueness** is used here in the factor analytic sense to mean a composite of random measurement error, and specific measurement error associated with a particular measuring instrument; in cross-sectional studies the two cannot be separated (Gerbing & Anderson, 1984).

2. A set of measures is said to be **congeneric** if each measure in the set purports to assess the same construct, except for errors of measurement (Jöreskog, 1971).

3. It is important to note that the mere inclusion of standard deviations does not cause the covariance matrix to be analyzed. Had we chosen to analyze the covariance matrix, the specification of **MA=COR** would still have been necessary since EQS assumes that the input matrix is a covariance matrix.

4. This aspect of the LM Test will be discussed in Part 3, where we examine multiple-group applications.

5. For a more comprehensive breakdown and discussion of these matrices and their component parts, see the manual (Bentler, 1989, 1992a).

6. One notable exception is the exclusion of the first page, which echoes back the input file (already presented in Table 3.2).

7. Readers are referred to the EQS Manual (Bentler, 1989, 1992a) for an explanation of the CAIC.

8. This index is given the acronym **BBI** in the Byrne and Shavelson (1986) article.

9. A negative variance is another example of an atypical parameter estimate. As noted earlier, EQS prevents the estimation of such parameters by constraining the value of the offending parameter to zero; the message **"PARAMETER XX,XX CONSTRAINED AT LOWER BOUND"** will appear on the output.

10. It is important to note that the standardized solution produced by EQS differs from that for LISREL 7 (Jöreskog & Sörbom, 1988); in the latter, measured variables, errors in variables, and disturbances in equations are not standardized (Bentler, 1989, 1992a).

11. Nested models are hierarchically related to one another in the sense that one is a subset of another; for example, particular parameters are freely estimated in one model but fixed to zero in a second model (Bentler & Chou, 1987).

12. You will note in the Byrne and Shavelson (1986) study that additional post hoc models were specified that included the cross-loading determined here (V3,F1), as well as other error covariances. However, more extensive knowledge of model-fitting procedures at this point in time leads me now to consider the final model reported to represent a certain degree of overfit.

13. The differential goodness-of-fit statistics for this EQS analysis versus the LISREL analysis conducted in the original study derive from an unequal number of parameters defining the final model.

4

Application 2
Testing the Factorial Validity
of a Measuring Instrument
(First-Order CFA Model)

Our second application is a first-order CFA model that this time tests hypotheses bearing on the Maslach Burnout Inventory (MBI; Maslach & Jackson, 1981, 1986), an instrument designed to measure three dimensions of burnout that the authors term Emotional Exhaustion (EE), Depersonalization (DP), and Reduced Personal Accomplishment (PA). The term **burnout** denotes the inability to function effectively in one's job as a consequence of prolonged and extensive job-related stress; **emotional exhaustion** represents feelings of fatigue that develop as one's energies become drained; **depersonalization** denotes the development of negative and uncaring attitudes towards others; and **reduced personal accomplishment** denotes a deterioration of self-confidence, and dissatisfaction in one's achievements. The escalation and prevalence of burnout among members of the teaching profession over this past decade has been of great concern to both educational administrators and clinicians, and has precipitated a plethora of research on the topic.

The purposes of the original study (Byrne, 1992), from which this example is taken, were to test for the validity and invariance of factorial structure within and across gender for elementary and secondary teachers. For the purposes of this chapter, however, we focus on testing the factorial validity of the MBI for elementary male teachers only.

Confirmatory factor analysis of a measuring instrument is most appropriately applied to assessment measures that have been fully developed and have had their factor structures validated. In other words, application of CFA procedures to measures that are still in the initial stages of development represents a serious misuse of the technique. This is because, in using CFA, the researcher tests hypotheses related to the factorial structure of the instrument under study. Specifically, he or she seeks to determine the extent to which items designed to measure a particular factor (i.e., dimension or facet of a construct) actually do so. In general, subscales of a measuring instrument are considered to represent the factors; all items comprising a particular subscale are therefore expected to load onto its related factor. Thus the viability of the CFA procedure depends importantly on the ability to specify a priori a factorial structure that is grounded in theory or empirical research, or both.

In this regard, the MBI most certainly qualifies for CFA research. It has been commercially marketed since 1981, is the most widely used measure of occupational burnout, and has undergone substantial testing of its psychometric properties over the years (see, e.g., Byrne 1991, 1992, 1993). Interestingly, until my 1991 study of the MBI, virtually all previous factor analytic work had involved exploratory procedures. Readers interested in more details related to this MBI research can refer to the original papers cited above. We turn now to a description of the instrument of central concern in this chapter.

THE MEASURING INSTRUMENT UNDER STUDY

The MBI is a 22-item instrument structured on a 7-point Likert scale ranging from 0 ("feeling has never been experienced") to 6 ("feeling experienced daily"). It is composed of three subscales, each measuring one facet of burnout; the EE subscale comprises nine items, the DP subscale five, and the PA subscale eight. The original version of the MBI (Maslach & Jackson, 1981) was constructed from data based on samples of workers from a wide range of human service organizations. Recently, however, Maslach and Jackson (1986), in collaboration with Schwab, developed the Educators' Survey (MBI Form Ed), a version of the instrument specifically designed for use with teachers. The MBI Form Ed parallels the original version of the MBI except for the modified wording of certain items to make them more appropriate to a teacher's work environment. Specifically, the generic term **recipients,** used in reference to clients, was replaced by the term **students**.

THE HYPOTHESIZED MODEL

The CFA model in the present example hypothesized a priori that (a) responses to the MBI could be explained by three factors, (b) each item would have a nonzero loading on the burnout factor it was designed to measure and zero loadings on all other factors, (c) the three factors would be correlated, and (d) measurement error terms would be uncorrelated. A schematic representation of this model is presented in Figure 1.[1]

THE EQS INPUT FILE

In this second application, we'll use a raw data matrix that is treated as an external file. Because many users work within a mainframe environment and because certain aspects of the EQS input file differ for the mainframe and microcomputer environments, I consider it worthwhile to include at least one example that addresses this issue. Nonetheless, because specific aspects of the job language shown here will vary from one institution to another, you will need to tailor this input to your own needs. The present input file, then, is structured for a mainframe system, but adaptation to the microcomputer environment is described. Also included in the file are two other features of the EQS program. Let's turn now to this EQS file, which is presented in Table 4.1.

The first six lines preceding the **/TITLE** paragraph contain information needed in order to run this EQS file on the mainframe. Although the specific job language will vary according to the particular system being used, the basic structure will remain the same. Each of these lines is now described separately.

- Line 1: This is a basic job card.
- Line 2: The **EXEC** card indicates that the job will use the EQS program; **PARM=500000** indicates the amount of storage space allocated for the job.
- Line 3: The term DATA indicates that this job will use a data set that is external to the present file; it is equivalent to the term **IN** when using the SPSS and BMDP packages. Thus this card is used to identify the external data file. The letters **DSN** stand for **data set name**; **IAVPBMB** indicates the computer account ID, and **ELEMM1.DATA** is the name of the external data file.
- Line 4: You will note again that no start values are included in this input file. This time, however, we are going to make use of the **RE-TEST** option, which automatically calculates start values based on

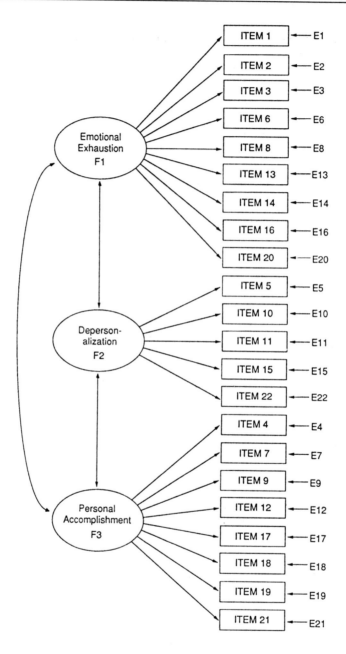

FIGURE 4.1. Hypothesized Model of Factorial Structure for the Maslach Burnout Inventory

Note: Item numbers correspond to variable numbers (e.g., ITEM 1 = V1).

TABLE 4.1. EQS Input for Initially Hypothesized Model of Maslach Burnout
Inventory: No Start Values

```
//    JOB
//    EXEC    EQS,PARM=500000
//DATA  DD    DSN=IAVPBMB.ELEMM1.DATA,DISP=SHR
//RETEST DD    DSN=IAVPBMB.STARTEM,
//      DCB=(RECFM=FB,LRECL=80,BLKSIZE=6160),
//      SPACE=(TRK,(20,20),RLSE),UNIT=DATA,DISP=(NEW,CATLG)
/TITLE
CFA OF MBI FOR ELEM MALE TCHRS (GRP 1; CALIBRATION) "MBIELM1I"
INITIAL MODEL              (INITIAL RUN TO GET START VALUES)
/SPEC
CASE=372; VAR=22; ME=ML; MA=RAW; UN=9; FO='(22F1.0)';
/LABELS
V1=MBI1;      V2=MBI2;      V3=MBI3;      V4=MBI4;
V5=MBI5;      V6=MBI6;      V7=MBI7;      V8=MBI8;      V9=MBI9;
V10=MBI10;    V11=MBI11;    V12=MBI12;    V13=MBI13;    V14=MBI14;
V15=MBI15;    V16=MBI16;    V17=MBI17;    V18=MBI18;    V19=MBI19;
V20=MBI20;    V21=MBI21;    V22=MBI22;
F1=EE;      F2=DP;      F3=PA;

/EQU
V1=     F1+E1;
V2=    *F1+E2;
V3=    *F1+E3;
V6=    *F1+E6;
V8=    *F1+E8;
V13=   *F1+E13;
V14=   *F1+E14;
V16=   *F1+E16;
V20=   *F1+E20;
              V5=     F2+E5;
              V10=   *F2+E10;
              V11=   *F2+E11;
              V15=   *F2+E15;
              V22=   *F2+E22;
                       V4=     F3+E4;
                       V7=    *F3+E7;
                       V9=    *F3+E9;
                       V12=   *F3+E12;
                       V17=   *F3+E17;
                       V18=   *F3+E18;
                       V19=   *F3+E19;
                       V21=   *F3+E21;
/VAR
F1 TO F3= *;
E1 TO E22= *;
/COVARIANCES
F1 TO F3= *;
/PRINT
RETEST=RETEST;
/END
```

the initial run. These values are then stored in a separate external file
containing only the /EQUATION, /VARIANCE, and /COVARIANCE
paragraphs; the name of this file is defined by the user. Use of the
keyword **RETEST** is analogous to the term **OUT** when creating an

external file with the SPSS or BMDP packages. Thus Line 4 indicates that the **RETEST** option is to be implemented and that the name of the file containing the start values will be **STARTEM**.

■ Lines 5/6: These two lines contain job language that describe the size of the new file to be created from the **RETEST** option.

Application of the present example to a microcomputer environment requires two very important changes to the above input file; they pertain to (a) use of an external data set, and (b) the **RETEST** option. If an external data set is to be used, the name of the data file must be stated in the **/SPEC** paragraph; the command would be **DA=ELEMM1.DAT**.[2] Use of the **/RETEST** option requires that the name of the external file to be created by the program be stated in the **/PRINT** paragraph. Thus, instead of stating that **RETEST=RETEST,** as with the current mainframe setup, you would need to specify that **RETEST=STARTEM.** Let's turn our attention now to the remainder of the input file.

As indicated in the **/TITLE** paragraph, the input file shown in Table 4.1 represents the initially hypothesized model of the MBI, and the first EQS run will be used to obtain start values that will be included in all subsequent input files related to this example. The **/SPEC** paragraph states that the data (a) comprise 22 variables for each of 372 cases, (b) are to be analyzed using the maximum likelihood method, (c) are in the form of a raw data matrix, (d) reside externally to the current file on Unit 9, and (e) are formatted such that the score for each variable occupies one column. In the **/LABELS** paragraph, we see that the labels for V1 through V22 are consistent with the item numbers comprising the MBI; those for F1 through F3 represent the EE, DP, and PA factors, respectively.

We turn now to the model specifications. The **/EQU** paragraph, as presented here, makes it easy to identify the pattern by which the items load onto each factor. As with the previous example, the first of each congeneric set of factor loadings and the error/uniqueness term associated with each observed variable are specified as fixed parameters; all other factors, as indicated by the asterisks, are to be freely estimated. The **/VAR** paragraph specifies that the variance of each factor and error term is to be estimated, and the **/COV** paragraph specifies that covariances among the three factors are to be estimated. Finally, the **/PRINT** paragraph indicates that the **RETEST** option is to be invoked. However, because the present application simulates a mainframe environment and because the name of the **RETEST** file is thus stated in the job language, as above, we state that **RETEST= RETEST.**

EQS OUTPUT FILES

Two output files are of immediate interest here: (a) the external file that was generated from the **RETEST** option, and (b) the output related to the specified model. We now examine each of these files.

RETEST External File (STARTEM)

This file, created by EQS as a separate file after running the job corresponding to Table 4.1, is shown partially in Table 4.2; not shown is the top part of the file, which is exactly that given in Table 4.1 (except for the **//** statements).

The important part of the file follows the **!** statements. As you will note, it contains a replication of the model specifications, but with start values implemented for all estimated parameters; each fixed parameter is constrained to 1.00. With minor editing, this file can now be used as a replacement for the original input file (Table 4.1). Specifically, you will need to block and delete the original specifications (the **/EQU, /VAR,** and **/COV** paragraphs), in addition to the first three comment lines (indicated with **!**s) of the retest output file. To complete your editing, you will then most likely wish to add **/PRINT** and **/LMTEST** paragraphs to the file. So edited, the input file for the initially hypothesized model will now appear as shown in Table 4.3.

Initially Hypothesized Model

Once the start values were added to the original file (Table 4.3), the job was executed. Selected components of the resulting output are presented in Table 4.4.

Sample Statistics

Because the input data were in the form of a raw score matrix, EQS automatically provides an abundance of information related to univariate as well as multivariate sample statistics. Given the strong underlying assumption of multivariate normality associated with SEM, such information bears importantly on the interpretability of the findings. Turning first to the **univariate statistics,** we find mean, skewness, and kurtosis coefficients printed for each MBI item. In general, skewness values for all items and kurtosis values for all except five items (4, 7, 15, 17, 19) can be considered satisfactory. When variables demonstrate significant nonzero univariate kurtosis, it is certain that they will not be multivariately normally distributed. Although the aberrant items here are not excessively kurtotic, they may be sufficiently

TABLE 4.2. EQS Start Values From **RETEST** Option

```
!
! Following lists are generated from RETEST
!
/EQUATION
    V1  =  1.000 F1   +  1.000 E1    ;
    V2  =   .887*F1   +  1.000 E2    ;
    V3  =  1.021*F1   +  1.000 E3    ;
    V4  =  1.000 F3   +  1.000 E4    ;
    V5  =  1.000 F2   +  1.000 E5    ;
    V6  =   .764*F1   +  1.000 E6    ;
    V7  =   .970*F3   +  1.000 E7    ;
    V8  =  1.143*F1   +  1.000 E8    ;
    V9  =  1.779*F3   +  1.000 E9    ;
   V10  =  1.141*F2   +  1.000 E10   ;
   V11  =  1.352*F2   +  1.000 E11   ;
   V12  =  1.498*F3   +  1.000 E12   ;
   V13  =  1.017*F1   +  1.000 E13   ;
   V14  =   .848*F1   +  1.000 E14   ;
   V15  =   .905*F2   +  1.000 E15   ;
   V16  =   .715*F1   +  1.000 E16   ;
   V17  =  1.348*F3   +  1.000 E17   ;
   V18  =  1.917*F3   +  1.000 E18   ;
   V19  =  1.715*F3   +  1.000 E19   ;
   V20  =   .753*F1   +  1.000 E20   ;
   V21  =  1.356*F3   +  1.000 E21   ;
   V22  =   .768*F2   +  1.000 E22   ;
/VARIANCES
       F1=  1.630*  ;
       F2=   .707*  ;
       F3=   .193*  ;
       E1=  1.131*  ;
       E2=  1.108*  ;
       E3=  1.304*  ;
       E4=   .804*  ;
       E5=  1.507*  ;
       E6=  1.557*  ;
       E7=   .524*  ;
       E8=   .854*  ;
       E9=  1.120*  ;
      E10=  1.173*  ;
      E11=  1.047*  ;
      E12=   .990*  ;
      E13=  1.145*  ;
      E14=  1.809*  ;
      E15=  1.108*  ;
      E16=  1.239*  ;
      E17=   .376*  ;
      E18=   .912*  ;
      E19=   .846*  ;
      E20=  1.078*  ;
      E21=  1.248*  ;
      E22=  2.081*  ;
/COVARIANCES
      F2,F1  =   .703*  ;
      F3,F1  =  -.193*  ;
      F3,F2  =  -.173*  ;
/END
```

TABLE 4.3. EQS Input for Initially Hypothesized Model of Maslach Burnout Inventory: Start Values Added

```
/TITLE
CFA OF MBI FOR ELEMENTARY MALE TCHRS (GRP 1; CALIBRATION) "MBIELM11"
INITIAL MODEL (START VALUES ADDED)
/SPEC
CASE=372; VAR=22; ME=ML; MA=RAW; UN=9; FO='(22F1.0)';
/LABELS
V1=MBI1;      V2=MBI2;      V3=MBI3;      V4=MBI4;
V5=MBI5;      V6=MBI6;      V7=MBI7;      V8=MBI8;      V9=MBI9;
V10=MBI10;    V11=MBI11;    V12=MBI12;    V13=MBI13;    V14=MBI14;
V15=MBI15;    V16=MBI16;    V17=MBI17;    V18=MBI18;    V19=MBI19;
V20=MBI20;    V21=MBI21;    V22=MBI22;
F1=EE;     F2=DP;     F3=PA;
/EQUATION
V1   =   1.000 F1   +   1.000 E1    ;
V2   =    .887*F1   +   1.000 E2    ;
V3   =   1.021*F1   +   1.000 E3    ;
V4   =   1.000 F3   +   1.000 E4    ;
V5   =   1.000 F2   +   1.000 E5    ;
V6   =    .764*F1   +   1.000 E6    ;
V7   =    .970*F3   +   1.000 E7    ;
V8   =   1.143*F1   +   1.000 E8    ;
V9   =   1.779*F3   +   1.000 E9    ;
V10  =   1.141*F2   +   1.000 E10   ;
V11  =   1.352*F2   +   1.000 E11   ;
V12  =   1.498*F3   +   1.000 E12   ;
V13  =   1.017*F1   +   1.000 E13   ;
V14  =    .848*F1   +   1.000 E14   ;
V15  =    .905*F2   +   1.000 E15   ;
V16  =    .715*F1   +   1.000 E16   ;
V17  =   1.348*F3   +   1.000 E17   ;
V18  =   1.917*F3   +   1.000 E18   ;
V19  =   1.715*F3   +   1.000 E19   ;
V20  =    .753*F1   +   1.000 E20   ;
V21  =   1.356*F3   +   1.000 E21   ;
V22  =    .768*F2   +   1.000 E22   ;
/VARIANCES
F1=  1.630* ;
F2=   .707* ;
F3=   .193* ;
E1=  1.131* ;
E2=  1.108* ;
E3=  1.304* ;
E4=   .804* ;
E5=  1.507* ;
E6=  1.557* ;
E7=   .524* ;
E8=   .854* ;
E9=  1.120* ;
E10= 1.173* ;
E11= 1.047* ;
E12=  .990* ;
E13= 1.145* ;
E14= 1.809* ;
E15= 1.108* ;
E16= 1.239* ;
```

(Continued)

TABLE 4.3. (Continued)

```
E17=    .376* ;
E18=    .912* ;
E19=    .846* ;
E20=   1.078* ;
E21=   1.248* ;
E22=   2.081* ;
/COVARIANCES
F2,F1   =    .703* ;
F3,F1   =   -.193* ;
F3,F2   =   -.173* ;
/PRINT
 CORRELATION=YES;
/LMTEST
 SET=PEE, GVF;
/END
```

nonnormal to make interpretations based on the usual χ^2 statistic and CFI problematic, an issue that I address in the specification of Model 2.

The **multivariate sample statistics** all relate to kurtosis only and are variants of Mardia's (1970, 1974) coefficient that bear on normal theory. Elliptical theory estimates also are shown but are not typically relevant unless that theory is invoked. When the sample is very large and multivariately normal, the normalized estimate is distributed as a unit normal variate. Although there is still no absolute determinant of the extent to which a sample can be considered nonnormal, Bentler (1989, 1992a) suggests that large values of the normalized estimate indicate significant positive kurtosis; large negative values are indicative of significant negative kurtosis. In this example, a z statistic of 37.1380 is highly suggestive of nonnormality in the population.

Another important aspect of the EQS program is its capability to identify outliers with respect to multivariate kurtosis; this information is presented next. In this section of the output, the program automatically prints out the five cases contributing most to the normalized multivariate kurtosis estimate. However, it is entirely possible that none of the five cases is actually an outlier. Identification of an outlier is based on the estimate presented for one case relative to those for the other four cases; there is no absolute value upon which to make this judgment. In reviewing the output in Table 4.4, we would conclude no evidence of an outlying case. This assessment is based on the observation that all five estimates fall approximately within the same range of values; typically, estimates for outlying cases are distinctively different from those representing the other cases. (For more extensive discussion of the detection and treatment of outliers in structural equation modeling, see Berkane & Bentler, 1988; Bollen, 1989.)

TABLE 4.4. Selected EQS Output for Initially Hypothesized Model of Maslach
Burnout Inventory

SAMPLE STATISTICS

UNIVARIATE STATISTICS

VARIABLE		MBI1	MBI2	MBI3	MBI4	MBI5
MEAN		4.3656	4.8683	3.5269	6.2984	2.1989
SKEWNESS	(G1)	-0.1151	-0.5070	0.3169	-1.8111	1.3283
KURTOSIS	(G2)	-1.1562	-0.6926	-1.0997	3.6665	0.9305
VARIABLE		MBI6	MBI7	MBI8	MBI9	MBI10
MEAN		2.7070	6.3118	3.0430	6.0349	2.2043
SKEWNESS	(G1)	0.9238	-1.6490	0.7407	-1.5422	1.2025
KURTOSIS	(G2)	0.0071	3.8021	-0.5971	1.8694	0.5827
VARIABLE		MBI11	MBI12	MBI13	MBI14	MBI15
MEAN		2.2392	5.6989	3.5860	4.0269	1.7688
SKEWNESS	(G1)	1.2731	-1.3195	0.3472	0.0309	2.0963
KURTOSIS	(G2)	0.8159	1.8669	-0.7803	-0.9253	4.2790
VARIABLE		MBI16	MBI17	MBI18	MBI19	MBI20
MEAN		2.4731	6.4059	5.7016	5.9462	2.2446
SKEWNESS	(G1)	0.9714	-1.9783	-1.2309	-1.4839	1.3001
KURTOSIS	(G2)	0.1735	5.1001	1.3641	2.2408	1.1929
VARIABLE		MBI21	MBI22			
MEAN		5.8522	2.5806			
SKEWNESS	(G1)	-1.3000	1.0662			
KURTOSIS	(G2)	1.1823	0.1986			

MULTIVARIATE KURTOSIS

MARDIA'S COEFFICIENT (G2,P) =   125.1437
NORMALIZED ESTIMATE =   37.1380

ELLIPTICAL THEORY KURTOSIS ESTIMATES

MARDIA-BASED KAPPA =   0.2370 MEAN SCALED UNIVARIATE KURTOSIS =   0.3640
MARDIA-BASED KAPPA IS USED IN COMPUTATION. KAPPA=   0.2370

CASE NUMBERS WITH LARGEST CONTRIBUTION TO NORMALIZED MULTIVARIATE KURTOSIS:

CASE NUMBER	26	30	84	171	200
ESTIMATE	1194.8267	1446.5683	1221.4445	1136.6243	1078.3868

(Continued)

TABLE 4.4. (Continued)

BENTLER-WEEKS STRUCTURAL REPRESENTATION:

```
NUMBER OF DEPENDENT VARIABLES = 22
    DEPENDENT V'S :    1    2    3    4    5    6    7    8    9   10
    DEPENDENT V'S :   11   12   13   14   15   16   17   18   19   20
    DEPENDENT V'S :   21   22

NUMBER OF INDEPENDENT VARIABLES = 25
    INDEPENDENT F'S :    1    2    3
    INDEPENDENT E'S :    1    2    3    4    5    6    7    8    9   10
    INDEPENDENT E'S :   11   12   13   14   15   16   17   18   19   20
    INDEPENDENT E'S :   21   22
```

PARAMETER ESTIMATES APPEAR IN ORDER,
NO SPECIAL PROBLEMS WERE ENCOUNTERED DURING OPTIMIZATION.

GOODNESS OF FIT SUMMARY

INDEPENDENCE MODEL CHI-SQUARE =   3442.988 ON   231 DEGREES OF FREEDOM

INDEPENDENCE AIC = 2980.98835   INDEPENDENCE CAIC = 1844.72387
      MODEL AIC =   281.84886   MODEL CAIC = -731.44328

CHI-SQUARE =   693.849 BASED ON   206 DEGREES OF FREEDOM
PROBABILITY VALUE FOR THE CHI-SQUARE STATISTIC IS LESS THAN 0.001
THE NORMAL THEORY RLS CHI-SQUARE FOR THIS ML SOLUTION IS   725.079.

BENTLER-BONETT NORMED   FIT INDEX=   0.798
BENTLER-BONETT NONNORMED FIT INDEX=   0.830
COMPARATIVE FIT INDEX   =   0.848

MULTIVARIATE LAGRANGE MULTIPLIER TEST BY SIMULTANEOUS PROCESS IN STAGE

PARAMETER SETS (SUBMATRICES) ACTIVE AT THIS STAGE ARE:

    PEE GVF

		CUMULATIVE MULTIVARIATE STATISTICS			UNIVARIATE INCREMENT	
STEP	PARAMETER	CHI-SQUARE	D.F.	PROBABILITY	CHI-SQUARE	PROBABILITY
1	E16,E6	91.029	1	0.000	91.029	0.000
2	E2,E1	169.785	2	0.000	78.757	0.000
3	V12,F1	211.195	3	0.000	41.409	0.000
4	E11,E10	249.165	4	0.000	37.970	0.000
5	E21,E7	281.857	5	0.000	32.693	0.000
6	E7,E4	319.406	6	0.000	37.549	0.000
7	V1,F3	344.596	7	0.000	25.189	0.000
8	E21,E4	365.386	8	0.000	20.791	0.000
9	E6,E5	382.052	9	0.000	16.666	0.000
10	E3,E1	397.787	10	0.000	15.735	0.000
11	V2,F3	413.132	11	0.000	15.345	0.000
12	E13,E12	428.102	12	0.000	14.970	0.000
13	E14,E2	441.833	13	0.000	13.732	0.000
14	E19,E18	453.140	14	0.000	11.307	0.001
15	E19,E9	463.212	15	0.000	10.072	0.002
16	V14,F3	473.226	16	0.000	10.014	0.002
17	E20,E13	481.640	17	0.000	8.414	0.004
18	E20,E8	493.323	18	0.000	11.683	0.001
19	E12,E5	501.675	19	0.000	8.352	0.004
20	E14,E6	509.896	20	0.000	8.221	0.004
21	E14,E8	520.132	21	0.000	10.237	0.001
22	E17,E3	527.713	22	0.000	7.581	0.006
23	E16,E5	535.178	23	0.000	7.465	0.006

```
     .
     .
Execution begins at 21:18:47.23
Execution ends   at 21:19:42.32
Elapsed time =      55.09 seconds
```

Bentler-Weeks Structural Representation

In examining the Bentler-Weeks summary of the model, it may be helpful to review, concomitantly, the graphic representation of the model in Figure 4.1. We see first, that there are 22 dependent variables; these represent the observed indicator variables (MBI items). The number of independent variables is 25; 22 represent the error/uniquenesses associated with each observed variable, and 3 represent the underlying factors of EE, DP, and PA.

Goodness-of-Fit Summary

Because the various criteria of model fit were all discussed in Chapter 3, my evaluation here will be limited to only two criteria: the χ^2 statistic and the CFI. Indeed, both of these values ($\chi^2_{(206)} = 693.849$; CFI $= .848$), as shown in Table 4.4, are clearly indicative of an ill-fitting model. Thus it is apparent that some modification in specification is needed in order to determine a model that better represents the sample data. Clues to these modifications are derived from LM statistics presented next in the output.

Modification Indices

Recall that in the initial EQS input file, the **SET** command was used to limit the search for malfitting parameters to only factor loadings (GVF) and error covariances (PEE); these parameters, then, are the only ones identified here. In reviewing the univariate increments for the fixed parameters listed, we see that the three largest increments are associated with two covariances and one factor loading. The cumulative multivariate $\chi^2_{(3)}$ of 211.195 indicates that if these parameters were to be freely estimated, the χ^2 statistic representing overall model fit would drop by that amount. The estimation of these three parameters is well substantiated based on previous validity research bearing on the MBI (e.g., Byrne, 1991, 1993).

Nonetheless, in selecting which parameters to free in subsequent models, the researcher walks a thin line between adequately fitting the model and overfitting the model. Thus, as noted in Chapter 3, it is imperative that such decisions be grounded in theory or based on past empirical research or both. This is exactly the dilemma here with respect to the next three parameters; each represents an error covariance and demonstrates a potentially substantial drop in χ^2 should the parameter be set free. In the original study (Byrne, 1992), I made the decision to free up the fourth parameter (E11,E10) on the basis of two factors: (a) the consistency of this specification with two previous studies of the MBI that demonstrated an abnormally large correlated error between Items 11 and 10 (Byrne, 1991, 1993), and (b) the large drop in χ^2 value from Parameter 4 to Parameter 5, and then the upturn in that value for Parameter 6. Wary of overfitting the model on the basis of correlated errors, I considered it most appropriate to respecify only the first four fixed parameters as freely estimated. Let's turn now to this respecified model, which is labeled as Model 2.

Specification and Analysis of Model 2

EQS Input

The model specification portion of the input file for Model 2 is presented in Table 4.5. As you will note, the only difference between this input and that for the hypothesized model involves the cross-loading of Item 12 (V12) on Factor 1, and the specification of three error covariances (E16,E6; E2,E1; E11,E10).

Recall that in reviewing the descriptive sample statistics presented earlier, we noted evidence of moderate kurtosis associated with five MBI items. The effect of these kurtotic variables may be sufficient for the distribution to be multivariately nonnormal, thereby violating the underlying assumption of normality associated with the maximum likelihood method of estimation. Violation of this assumption can seriously invalidate statistical hypothesis testing, with the result that the normal theory test statistic (χ^2) may not reflect an adequate evaluation of the model under study (Hu et al., 1992). Although other estimation methods have been developed for use when the normality assumption does not hold (e.g., asymptotic distribution-free; elliptical; heterogeneous kurtotic), Bentler and associates (Chou et al., 1991; Hu et al., 1992) have argued that it may be more appropriate to correct the test statistic than to use a different mode of estimation. In other words, when there is evidence that the sample distribution is nonnormal, one of the following two approaches will yield the more valid result in addressing the problem: (a) use of an estimation method that assumes an underlying nonnormal distribution of the sample data and bases evaluation of model fit on the corresponding χ^2 statistic, or (b) use of an estimation method that assumes an underlying normal distribution (ML; GLS) but bases evaluation of model fit on a test statistic that has been corrected to take nonnormality into account. Hu et al. (1992) have recently provided strong evidence to substantiate the latter.

Satorra and Bentler (1988a, 1988b) developed such a statistic that incorporates a scaling correction for the χ^2 statistic when distributional assumptions are violated; its computation takes into account the model, the estimation method, and the sample kurtosis values. This Satorra-Bentler Scaled Statistic (S-Bχ^2) has been shown to be the most reliable test statistic for evaluating covariance structure models under various distributions and sample sizes. In EQS, when this option is chosen, robust standard errors are also computed.[3]

TABLE 4.5. Selected EQS Input for Modified Model of Maslach Burnout Inventory

```
/EQUATION
    V1  =  1.000 F1  +  1.000 E1   ;
    V2  =   .887*F1  +  1.000 E2   ;
    V3  =  1.021*F1  +  1.000 E3   ;
    V4  =  1.000 F3  +  1.000 E4   ;
    V5  =  1.000 F2  +  1.000 E5   ;
    V6  =   .764*F1  +  1.000 E6   ;
    V7  =   .970*F3  +  1.000 E7   ;
    V8  =  1.143*F1  +  1.000 E8   ;
    V9  =  1.779*F3  +  1.000 E9   ;
    V10 =  1.141*F2  +  1.000 E10  ;
    V11 =  1.352*F2  +  1.000 E11  ;
    V12 =  1.498*F3  +  *F1 + 1.000 E12  ;
    V13 =  1.017*F1  +  1.000 E13  ;
    V14 =   .848*F1  +  1.000 E14  ;
    V15 =   .905*F2  +  1.000 E15  ;
    V16 =   .715*F1  +  1.000 E16  ;
    V17 =  1.348*F3  +  1.000 E17  ;
    V18 =  1.917*F3  +  1.000 E18  ;
    V19 =  1.715*F3  +  1.000 E19  ;
    V20 =   .753*F1  +  1.000 E20  ;
    V21 =  1.356*F3  +  1.000 E21  ;
    V22 =   .768*F2  +  1.000 E22  ;
/VARIANCES
        F1=  1.630* ;
        F2=   .707* ;
        F3=   .193* ;
        E1=  1.131* ;
        E2=  1.108* ;
        E3=  1.304* ;
        E4=   .804* ;
        E5=  1.507* ;
        E6=  1.557* ;
        E7=   .524* ;
        E8=   .854* ;
        E9=  1.120* ;
       E10=  1.173* ;
       E11=  1.047* ;
       E12=   .990* ;
       E13=  1.145* ;
       E14=  1.809* ;
       E15=  1.108* ;
       E16=  1.239* ;
       E17=   .376* ;
       E18=   .912* ;
       E19=   .846* ;
       E20=  1.078* ;
       E21=  1.248* ;
       E22=  2.081* ;
 /COVARIANCES
       F2,F1  =   .703* ;
       F3,F1  =  -.193* ;
       F3,F2  =  -.173* ;
   E16,E6 = *;
   E2,E1 = *;
   E11,E10 = *;
/PRINT
 CORRELATION=YES;
/LMTEST
 SET=PEE, GVF;
/END
```

The EQS program, once again, is unique in its provision of robust statistics for any method specified, except the arbitrary distribution GLS. The user first specifies the normal theory estimation method and then requests that robust statistics be provided. For example, the method specification for Model 2 is stated as **ME=ML, ROBUST;**. Let's turn now to the computer output for the respecified model.

EQS Output

The results for Model 2 are presented in Table 4.6. Turning first to the **goodness-of-fit summary,** we can see that the overall χ^2 value has now dropped to 445.219, with 202 degrees of freedom.[4] This indicates a highly significant improvement in model fit ($\Delta\chi^2_{(4)} = 248.63$). The figure is consistent with that predicted by the cumulative LM statistics provided in our initial EQS output. As expected, the CFI value also reflects a better fit of the model to the sample data.[5] Once again, the difference in CFI values (.08) reflects a substantial improvement in model fit.

Let's turn our attention now to the S-Bχ^2 which, at a value of 370.99, is substantially lower than the uncorrected χ^2 statistic. The size of this differential bears evidence that the sample was indeed somewhat nonnormally distributed. Although the S-Bχ^2 value is indicative of a better fitting model, this corrected χ^2 statistic, like its uncorrected counterpart, remains sensitive to sample size. Thus it would be helpful to the researcher to be able to assess the adequacy of the model using some practical index of fit. In this regard, the CFI is inappropriate because it is based on the usual χ^2 statistic. However, it is easy to compute a corrected version of the CFI (CFI*) by simply substituting the S-Bχ^2 for the usual χ^2 statistic. In order to illustrate the ease with which this criterion can be obtained, and to provide you with a complete picture of the final MBI model, specification and analysis of the null model is detailed at the end of the chapter. But first we need to review the remainder of the EQS output for Model 2.

Following the goodness-of-fit statistics we find the **iterative summary.** The fact that the estimates converged after only five iterations, with negligible change following the second one, is a good indication that model specification was on target (i.e., elements in the residual covariance matrix are small).

The **measurement equations with standard errors and test statistics** are presented next. Again, for each estimated variable, the ML estimate is presented first, followed below by the standard error and the z value. However, because we requested robust statistics, these values are also provided, albeit within parentheses; the first robust statistic represents the corrected standard error, and the second the corrected test statistic. As you will note,

TABLE 4.6. Selected EQS Output for Modified Model of Maslach Burnout
Inventory

PARAMETER ESTIMATES APPEAR IN ORDER,
NO SPECIAL PROBLEMS WERE ENCOUNTERED DURING OPTIMIZATION.

GOODNESS OF FIT SUMMARY

```
INDEPENDENCE MODEL CHI-SQUARE =       3442.988 ON    231 DEGREES OF FREEDOM

INDEPENDENCE AIC =  2980.98835    INDEPENDENCE CAIC =  1844.72387
        MODEL AIC =    41.21939          MODEL CAIC =  -952.39717

CHI-SQUARE =      445.219 BASED ON    202 DEGREES OF FREEDOM
PROBABILITY VALUE FOR THE CHI-SQUARE STATISTIC IS LESS THAN 0.001
THE NORMAL THEORY RLS CHI-SQUARE FOR THIS ML SOLUTION IS          448.816.

SATORRA-BENTLER SCALED CHI-SQUARE =      370.9944
PROBABILITY VALUE FOR THE CHI-SQUARE STATISTIC IS      0.00000

BENTLER-BONETT NORMED     FIT INDEX=       0.871
BENTLER-BONETT NONNORMED FIT INDEX=       0.913
COMPARATIVE FIT INDEX          =          0.924
```

ITERATIVE SUMMARY

ITERATION	PARAMETER ABS CHANGE	ALPHA	FUNCTION
1	0.181982	1.00000	1.78453
2	0.077792	1.00000	1.20126
3	0.007116	1.00000	1.20008
4	0.001046	1.00000	1.20005
5	0.000210	1.00000	1.20005

MEASUREMENT EQUATIONS WITH STANDARD ERRORS AND TEST STATISTICS
(ROBUST STATISTICS IN PARENTHESES)

```
MBI1  =V1  =    1.000 F1     + 1.000 E1
MBI2  =V2  =     .878*F1     + 1.000 E2
                .049
              17.945
           (   .041)
           ( 21.344)
MBI3  =V3  =    1.073*F1     + 1.000 E3
                .075
              14.284
           (   .058)
           ( 18.484)
MBI4  =V4  =    1.000 F3     + 1.000 E4
MBI5  =V5  =    1.000 F2     + 1.000 E5
MBI6  =V6  =     .764*F1     + 1.000 E6
                .069
              10.996
           (   .076)
           ( 10.005)
MBI7  =V7  =     .973*F3     + 1.000 E7
                .147
               6.603
           (   .128)
           (  7.613)
MBI8  =V8  =    1.215*F1     + 1.000 E8
                .075
              16.277
           (   .066)
           ( 18.407)
```

(Continued)

TABLE 4.6. (Continued)

```
MBI9    =V9  =     1.763*F3    + 1.000 E9
                     .248
                    7.096
                 (   .317)
                 (  5.569)
MBI10   =V10 =      .889*F2    + 1.000 E10
                     .114
                    7.818
                 (   .124)
                 (  7.188)
MBI11   =V11 =     1.105*F2    + 1.000 E11
                     .125
                    8.808
                 (   .129)
                 (  8.542)
MBI12   =V12 =     -.316*F1    + 1.131*F3    + 1.000 E12
                     .050          .188
                   -6.356         6.014
                 (   .054)     (   .201)
                 ( -5.897)     (  5.614)
MBI13   =V13 =     1.072*F1    + 1.000 E13
                     .073
                   14.719
                 (   .069)
                 ( 15.436)
MBI14   =V14 =      .880*F1    + 1.000 E14
                     .075
                   11.657
                 (   .062)
                 ( 14.090)
MBI15   =V15 =      .921*F2    + 1.000 E15
                     .105
                    8.779
                 (   .120)
                 (  7.681)
MBI16   =V16 =      .727*F1    + 1.000 E16
                     .063
                   11.541
                 (   .072)
                 ( 10.045)
MBI17   =V17 =     1.327*F3    + 1.000 E17
                     .176
                    7.545
                 (   .197)
                 (  6.727)
MBI18   =V18 =     1.890*F3    + 1.000 E18
                     .255
                    7.411
                 (   .290)
                 (  6.507)
MBI19   =V19 =     1.695*F3    + 1.000 E19
                     .232
                    7.291
                 (   .285)
                 (  5.941)
```

TABLE 4.6. (Continued)

```
MBI20    =V20 =      .806*F1      + 1.000 E20
                     .062
                   13.095
                   (   .066)
                   ( 12.144)
MBI21    =V21 =     1.342*F3      + 1.000 E21
                     .214
                    6.282
                   (   .224)
                   (  6.002)
MBI22    =V22 =      .776*F2      + 1.000 E22
                     .116
                    6.721
                   (   .116)
                   (  6.677)
```

COVARIANCES AMONG INDEPENDENT VARIABLES

```
                         V                          F
                         ---                        ---
                               I F2  -  DP              .749*I
                               I F1  -  EE              .104 I
                               I                       7.188 I
                               I                     (   .106)I
                               I                     (  7.048)I
                               I                            I
                               I F3  -  PA             -.167*I
                               I F1  -  EE              .040 I
                               I                      -4.163 I
                               I                     (   .038)I
                               I                     ( -4.362)I
                               I                            I
                               I F3  -  PA             -.181*I
                               I F2  -  DP              .038 I
                               I                      -4.762 I
                               I                     (   .038)I
                               I                     ( -4.795)I
                               I                            I

                         E                          D
                         ---                        ---
E2   -  MBI2              .590*I                          I
E1   -  MBI1              .083 I                          I
                        7.122 I                          I
                      (   .086)I                          I
                      (  6.880)I                          I
                            I                          I
E16  -MBI16              .708*I                          I
E6   -  MBI6             .090 I                          I
                        7.858 I                          I
                      (   .122)I                          I
                      (  5.781)I                          I
                            I                          I
E11  -MBI11              .518*I                          I
E10  -MBI10             .102 I                          I
                        5.099 I                          I
                      (   .110)I                          I
                      (  4.726)I                          I
                            I                          I
```

(Continued)

TABLE 4.6. (Continued)

```
STANDARDIZED SOLUTION:
    MBI1  =V1  =    .735 F1    + .678 E1
    MBI2  =V2  =    .693*F1    + .721 E2
    MBI3  =V3  =    .756*F1    + .655 E3
    MBI4  =V4  =    .448 F3    + .894 E4
    MBI5  =V5  =    .602 F2    + .798 E5
    MBI6  =V6  =    .589*F1    + .808 E6
    MBI7  =V7  =    .518*F3    + .855 E7
    MBI8  =V8  =    .859*F1    + .513 E8
    MBI9  =V9  =    .599*F3    + .801 E9
    MBI10 =V10 =    .551*F2    + .835 E10
    MBI11 =V11 =    .647*F2    + .762 E11
    MBI12 =V12 =   -.323*F1    + .424*F3   + .795 E12
    MBI13 =V13 =    .778*F1    + .628 E13
    MBI14 =V14 =    .622*F1    + .783 E14
    MBI15 =V15 =    .635*F2    + .772 E15
    MBI16 =V16 =    .616*F1    + .787 E16
    MBI17 =V17 =    .696*F3    + .718 E17
    MBI18 =V18 =    .663*F3    + .748 E18
    MBI19 =V19 =    .637*F3    + .771 E19
    MBI20 =V20 =    .696*F1    + .718 E20
    MBI21 =V21 =    .474*F3    + .881 E21
    MBI22 =V22 =    .440*F2    + .898 E22
```

```
CORRELATIONS AMONG INDEPENDENT VARIABLES
-----------------------------------------
                       V                              F
                      ---                            ---
                              I F2  -  DP          .685*I
                              I F1  -  EE             I
                              I                       I
                              I F3  -  PA         -.306*I
                              I F1  -  EE             I
                              I                       I
                              I F3  -  PA         -.453*I
                              I F2  -  DP             I
                              I                       I
                       E                              D
                      ---                            ---
  E2  -  MBI2              .469*I                     I
  E1  -  MBI1                  I                      I
                              I                       I
  E16 -MBI16               .488*I                     I
  E6  -  MBI6                  I                      I
                              I                       I
  E11 -MBI11               .368*I                     I
  E10 -MBI10                   I                      I
                              I                       I
```

all estimates are statistically significant, including the one cross-loading and the three error covariances. In this instance, the ML and robust statistics yield the same conclusions regarding parameter significance. However, this will

TABLE 4.6. (Continued)

STEP	PARAMETER	CUMULATIVE MULTIVARIATE STATISTICS CHI-SQUARE	D.F.	PROBABILITY	UNIVARIATE INCREMENT CHI-SQUARE	PROBABILITY
1	E21,E7	32.417	1	0.000	32.417	0.000
2	E7,E4	69.546	2	0.000	37.128	0.000
3	E21,E4	90.785	3	0.000	21.239	0.000
4	V1,F3	105.394	4	0.000	14.609	0.000
5	E13,E12	118.656	5	0.000	13.262	0.000
.						
.						
.						
22						

```
Execution begins at 22:10:28.76
Execution ends   at 22:50:33.40
Elapsed time =     2404.64 seconds
```

not always be the case. Moreover, a review of the **standardized solution** reveals each of the correlated errors to be substantial, ranging from $r = .37$ to $r = .49$. These findings are very suggestive of redundant content across items.

Presented next in Table 4.6, are the **LM statistics**. Not surprisingly, misspecification in the model was due for the most part to error covariances between MBI items. (In the interest of space, only the first five are presented here.) Although from a statistical perspective, respecification that includes the first two parameters is justified, substantive considerations do not support this decision. Thus, for reasons described earlier, I consider it inappropriate to continue fitting the model beyond this point.

Finally, as an indication of the amount of time needed to execute a job in which robust statistics are requested (see caveat in Chapter 2), you will note that this run required 2404.64 seconds, compared with 55.09 seconds for the previous one based only on maximum likelihood estimation.

Specification and Analysis
of the Null Model

An explanation of the null model and its underlying rationale was presented in Chapter 3; the formula for computation of the CFI was also described. In order to compute the corrected version of this index, (CFI*), we need to obtain the S-Bχ^2 for the null model, which is not provided by the current release. Accordingly, the input file is presented in Table 4.7.

TABLE 4.7. EQS Input for Null Model of Maslach Burnout Inventory

```
/TITLE
CFA OF MBI FOR ELEMENTARY MALE TCHRS (GRP 1; CALIBRATION) "MBIELM1N"
NULL MODEL
/SPEC
CASE=372; VAR=22; ME=ML,ROBUST; MA=RAW; UN=9; FO='(22F1.0)';
/LABELS
V1=MBI1;       V2=MBI2;       V3=MBI3;       V4=MBI4;
V5=MBI5;       V6=MBI6;       V7=MBI7;       V8=MBI8;       V9=MBI9;
V10=MBI10;     V11=MBI11;     V12=MBI12;     V13=MBI13;     V14=MBI14;
V15=MBI15;     V16=MBI16;     V17=MBI17;     V18=MBI18;     V19=MBI19;
V20=MBI20;     V21=MBI21;     V22=MBI22;
/EQUATION
    V1  =  F1;
    V2  =  F2;
    V3  =  F3;
    V4  =  F4;
    V5  =  F5;
    V6  =  F6;
    V7  =  F7;
    V8  =  F8;
    V9  =  F9;
    V10 =  F10;
    V11 =  F11;
    V12 =  F12;
    V13 =  F13;
    V14 =  F14;
    V15 =  F15;
    V16 =  F16;
    V17 =  F17;
    V18 =  F18;
    V19 =  F19;
    V20 =  F20;
    V21 =  F21;
    V22 =  F22;
/VARIANCES
    F1 TO F22 = *;
/END
```

A peculiarity of the current EQS release is that a model must have equations. Thus each observed variable is taken as a factor; a 22-factor model is therefore specified. Because each $V_i = F_i$ exactly, freely estimated variances of the factors are identically equal to the variances of the variables. The independence (or uncorrelated variable model), of course, has no covariances.[6] Results for this model are presented in Table 4.8.

The **Bentler-Weeks structural representation** once again is helpful as a double check on model specification. As indicated, there are 22 **dependent** variables (the observed measures) and 22 **independent** variables (the latent factors).

Finally, the reported S-Bχ^2 is shown to be 2919.31 with 231 degrees of freedom. Now that we have this information, we can proceed in formulating the CFI* for our final MBI model.

TABLE 4.8. Selected EQS Output for Null Model of Maslach Burnout Inventory

BENTLER-WEEKS STRUCTURAL REPRESENTATION:

```
NUMBER OF DEPENDENT VARIABLES = 22
    DEPENDENT V'S :      1    2    3    4    5    6    7    8    9   10
    DEPENDENT V'S :     11   12   13   14   15   16   17   18   19   20
    DEPENDENT V'S :     21   22


NUMBER OF INDEPENDENT VARIABLES = 22
    INDEPENDENT F'S :    1    2    3    4    5    6    7    8    9   10
    INDEPENDENT F'S :   11   12   13   14   15   16   17   18   19   20
    INDEPENDENT F'S :   21   22
```

GOODNESS OF FIT SUMMARY

```
INDEPENDENCE MODEL CHI-SQUARE =        3442.988 ON    231 DEGREES OF FREEDOM

INDEPENDENCE AIC =  2980.98835   INDEPENDENCE CAIC =  1844.72387
         MODEL AIC =  2980.98852          MODEL CAIC =  1844.72404

CHI-SQUARE =      3442.989 BASED ON    231 DEGREES OF FREEDOM
PROBABILITY VALUE FOR THE CHI-SQUARE STATISTIC IS LESS THAN 0.001
THE NORMAL THEORY RLS CHI-SQUARE FOR THIS ML SOLUTION IS         7954.780.

SATORRA-BENTLER SCALED CHI-SQUARE =    2919.3142
PROBABILITY VALUE FOR THE CHI-SQUARE STATISTIC IS       0.00000

BENTLER-BONETT NORMED    FIT INDEX=      0.000
BENTLER-BONETT NONNORMED FIT INDEX=      0.000
COMPARATIVE FIT INDEX            =       0.000
```

Recall that when each χ_i^2 is greater than or equal to df_i,

$$\text{CFI} = \frac{(\chi_0^2 - df_0) - (\chi_k^2 - df_k)}{(\chi_0^2 - df_0)}$$

where df_0 = degrees of freedom for the null model and df_k = degrees of freedom for the hypothesized model. Thus

$$\text{CFI}^* = \frac{(2919.31 - 231) - (370.99 - 202)}{(2919.31 - 231)} = .94$$

In conclusion, relying on sound statistical and theoretical rationales, we can feel confident that the modified model of MBI structure, as determined through post hoc model-fitting procedures, stands as a very adequate representation of the sample data. A schematic summary of this final model is presented in Figure 4.2.

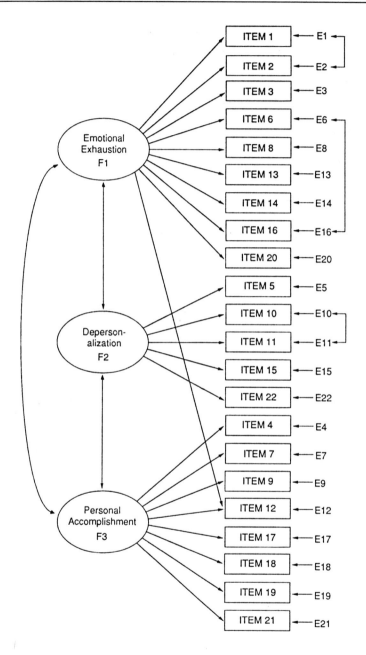

FIGURE 4.2. Final Model of Factorial Structure for the Maslach Burnout Inventory

Note: Item numbers correspond to variable numbers (e.g., ITEM 1 = V1).

Applications Related to Other Disciplines

BUSINESS: Shore, L. M., & Tetrick, L. E. (1991). A construct validity study of the Survey of Perceived Organizational Support. *Journal of Applied Psychology, 76,* 636-643.

EDUCATION: O'Grady, K. E. (1989). Factor structure of the WISC-R *Multivariate Behavioral Research, 24,* 177-193.

KINESIOLOGY: Pelletier, L. G., Vallerand, R. J., Briere, N. M., Tuson, K. M., & Blais, M. R. (in press). The Sport Motivation Scale: A measure of intrinsic, extrinsic, and amotivation in sport. *Journal of Sport and Exercise Psychology.*

Notes

1. As was the case in Chapter 3, the first of each congeneric set of items was fixed to 1.00 for purposes of statistical identification.

2. EQS automatically truncates labels that follow the dotted extension to three letters.

3. That the S-Bχ^2 and its standard errors are robust means that their computed values are valid, despite violation of the normality assumption underlying the estimation method.

4. Four parameters previously specified as fixed in the initially hypothesized model were specified as free in the present model, thereby using up four degrees of freedom (i.e., 4 fewer degrees of freedom).

5. Although a CFI equal to .92 indicates that there is still some misfit in the model, I chose not to continue fitting the model, given that the bulk of the misfitting parameters represented correlated errors among MBI items. Although familiarity with MBI item content provides clear evidence as to why these correlated errors are so prominent, post hoc fitting of the model to these parameters would probably generate abundant criticism (see, e.g., Cliff, 1983).

6. Instead of using F_j, we could have used E_i or D_i equally well in the specification because they are assumed to be uncorrelated.

5

Application 3
Testing the Factorial Validity
of a Measuring Instrument
(Second-Order CFA Model)

In contrast to the two previous applications, this one examines a CFA model that comprises a second-order factor. Specifically, we test hypotheses related to a French version of the Beck Depression Inventory (FR-BDI: Bourque & Beaudette, 1982). The example comes from one of a series of studies by Byrne and colleagues (Byrne & Baron, 1993, in press; Byrne, Baron, & Campbell, in press, 1993) that tested for the validity of a second-order factorial structure of the BDI (Beck, Ward, Mendelson, Mock, & Erbaugh, 1961) for nonclinical adolescents; we concentrate here on the Byrne et al. (in press) study. Although the purposes of this study were to cross-validate and test for an invariant FR-BDI structure across gender for French Canadian high school students, we focus only on factorial validity as it relates to the female calibration sample.

As noted in Chapter 4, the CFA of a measuring instrument is most appropriately conducted with fully developed assessment measures that have demonstrated satisfactory factorial validity. Justification for CFA procedures in the present instance is based on evidence provided by Tanaka and Huba (1984) and replicated studies by Byrne and associates (see above) that BDI (and FR-BDI) score data are most adequately represented by a hierarchical factorial structure. That is to say, the first-order factors are explained by some higher order structure that, in the case of the BDI, is a single second-order factor of general depression. So let's turn now to a description of the BDI and its postulated structure.

THE MEASURING INSTRUMENT UNDER STUDY

The Beck Depression Inventory (BDI) is a 21-item scale that measures symptoms related to cognitive, behavioral, affective, and somatic components of depression. Although originally designed for use by trained interviewers, it is now most typically used as a self-report measure. For each item, respondents are presented with four statements rated from 0 to 3 in terms of intensity and are asked to select the one that most accurately describes their own feelings; higher scores represent a more severe level of reported depression.

Less well known than the original instrument, however, is a French version of the BDI (BDI-FR) developed and validated by Bourque and Beaudette (1982) for use with French-speaking adults. Basically, the only difference between the BDI and the FR-BDI lies in the translation of the items into French. In a recent CFA study that included cross-validation based on three independent samples, Byrne and Baron (in press) concluded that, consistent with the English version of the BDI, the FR-BDI was most adequately described by a second-order factorial structure.

THE HYPOTHESIZED MODEL

The model to be tested in the present application derives from the work of Byrne and Baron (in press). As such, the CFA model hypothesizes a priori that (a) responses to the BDI-FR can be explained by three first-order factors (Negative Attitude, Performance Difficulty, Somatic Elements) and one second-order factor (General Depression), (b) each item will have a nonzero loading on the first-order factor it was designed to measure and zero loadings on the other two first-order factors, (c) error terms associated with each item will be uncorrelated, and (d) covariation among the three first-order factors will be explained fully by their regression on the second-order factor. A diagrammatic representation of this model is presented in Figure 5.1.

The EQS Input File

For this application, we'll again use a raw data matrix that is treated as an external file. However, in contrast to the mainframe setup simulated in Chapter 4, the present example will be consistent with a microcomputer environment. In this first input file, presented in Table 5.1, we impose the second-order

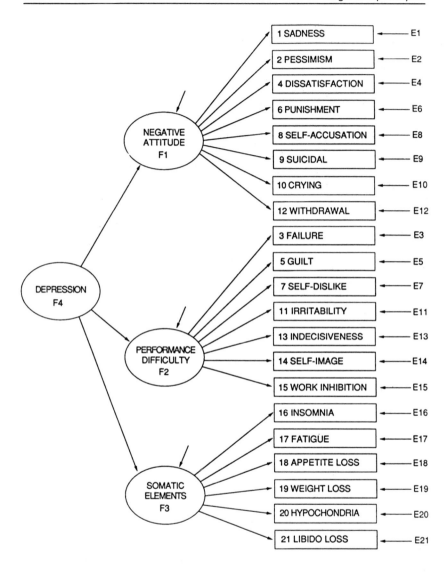

FIGURE 5.1. Initially Hypothesized Second-Order Model of Factorial Structure for the Beck Depression Inventory (French Version)

Note: Item numbers correspond to variable numbers (e.g., 1 SADNESS = V1).
Source: Adapted from Byrne, Baron, & Campbell (in press). Reprinted by permission.

structure determined from the Byrne and Baron study (in press-b) on the present data comprising 301 female French-speaking adolescents. (For further details regarding the sample, analyses, and results, see Byrne et al., in press.)

TABLE 5.1. Hypothesized Second-Order Model of Beck Depression Inventory
(French Version)

```
/TITLE
CFA OF FR BDI FOR FEMALES (GRP 1; CALIBRATION) "FRBDIF1H"
HYPOTHESIZED 2ND-ORDER MODEL
/SPECIFICATIONS
CASE=301; VAR=21; ME=ML; MA=RAW; FO=' (21F1.0)';
DATA='FRBDIF1.DAT';
/LABELS
V1=BDI1;       V2=BDI2;       V3=BDI3;       V4=BDI4;      V5=BDI5;
V6=BDI6;       V7=BDI7;       V8=BDI8;       V9=BDI9;      V10=BDI10;
V11=BDI11;     V12=BDI12;     V13=BDI13;     V14=BDI14;    V15=BDI15;
V16=BDI16;     V17=BDI17;     V18=BDI18;     V19=BDI19;    V20=BDI20;
V21=BDI21;
F1=NEGATT;     F2=PERFDIFF;   F3=SOMELEM;    F4=DEPRESS;
/EQUATIONS
V1=    F1+E1;
V2=   *F1+E2;
V4=   *F1+E4;
V6=   *F1+E6;
V8=   *F1+E8;
V9=   *F1+E9;
V10=  *F1+E10;
V12=  *F1+E12;
            V3=    F2+E3;
            V5=   *F2+E5;
            V7=   *F2+E7;
            V11=  *F2+E11;
            V13=  *F2+E13;
            V14=  *F2+E14;
            V15=  *F2+E15;
                        V16=   F3+E16;
                        V17=  *F3+E17;
                        V18=  *F3+E18;
                        V19=  *F3+E19;
                        V20=  *F3+E20;
                        V21=  *F3+E21;
            F1 = *F4 + D1;
            F2 = *F4 + D2;
            F3 = *F4 + D3;
/VARIANCES
    F4 = 1.0;
    D1 to D3 = *;
    E1 to E21 = *;
/CONSTRAINTS
    (D1,D1) = (D2,D2);
/END
```

Turning first to the **/SPECIFICATIONS** paragraph, we see that there
are 301 cases and 21 variables, the method of analysis is maximum likelihood,[1] and the data are in the form of a raw matrix; the Fortran statement for
reading the data is provided. On the second line of this paragraph is the name
of the data file, which must be provided here for microcomputer applications.
The **UN=9** statement is not needed in PC environments.

In the **/EQUATIONS** paragraph, the three indented groups of variables represent the first-order factor structure; each represents a congeneric set of observed measures that all tap the same factor. Consistent with our previous CFA models, the first of each variable set is fixed for purposes of statistical identification. The second-order structure is represented by the three statements involving Factor 4 (F4). In contrast to the lower order structure, however, all of the higher order factor loadings are to be freely estimated. Finally, the residual terms associated with the regression of each of the three lower order factors on Factor 4 are represented by the Ds.

In the **/VARIANCES** paragraph, you will note first of all that the variance for the higher order factor (F4) is fixed to 1.00. This, of course, is necessary because the three factor loadings are free to be estimated (see Chapter 1). You will also observe that the variances of the second-order disturbance terms (Ds) and first-order error terms (Es) are to be freely estimated.

Finally, note the addition of a **/CONSTRAINTS** paragraph within which the variance of D1 is held equal to that of D2. The reason for this specification is that unless a constraint is placed on at least one parameter in the higher order structure, this part of the model will be just-identified (see e.g., Bentler, 1989, 1992a; Rindskopf & Rose, 1988). The decision to equate D1 with D2 was based on other analyses that showed the variances of these parameters to be small and approximately equivalent. Three important points need to be noted with respect to the imposition of equality constraints: they must (a) exist in the model, (b) be free parameters in the model, and (c) start at the same value. Because we have not specified start values in this initial run, the estimate for D2 (as a consequence of the constraint) will automatically be identical to D1. Results are presented in Table 5.2.

The EQS Output File

Presented with findings of $\chi^2_{(187)} = 402.653$ and CFI = .853, it is clear that the initially hypothesized second-order model does not represent a good fit to the present data. Thus we need to locate the source of misfit in the model. Because it is most probable that model misfit derives from the misspecification of factor loadings or measurement errors at the first-order level or both, it is most expedient to reformulate the hypothesized model as a first-order CFA structure and then to examine the LM statistics for clues to possible misfit. Model misfit may also be a consequence of outliers in the data. To investigate both of these possibilities, the hypothesized second-order model was restructured and analyzed as a first-order model (Model 2); the related input file is presented in Table 5.3.

TABLE 5.2. Goodness-of-Fit Statistics for Hypothesized Second-Order Model of Beck Depression Inventory (French Version)

```
MAXIMUM LIKELIHOOD SOLUTION (NORMAL DISTRIBUTION THEORY)

PARAMETER ESTIMATES APPEAR IN ORDER,
NO SPECIAL PROBLEMS WERE ENCOUNTERED DURING OPTIMIZATION.

ALL EQUALITY CONSTRAINTS WERE CORRECTLY IMPOSED


GOODNESS OF FIT SUMMARY

  INDEPENDENCE MODEL CHI-SQUARE =      1662.857 ON    210 DEGREES OF FREEDOM

   INDEPENDENCE AIC =  1242.85715   INDEPENDENCE CAIC =   254.36399
           MODEL AIC =    28.65268         MODEL CAIC =  -851.57694

   CHI-SQUARE =     402.653 BASED ON    187 DEGREES OF FREEDOM
   PROBABILITY VALUE FOR THE CHI-SQUARE STATISTIC IS LESS THAN 0.001
   THE NORMAL THEORY RLS CHI-SQUARE FOR THIS ML SOLUTION IS       385.842.

   BENTLER-BONETT NORMED    FIT INDEX=     0.758
   BENTLER-BONETT NONNORMED FIT INDEX=     0.833
   COMPARATIVE FIT INDEX          =        0.852
```

POST HOC MODEL FITTING

Respecification and Analysis of First-Order Model

The initial run of Model 2 was used mainly as a check on the presence of outliers and also to obtain start values for subsequent runs. Thus you will note that the **"RETEST"** command has been implemented but that neither the robust statistics nor the LM statistics have been requested. Let's turn to Table 5.4, then, to see the output related to this initial first-order model.

Because the data are in raw form, we can benefit from information bearing on the sample statistics. Reviewing the univariate statistics related to each FR-BDI item, we can see a few severely kurtotic items (e.g., BDI12, BDI19, BDI21), suggesting that the S-Bχ^2, which corrects for this distributional abnormality, should be substantially lower than the usual χ^2 statistic. In determining possible outliers in the data, we compare estimates for the five cases selected by the program as contributing most to multivariate kurtosis. Relative to estimates for the other cases, I regard Subject 63 to be an outlier and thus elegible for deletion on subsequent runs. Finally, if you examine the goodness-of-fit statistics you will note that the χ^2 statistic and CFI values are almost the same as for the second-order model. This is as it should be, given that the second-order model merely specifies a higher order factor to account for correlation among the lower order factors, rather than

TABLE 5.3. First-Order Model of Beck Depression Inventory (French Version): No Start Values

```
/TITLE
CFA OF FR BDI FOR FEMALES (GRP 1; CALIBRATION) "FRBDIF1I"
1ST ORDER INITIAL MODEL (INITIAL RUN TO GET START VALUES)

/SPECIFICATIONS
CASE=301; VAR=21; ME=ML; MA=RAW; FO='(21F1.0)';
DATA='FRBDIF1.DAT';

/LABELS
V1=BDI1;      V2=BDI2;      V3=BDI3;      V4=BDI4;      V5=BDI5;
V6=BDI6;      V7=BDI7;      V8=BDI8;      V9=BDI9;      V10=BDI10;
V11=BDI11;    V12=BDI12;    V13=BDI13;    V14=BDI14;    V15=BDI15;
V16=BDI16;    V17=BDI17;    V18=BDI18;    V19=BDI19;    V20=BDI20;
V21=BDI21;
F1=NEGATT;    F2=PERFDIFF;  F3=SOMELEM;   F4=DEPRESS;

/EQUATIONS
V1=    F1+E1;
V2=   *F1+E2;
V4=   *F1+E4;
V6=   *F1+E6;
V8=   *F1+E8;
V9=   *F1+E9;
V10=  *F1+E10;
V12=  *F1+E12;
          V3=    F2+E3;
          V5=   *F2+E5;
          V7=   *F2+E7;
          V11=  *F2+E11;
          V13=  *F2+E13;
          V14=  *F2+E14;
          V15=  *F2+E15;
                    V16=   F3+E16;
                    V17=  *F3+E17;
                    V18=  *F3+E18;
                    V19=  *F3+E19;
                    V20=  *F3+E20;
                    V21=  *F3+E21;

/VARIANCES
F1 TO F3= *;
E1 TO E21= *;

/COVARIANCES
F1 TO F3= *;

/PRINT
RETEST='START';

/END
```

the correlation of these factors among themselves, as is the case with a first-order structure.[2]

Following this preliminary check for outliers, Model 2 was modified (a) to include start values, as derived from the program, (b) to include both the robust and LM Test statistics, (c) to delete Case 63, and (d) to include a

TABLE 5.4. Selected EQS Output for First-Order Model of Beck Depression
Inventory (French Version): Initial Run

SAMPLE STATISTICS

UNIVARIATE STATISTICS

VARIABLE		BDI1	BDI2	BDI3	BDI4	BDI5
MEAN		1.3555	1.4817	1.4219	1.5880	1.4219
SKEWNESS	(G1)	1.8575	1.8217	1.7594	1.5952	1.5742
KURTOSIS	(G2)	3.7988	2.3854	1.7161	1.4753	2.0804
VARIABLE		BDI6	BDI7	BDI8	BDI9	BDI10
MEAN		1.6578	1.4485	1.6944	1.4551	1.5515
SKEWNESS	(G1)	1.3667	1.8684	1.2260	1.6964	1.6620
KURTOSIS	(G2)	0.6046	3.6975	0.6821	3.4186	1.8470
VARIABLE		BDI11	BDI12	BDI13	BDI14	BDI15
MEAN		1.7176	1.2791	1.7907	1.8339	1.5449
SKEWNESS	(G1)	1.3539	2.2585	0.5411	0.9705	1.0607
KURTOSIS	(G2)	0.7935	5.2350	-1.1012	-0.7401	0.5563
VARIABLE		BDI16	BDI17	BDI18	BDI19	BDI20
MEAN		1.6844	1.7143	1.5714	1.2226	1.4086
SKEWNESS	(G1)	1.1719	1.0652	1.1893	2.9602	1.6366
KURTOSIS	(G2)	0.7000	1.0437	0.3236	9.0310	2.2009
VARIABLE		BDI21				
MEAN		1.1894				
SKEWNESS	(G1)	3.2583				
KURTOSIS	(G2)	11.3725				

MULTIVARIATE KURTOSIS

MARDIA'S COEFFICIENT (G2,P) =   166.7914
NORMALIZED ESTIMATE =   46.5520

ELLIPTICAL THEORY KURTOSIS ESTIMATES

MARDIA-BASED KAPPA =   0.3453 MEAN SCALED UNIVARIATE KURTOSIS =   0.8114

MARDIA-BASED KAPPA IS USED IN COMPUTATION. KAPPA=   0.3453

CASE NUMBERS WITH LARGEST CONTRIBUTION TO NORMALIZED MULTIVARIATE KURTOSIS:

CASE NUMBER	60	63	74	114	132
ESTIMATE	781.9579	1225.9203	961.6606	787.1015	1026.7931

(Continued)

TABLE 5.4. (Continued)

GOODNESS OF FIT SUMMARY

INDEPENDENCE MODEL CHI-SQUARE =   1662.857 ON   210 DEGREES OF FREEDOM

INDEPENDENCE AIC = 1242.85715   INDEPENDENCE CAIC =   254.36399
        MODEL AIC =   26.17239   MODEL CAIC = -849.35012

CHI-SQUARE =   398.172 BASED ON   186 DEGREES OF FREEDOM
PROBABILITY VALUE FOR THE CHI-SQUARE STATISTIC IS LESS THAN 0.001
THE NORMAL THEORY RLS CHI-SQUARE FOR THIS ML SOLUTION IS   380.013.

BENTLER-BONETT NORMED   FIT INDEX=   0.761
BENTLER-BONETT NONNORMED FIT INDEX=   0.835
COMPARATIVE FIT INDEX   =   0.854

/PRINT paragraph that requested the model correlation matrix. Specifically, the adjusted and new paragraphs are as follows:

```
/SPECIFICATIONS
CASE=301; VAR=21; ME=ML,ROBUST; MA=RAW; UN=9; FO= '21F1.0)';
DEL=63; DATA='FRBDIF1.DAT';
/PRINT
CORRELATION=YES;
/LMTEST
SET=PEE,GVF;
```

In the **/SPECIFICATIONS** paragraph, you will see that Case 63 has been deleted. It is important to know that in the deletion of outliers there is no need to adjust the number of cases; EQS will automatically delete any specified cases. Because it is often worthwhile to examine the model correlation matrix, we have added the **/PRINT** paragraph in which this information is requested. Finally, we have included the **/LMTEST** paragraph in which we request that LM statistics be computed only for factor loadings (**GVF**) and correlated errors (**PEE**). Important results related to this modified input file are presented in Table 5.5.

The first thing to note here is that with Subject 63 deleted, estimates for the five selected cases are now relatively close to one another; no further deletions were therefore specified. Turning to the goodness-of-fit summary, we see that both the χ^2 and CFI values dropped negligibly, indicating that misfit in the model must be a consequence of misspecified parameters. Of primary import, however, is the large difference in the size of the usual χ^2 (393.513) and the S-Bχ^2 (296.991); the corrected CFI (CFI*) for the latter is 0.88. A differential of this magnitude is a clear indication that kurtosis is,

TABLE 5.5. Selected EQS Output for First-Order Model of Beck Depression
Inventory (French Version): Second Run

CASE NUMBERS WITH LARGEST CONTRIBUTION TO NORMALIZED MULTIVARIATE KURTOSIS:

CASE NUMBER	23	60	73	113	131
ESTIMATE	810.5492	780.9698	955.2268	823.8058	1017.8256

GOODNESS OF FIT SUMMARY

INDEPENDENCE MODEL CHI-SQUARE =   1612.940 ON   210 DEGREES OF FREEDOM

INDEPENDENCE AIC = 1192.93980   INDEPENDENCE CAIC =   205.14548
     MODEL AIC =   21.51333   MODEL CAIC = -853.39021

CHI-SQUARE =   393.513 BASED ON   186 DEGREES OF FREEDOM
PROBABILITY VALUE FOR THE CHI-SQUARE STATISTIC IS LESS THAN 0.001
THE NORMAL THEORY RLS CHI-SQUARE FOR THIS ML SOLUTION IS   374.791.

SATORRA-BENTLER SCALED CHI-SQUARE =   296.9913
PROBABILITY VALUE FOR THE CHI-SQUARE STATISTIC IS   0.00000

BENTLER-BONETT NORMED   FIT INDEX=   0.756
BENTLER-BONETT NONNORMED FIT INDEX=   0.833
COMPARATIVE FIT INDEX   =   0.852

MULTIVARIATE LAGRANGE MULTIPLIER TEST BY SIMULTANEOUS PROCESS IN STAGE   1
   PARAMETER SETS (SUBMATRICES) ACTIVE AT THIS STAGE ARE:
      PEE GVF

		CUMULATIVE MULTIVARIATE STATISTICS			UNIVARIATE INCREMENT	
STEP	PARAMETER	CHI-SQUARE	D.F.	PROBABILITY	CHI-SQUARE	PROBABILITY
1	V17,F1	24.104	1	0.000	24.104	0.000
2	E8,E5	47.669	2	0.000	23.566	0.000
3	E4,E2	67.984	3	0.000	20.315	0.000
4	E18,E2	83.107	4	0.000	15.123	0.000
5	E14,E7	96.938	5	0.000	13.831	0.000
6	E17,E15	106.612	6	0.000	9.674	0.002
7	E15,E13	115.473	7	0.000	8.861	0.003
8	V13,F3	126.653	8	0.000	11.181	0.001
9	E8,E3	133.737	9	0.000	7.084	0.008
10	E15,E2	140.428	10	0.000	6.691	0.010
11	E16,E8	147.020	11	0.000	6.592	0.010
12	E20,E6	153.496	12	0.000	6.476	0.011
13	E14,E10	159.572	13	0.000	6.075	0.014
14	E18,E12	165.313	14	0.000	5.741	0.017
15	E18,E5	171.666	15	0.000	6.353	0.012
16	E6,E3	177.418	16	0.000	5.751	0.016
17	E15,E3	183.221	17	0.000	5.803	0.016
18	E19,E18	188.780	18	0.000	5.559	0.018
19	E11,E7	194.172	19	0.000	5.392	0.020
20	E20,E14	198.755	20	0.000	4.582	0.032
21	E13,E6	203.153	21	0.000	4.398	0.036
22	E21,E13	207.580	22	0.000	4.427	0.035
23	E17,E16	211.956	23	0.000	4.376	0.036
24	E16,E7	216.685	24	0.000	4.729	0.030
25	E10,E9	220.767	25	0.000	4.082	0.043

in large part, responsible for the nonnormality of the data, and also shows the extent to which the usual χ^2 statistic would have been in error. Thus subsequent evaluations of model fit will be based on both the corrected S-Bχ^2 and CFI*.

Finally, to review parameters identified as those contributing most to model misfit, we examine the LM statistics. Here we can see a definite split between the first five parameters and the remaining ones. The largest malfitting parameter represents a cross-loading of BDI Item 17 (V17) on Factor 1. In other words, although this item was hypothesized to load on Factor 3, it is also loading substantially on Factor 1. The next four misspecified parameters represent error covariances between particular FR-BDI items, a finding that is consistent with previous gender-difference factor analyses of the English version of the instrument (Byrne et al., 1993). Except for one additional cross-loading (V13,F3), all remaining LM statistics relate to error covariances.

Given findings of inadequate fit, the hypothesized first-order model was subsequently respecified taking into account the LM statistics. Specifically, this model (Model 3) was modified to include the cross-loading of Item 17 on Factor 1, and error covariances between Items 8 and 5, Items 4 and 2, Items 18 and 2, and Items 14 and 7. Given that (a) the cross-loading of Item 13 on Factor 3 was neither theoretically nor substantively meaningful, (b) there was a substantial drop in the univariate LM χ^2 from Step 5 to Step 6, and (c) all remaining parameters represented error covariances that appeared likely to improve model fit only trivially while concomitantly rendering the model less parsimonious, no additional parameters were incorporated into the model.

Goodness-of-fit results for Model 3 demonstrated a striking improvement in overall fit (S-B$\chi^2_{(181)}$ = 229.99; CFI* = .95). Indeed, incorporation of these five parameters into the model resulted in a statistically significant better fitting model than was the case for Model 2 (ΔS-B$\chi^2_{(5)}$ = 67.64; the difference in CFI* values was also substantial (.07).[3] Furthermore, results bearing on the individual estimates revealed the cross-loading of Item 17 onto Factor 1 to be statistically significant ($p < .001$), as were the error covariances ($p < .01$). However, the initial loading of Item 17 onto Factor 3 was found to be nonsignificant ($p = .08$). Given this nonsignificant finding, and because parsimony is always an important criterion in model building, the model was once again reestimated (Model 4), with Item 17 loading onto Factor 1 in lieu of Factor 3 (i.e., the loading of V17 was limited to one factor only, resulting in a more parsimonious model). Model specification related to the input file for Model 4 is presented in Table 5.6.

It is easy to identify the respecified loading and the added error covariances by their absence of start values. Furthermore, to conserve space, only

TABLE 5.6. Model Specifications for Final First-Order Model of Beck
Depression Inventory (French Version)

```
/EQUATIONS
       V1  =  1.000  F1   +   1.000  E1    ;
       V2  =  1.186*F1    +   1.000  E2    ;
       V3  =  1.000  F2   +   1.000  E3    ;
       V4  =  1.443*F1    +   1.000  E4    ;
       V5  =   .303*F2    +   1.000  E5    ;
       V6  =  1.060*F1    +   1.000  E6    ;
       V7  =   .358*F2    +   1.000  E7    ;
       V8  =  1.043*F1    +   1.000  E8    ;
       V9  =  1.069*F1    +   1.000  E9    ;
      V10  =  1.111*F1    +   1.000  E10   ;
      V11  =   .209*F2    +   1.000  E11   ;
      V12  =   .842*F1    +   1.000  E12   ;
      V13  =   .094*F2    +   1.000  E13   ;
      V14  =   .483*F2    +   1.000  E14   ;
      V15  =   .223*F2    +   1.000  E15   ;
      V16  =  1.000  F3   +   1.000  E16   ;
      V17  =        *F1   +   1.000  E17   ;
      V18  =   .856*F3    +   1.000  E18   ;
      V19  =   .363*F3    +   1.000  E19   ;
      V20  =   .490*F3    +   1.000  E20   ;
      V21  =   .326*F3    +   1.000  E21   ;

/VARIANCES
       F1=    .164*  ;
       F2=    .698*  ;
       F3=    .230*  ;
       E1=    .205*  ;
        .
        .
        .
      E21=    .256*  ;

/COVARIANCES
       F2,F1  =   .225*  ;
       F3,F1  =   .151*  ;
       F3,F2  =   .166*  ;
       E8,E5  =  *;
       E4,E2  =  *;
      E18,E2  =  *;
      E14,E7  =  *;

/END
```

the first and last error variance parameters have been listed. Goodness-of-fit
statistics for this model are shown in Table 5.7.

As you will note, the difference in S-$B\chi^2$ values between Models 3 and
4 was not statistically significant (ΔS-$B\chi^2_{(1)} = 2.94$); essentially the fit of the
two models was equivalent and represented a good fit to the data. Model 4,
however, was considered the better fitting first-order model of BDI structure
because it was the more parsimonious model of the two and as such represented a psychometrically sounder parameterization of the instrument.

TABLE 5.7. Goodness-of-fit Statistics for Final First-Order Model of Beck
Depression Inventory (French Version)

```
GOODNESS OF FIT SUMMARY

INDEPENDENCE MODEL CHI-SQUARE =         1612.940 ON    210 DEGREES OF FREEDOM

INDEPENDENCE AIC =  1192.93980   INDEPENDENCE CAIC =    205.14548
        MODEL AIC =   -62.07088          MODEL CAIC =  -918.15929

CHI-SQUARE =     301.929 BASED ON    182 DEGREES OF FREEDOM
PROBABILITY VALUE FOR THE CHI-SQUARE STATISTIC IS LESS THAN 0.001
THE NORMAL THEORY RLS CHI-SQUARE FOR THIS ML SOLUTION IS          283.524.

SATORRA-BENTLER SCALED CHI-SQUARE =     232.2894
PROBABILITY VALUE FOR THE CHI-SQUARE STATISTIC IS      0.00694

BENTLER-BONETT NORMED    FIT INDEX=     0.813
BENTLER-BONETT NONNORMED FIT INDEX=     0.901
COMPARATIVE FIT INDEX            =      0.915
```

Respecification and Estimation
of Second-Order Model

Having determined the best fitting lower order factor structure, the final
task was to reparameterize the model as a second-order structure. Specification related to this model (Model 5) is presented in Table 5.8.

Although estimation of this model yielded fit statistics that were comparable to those for Model 4 ($\chi^2_{(183)}$ = 308.06; CFI = .92), the output also
included the following error message:

```
PARAMETER CONDITION CODE
D1,D1 CONSTRAINED AT LOWER BOUND
ALL EQUALITY CONSTRAINTS WERE CORRECTLY IMPOSED
D2,D2 VARIANCE OF PARAMETER ESTIMATE IS SET TO ZERO.
*** WARNING *** TEST RESULTS MAY NOT BE APPROPRIATE DUE TO
CONDITION CODE
```

Within the context of the present application, it seems likely that the
variance of D1 was a boundary parameter with a value close to zero. As noted
in Chapter 3, to prevent the tendency for such parameters to manifest themselves as negative values, as can happen with LISREL, EQS automatically
constrains these parameters to be nonnegative. Of course, since the variance
of D2 was constrained equal to that of D1, its value too was fixed to zero.

Model 5 was subsequently reestimated, with the variance of D1 fixed to
a small positive number (.001).[4] The results and diagrammatic portrayal of
this final model are presented in Table 5.9 and Figure 5.2, respectively.

TABLE 5.8. Model Specifications for Final Second-Order Model of Beck
Depression Inventory (French Version)

```
/EQUATIONS
    V1   =   1.000 F1   +   1.000 E1    ;
    V2   =   1.186*F1   +   1.000 E2    ;
    V3   =   1.000 F2   +   1.000 E3    ;
    V4   =   1.443*F1   +   1.000 E4    ;
    V5   =    .303*F2   +   1.000 E5    ;
    V6   =   1.060*F1   +   1.000 E6    ;
    V7   =    .358*F2   +   1.000 E7    ;
    V8   =   1.043*F1   +   1.000 E8    ;
    V9   =   1.069*F1   +   1.000 E9    ;
    V10  =   1.111*F1   +   1.000 E10   ;
    V11  =    .209*F2   +   1.000 E11   ;
    V12  =    .842*F1   +   1.000 E12   ;
    V13  =    .094*F2   +   1.000 E13   ;
    V14  =    .483*F2   +   1.000 E14   ;
    V15  =    .223*F2   +   1.000 E15   ;
    V16  =   1.000 F3   +   1.000 E16   ;
    V17  =        *F1   +   1.000 E17   ;
    V18  =    .856*F3   +   1.000 E18   ;
    V19  =    .363*F3   +   1.000 E19   ;
    V20  =    .490*F3   +   1.000 E20   ;
    V21  =    .326*F3   +   1.000 E21   ;
    F1= *F4 + D1;
    F2= *F4 + D2;
    F3= *F4 + D3;
/VARIANCES
      F4=   1.0;
      D1=   *;
      D2=   *;
      D3=   *;
      E1=    .205*  ;
      .
      .
      .
      E21=    .256*  ;
/COVARIANCES
    E8,E5  =  *;
    E4,E2  =  *;
    E14,E7 =  *;
    E18,E2 =  *;
/CONSTRAINTS
    (D1,D1)=(D2,D2) ;
/END
```

As was the case in the previous run, the fit of this final second-order
model is, for all intents and purposes, the same as that for the first-order
structure. The very slight difference between the usual fit statistic ($\chi^2_{(183)} =$
307.52 vs $\chi^2_{(182)}$ = 301.18) and the corrected fit statistic (S-B$\chi^2_{(183)}$ = 236.75
vs S-B$\chi^2_{(182)}$ = 232.29) was undoubtedly due to the constraint placed on the
first disturbance term (D1). Next, in reviewing information related to the
measurement equations, you will note that all estimates are both reasonable
and statistically significant (including the error covariances), and all standard

TABLE 5.9. Selected EQS Output for Final Second-Order Model of Beck
Depression Inventory (French Version)

GOODNESS OF FIT SUMMARY

INDEPENDENCE MODEL CHI-SQUARE =   1612.940 ON   210 DEGREES OF FREEDOM

INDEPENDENCE AIC =   1192.93980   INDEPENDENCE CAIC =   205.14548
        MODEL AIC =   -58.48482   MODEL CAIC = -919.27701

CHI-SQUARE =   307.515 BASED ON   183 DEGREES OF FREEDOM
PROBABILITY VALUE FOR THE CHI-SQUARE STATISTIC IS LESS THAN 0.001
THE NORMAL THEORY RLS CHI-SQUARE FOR THIS ML SOLUTION IS   290.632.

SATORRA-BENTLER SCALED CHI-SQUARE =   236.7543
PROBABILITY VALUE FOR THE CHI-SQUARE STATISTIC IS   0.00455

BENTLER-BONETT NORMED   FIT INDEX=   0.809
BENTLER-BONETT NONNORMED FIT INDEX=   0.898
COMPARATIVE FIT INDEX   =   0.911

**MEASUREMENT EQUATIONS WITH STANDARD ERRORS AND TEST STATISTICS
(ROBUST STATISTICS IN PARENTHESES)**

```
BDI1  =V1  =    1.000 F1    + 1.000 E1

BDI2  =V2  =    1.189*F1    + 1.000 E2
                 .149
                7.992
           (    .177)
           (  6.722)

BDI3  =V3  =    1.000 F2    + 1.000 E3

BDI4  =V4  =    1.476*F1    + 1.000 E4
                 .167
                8.828
           (    .193)
           (  7.660)

BDI5  =V5  =     .671*F2    + 1.000 E5
                 .091
                7.353
           (    .124)
           (  5.392)

BDI6  =V6  =    1.170*F1    + 1.000 E6
                 .170
                6.900
           (    .213)
           (  5.506)

BDI7  =V7  =     .872*F2    + 1.000 E7
                 .100
                8.760
           (    .137)
           (  6.359)

BDI8  =V8  =    1.098*F1    + 1.000 E8
                 .154
                7.142
           (    .207)
           (  5.293)
```

TABLE 5.9. (Continued)

```
BDI9   =V9   =    1.081*F1   + 1.000 E9
                    .118
                   9.148
                 (   .153)
                 ( 7.067)
BDI10  =V10  =    1.130*F1   + 1.000 E10
                    .154
                   7.336
                 (   .179)
                 ( 6.317)
BDI11  =V11  =     .441*F2   + 1.000 E11
                    .123
                   3.582
                 (   .121)
                 ( 3.641)
BDI12  =V12  =     .930*F1   + 1.000 E12
                    .104
                   8.948
                 (   .133)
                 ( 6.971)
BDI13  =V13  =     .566*F2   + 1.000 E13
                    .111
                   5.090
                 (   .126)
                 ( 4.490)
BDI14  =V14  =    1.107*F2   + 1.000 E14
                    .159
                   6.957
                 (   .176)
                 ( 6.285)
BDI15  =V15  =     .810*F2   + 1.000 E15
                    .097
                   8.374
                 (   .133)
                 ( 6.096)
BDI16  =V16  =    1.000 F3   + 1.000 E16
BDI17  =V17  =    1.234*F1   + 1.000 E17
                    .138
                   8.926
                 (   .155)
                 ( 7.943)
BDI18  =V18  =     .929*F3   + 1.000 E18
                    .147
                   6.318
                 (   .155)
                 ( 5.985)
BDI19  =V19  =     .330*F3   + 1.000 E19
                    .082
                   4.043
                 (   .099)
                 ( 3.330)
```

(Continued)

TABLE 5.9. (Continued)

```
BDI20    =V20 =      .487*F3    + 1.000 E20
                     .103
                    4.746
                  (  .120)
                  ( 4.064)
BDI21    =V21 =      .329*F3    + 1.000 E21
                     .079
                    4.195
                  (  .082)
                  ( 3.996)
NEGATT   =F1  =      .377*F4    + 1.000 D1
                     .033
                   11.592
                  (  .044)
                  ( 8.551)
PERFDIFF=F2   =      .492*F4    + 1.000 D2
                     .046
                   10.642
                  (  .056)
                  ( 8.755)
SOMELEM  =F3  =      .325*F4    + 1.000 D3
                     .047
                    6.911
                  (  .052)
                  ( 6.252)
```

VARIANCES OF INDEPENDENT VARIABLES

```
                         V                              F
                        ---                            ---
                                  I F4  -DEPRESS           1.000 I
                                  I                              I
                         E                              D
                        ---                            ---
E1  -  BDI1                 .205*I D1  -NEGATT            .001 I
                           .019 I                              I
                         10.875 I                              I
                        (  .025)I                              I
                        ( 8.327)I                              I
                               I                              I
E2  -  BDI2                 .508*I D2  -PERFDIFF          .012*I
                           .044 I                         .015 I
                         11.431 I                         .848 I
                        (  .069)I                       (  .018)I
                        ( 7.369)I                       (  .686)I
                               I                              I
E3  -  BDI3                 .423*I D3  -SOMELEM           .159*I
                           .039 I                         .041 I
                         10.813 I                        3.856 I
                        (  .049)I                       (  .052)I
                        ( 8.616)I                       ( 3.074)I
                               I                              I
E4  -  BDI4                 .553*I                              I
                           .050 I                              I
                         11.089 I                              I
                        (  .067)I                              I
                        ( 8.198)I                              I
```

TABLE 5.9. (Continued)

```
                                      I                                    I
E5   -   BDI5                   .336*I                                    I
                               .029 I                                     I
                             11.456 I                                     I
                           (   .040)I                                     I
                           (  8.375)I                                     I
                                      I                                    I
E6   -   BDI6                   .768*I                                    I
                               .065 I                                     I
                             11.737 I                                     I
                           (   .078)I                                     I
                           (  9.791)I                                     I
                                      I                                    I
E7   -   BDI7                   .294*I                                    I
                               .028 I                                     I
                             10.620 I                                     I
                           (   .043)I                                     I
                           (  6.838)I                                     I
                                      I                                    I
E8   -   BDI8                   .612*I                                    I
                               .052 I                                     I
                             11.675 I                                     I
                           (   .061)I                                     I
                           ( 10.067)I                                     I
                                      I                                    I
E9   -   BDI9                   .261*I                                    I
                               .024 I                                     I
                             10.990 I                                     I
                           (   .032)I                                     I
                           (  8.273)I                                     I
                                      I                                    I
E10  -BDI10                     .601*I                                    I
                               .052 I                                     I
                             11.643 I                                     I
                           (   .080)I                                     I
                           (  7.467)I                                     I
                                      I                                    I

E11  -BDI11                     .897*I                                    I
                               .074 I                                     I
                             12.109 I                                     I
                           (   .096)I                                     I
                           (  9.307)I                                     I
                                      I                                    I
E12  -BDI12                     .211*I                                    I
                               .019 I                                     I
                             11.093 I                                     I
                           (   .026)I                                     I
                           (  8.227)I                                     I
                                      I                                    I
E13  -BDI13                     .658*I                                    I
                               .055 I                                     I
                             11.959 I                                     I
                           (   .043)I                                     I
                           ( 15.374)I                                     I
                                      I                                    I
E14  -BDI14                    1.069*I                                    I
                               .093 I                                     I
```

(Continued)

TABLE 5.9. (Continued)

```
                                    11.505 I                           I
                                   (  .096)I                           I
                                   ( 11.190)I                          I
                                          I                            I
E15 -BDI15                            .309*I                           I
                                     .028 I                            I
                                   10.969 I                            I
                                   (  .029)I                           I
                                   ( 10.728)I                          I
                                          I                            I
E16 -BDI16                            .443*I                           I
                                     .052 I                            I
                                    8.517 I                            I
                                   (  .062)I                           I
                                   (  7.151)I                          I
                                          I                            I
E17 -BDI17                            .375*I                           I
                                     .034 I                            I
                                   11.104 I                            I
                                   (  .042)I                           I
                                   (  8.908)I                          I
                                          I                            I
E18 -BDI18                            .433*I                           I
                                     .049 I                            I
                                    8.889 I                            I
                                   (  .053)I                           I
                                   (  8.124)I                          I
                                          I                            I
E19 -BDI19                            .280*I                           I
                                     .024 I                            I
                                   11.614 I                            I
                                   (  .057)I                           I
                                   (  4.913)I                          I
                                          I                            I
E20 -BDI20                            .393*I                           I
                                     .035 I                            I
                                   11.275 I                            I
                                   (  .051)I                           I
                                   (  7.780)I                          I
                                          I                            I
E21 -BDI21                            .253*I                           I
                                     .022 I                            I
                                   11.552 I                            I
                                   (  .052)I                           I
                                   (  4.876)I                          I
                                          I                            I
    COVARIANCES AMONG INDEPENDENT VARIABLES
    ----------------------------------------
                        E                          D
                       ---                        ---
E4  -  BDI4             .136*I                           I
E2  -  BDI2             .035 I                           I
                      3.946 I                            I
                     (  .044)I                           I
                     (  3.114)I                          I
E18 -BDI18            -.115*I                            I
E2  -  BDI2             .030 I                           I
                     -3.832 I                            I
                     (  .031)I                           I
                     ( -3.677)I                          I
                            I                            I
```

TABLE 5.9. (Continued)

E8	–	BDI8	.133*I	I
E5	–	BDI5	.029 I	I
			4.585 I	I
			(.036)I	I
			(3.688)I	I
			I	I
E14	–	BDI14	.142*I	I
E7	–	BDI7	.038 I	I
			3.751 I	I
			(.048)I	I
			(2.972)I	I

errors are acceptable. Finally, to help you perhaps develop a better sense of how each of the above models compared with one another, goodness-of-fit statistics for each are summarized below in Table 5.10.

TABLE 5.10. Summary of Goodness-of-Fit Statistics for Comparative Models of Beck Depression Inventory (French Version)

	Model	χ^2	df	CFI	S-Bχ^2	CFI[*a]
1	Initial (second-order)	402.65	187[b]	.85	—	—
2	Initial (first-order)	393.51	186	.85	296.99	.88
3	Model 2 with: Item 17 cross- loaded on F1 4 correlated errors	297.25	181	.92	229.35	.95
4	Model 2 with: Item 17 loaded on F1 instead of on F3 4 correlated errors	301.18	182	.92	232.29	.95
5	Model 4 (second-order)	307.52	183[c]	.92	236.75	.95

NOTE: F1 = Factor 1 (Negative Attitude); F2 = Factor 2 (Performance Difficulty); F3 = Factor 3 (Somatic Elements).
a. Corrected Comparative Fit Index based on Satorra-Bentler χ^2 fit for the null model
b. Disturbance terms for F1 and F2 equated
c. Disturbance term for F1 fixed to .001

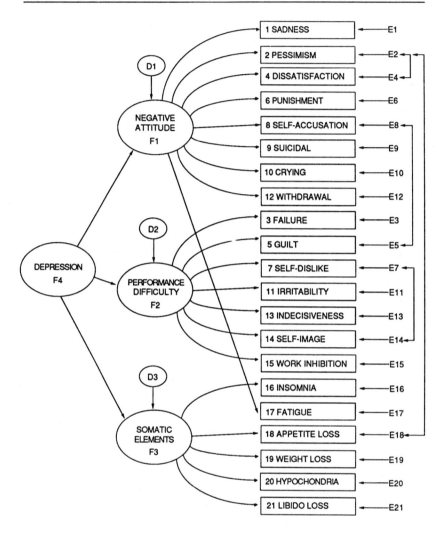

FIGURE 5.2. Final Second-Order Model of Factorial Structure for the Beck Depression Inventory (French Version)

Source: Adapted from Byrne, Baron, & Campbell (in press). Copyright by Sage Publications, Inc. Reprinted by permission.
Note: Error labels (Es) have been omitted for the sake of simplicity.

An important point to note with respect to the application presented in this chapter is that, given the same number of parameters to be estimated, fit statistics related to a model parameterized first as a first-order structure and then as a second-order structure will be equivalent. The difference between the two specifications here is that the second-order model is a special case of the first-order model, with the added restriction that structure be imposed on correlational pattern among the first-order factors (Rindskopf & Rose, 1988). However, judgment as to whether a measuring instrument should be modeled as a first-order or a second-order structure ultimately rests on substantive meaningfulness as dictated by the underlying theory.

Applications Related to Other Disciplines

BUSINESS: Goffin, R. D., & Jackson, D. N. (1988). The structural validity of the Index of Organizational Reactions. *Multivariate Behavioral Research, 23,* 327-347.

EDUCATION: Marsh, H. W. (1991). Multidimensional students' evaluations of teaching effectiveness: A test of alternative higher-order structures. *Journal of Educational Psychology, 83,* 285-296.

SOCIOLOGY: Kerlinger, F. N. (1984). *Liberalism and conservatism: The nature and structure of social attitudes.* Hillsdale, NJ: Lawrence Erlbaum.

Notes

1. For pedagogical purposes related to the introduction of various aspects of EQS programming and CFA model building, robust statistics have not been included here.

2. The additional degree of freedom for the second-order model is a consequence of the equality constraint placed on D1 and D2.

3. Recall that to assess the extent to which a respecified model exhibits an improvement in fit, we can examine the difference in χ^2 ($\Delta\chi^2$) between the two models. Because this difference is itself χ^2-distributed, with degrees of freedom equal to the difference in degrees of freedom (Δdf), it can be tested statistically, a significant $\Delta\chi^2$ indicating a substantial improvement in model fit.

4. The model was also estimated with D1 left constrained to zero (see Bentler, 1989, 1992a; Bentler & Chou, 1987; Dijkstra, 1992; Dillon, Kumar, & Mulani, 1987; Gerbing & Anderson, 1987). However, due to computation problems, probably as a consequence of the fixed value of zero for D1, the S-Bχ^2 was computed incorrectly.

6

Application 4
Testing for Construct Validity:
The Multitrait-Multimethod Model

In this chapter, we use CFA procedures to test hypotheses related to a more complex model structure known as the multitrait-multimethod (MTMM) model. As the name implies, this CFA framework models multiple traits assessed by multiple methods. The purpose of the MTMM model is to provide a means for testing hypotheses related to construct validity. Following from the seminal work of Campbell and Fiske (1959), construct validity research typically focuses on the extent to which data exhibit evidence of (a) convergent validity, (b) discriminant validity, and (c) method effects, an extension of the discriminant validity issue.

In the time since its inception, the original Campbell-Fiske approach to MTMM research has been the target of much criticism as methodologists have uncovered a growing number of limitations in its basic analytic strategy. Although several alternative MTMM approaches have been proposed over the years (for a review, see Schmitt & Stults, 1986), those based on the analysis of covariance structures have gained the most salience; of these, the most commonly applied is the general CFA approach to MTMM analyses.

The present application is taken from a study designed to assess the extent to which findings from three prominent covariance structure MTMM models were concordant (Byrne & Goffin, 1993). For our purposes here, however, we focus solely on only one of these: the CFA approach. Specifically, we test for evidence of construct validity related to four facets of perceived competence (social, academic, English, mathematics), as measured by self-, teacher, parent, and peer ratings. In other words, the MTMM model to be examined here is composed of four traits (social competence, academic competence, English competence, mathematic competence) and four methods (self-ratings, teacher ratings, parent ratings, peer ratings). Data comprise scores on these eight variables for 158 11th-grade high school students. (For further elaboration of the sample, instrumentation, and analytic strategy, see Byrne & Goffin, 1993.) A schematic summary of the eight-factor MTMM CFA model under study is presented in Figure 6.1.

THE CFA APPROACH
TO MTMM ANALYSES

In testing for evidence of construct validity within the context of the CFA framework, it has become customary to follow guidelines set forth by Widaman (1985). Accordingly, the postulated MTMM model is compared with a nested series of more restrictive models in which specific parameters are either eliminated or constrained equal to zero or 1.0. The difference in χ^2 ($\Delta\chi^2$), as discussed previously, then provides the yardstick by which to judge evidence of convergent and discriminant validity. This evaluative approach, as suggested by Widaman, is determined solely at the matrix level. Beyond these criteria, however, the CFA format allows for an assessment of construct validity at the individual parameter level; the postulated model provides the basis for this assessment. In testing for evidence of construct validity using the CFA approach, assessment is typically formulated at both the matrix and the individual parameter levels. We examine both in the present application.

The MTMM model shown in Figure 6.1 represents the hypothesized model. Clearly, it is a much more complex structure than either of the two models studied earlier. The complexity arises primarily from the loading of each observed variable onto both a trait and a method factor. Typically, in working through Widaman's nested model comparisons, one's hypothesized model is the least restrictive among those with which it is compared.

For our purposes here, we shall proceed first to test for evidence of construct validity at the matrix level and then base our judgment on individual parameters related to the hypothesized model presented in Figure 6.1. We turn now to a salient subset of nested MTMM models from those proposed by Widaman (1985).

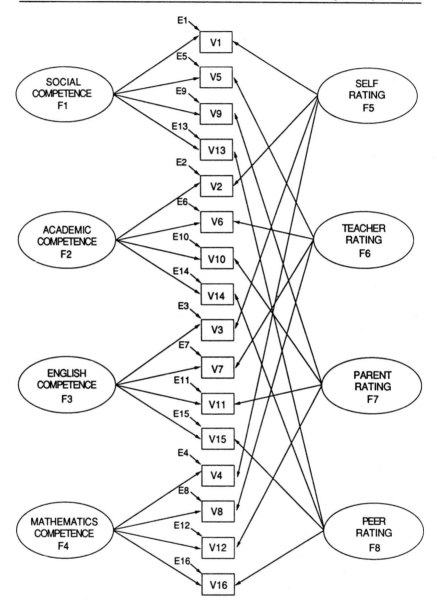

FIGURE 6.1. Hypothesized MTMM Model of Self-Concept (Model 1)

Source: Adapted from Byrne & Goffin (1993). Copyright 1993 by Erlbaum. Reprinted by permission.
Note: For sake of clarity, factor intercorrelations not shown.

FORMULATION OF MTMM MODELS

Model 1: Correlated Traits/Correlated Methods

This first model represents the hypothesized model and serves as the baseline against which all alternative MTMM models are compared. As noted earlier, it is typically the least restrictive model. This is because its specification includes both trait and method factors and allows for correlations among traits and among methods.[1] The related EQS input file is presented in Table 6.1.

EQS Input File

For this application, we work within the microcomputer environment; the data are in the form of a correlation matrix and reside as an external file. For purposes of consistency with the original study, analyses are also based on the correlation matrix. Nonetheless, readers are urged to review Cudeck's (1989) caveat regarding the analysis of correlation matrices.

Considering the input file presented in Table 6.1, let's focus first on the **/SPEC** paragraph, for which there are several specification points of interest. First, as with the previous applications, the name of the data file is specified here. This is a necessary requirement because the data are external to the input file. Second, no format statement is necessary because the data are in the form of a lower triangular matrix, and also in free format; both conditions are defaulted in EQS. Third, by default, EQS will analyze the correlation matrix because no standard deviations have been specified. Finally, some mention needs to be made regarding the small sample size of 158; admittedly, it was less than optimal and could possibly contribute to unstable asymptotic properties of the estimates. However, as noted in the original paper, we considered it less onerous to base the analyses on a small sample that comprised complete data than to base them on the full sample ($N = 335$), which contained missing data resulting from the nonreturn of parent rating forms (see e.g., Muthén, Kaplan, & Hollis, 1987).

Because the **/LABELS** paragraph is self-explanatory, let's focus next on specifications related to the hypothesized model. First, in the **/EQU** paragraph, you will see that in this example, unlike our previous examples, all factor loadings are to be freely estimated. In order for the model to be identified statistically, then, all factor variances have been constrained to equal 1.00 (see **/VAR** paragraph). Second, as specified in the **/COV** paragraph, all trait (F1 to F4) and method (F5 to F8) correlations are freely estimated.[2]

TABLE 6.1. EQS Input for MTMM Model 1 of Self-Concept: Correlated
                Traits/Correlated Methods

```
/TITLE
MTMM - CORRELATED TRAITS/CORRELATED METHODS "CTCMI.EQS"
/SPEC
CASE=158; VAR=16; ME=ML; MA=COR;
DATA='MTMM4APS.DAT';

/LABELS
V1=SCSELF;      V2=ACSELF;      V3=ECSELF;      V4=MCSELF;
V5=SCTCH;       V6=ACTCH;       V7=ECTCH;       V8=MCTCH;
V9=SCPAR;       V10=ACPAR;      V11=ECPAR;      V12=MCPAR;
V13=SCPEER;     V14=ACPEER;     V15=ECPEER;     V16=MCPEER;
F1=SC; F2=AC; F3=EC; F4=MC; F5=SELF; F6=TCHR; F7=PAR; F8=PEER;

/EQU
V1  = *F1 + *F5 + E1;
V5  = *F1 + *F6 + E5;
V9  = *F1 + *F7 + E9;
V13 = *F1 + *F8 + E13;
            V2  = *F2 + *F5 +E2;
            V6  = *F2 + *F6 +E6;
            V10 = *F2 + *F7 +E10;
            V14 = *F2 + *F8 +E14;
                    V3  = *F3 + *F5+ E3;
                    V7  = *F3 + *F6+ E7;
                    V11 = *F3 + *F7+ E11;
                    V15 = *F3 + *F8+ E15;
                            V4  = *F4 + *F5 + E4;
                            V8  = *F4 + *F6 + E8;
                            V12 = *F4 + *F7 + E12;
                            V16 = *F4 + *F8 + E16;
/VAR
F1 TO F8= 1;
E1 TO E16= *;
/COV
F1 TO F4= *; F5 TO F8=*;

/END
```

Note, however, that correlations among traits and methods have **not** been
specified (F1 to F8).

Let's turn now to the result of this Model 1 specification; relevant output
is shown in Table 6.2.

EQS Output File

Of great importance here is the fact that although model fit appeared
to be adequate, the number of iterations exceeded the default limit of 30,
thereby indicating nonconvergence of estimates on the parameters. Nonconvergence is a consequence of these values' being insufficiently close after
repeated iterations (Bollen, 1989).[3] Indeed, perusal of the iterative functions
and the parameter absolute changes reveals substantial fluctuation from one

TABLE 6.2. Selected EQS Output for MTMM Model 1 of Self-Concept
(No Start Values)

```
GOODNESS OF FIT SUMMARY
INDEPENDENCE MODEL CHI-SQUARE =        1076.725 ON    120 DEGREES OF FREEDOM
INDEPENDENCE AIC =    836.72516   INDEPENDENCE CAIC =    349.21375
      MODEL AIC =    -23.13164         MODEL CAIC =   -331.88886
CHI-SQUARE =      128.868 BASED ON   76 DEGREES OF FREEDOM
PROBABILITY VALUE FOR THE CHI-SQUARE STATISTIC IS LESS THAN 0.001
THE NORMAL THEORY RLS CHI-SQUARE FOR THIS ML SOLUTION IS        124.565.
BENTLER-BONETT NORMED     FIT INDEX=      0.880
BENTLER-BONETT NONNORMED FIT INDEX=      0.913
COMPARATIVE FIT INDEX          =         0.945

                         ITERATIVE SUMMARY
                       PARAMETER
ITERATION              ABS CHANGE         ALPHA            FUNCTION
    1                   0.350795        1.00000            2.58574
    2                   0.166637        1.00000            1.27602
    3                   0.094467        1.00000            0.94850
    4                   0.059219        1.00000            0.87906
    5                   0.049190        1.00000            0.85341
    6                   0.031489        1.00000            0.84187
    7                   0.028533        1.00000            0.83491
    8                   0.018352        1.00000            0.83159
    9                   0.017269        1.00000            0.82918
   10                   0.010780        1.00000            0.82782
   11                   0.010883        1.00000            0.82685
   12                   0.006349        1.00000            0.82620
   13                   0.007131        1.00000            0.82571
   14                   0.003806        1.00000            0.82534
   15                   0.004904        1.00000            0.82504
   16                   0.002340        1.00000            0.82479
   17                   0.003632        1.00000            0.82456
   18                   0.001676        1.00000            0.82434
   19                   0.002926        1.00000            0.82413
   20                   0.001563        1.00000            0.82393
   21                   0.002554        1.00000            0.82371
   22                   0.001740        1.00000            0.82349
   23                   0.002432        1.00000            0.82326
   24                   0.002016        1.00000            0.82300
   25                   0.002510        1.00000            0.82272
   26                   0.002331        1.00000            0.82241
   27                   0.002713        1.00000            0.82207
   28                   0.002686        1.00000            0.82170
   29                   0.003003        1.00000            0.82128
   30                   0.003053        1.00000            0.82082
************************************************************************
** NOTE: DO NOT TRUST THIS OUTPUT.  ITERATIVE PROCESS HAS NOT CONVERGED.
MAXIMUM NUMBER OF ITERATIONS WAS REACHED. **
  **
      **
  **   30 ITERATIONS HAVE BEEN COMPLETED AND THE PROGRAM STOPPED. CHECK
       PARAMETER IDENTIFICATION.
      **
  **   IF IDENTIFIED, USE THE UPDATED PARAMETERS TO START AGAIN.
      **
  **
      **
  **   SUBSEQUENT METHODS WILL NOT BE COMPUTED DUE TO ITERATIVE FAILURE.
      **
```

iteration to the next, with the smallest difference exceeding the convergence criterion of .001. Because nonconvergence can lead to unstable estimates, EQS prints out an error message warning users not to trust the output, which at this point pertains only to the goodness-of-fit summary.

Although EQS allows the cutoff limit for iterations to be set as high as 500, there seems to be little justification for doing this. In general, if estimates have not converged after 30 iterations, this is usually a good indication that either the model is in some way misspecified or the starting points for the iterative process are very distant from the final estimated values. In the case of our application here, the problem appears clearly to be a consequence of the latter. Given the complex specification of the MTMM model and the fact that we did not provide start values as a guide for the iterative process, the finding of nonconvergence was not unexpected. Thus start values were subsequently added to the input file, and the job was reexecuted. Because it seemed interesting to compare the final estimates from both the original study (Byrne & Goffin, 1993)[4] and the present application, estimates from the former were used as start values in lieu of those that could have been obtained from the RETEST feature.[5] Goodness-of-fit results from this second run are presented in Table 6.3.

Three important aspects of this output are of interest. First, note the two warning messages printed immediately before the goodness-of-fit summary. The first one notes that because standard deviations were not provided and **ANAL=COR** was not specified, the analysis will be based on the correlation matrix. The second message is in consonance with Cudeck's (1989) caveat regarding the analysis of correlation rather than covariance matrices. Second, although the χ^2 and CFI values border on those produced by the previous run, they are nonetheless different from those obtained from the nonconvergent solution. Indeed, the goodness-of-fit information lead us to conclude that the hypothesized model, in which both the traits and methods are correlated among themselves, represents a very reasonable fit to the sample data. Finally, you will observe that in this run only 12 iterations were needed before a final solution was reached. Thus the input of start values served the iteration process well.

Because the hypothesized MTMM model (Model 1) is typically the one that is least restrictive and best fitting, it serves as the standard against which to compare alternative models in the determination of construct validity. We turn now to these other MTMM models. In the interest of space, only model specification input and goodness-of-fit output will be tabled for each; Model 1 start values were used throughout, and no convergence problems were encountered.

TABLE 6.3 EQS Goodness-of-Fit Statistics for MTMM Model 1 of Self-Concept

```
*** WARNING *** ANALYZE COVARIANCE MATRIX FROM INPUT CORRELATION MATRIX
                BUT NO /STANDARD DEVIATION FOUND ANALYSIS=CORRELATION;
                IS ASSUMED

CORRELATION MATRIX TO BE ANALYZED:    16 VARIABLES (SELECTED FROM
 16 VARIABLES) BASED ON    158 CASES.

*** WARNING *** STATISTICS MAY NOT BE MEANINGFUL
                DUE TO ANALYZING CORRELATION MATRIX


GOODNESS OF FIT SUMMARY

INDEPENDENCE MODEL CHI-SQUARE =        1076.725 ON    120 DEGREES OF FREEDOM
INDEPENDENCE AIC =    836.72516    INDEPENDENCE CAIC =    349.21375
          MODEL AIC =   -24.41710        MODEL CAIC =   -333.17432
CHI-SQUARE =      127.583 BASED ON    76 DEGREES OF FREEDOM
PROBABILITY VALUE FOR THE CHI-SQUARE STATISTIC IS LESS THAN 0.001
THE NORMAL THEORY RLS CHI-SQUARE FOR THIS ML SOLUTION IS         124.400.
BENTLER-BONETT NORMED    FIT INDEX=        0.882
BENTLER-BONETT NONNORMED FIT INDEX=        0.915
COMPARATIVE FIT INDEX            =         0.946

                       ITERATIVE SUMMARY

                    PARAMETER
ITERATION           ABS CHANGE          ALPHA                 FUNCTION
    1                0.043527          1.00000                0.83004
    2                0.017336          1.00000                0.81632
    3                0.010041          1.00000                0.81398
    4                0.005822          1.00000                0.81335
    5                0.004788          1.00000                0.81308
    6                0.003067          1.00000                0.81292
    7                0.002992          1.00000                0.81283
    8                0.001749          1.00000                0.81276
    9                0.002027          1.00000                0.81271
   10                0.001099          1.00000                0.81268
   11                0.001443          1.00000                0.81265
   12                0.000750          1.00000                0.81263
```

Model 2: No Traits/Correlated Methods

Specification of parameters for this model is presented in Table 6.4, and the goodness-of-fit statistics are presented in Table 6.5. Of major importance with the **input file** is the absence of Factors 1 through 4 (the traits). As a result, each statement in the /EQU paragraph comprises only one factor loading (for methods). Relatedly, the /COV paragraph has been altered to include correlations among the methods only. As indicated by the χ^2 and CFI values in the **output file,** the goodness of fit for Model 2 was extremely poor ($\chi^2_{(98)} = 320.961$; CFI = .767).

TABLE 6.4. EQS Input for MTMM Model 2 of Self-Concept: No Traits/Correlated Methods

```
/EQU
 V1  = *F5 + E1;
 V5  = *F6 + E5;
 V9  = *F7 + E9;
 V13 = *F8 + E13;
             V2  = *F5 + E2;
             V6  = *F6 + E6;
             V10 = *F7 + E10;
             V14 = *F8 + E14;
                         V3  = *F5 + E3;
                         V7  = *F6 + E7;
                         V11 = *F7 + E11;
                         V15 = *F8 + E15;
                                     V4  = *F5 + E4;
                                     V8  = *F6 + E8;
                                     V12 = *F7 + E12;
                                     V16 = *F8 + E16;
/VAR
 F5 TO F8= 1;
 E1 TO E16= *;
/COV
 F5 TO F8= *;
/END
```

Model 3: Perfectly Correlated Traits/ Freely Correlated Methods

Input specifications and **output** results for Model 3 are illustrated in Tables 6.6 and 6.7, respectively. As with Model 1, the hypothesized model, each observed variable loads on both a trait and a method factor. In contrast, however, correlations among the trait factors are fixed to 1.0, as shown in the /COV paragraph. Viewing the results in Table 6.7, we see that the fit of this model ($\chi^2_{(82)}$ = 151.318; CFI = .928) is fairly good, albeit slightly less well fitting than for Model 1.

TABLE 6.5. EQS Goodness-of-Fit Statistics for MTMM Model 2 of Self-Concept

```
GOODNESS OF FIT SUMMARY
INDEPENDENCE MODEL CHI-SQUARE =        1076.725 ON    120 DEGREES OF FREEDOM
INDEPENDENCE AIC =     836.72516   INDEPENDENCE CAIC =     349.21375
        MODEL AIC =    124.96110          MODEL CAIC =    -273.17321
CHI-SQUARE =         320.961 BASED ON    98 DEGREES OF FREEDOM
PROBABILITY VALUE FOR THE CHI-SQUARE STATISTIC IS LESS THAN 0.001
THE NORMAL THEORY RLS CHI-SQUARE FOR THIS ML SOLUTION IS         386.342.
BENTLER-BONETT NORMED     FIT INDEX=       0.702
BENTLER-BONETT NONNORMED FIT INDEX=       0.715
COMPARATIVE FIT INDEX            =        0.767
```

TABLE 6.6. EQS Input for MTMM Model 3 of Self-Concept: Perfectly Correlated Traits/Freely Correlated Methods

```
/EQU
V1   = *F1 + *F5 + E1;
V5   = *F1 + *F6 + E5;
V9   = *F1 + *F7 + E9;
V13  = *F1 + *F8 + E13;
         V2   = *F2 + *F5 + E2;
         V6   = *F2 + *F6 + E6;
         V10  = *F2 + *F7 + E10;
         V14  = *F2 + *F8 + E14;
                  V3   = *F3 + *F5 + E3;
                  V7   = *F3 + *F6 + E7;
                  V11  = *F3 + *F7 + E11;
                  V15  = *F3 + *F8 + E15;
                           V4   = *F4 + *F5 + E4;
                           V8   = *F4 + *F6 + E8;
                           V12  = *F4 + *F7 + E12;
                           V16  = *F4 + *F8 + E16;
/VAR
F1 TO F8= 1;
E1 TO E16= *;
/COV
F1 TO F4= 1.0;F5 TO F8=*;
/END
```

Model 4: Freely Correlated Traits/ Perfectly Correlated Methods

The only change to be made in this model from the previous one takes place in the **/COV** paragraph. As shown in Table 6.8, F5 through F8 are now specified as fixed to 1.0, while F1 through F4 are freely estimated. Goodness-of-fit results from this run are presented in Table 6.9. As indicated by both the χ^2 and CFI values, the fit of Model 4 ($\chi^2_{(82)}$ = 231.402; CFI = .844) was much less well fitting than was the case for both Models 1 and 3.

TABLE 6.7. EQS Goodness-of-Fit Statistics for MTMM Model 3 of Self-Concept

```
GOODNESS OF FIT SUMMARY
INDEPENDENCE MODEL CHI-SQUARE =      1076.725 ON  120 DEGREES   OF FREEDOM
INDEPENDENCE AIC =   836.72516   INDEPENDENCE CAIC =   349.21375
       MODEL AIC =   -12.68212        MODEL CAIC =  -345.81491
CHI-SQUARE =       151.318 BASED ON    82 DEGREES OF FREEDOM
PROBABILITY VALUE FOR THE CHI-SQUARE STATISTIC IS LESS THAN 0.001
THE NORMAL THEORY RLS CHI-SQUARE FOR THIS ML SOLUTION IS         153.466.
BENTLER-BONETT NORMED    FIT INDEX=      0.859
BENTLER-BONETT NONNORMED FIT INDEX=      0.894
COMPARATIVE FIT INDEX          =         0.928
```

TABLE 6.8 EQS Input for MTMM Model 4 of Self-Concept: Freely Correlated
Traits/Perfectly Correlated Methods

```
/EQU
 V1  = *F1 + *F5 + E1;
 V5  = *F1 + *F6 + E5;
 V9  = *F1 + *F7 + E9;
 V13 = *F1 + *F8 + E13;
            V2  = *F2 + *F5 + E2;
            V6  = *F2 + *F6 + E6;
            V10 = *F2 + *F7 + E10;
            V14 = *F2 + *F8 + E14;
                       V3  = *F3 + *F5 + E3;
                       V7  = *F3 + *F6 + E7;
                       V11 = *F3 + *F7 + E11;
                       V15 = *F3 + *F8 + E15;
                                  V4  = *F4 + *F5 + E4;
                                  V8  = *F4 + *F6 + E8;
                                  V12 = *F4 + *F7 + E12;
                                  V16 = *F4 + *F8 + E16;
/VAR
 F1 TO F8= 1;
 E1 TO E16= *;
/COV
 F1 TO F4= *;F5 TO F8=1.0;
/END
```

TESTING FOR CONSTRUCT VALIDITY:
COMPARISON OF MODELS

Now that we have examined goodness-of-fit results for each of our
MTMM models, we can turn to the task of determining evidence of construct
validity. In this section, we'll ascertain information at the matrix level only
by comparing particular pairs of models. A summary of fit related to all
MTMM models is presented in Table 6.10, and results of model comparisons
are summarized in Table 6.11.

TABLE 6.9. EQS Goodness-of-Fit Statistics for MTMM Model 4 of Self-Concept

```
GOODNESS OF FIT SUMMARY
INDEPENDENCE MODEL CHI-SQUARE =        1076.725 ON   120 DEGREES OF FREEDOM
INDEPENDENCE AIC =     836.72516   INDEPENDENCE CAIC =    349.21375
       MODEL AIC =      67.40162         MODEL CAIC =   -265.73117
CHI-SQUARE =       231.402 BASED ON    82 DEGREES OF FREEDOM
PROBABILITY VALUE FOR THE CHI-SQUARE STATISTIC IS LESS THAN 0.001
THE NORMAL THEORY RLS CHI-SQUARE FOR THIS ML SOLUTION IS        243.407.
BENTLER-BONETT NORMED    FIT INDEX=       0.785
BENTLER-BONETT NONNORMED FIT INDEX=       0.771
COMPARATIVE FIT INDEX          =          0.844
```

TABLE 6.10. Summary of Goodness-of-Fit Indices for MTMM Models of
Self-Concept

Model	χ^2	df	CFI
1 Freely correlated traits; Freely correlated methods	127.58	76	.95
2 No traits; Freely correlated methods	320.96	98	.77
3 Perfectly correlated traits; Freely correlated methods	151.32	82	.93
4 Freely correlated traits; Perfectly correlated methods	231.40	82	.84

Evidence of Convergent Validity

As noted earlier, one criterion of construct validity bears on the issue of
convergent validity, the extent to which **independent measures** of the **same
trait** are correlated (e.g., teacher and self-ratings of social competence); these
values should be substantial and statistically significant (Campbell & Fiske,
1959). Using Widaman's (1985) paradigm, evidence of convergent validity
can be tested by comparing a model in which traits are specified (Model 1)
with one in which they are not (Model 2), the difference in χ^2 between the
two models providing the basis for judgment; a significant difference in χ^2
supports evidence of convergent validity. As shown in Table 6.11, the $\Delta\chi^2$
was highly significant ($p < .01$), and the difference in practical fit (ΔCFI =
.18) substantial, thereby arguing for the tenability of this criterion.[6]

TABLE 6.11. Differential Goodness-of-Fit Indices for MTMM Model
Comparisons

| Model Comparisons | Difference in | | |
	χ^2	df	CFI
Test of Convergent Validity			
Model 1 vs. Model 2 (traits)	193.38	22	.18
Test of Discriminant Validity			
Model 1 vs. Model 3 (traits)	23.74	6	.02
Model 1 vs. Model 4 (methods)	103.82	6	.11

Evidence of Discriminant Validity

Discriminant validity is typically assessed in terms of both traits and methods. In testing for evidence of trait discriminant validity, one is interested in the extent to which **independent measures** of **different traits** are correlated; these values should be negligible. When the independent measures represent different methods, correlations bear on the discriminant validity of traits; when they represent the same method, correlations bear on the presence of method effects, another aspect of discriminant validity.

In testing for evidence of discriminant validity among traits, we compare a model in which traits correlate freely (Model 1) with one in which they are perfectly correlated (Model 3); the larger the discrepancy between the χ^2 and CFI values, the stronger the support for evidence of discriminant validity. Although this comparison yielded a significant $\Delta\chi^2$ value, the ΔCFI was small.[7] These results, at face value, indicate little difference between the two models and thus argue for weak evidence of discriminant validity. In light of the traits under study, however, these findings are consistent with previous construct validity research in this area (for an elaboration, see Byrne & Goffin, 1993).

Based on the same logic, evidence of discriminant validity related to method effects was tested by comparing a model in which method factors were freely correlated (Model 1) with one in which the method factor correlations were specified as unity (Model 4); a nonsignificant $\Delta\chi^2$ (or minimal CFI) argues for the lack of discriminant validity and thus for common method bias across methods of measurement.[8] On the strength of both statistical ($\Delta\chi^2$ = 103.82) and nonstatistical (ΔCFI = .11) criteria, as shown in Table 6.11, it seems reasonable to conclude that evidence of discriminant validity for the methods was stronger than it was for the traits.

TESTING FOR CONSTRUCT VALIDITY: EXAMINATION OF PARAMETERS

A more precise assessment of trait- and method-related variance can be ascertained by examining individual parameter estimates. Specifically, the factor loadings and factor correlations of the hypothesized model (Model 1) provide the focus here. These results, as produced in the EQS output, are presented in Table 6.12. However, because it is difficult to envision the MTMM pattern of factor loadings and correlations from the printout, these values have been reordered and tabled to facilitate the assessment of convergent and discriminant validity; factor loadings are summarized in Table 6.13 and factor correlations in Table 6.14. (For a more extensive discussion of these MTMM findings, see Byrne & Goffin, 1993.)

TABLE 6.12. EQS Factor loading and Factor Correlation Estimates for MTMM
Model 1 of Self-Concept

MEASUREMENT EQUATIONS WITH STANDARD ERRORS AND TEST STATISTICS

```
SCSELF  =V1  =    .555*F1    +  .210*F5   + 1.000 E1
                  .106          .100
                 5.246         2.099

ACSELF  =V2  =    .499*F2    +  .593*F5   + 1.000 E2
                  .089          .096
                 5.615         6.181

ECSELF  =V3  =    .520*F3    +  .140*F5   + 1.000 E3
                  .090          .101
                 5.798         1.387

MCSELF  =V4  =    .467*F4    +  .656*F5   + 1.000 E4
                  .088          .094
                 5.291         6.980

SCTCH   =V5  =    .281*F1    +  .453*F6   + 1.000 E5
                  .099          .091
                 2.836         5.001

ACTCH   =V6  =    .423*F2    +  .716*F6   + 1.000 E6
                  .086          .082
                 4.891         8.688

ECTCH   =V7  =    .257*F3    +  .641*F6   + 1.000 E7
                  .090          .088
                 2.875         7.256

MCTCH   =V8  =    .697*F4    +  .527*F6   + 1.000 E8
                  .077          .076
                 9.101         6.924

SCPAR   =V9  =    .598*F1    +  .109*F7   + 1.000 E9
                  .109          .100
                 5.504         1.088

ACPAR   =V10 =    .626*F2    +  .342*F7   + 1.000 E10
                  .086          .107
                 7.256         3.203

ECPAR   =V11 =    .848*F3    +  .055*F7   + 1.000 E11
                  .099          .100
                 8.608          .548

MCPAR   =V12 =    .579*F4    +  .720*F7   + 1.000 E12
                  .087          .130
                 6.633         5.552

SCPEER  =V13 =    .127*F1    +  .826*F8   + 1.000 E13
                  .075          .069
                 1.685        12.020

ACPEER  =V14 =    .505*F2    +  .737*F8   + 1.000 E14
                  .065          .066
                 7.780        11.242
```

(Continued)

TABLE 6.12. (Continued)

```
ECPEER   =V15 =     .212*F3    +   .830*F8    + 1.000 E15
                    .069            .069
                   3.055          12.087

MCPEER   =V16 =     .474*F4    +   .568*F8    + 1.000 E16
                    .075            .072
                   6.353           7.881
```

COVARIANCES AMONG INDEPENDENT VARIABLES
```
------------------------------------------
              V                          F
             ---                        ---
                      I F2  -  AC              .095*I
                      I F1  -  SC              .152 I
                      I                        .628 I
                      I                            I
                      I F3  -  EC              .504*I
                      I F1  -  SC              .117 I
                      I                       4.315 I
                      I                            I
                      I F4  -  MC             -.148*I
                      I F1  -  SC              .149 I
                      I                        -.990 I
                      I                            I
                      I F3  -  EC              .719*I
                      I F2  -  AC              .087 I
                      I                       8.264 I
                      I                            I
                      I F4  -  MC              .871*I
                      I F2  -  AC              .052 I
                      I                      16.633 I
                      I                            I
                      I F4  -  MC              .329*I
                      I F3  -  EC              .114 I
                      I                       2.874 I
                      I                            I
                      I F6  -  TCHR            .492*I
                      I F5  -  SELF            .106 I
                      I                       4.646 I
                      I                            I
                      I F7  -  PAR             .595*I
                      I F5  -  SELF            .131 I
                      I                       4.527 I
                      I                            I
                      I F8  -  PEER            .309*I
                      I F5  -  SELF            .105 I
                      I                       2.938 I
                      I                            I
                      I F7  -  PAR             .498*I
                      I F6  -  TCHR            .125 I
                      I                       3.983 I
                      I                            I
                      I F8  -  PEER            .155*I
                      I F6  -  TCHR            .103 I
                      I                       1.503 I
                      I                            I
                      I F8  -  PEER            .169*I
                      I F7  -  PAR             .112 I
                      I                       1.512 I
```

TABLE 6.13. Trait and Method Loadings for MTMM Model 1 of Self-Concept

	SC	AC	EC	MC	SR	TR	PAR	PER
Self Ratings (SR)								
Social Competence	.56				.21			
Academic Competence		.50			.59			
English Competence			.52		.14[a]			
Mathematics Competence				.47	.66			
Teacher Ratings (TR)								
Social Competence	.28					.45		
Academic Competence		.42				.72		
English Competence			.25			.64		
Mathematics Competence				.70		.53		
Parent Ratings (PAR)								
Social Competence	.60						.11[a]	
Academic Competence		.63					.34	
English Competence			.85				.06[a]	
Mathematics Competence				.58			.72	
Peer Ratings (PER)								
Social Competence	.13[a]							.83
Academic Competence		.51						.74
English Competence			.21					.83
Mathematics Competence				.47				.57

a. Not statistically significant

Evidence of Convergent Validity

In examining individual parameters, we find convergent validity reflected in the magnitude of the trait loadings. As indicated in Table 6.13, all but one trait loading was significant. However, in a comparison of factor loadings across traits and methods, we see that the proportion of method variance exceeds that of trait variance for 10 of the 16 variables.[9] Thus although at first blush evidence of convergent validity appears to be fairly good, further scrutiny of the loadings reveals the tendency for method effects to attenuate the trait effects, thereby tempering evidence of convergent validity; these effects are most salient for the peer and teacher ratings.

Evidence of Discriminant Validity

Discriminant validity bearing on particular traits and methods is determined by examining the factor correlation matrices. Although, conceptually, correlations among traits should be negligible in order to satisfy evidence of

TABLE 6.14. Trait and Method Correlations for MTMM Model 1 of Self-Concept

Measures	Traits				Methods			
	SC	AC	EC	MC	SR	TR	PAR	PER
Social Competence (SC)	1.00							
Academic Competence (AC)	.10[a]	1.00						
English Competence (EC)	.50	.72	1.00					
Mathematics Competence (MC)	−.15[a]	.87	.44	1.00				
Self Ratings (SR)					1.00			
Teacher Ratings (TR)					.49	1.00		
Parent Ratings (PAR)					.60	.50	1.00	
Peer Ratings (PER)					.31	.16[a]	.17[a]	1.00

a. Not statistically significant

discriminant validity, such findings are highly unlikely in general, and with respect to psychological data in particular. Although these findings, as shown in Table 6.14, suggest that relations between academic competence and the specific subject areas of English and mathematics are most detrimental to the attainment of trait discriminant validity, they are nonetheless consistent with construct validity research in this area (see Byrne, 1986; Byrne & Shavelson, 1986; for additional references, see Byrne & Goffin, 1993).

Finally, an examination of method factor correlations in Table 6.14 reflects on their discriminability, and thus on the extent to which the methods are maximally dissimilar; this factor is an important underlying assumption of the MTMM strategy (see Campbell & Fiske, 1959). Given the obvious dissimilarity of self-, teacher, parent, and peer ratings, it might seem somewhat surprising to find correlations of .49 and .59. However, as noted in the Byrne and Goffin paper, these values are probably explained by the fact that the substantive content of all comparable items in the self, teacher, and parent scales were identically worded in order to maximize responses by different raters of the same student.

Applications Related to Other Disciplines

BUSINESS: Phillips, L. W. (1982). Assessing measurement error in key informant reports: A methodological note on organizational analysis in marketing. *Journal of Marketing Research, 18,* 395-415.

MEDICINE: Stein, J. A., Newcomb, M. D., & Bentler, P. M. (1988). Structure of drug use behaviors and consequences among young adults:

Multitrait-multimethod assessment of frequency, quantity, work site, and problem substance use. *Journal of Applied Psychology, 73,* 595-605.

LINGUISTICS: Bachman, L. F., & Palmer, A. S. (1981). The construct validation of the FSI Oral Interview. *Language Learning, 31,* 67-86.

Notes

1. As a consequence of problems related to both the identification and estimation of CFA models, trait-method correlations cannot be freely estimated (see Schmitt & Stults, 1986; Widaman, 1985).

2. The estimates will be correlations and not covariances, because the correlation matrix is to be analyzed.

3. **Insufficiently close** is defined by the convergence criterion established for a particular program. In EQS, the criterion is based on a mean of parameter absolute differences in estimates between two iterations; a value equal to .001 constitutes the criterion (Bentler, 1989, 1992a).

4. The original study was based on the LISREL 7 program (Jöreskog & Sörbom, 1988).

5. Had we invoked the **RETEST** command, this would have functioned in the same way as increasing the number of iterations. In comparing the number of iterations shown in Table 6.3 with those in Table 6.2, it appears that use of the **/TECH** paragraph, with **ITR=50,** would have yielded the same results (Bentler, Personal communication, June, 1993).

6. As we note in the article (Byrne & Goffin, 1993), there is not yet any firm standard for assessing the difference in indices of practical fit. However, such differentials have been used heuristically in order to provide more realistic indications of nested model comparisons than those based on the χ^2 statistic (see e.g., Bagozzi & Yi, 1990; Widaman, 1985); it is in this sense that they are used here.

7. Alternatively, we could compare Model 1 with one in which trait factors are specified as orthogonal factors (i.e., they are uncorrelated). In this case a large difference in $\Delta\chi^2$ would argue **against** evidence of discriminant validity (i.e., large $\chi^2 \equiv$ Reject H_0: factors are uncorrelated).

8. As was noted for the traits (note 7), we could alternatively specify a model in which uncorrelated method factors are specified, a large difference in χ^2 arguing **against** evidence of discriminant validity.

9. Trait variance equals the factor loading squared.

7

Application 5
Testing the Validity
of a Causal Structure

In this chapter, we take our first look at a full structural equation model (SEM). The hypothesis to be tested relates to the pattern of causal structure linking several stressor variables that bear on the construct of burnout. The original study from which this application is taken (Byrne, in press) tested and cross-validated the impact of organizational and personality variables on three dimensions of burnout for elementary, intermediate, and secondary teachers. For purposes of illustration here, however, the application is limited to the calibration sample of secondary teachers only.

As was the case with our factor analytic applications, those involving full SEMs are presumed to be of a confirmatory nature. That is to say, causal relations among all variables in the hypothesized model must be grounded in theory or empirical research or both. Typically, the hypothesis to be tested argues for the validity of postulated causal linkages among the variables of interest. Let's turn now to an in-depth examination of the hypothesized model under study in the current chapter.

THE HYPOTHESIZED MODEL

Consensus of findings from a literature review of burnout, as it bears on the teaching profession, led to the hypothesized model presented in Figure 7.1.

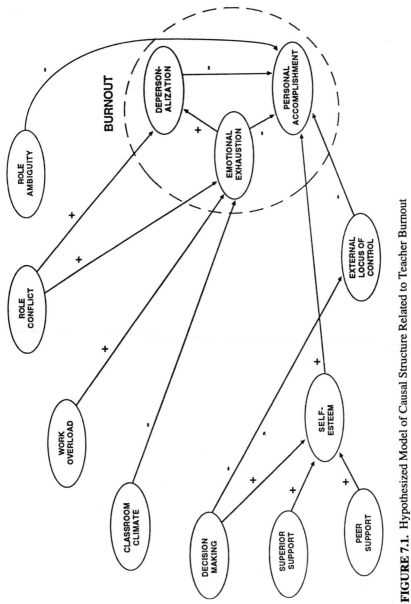

FIGURE 7.1. Hypothesized Model of Causal Structure Related to Teacher Burnout

Source: Copyright (in press) by the American Educational Research Association. Reprinted by permission.

139

(Readers wishing a more detailed summary of this research are referred to the original paper [Byrne, in press]). In reviewing this model, you will note that burnout is represented as a multidimensional construct, with Emotional Exhaustion (EE), Depersonalization (DP), and Personal Accomplishment (PA) operating as conceptually distinct factors. This part of the model is based on the work of Leiter (1991) in conceptualizing burnout as a cognitive-emotional reaction to chronic stress. Accordingly, EE holds the central position because it is considered to be most responsive to various stressors in the teacher's work environment. Depersonalization and reduced PA represent the cognitive aspects of burnout; they are indicative of the extent to which teachers' valuations of their students, their colleagues, and themselves become diminished. As indicated by the signs associated with each path in the model, EE is hypothesized to impact positively on DP, but negatively on PA; DP is hypothesized to impact negatively on PA.

The paths (and their associated signs) leading from the organizational (role ambiguity, role conflict, work overload, classroom climate, decision making, superior support, peer support) and personality (self-esteem, external locus of control) variables to the three dimensions of burnout reflect findings in the literature.[1] For example, high levels of work overload are expected to cause high levels of emotional exhaustion; in contrast, high (i.e., good) levels of classroom climate are expected to generate low levels of emotional exhaustion.

Preliminary Analyses

Of course, the model shown in Figure 7.1 represents only the structural portion of the full structural equation model. What we need to know now, however, is how each of the constructs in the above model is to be measured; this information represents the measurement portion of the structural equation model (see Chapter 1). The task involved in developing the measurement model is to determine (a) the number of indicators to use in measuring each construct, and (b) which items to use in formulating each indicator.

Formulation of Indicator Variables

In the applications examined in Chapters 3 through 6, the formulation of measurement indicators has been relatively straightforward; all examples have involved CFA models and have thus comprised only measurement models. In the measurement of multidimensional facets of self-concept (Chapters 3 and 6), each indicator represented a subscale score (i.e., the sum of all items designed to measure a particular SC dimension). In Chapters 4 and 5, our interest focused on the factorial validity of a measuring instrument. Accordingly, we were concerned with the extent to which items loaded onto their targeted factor. Adequate assessment of this phenomenon demanded that each item be included in the model. Thus the indicator variables in these cases each represented one item in the measuring instrument under study.

In contrast to these previous examples, formulation of the indicator variables in the present case was slightly more complex. Specifically, multiple indicators of each construct were formulated through the judicious combination of particular items. Thus items were carefully grouped according to content in order to equalize the measurement weighting across indicators. For example, the Classroom Environment Scale (Bacharach, Bauer, & Conley, 1986), used to measure classroom climate, comprises items that tap classroom size, ability and interest of students, and various types of abuse by students. Indicators of this construct were formed such that each item in the composite of items measured a different aspect of classroom climate. In the measurement of classroom climate, self-esteem, and external locus of control, indicator variables comprised items from a single unidimensional scale; all other indicators comprised items from subscales of multidimensional scales. (For an extensive description of the measuring instruments, see Byrne [in press].) In total, 32 indicators were used to measure the hypothesized structural model. A schematic presentation of the full structural equation model is presented in Figure 7.2.

Confirmatory Factor Analyses

Because (a) the structural portion of a standard full structural equation model involves relations among only latent variables, and (b) the primary concern in working with a standard full model is to assess the extent to which these relations are valid, it is critical that the measurement of each latent variable is psychometrically sound.[2] Thus an important preliminary step in the analysis of such models is to test first for the validity of the measurement model before making any attempt to evaluate the structural model. Consequently the indicator variables are tested using CFA procedures. Once it is known that the measurement model is operating adequately,[3] one can then have more confidence in findings related to the assessment of the hypothesized structural model.

In the present case, CFAs were conducted for indicator variables derived from each of the two multidimensional scales: these were the Teacher Stress Scale (TSS; Pettegrew & Wolf, 1982), measuring all organizational variables except classroom climate, and the Maslach Burnout Inventory (MBI; Maslach & Jackson, 1986), measuring the three facets of burnout. Whereas fit for the MBI was satisfactory (CFI = .97), that for the TSS was less so (CFI = .89); specification of four cross-loadings resulted in a more valid TSS instrument (CFI = .92). The final measurement model retained this revised

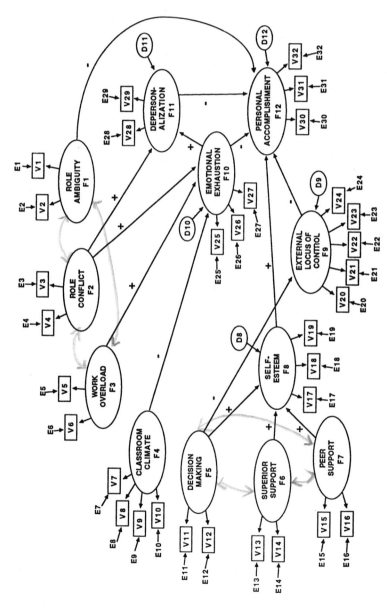

FIGURE 7.2. Hypothesized Model of Teacher Burnout: Measurement and Structural Components

Note: Two-way arrows linking correlated exogenous factors are not shown for sake of clarity.

specification throughout all analyses of the structural model. Finally, one case was identified as an outlier and subsequently deleted. Let's turn now to the EQS input file for the hypothesized model, which is presented in Table 7.1.

THE EQS INPUT FILE

Turning first to the /SPEC paragraph, we see that there are 716 cases, that the model includes 32 indicator variables, and that analyses are based on maximum likelihood estimates.[4] We can also determine that the data are in the form of a raw matrix that resides external to the input file and that Case 298 is to be excluded from all analyses.

In the /EQU paragraph, you will note that start values have been included. However, in contrast to previous examples, these values were inserted as "best guess" estimates. It will appear that there are two sections to this paragraph. The first set of equations, easily identified by their augmenting indentation, define the measurement model; as such, each equation is specified in terms of the indicator variables (the Vs). In particular, note the cross-loadings associated with V1, V3, V4, and V11. The second set of equations pertain to the structural model. They define the model in terms of the latent variables; specifically, they specify the causal network encompassing these variables, as depicted in Figure 7.1.

The /VAR paragraph specifies the estimation of variances for the independent factors (F1 to F7), error terms associated with each of the indicator variables (E1 to E32), and disturbance terms associated with each of the dependent factors (F8 to F12). Estimated covariances, as specified in the /COV paragraph, are based on reported findings in the literature. Specifically, these involve relations among Role Conflict, Role Ambiguity, and Work Overload factors, and among the factors of Decision Making and the two Support variables (Superior, Peer).

Finally, the /LMTEST paragraph has incorporated the SET command to limit LM statistics to (a) misspecified paths (i.e., paths that are not specified, but should be) that flow from independent to dependent factors (GFF) and from one dependent factor to another (BFF), and (b) misspecified covariances among the disturbance terms (PDD). Selected results from the execution of this input file are presented in Table 7.2.

EQS OUTPUT FOR HYPOTHESIZED MODEL

Turning first to the goodness-of-fit statistics, we can conclude that with a CFI of .89 there is some degree of misfit in the model. Of course, the χ^2 value is also indicative of a malfitting model. However, given the known sensitivity of this statistic to sample size, use of the χ^2 index provides little

TABLE 7.1. EQS Input for Hypothesized Model of Causal Structure Related to
Teacher Burnout

```
/TITLE
FULL BURNOUT MODEL FOR SECONDARY TCHRS (GRP1); "BURNHS1I.EQS"
OUTLIER CASE (298) DELETED)
INITIAL MODEL
CROSS-LOADINGS: F1 TO V11 (ROLEA TO DEC1); F7 TO V1 (PSUP TO ROLEA1);
F6 TO V4 (SSUP TO ROLEC2); F5 TO V3 (DEC TO ROLEC1)
/SPEC
CASE=716; VAR=32; ME=ML; MA=RAW; FO='(19F4.2/13F4.2)';
DEL= 298; DATA= 'SECIND1.DAT';
/LABELS
V1=ROLEA1;    V2=ROLEA2;    V3=ROLEC1;    V4=ROLEC2;    V5=WORK1;
V6=WORK2;     V7=CLIMATE1;  V8=CLIMATE2;  V9=CLIMATE3;  V10=CLIMATE4;
V11=DEC1;     V12=DEC2;     V13=SSUP1;    V14=SSUP2;    V15=PSUP1;
V16=PSUP2;    V17=SELF1;    V18=SELF2;    V19=SELF3;    V20=XLOC1;
V21=XLOC2;    V22=XLOC3;    V23=XLOC4;    V24=XLOC5;    V25=EE1;
V26=EE2;      V27=EE3;      V28=DP1;      V29=DP2;      V30=PA1;
V31=PA2;      V32=PA3;
F1=ROLEA; F2=ROLEC; F3=WORK; F4=CLIMATE; F5=DEC; F6=SSUP; F7=PSUP;
F8=SELF; F9=XLOC; F10=EE; F11=DP; F12=PA;
/EQU
V1= F1+ -.1*F7+E1;
V2= 1.*F1+E2;
  V3= F2+ -.4*F5+E3;
  V4= 1.7*F2+ -.2*F6+E4;
    V5= F3+E5;
    V6= .9*F3+E6;
      V7= F4+E7;
      V8= .6*F4+E8;
      V9= .6*F4+E9;
      V10= .6*F4+E10;
        V11= F5+ *F1+E11;
        V12= 1.*F5+E12;
          V13= F6+E13;
          V14= 1.*F6+E14;
            V15= F7+E15;
            V16= 1.*F7+E16;
              V17= F8+E17;
              V18= .8*F8+E18;
              V19= .8*F8+E19;
                V20= F9+E20;
                V21= .8*F9+E21;
                V22= .8*F9+E22;
                V23= .8*F9+E23;
                V24= .8*F9+E24;
                  V25= F10+E25;
                  V26= 1.*F10+E26;
                  V27= .9*F10+E27;
                    V28= F11+E28;
                    V29= .9*F11+E29;
                      V30= F12+E30;
                      V31= .8*F12+E31;
                      V32= .9*F12+E32;
F8= .5*F5+ -.1*F6+.08*F7+D8;
F9= -.2*F5+D9;
F10= .6*F2+ 1.1*F3+ -.8*F4+D10;
F11= .1*F2+ .4*F10+D11;
F12= -.05*F1+ .5*F2+ -.5*F9+ -.54*F10+ -.2*F11+D12;
```

TABLE 7.1. (Continued)

```
/VAR
 F1 TO F2= .3*;
 F3= .9*; F4=.09*; F5=.2*; F6=1.1*; F7=.6*;              /
 E1, E12, E13, E25, E27,E32=.4*; E2, E10, E15, E31=.3*; E3, E6=.6*;
 E4, E5, E11=.5*; E7 TO E9, E14, E16, E22, E24=.1*; E17 TO E19=.07*;
 E20 TO E21, E23, E26, E28, E30=.2*; E29=.7*;
 D8 TO D9=.1*; D10 TO D11=.6*; D12=.3*;
/COV
 F2,F1=.2*; F3,F1=.3*; F3,F2=.6*; F6,F5=.5*; F7,F5=.2*; F7,F6=.4*;
/PRINT
 CORRELATION=YES;
/LMTEST
 SET=GFF, BFF, PDD;
/END
```

guidance in determining the extent to which the model does not fit; it is more beneficial at this point to rely on fit as represented by the CFI.

As a point of interest, I also include the iterative summary here. As you will see, only 12 iterations were needed for a convergent solution, thereby indicating that in general the specified model and the initial start values were fairly good.

Of substantial interest in this computer output are the LM statistics. As you examine this section of the output, notice that after the fourth step the univariate increment drops sharply from $\chi^2_{(4)} = 48.63$ to $\chi^2_{(5)} = 18.02$. Considering this finding, it seems most reasonable to concentrate on only the first four parameters pinpointed as malfitting; all represent structural paths that were not specified in the originally hypothesized model.

These omitted paths leading from one latent variable to another are listed in the column labeled **Parameter**. The easiest way to identify the path being targeted as a misspecified parameter is to conceptualize the causal flow as going **from** the second factor in a pair of latent factors **to** the first factor in the pair. For example, the first parameter specified in the output is F8,F10; we interpret this parameter as the structural path flowing **from** F10 (EE) **to** F8 (Self-Concept). These results suggest that if this path were to be specified in the model, emotional exhaustion would have a substantial impact on self-concept. However, as emphasized in Chapter 3, parameters identified by EQS as belonging in a model are based on statistical criteria only; of more import is that their inclusion be substantively meaningful. In the present instance, the incorporation of this path into the model would make no sense whatsoever because the purpose of the model is to validate the impact of organizational and personality variables on burnout, and not the reverse. Thus the F8,F10 parameter was ignored with respect to model respecification.

Incorporation of the next three parameters, however, is theoretically reasonable. The first one (F11,F4) argues for the impact of classroom climate

TABLE 7.2. Goodness-of-Fit and LM Statistics for Hypothesized Model of
Teacher Burnout

GOODNESS OF FIT SUMMARY

INDEPENDENCE MODEL CHI-SQUARE =   12416.419 ON   496 DEGREES OF FREEDOM
INDEPENDENCE AIC = 11424.41883   INDEPENDENCE CAIC =   8660.56669
        MODEL AIC =   826.32083   MODEL CAIC = -1625.48349
CHI-SQUARE =   1706.321 BASED ON   440 DEGREES OF FREEDOM
PROBABILITY VALUE FOR THE CHI-SQUARE STATISTIC IS LESS THAN 0.001
THE NORMAL THEORY RLS CHI-SQUARE FOR THIS ML SOLUTION IS   1672.179.
BENTLER-BONETT NORMED   FIT INDEX=   0.863
BENTLER-BONETT NONNORMED FIT INDEX=   0.880
COMPARATIVE FIT INDEX   =   0.894

ITERATIVE SUMMARY

ITERATION	PARAMETER ABS CHANGE	ALPHA	FUNCTION
1	0.315266	1.00000	8.71395
2	0.184197	0.50000	4.85312
3	0.291220	1.00000	12.28536
4	0.223702	1.00000	10.35995
5	0.151064	1.00000	4.21289
6	0.124315	1.00000	3.57956
7	0.125226	1.00000	3.39706
8	0.076039	1.00000	3.04311
9	0.019205	1.00000	2.44229
10	0.004348	1.00000	2.39039
11	0.001888	1.00000	2.38987
12	0.000798	1.00000	2.38981

	CUMULATIVE MULTIVARIATE STATISTICS				UNIVARIATE INCREMENT	
STEP	PARAMETER	CHI-SQUARE	D.F.	PROBABILITY	CHI-SQUARE	PROBABILITY
1	F8,F10	83.778	1	0.000	83.778	0.000
2	F11,F4	157.404	2	0.000	73.626	0.000
3	F9,F2	209.320	3	0.000	51.915	0.000
4	F9,F8	257.950	4	0.000	48.630	0.000
5	F12,F8	275.971	5	0.000	18.021	0.000
6	F11,F5	292.651	6	0.000	16.680	0.000
7	F10,F5	304.526	7	0.000	11.876	0.001
8	F10,F11	312.272	8	0.000	7.745	0.005
9	F9,F7	319.188	9	0.000	6.917	0.009
10	F9,F4	324.890	10	0.000	5.702	0.017
11	F9,F3	330.482	11	0.000	5.592	0.018
12	F8,F11	336.012	12	0.000	5.530	0.019
13	F8,F1	340.265	13	0.000	4.254	0.039

on perceptions of depersonalization, the second one (F9,F2) for the impact
of role conflict on external locus of control, and the last one (F9,F8) for the
impact of self-concept on external locus of control. Because all of these paths
are meaningful, they were subsequently added to the model, and the model
reestimated. The EQS input file for this respecified model (Model 2) is presented in Table 7.3; the additional structural paths are highlighted.

TABLE 7.3. EQS Input for Model 2 of Teacher Burnout

```
/TITLE
FULL BURNOUT MODEL FOR SECONDARY TCHRS (GRP1); "BURNHS12.EQS"
OUTLIER CASE (298) DELETED
MODIFYING MODEL
ADDED PATHS: F4 TO F11 (CLASS CLIM TO DP); F2 TO F9 (ROLEC TO XLOC);
F8 TO F9 (SELF TO XLOC)
CROSS-LOADINGS: F1 TO V11 (ROLEA TO DEC1); F6 TO V4 (SSUP TO ROLEC2);
F7 TO V1 (PSUP TO ROLEA1); F5 TO V3 (DEC TO ROLEC1)
/SPEC
CASE=716; VAR=32; ME=ML,ROBUST; MA=RAW; FO='(19F4.2/13F4.2)';
DEL= 298; DATA='SECIND1.DAT';
/LABELS
V1=ROLEA1;    V2=ROLEA2;    V3=ROLEC1;    V4=ROLEC2;    V5=WORK1;
V6=WORK2;     V7=CLIMATE1; V8=CLIMATE2; V9=CLIMATE3; V10=CLIMATE4;
V11=DEC1;     V12=DEC2;     V13=SSUP1;    V14=SSUP2;    V15=PSUP1;
V16=PSUP2;    V17=SELF1;    V18=SELF2;    V19=SELF3;    V20=XLOC1;
V21=XLOC2;    V22=XLOC3;    V23=XLOC4;    V24=XLOC5;    V25=EE1;
V26=EE2;      V27=EE3;      V28=DP1;      V29=DP2;      V30=PA1;
V31=PA2;      V32=PA3;
F1=ROLEA; F2=ROLEC; F3=WORK; F4=CLIMATE; F5=DEC; F6=SSUP; F7=PSUP;
F8=SELF; F9=XLOC; F10=EE; F11=DP; F12=PA;
/EQU
V1= F1+ -.1*F7+E1;
V2= 1.*F1+E2;
  V3= F2+ -.4*F5+E3;
  V4= 1.7*F2+ -.2*F6+E4;
    V5= F3+E5;
    V6= .9*F3+E6;
      V7= F4+E7;
      V8= .6*F4+E8;
      V9= .6*F4+E9;
    V10= .6*F4+E10;
        V11= F5+ *F1+E11;
        V12= 1.*F5+E12;
          V13= F6+E13;
          V14= 1.*F6+E14;
            V15= F7+E15;
            V16= 1.*F7+E16;
              V17= F8+E17;
              V18= .8*F8+E18;
              V19= .8*F8+E19;
                V20= F9+E20;
                V21= .8*F9+E21;
                V22= .8*F9+E22;
                V23= .8*F9+E23;
                V24= .8*F9+E24;
                  V25= F10+E25;
                  V26= 1.*F10+E26;
                  V27= .9*F10+E27;
                    V28= F11+E28;
                    V29= .9*F11+E29;
                      V30= F12+E30;
                      V31= .8*F12+E31;
                      V32= .9*F12+E32;
F8= .3*F5+ -.1*F6+.1*F7+D8;
F9= -.1*F5+ -.2*F8+.1*F2+D9;
F10= -.6*F2+ 1.1*F3+ -.7*F4+D10;
F11= .1*F2+ .3*F10+ -1.2*F4+D11;
F12= -.01*F1+ .5*F8+ -.2*F9+ -.04*F10+ -.2*F11+D12;
```

(Continued)

TABLE 7.3. (Continued)

```
/VAR
 F1=.3*;  F2=.5*;  F3=.9*;  F4=.09*;  F5=.2*;  F6=1.1*;  F7=.6*;
 E1 TO E2= .3*;  E3 TO E6=.6*;  E7 TO E9=.1*;  E10 TO E13=.4*;  E14=.1*;
 E15=.3*;  E16=.1*;  E17 TO E19=.08*;  E20 TO E21=.2*;  E22=.1*;  E23=.2*;
 E24=.1*;  E25 TO E28=.3*;  E29=.7*;  E30 TO E32=.3*;
 D8 TO D9=.1*;  D10=.6*;  D11=.5*;  D12=.3*;
/COV
 F1,F2=.3*;  F3,F1=.3*;  F3,F2=.6*;  F6,F5=.5*;  F7,F5=.2*;  F7,F6=.4*;
/PRINT
 CORRELATION=YES;
/LMTEST
  SET=GFF, BFF, PDD;
/END
```

Goodness-of-fit and LM Test statistics for this modified model (Model 2) are presented in Table 7.4. As you will note, specification of the three additional parameters resulted in a highly significant drop in χ^2 values between the initially hypothesized and the revised models ($\Delta\chi^2_{(3)} = 199.94$). Indeed, a χ^2 difference of this magnitude is a clear indication that model fit has been improved substantially. Although it is difficult to get a good sense of fit from the χ^2 value, the CFI value of .91 provides evidence of the better fitting model. Because Model 2 also specified that robust statistics be provided, we can see the extent to which the Satorra-Bentler scaled statistic corrected the actual χ^2 value in addressing problems of multivariate kurtosis in the data ($\chi^2_{(437)} = 1339.43$ vs. $\chi^2_{(437)} = 1506.37$); interestingly, despite this decrease in χ^2, the corrected CFI value remained the same as that of the original CFI (CFI* = .91).

Turning to the LM statistics, we see that the structural path leading from emotional exhaustion to self-concept (F8,F10) remains the major indicator of misfit in the model. However, as discussed above, the incorporation of this path does not make sense in the present context, and thus we again dismiss specification of this parameter. Considering (a) the presently adequate fit of Model 2, and (b) the substantially smaller magnitude of the remaining LM χ^2 statistics compared with those of the three respecified structural parameters (in Model 2), I would argue for no further additions to the model.

In working with structural equation models, it is very important to know when to stop fitting a model. Although there are no firm rules or regulations to guide this decision, the researcher's best yardsticks include (a) a thorough knowledge of the substantive theory, (b) an adequate assessment of statistical criteria based on information pooled from various indices of fit, and (c) a watchful eye on parsimony. In this regard, the SEM researcher must walk a fine line between incorporating a sufficient number of parameters to yield a

TABLE 7.4. Goodness-of-Fit and LM Statistics for Model 2 of Teacher Burnout

```
GOODNESS OF FIT SUMMARY
INDEPENDENCE MODEL CHI-SQUARE =        12416.419 ON    496 DEGREES OF FREEDOM
INDEPENDENCE AIC = 11424.41883    INDEPENDENCE CAIC =   8660.56669
        MODEL AIC =   632.37310         MODEL CAIC = -1802.71437
CHI-SQUARE =      1506.373 BASED ON    437 DEGREES OF FREEDOM
PROBABILITY VALUE FOR THE CHI-SQUARE STATISTIC IS LESS THAN 0.001
THE NORMAL THEORY RLS CHI-SQUARE FOR THIS ML SOLUTION IS        1485.941.
SATORRA-BENTLER SCALED CHI-SQUARE =      1339.4325
PROBABILITY VALUE FOR THE CHI-SQUARE STATISTIC IS      0.00000
BENTLER-BONETT NORMED     FIT INDEX=       0.879
BENTLER-BONETT NONNORMED FIT INDEX=       0.898
COMPARATIVE FIT INDEX              =       0.910
```

		CUMULATIVE MULTIVARIATE STATISTICS			UNIVARIATE INCREMENT	
STEP	PARAMETER	CHI-SQUARE	D.F.	PROBABILITY	CHI-SQUARE	PROBABILITY
1	F8,F10	82.875	1	0.000	82.875	0.000
2	D12,D8	95.648	2	0.000	12.773	0.000
3	F10,F5	108.101	3	0.000	12.453	0.000
4	F11,F8	118.129	4	0.000	10.027	0.002
5	F11,F3	127.836	5	0.000	9.707	0.002
6	F9,F3	135.609	6	0.000	7.774	0.005
7	F12,F2	141.550	7	0.000	5.940	0.015
8	D9,D8	147.191	8	0.000	5.641	0.018
9	F8,F1	152.433	9	0.000	5.242	0.022
10	F12,F4	156.278	10	0.000	3.844	0.050

model that adequately represents the data and falling prey to the temptation of incorporating too many parameters in a zealous attempt to attain the best fitting model, statistically. Two major problems with the latter strategy are that (a) the model can comprise parameters that actually contribute only trivially to its structure, and (b) the more parameters there are in a model, the more difficult it is to replicate its structure should future validation research be conducted.

With these caveats in mind, then, I considered the incorporation of additional parameters into the model at this point definitely to run the risk of overparameterizing the model. Given the relatively small size of the univariate LM χ^2 statistics reported for Steps 2 through 10 in the output (Table 7.4), it seemed clear that incorporation of these parameters into the model would lead to only a trivial improvement in fit, while concomitantly eroding the parsimony of the model.

Thus far, discussion related to model fit has considered only the addition of parameters to the model. However, another side to the question of fit, particularly as it pertains to a full model, is the extent to which certain initially hypothesized paths may be redundant to the model. One way of determining such redundancy is to examine the statistical significance of all

TABLE 7.5. Estimates and Test Statistics for Structural Paths in Model 2 of Teacher Burnout

CONSTRUCT EQUATIONS WITH STANDARD ERRORS AND TEST STATISTICS
(ROBUST STATISTICS IN PARENTHESES)

```
SELF  =F8  =    .337*F5     + -.100*F6     +  .106*F7     + 1.000 D8
                .198           .086            .026
               1.703         -1.161          4.024
            (   .207)      (   .093)      (   .033)
            ( 1.629)      ( -1.070)      (  3.186)

XLOC  =F9  =   -.254*F8     +  .186*F2     + -.098*F5     + 1.000 D9
                .050           .025            .034
              -5.096          7.360         -2.890
            (   .064)      (   .026)      (   .036)
            ( -3.937)      (  7.025)      ( -2.703)

EE    =F10 =   -.597*F2     + 1.140*F3     + -.781*F4     + 1.000 D10
                .407           .320            .140
              -1.465          3.563         -5.574
            (   .440)      (   .342)      (   .133)
            ( -1.357)      (  3.333)      ( -5.890)

DP    =F11 =    .366*F10    +  .167*F2     +-1.199*F4     + 1.000 D11
                .041           .063            .147
               8.871          2.639         -8.138
            (   .049)      (   .075)      (   .166)
            ( 7.457)      (  2.236)      ( -7.211)

PA    =F12 =    .539*F8     + -.214*F9     + -.041*F10    + -.213*F11
                .083           .081            .033            .036
               6.456         -2.652         -1.254         -5.838
            (   .113)      (   .081)      (   .035)      (   .042)
            ( 4.752)      ( -2.644)      ( -1.181)      ( -5.082)

               -.016*F1     + 1.000 D12
                .060
               -.268
            (   .067)
            ( -.241)
```

structural parameter estimates. This information, as derived from the estimation of Model 2, is presented in Table 7.5.

Examining z statistics associated with these structural estimates, we can determine five that are nonsignificant: F8,F5 (1.703 [1.629]), F8,F6 (−1.161 [−1.070]), F10,F2 (−1.465 [−1.357]), F12,F1 (−.268 [−.241]), and F12,F10 (−1.254 [−1.181]). The limiting factor in using these statistics as a basis for pinpointing redundant parameters, however, is that they represent a univariate test of significance. When sets of parameters are to be evaluated, a more appropriate approach is to implement a multivariate test of statistical significance. Indeed, the EQS program is unique in its provision of the **Wald Test** for this very purpose. Essentially, the Wald Test ascertains whether sets of parameters, specified as free in the model, could in fact be simultaneously set to zero without substantial loss in model fit. It does so by taking the least

TABLE 7.6. Wald Test for Nonsignificant Parameters in Model 2 of Teacher Burnout

WALD TEST (FOR DROPPING PARAMETERS)
MULTIVARIATE WALD TEST BY SIMULTANEOUS PROCESS

		CUMULATIVE MULTIVARIATE STATISTICS			UNIVARIATE INCREMENT	
STEP	PARAMETER	CHI-SQUARE	D.F.	PROBABILITY	CHI-SQUARE	PROBABILITY
1	F12,F1	0.101	1	0.751	0.101	0.751
2	F8,F6	1.480	2	0.477	1.379	0.240
3	F10,F2	3.639	3	0.303	2.159	0.142
4	F12,F10	5.929	4	0.205	2.290	0.130

significant parameter (i.e., the one with the smallest z statistic) and adding other parameters in such a way that the overall multivariate test yields a set of free parameters that with high probability can simultaneously be dropped from the model in future EQS runs without a significant degradation in model fit (Bentler, 1989, 1992a). Implementation of the Wald Test is very simple and involves only the typing of a separate line as follows:

```
/WTEST
```

To test multivariately for redundant structural paths in the model, then, the /WTEST paragraph was added to the EQS input for Model 2 and the model reestimated; for this run also, there was no specification for robust or LM Test statistics. These Wald Test results are presented in Table 7.6.

Interestingly, in contrast to the univariate tests of statistical significance, the Wald Test identified only four of the five parameters as being redundant to the model; structural path F8,F5 remained in the model. Consistent with the process described above and with the univariate statistics in Table 7.5, the Wald Test identified path F12,F1 as the least significant parameter in the model. Each of the remaining parameters was added in rank order of small test statistic value.

Revision of the model in accordance with these results led to deletion of structural paths describing the impact of Role Ambiguity on Personal Accomplishment, Superior Support on Self-esteem, Role Conflict on Emotional Exhaustion, and Emotional Exhaution on Personal Accomplishment. To obtain fit statistics and estimates for this final model of burnout for secondary teachers, Model 2 was respecified and reestimated; the related EQS input file is presented in Table 7.7.

TABLE 7.7. EQS Input for Final Model of Teacher Burnout

```
/TITLE
FULL BURNOUT MODEL FOR SECONDARY TCHRS (GRP1); "BURNHS1F.EQS"
OUTLIER CASE (298) DELETED)
FINAL MODEL (4 NONSIGNIF PARAMETERS DELETED AS PER WALD TEST)
ADDED PATHS: F4 TO F11 (CLASS CLIM TO DP); F2 TO F9 (ROLEC TO
XLOC);
F8 TO F9 (SELF TO XLOC)
CROSS-LOADINGS: F1 TO V11 (ROLEA TO DEC1); F6 TO V4 (SSUP TO
ROLEC2);
F7 TO V1 (PSUP TO ROLEA1); F5 TO V3 (DEC TO ROLEC1)
/SPEC
CASE=716; VAR=32; ME=ML,ROBUST; MA=RAW; FO='(19F4.2/13F4.2)';
DEL= 298; DATA='SECIND1.DAT';
/LABELS
V1=ROLEA1;    V2=ROLEA2;    V3=ROLEC1;    V4=ROLEC2;    V5=WORK1;
V6=WORK2;     V7=CLIMATE1;  V8=CLIMATE2;  V9=CLIMATE3;  V10=CLIMATE4;
V11=DEC1;     V12=DEC2;     V13=SSUP1;    V14=SSUP2;    V15=PSUP1;
V16=PSUP2;    V17=SELF1;    V18=SELF2;    V19=SELF3;    V20=XLOC1;
V21=XLOC2;    V22=XLOC3;    V23=XLOC4;    V24=XLOC5;    V25=EE1;
V26=EE2;      V27=EE3;      V28=DP1;      V29=DP2;      V30=PA1;
V31=PA2;      V32=PA3;
F1=ROLEA; F2=ROLEC; F3=WORK; F4=CLIMATE; F5=DEC; F6=SSUP; F7=PSUP;
F8=SELF; F9=XLOC; F10=EE; F11=DP; F12=PA;
/EQU
V1= F1+ -.1*F7+E1;
V2= 1.*F1+E2;
  V3= F2+ -.4*F5+E3;
  V4= 1.7*F2+ -.2*F6+E4;
    V5= F3+E5;
    V6= .9*F3+E6;
      V7= F4+E7;
      V8= .6*F4+E8;
      V9= .6*F4+E9;
      V10= .6*F4+E10;      .
         V11= F5+ *F1+E11;
         V12= 1.*F5+E12;
           V13= F6+E13;
           V14= 1.*F6+E14;
             V15= F7+E15;
             V16= 1.*F7+E16;
               V17= F8+E17;
               V18= .8*F8+E18;
               V19= .8*F8+E19;
                 V20= F9+E20;
                 V21= .8*F9+E21;
                 V22= .8*F9+E22;
                 V23= .8*F9+E23;
                 V24= .8*F9+E24;
                   V25= F10+E25;
                   V26= 1.*F10+E26;
                   V27= .9*F10+E27;
                     V28= F11+E28;
                     V29= .9*F11+E29;
                       V30= F12+E30;
                       V31= .8*F12+E31;
                       V32= .9*F12+E32;
F8= .1*F5+.1*F7+D8;
F9= -.09*F5+ -.2*F8+ .1*F2+D9;
F10= .6*F3+ -.7*F4+D10;
F11= .1*F2+ .3*F10+ -1.1*F4+D11;
F12= .5*F8+ -.2*F9+ -.2*F11+D12;
```

TABLE 7.7. (Continued)

```
/VAR
 F1=.3*;  F2=.5*;  F3=.9*;  F4=.09*;  F5=.2*;  F6=1.1*;  F7=.6*;
 E1 TO E2= .3*;  E3 TO E6=.6*;  E7 TO E9=.1*;   E10 TO E13=.4*;
 E14=.1*;
 E15=.3*;  E16=.1*;  E17 TO E19=.08*;  E20 TO E21=.2*;  E22=.1*;
 E23=.2*;
 E24=.1*;  E25 TO E28=.3*;  E29=.7*;  E30 TO E32=.3*;
 D8 TO D9=.1*;  D10=.6*;  D11=.5*;  D12=.3*;
/COV
 F1,F2=.3*;  F3,F1=.3*;  F3,F2=.6*;  F6,F5=.5*;  F7,F5=.2*;  F7,F6=.4*;
/END
```

Estimation of this final model resulted in an overall $\chi^2_{(441)}$ value of 1514.09, with a CFI value of .91; the Satorra-Bentler corrected $\chi^2_{(441)}$ was 1347.53, with a CFI* of .91. At this point, you may have some concern over the slight erosion in model fit from $\chi^2_{(437)} = 1506.37$ for Model 2, to $\chi^2_{(441)} = 1514.09$ for Model 3, the final model. However, with deletion of any parameters from a model, such a change is to be expected. The important aspect of this change in model fit is that the χ^2 difference between the two models is not significant ($\Delta\chi^2_{(4)} = 7.72$). A schematic representation of this final structural model of burnout for secondary teachers that includes the standardized path coefficients is displayed in Figure 7.3.

In summary, of 14 causal paths specified in the hypothesized model (see Figure 7.2), 10 were found to be statistically significant for secondary teachers. These paths reflected the impact of (a) classroom climate and work overload on emotional exhaustion, (b) decision making on both self-esteem and external locus of control, (c) self-esteem, depersonalization, and external locus of control on perceived personal accomplishment, (d) role conflict and emotional exhaustion on depersonalization, and (e) peer support on self-esteem. Two paths not specified a priori (classroom climate → depersonalization; self-esteem → external locus of control) proved to be essential components of the causal structure; they were therefore added to the model. One path was found to be misspecified (role conflict → emotional exhaustion) and was subsequently respecified to flow from role conflict to external locus of control. Finally, three hypothesized paths (role ambiguity → personal accomplishment; superior support → self-esteem; emotional exhaustion → personal accomplishment) were not significant and were subsequently deleted from the model.

Overall, we can conclude from this study that role conflict, work overload, classroom climate, participation in the decisionmaking process, and the support of one's colleagues are potent organizational determinants of burnout for high school teachers. The process appears to be tempered, however, by one's general sense of self-worth and locus of control.

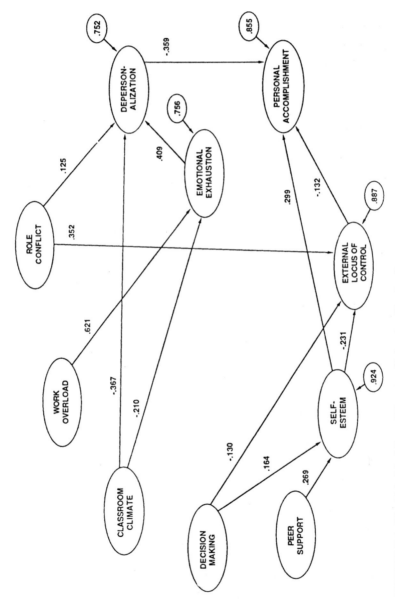

FIGURE 7.3. Final Model of Causal Structure Related to Teacher Burnout

Source: Copyright (in press) by the American Educational Research Association. Reprinted by permission.

Applications Related to Other Disciplines

BUSINESS: Niehoff, B. P., & Moorman, R. H. (1993). Justice as a mediator of the relationship between methods of monitoring and organizational citizenship behavior. *Academy of Management Journal, 36,* 527-556.

EDUCATION: Culver, S. M., Wolfle, L. M., & Cross, L. H. (1990). Testing a model of teacher satisfaction for blacks and whites. *American Educational Research Journal, 27,* 323-349.

MEDICINE: Stein, J. A., Fox, S. A., Murata, P. J., & Morisky, D. E. (1992). Mammography usage and the health belief model. *Health Education Quarterly, 19,* 447-462.

SOCIOLOGY: Fullager, C., McCoy, D., & Shull, C. (1992). The socialization of union loyalty. *Journal of Organizational Behavior, 13,* 13-26.

Notes

1. To facilitate interpretation, particular items were reflected such that high scores on role ambiguity, role conflict, work overload, EE, DP, and external locus of control represented negative perceptions, and high scores on the remaining constructs represented positive perceptions.

2. In a nonstandard model, various other types of paths such as V→V or V→F paths also may be of interest.

3. For example, it may be that to attain a better fitting CFA model, the specification of a cross-loading is needed.

4. Because this was the initial run, with the likelihood that certain parameters would be misspecified, thereby requiring a respecification and reestimation of the model, robust statistics were not requested at this time.

PART THREE

Multiple-Group Analyses

Confirmatory Factor Analytic Models

CHAPTER 8: APPLICATION 6
*Testing for Invariant Factorial Structure
of a Theoretical Construct (First-Order CFA Model)*

CHAPTER 9: APPLICATION 7
*Testing for Invariant Factorial Structure
of a Measuring Instrument (First-Order CFA Model)*

CHAPTER 10: APPLICATION 8
Testing for Invariant Latent Mean Structures

The Full Latent Variable Model

CHAPTER 11: APPLICATION 9
Testing for Invariant Causal Structure

8

Application 6
Testing for Invariant Factorial Structure
of a Theoretical Construct
(First-Order CFA Model)

T hus far, all examples have been based on single samples. In this section, however, we focus on applications involving more than one sample where the central concern is whether components of the measurement model, or the structural model, or both are invariant (i.e., equivalent) across particular groups.

In general, when researchers test for evidence of multigroup invariance, they do so in order to answer one of five questions. First, do the items comprising a particular measuring instrument operate equivalently across different populations (e.g., gender, age, ability)? In other words, is the measurement model group invariant? Second, is the factorial structure of a single instrument, or of a theoretical construct measured by multiple instruments, equivalent across populations? Here, invariance of the structural model is of primary interest, and in particular the equivalency of relations among the theoretical constructs. Third, are certain paths in a specified causal structure invariant across populations? Fourth, are the latent means of particular constructs in a model different across populations? Finally, does the factorial structure of a measuring instrument replicate across independent samples of the same population? This latter question, of course, addresses the issue of crossvalidation. Applications presented in the next four chapters provide you with specific examples of how each of these questions can be answered using structural equation modeling based on EQS.

In our first application of testing for invariance, we test hypotheses related to the equivalencies of self-concept measurement and structure across gender. Specifically, we wish to determine if multidimensional facets of self-concept (general, academic, English, mathematics) and the multiple assessment instruments used to measure them are equivalent across male and female high school adolescents. This example is taken from a study by Byrne and Shavelson (1987) as a follow-up to their earlier work that validated the structure of self-concept (Byrne & Shavelson, 1986), outlined in Chapter 3 of the present book.

TESTING FOR MULTIGROUP INVARIANCE

The General Framework

Seminal work in developing a procedure that can test for invariance simultaneously across groups is accorded Jöreskog (1971), first author of the LISREL program. In the Jöreskog tradition, all tests of invariance must begin with a global test of the equality of covariance structures across groups. In other words, one tests the null hypothesis (H_0) that $\Sigma_1 = \Sigma_2 = \ldots \Sigma_G$, where Σ is the population variance-covariance matrix, and G is the number of groups. Rejection of the null hypothesis then argues for the nonequivalence of the groups and thus for the subsequent testing of increasingly restrictive hypotheses in order to identify the source of noninvariance. On the other hand, if H_0 cannot be rejected, the groups are considered to be equivalent, and thus tests for invariance are unjustified; group data should be pooled and all subsequent investigative work based on single-group analyses.

Although this omnibus test appears reasonable and is fairly straightforward, it often leads to contradictory findings with respect to equivalencies across groups. For example, sometimes the null hypothesis is found tenable, yet subsequent tests of hypotheses related to the invariance of particular measurement or structural parameters must be rejected (see, e.g., Jöreskog, 1971). Alternatively, the global null hypothesis may be rejected, yet tests for the invariance of measurement and structural invariance hold (see, e.g., Byrne, 1988b).[1] Such inconsistencies in the global test for invariance stem from the fact that there is no baseline model for the test of invariant variance-covariance matrices, thereby making it substantially more stringent than tests of invariance related to sets of parameters in the model (B. Muthén, personal communication, October, 1988). Indeed, Muthén contends that the omnibus test provides little guidance in testing for equality across groups and thus should not be regarded as a necessary prerequisite to the testing of more specific hypotheses related to group invariance.

In testing for invariance across groups, sets of parameters are put to the test in a logically ordered and increasingly restrictive fashion. Depending on the model and hypotheses to be tested, the following sets of parameters are typically of interest in answering questions related to group invariance: (a) factor loading paths (F→V), (b) factor variances/covariances F,F; F↔F), (c) structural regression paths (F→F), (d) factor residuals (D,D; D↔D), and (e) error variances/covariances (E,E; E↔E). Except in particular instances when, for example, it might be of interest to test for the invariant reliability of an assessment measure across groups (see, e.g., Byrne, 1988b), the equality of error variances and covariances is probably the least important hypothesis to test (Bentler, 1989, 1992a). Although the Jöreskog tradition of invariance testing holds that the equality of these parameters should be tested, it is now widely accepted that to do so represents an overly restrictive test of the data.

The General Procedure

In the Jöreskog tradition, tests of hypotheses related to group invariance typically begin with scrutiny of the measurement model. In particular, the factor loadings of each measuring instrument are tested for their equivalence across the groups. Once it is known which items are group invariant, these parameters are constrained equal while subsequent tests of the structural parameters are conducted. (It is possible that not all items are equal across groups, as we shall see later.) As each new set of parameters is tested, those known to be group invariant are constrained equal. Thus the process of determining nonequivalence of measurement and structural parameters across groups involves the testing of a series of increasingly restrictive hypotheses. Given the univariate approach to testing these hypotheses using the LISREL program (Jöreskog & Sörbom, 1988), the orderly sequence of analytic steps is both necessary and strongly recommended.

The EQS approach to testing for invariance, however, differs importantly from LISREL in that it tests the validity of equality constraints multivariately rather than univariately, using the LM Test. The incorporation of this strategy into the program therefore makes it unnecessary to compare a series of restrictive versus less restrictive models in order to identify the source of noninvariance in the model. As a consequence, it is also not necessary first to test for the equality of the measurement model and then to conduct tests of the structural model (although the researcher can always do this if he or she wishes). All equality constraints can be put to the test simultaneously. Overall, procedures for testing invariance in EQS are very easy and straightforward. Indeed, for those of you who may be familiar with the approach taken by other statistical packages, I guarantee that you will be both amazed and relieved at the minimal amount of time involved in performing tests for invariance using EQS!

Preliminary Single-Group Analyses

Prior to testing hypotheses related to invariance, it is considered most appropriate to first establish a baseline model for each group separately. This model represents the best fitting one to the data both from the perspective of parsimony and from the perspective of substantive meaningfulness. Because the χ^2 statistic and its degrees of freedom are additive, the sum of the χ^2s reflects the extent to which the underlying structure fits the data across groups.

Because measuring instruments are often group specific in the way they operate, however, baseline models may not be identical across groups. For example, whereas the baseline model for one group might include cross-load-ings[2] or error covariances or both, this may not be the case for other groups under study. Of substantial import, however, is that such circumstances in no way negate the testing for invariance (Byrne, Shavelson, & Muthén, 1989). Rather, such a priori knowledge of group differences is critical to the appropriate conduct of these analyses.

Because the estimation of baseline models involves no between-group constraints, the data can be analyzed separately for each group. However, in testing for invariance, equality constraints are imposed on particular parameters, and thus the data for all groups must be analyzed simultaneously to obtain efficient estimates (Bentler, 1989, 1992a; Jöreskog & Sörbom, 1988); the pattern of fixed and free parameters nonetheless remains consistent with the baseline model specifications for each group.

Although the general principle underlying tests for invariance is fairly straightforward, the procedure involved is more difficult to grasp without the assistance of a concrete example. However, once you are walked through the basic steps, you will see that the actual procedure too is less complex than you may otherwise have thought. So now let's turn to the self-concept model under study in this chapter and to the task of testing for its equivalence across adolescent males and females.

THE HYPOTHESIZED MODEL

The model that was tested for its invariance across gender in the original study (Byrne & Shavelson, 1987) is the four-factor model of self-concept discussed in Chapter 3 and shown in Figure 3.1. The model argues for a four-factor structure comprising general self-concept, academic self-concept,

English self-concept, and mathematics self-concept, with the four constructs assumed to be intercorrelated.

Except for academic self-concept, each of the other dimensions is measured by three independent measures; findings from a preliminary factor analysis of the Affective Perception Inventory (Soares & Soares, 1979) revealing its inadequacy as a measure of academic self-concept resulted in its deletion from the analyses. It was originally hypothesized that each subscale measure would have a nonzero loading on the self-concept factor it was designed to measure and a zero loading on all other factors; error/uniquenesses associated with each of the measures were assumed to be uncorrelated. Relations among the four self-concept facets represent the structural model to be tested for its equivalency across groups.

At issue in the Byrne and Shavelson (1987) study was whether the structure of self-concept and the instruments used in measuring components of this structure, as presented in Figure 3.1, were equivalent across adolescent males and females. Of import, then, was the invariance of both the measurement and structural models.

THE BASELINE MODELS

As noted earlier, as a prerequisite to the testing of hypotheses related to invariance, it is customary to first establish baseline models separately for each group under study. The baseline self-concept models for adolescent males and females, as reported by Byrne and Shavelson (1987), are presented schematically in Figure 8.1.

In fitting the baseline model for each sex, Byrne and Shavelson (1987) reported a substantial drop in χ^2 when the English self-concept subscale (SDQESC) of the Self Description Questionnaire III (SDQIII; Marsh & O'Neill, 1984) was free to cross-load onto the general SC factor (V6,F1). Moreover, for males only, the mathematics SC subscale of the SDQ III (SDQMSC) was allowed to cross-load onto the English SC factor (V9,F1). Finally, error/uniquenesses between subscales of the same measuring instrument were free to covary, resulting in five error covariances for males and three for females. With the above specifications in place, these models were considered optimal in representing the data for adolescent males and females. Overall fit of the male model was $\chi^2_{(31)} = 60.96$, with a normed fit index (NFI; Bentler & Bonett, 1980) of .98; for the female model, it was $\chi^2_{(34)} = 77.30$, with NFI = .98. These NFI values translate into CFI values of .99 for both males and females.[3]

We are now ready to work with EQS in formally testing for the equivalence of these adolescent self-concept models across gender. The data we use are in the form of a correlation matrix, as presented in the Byrne and

MALES

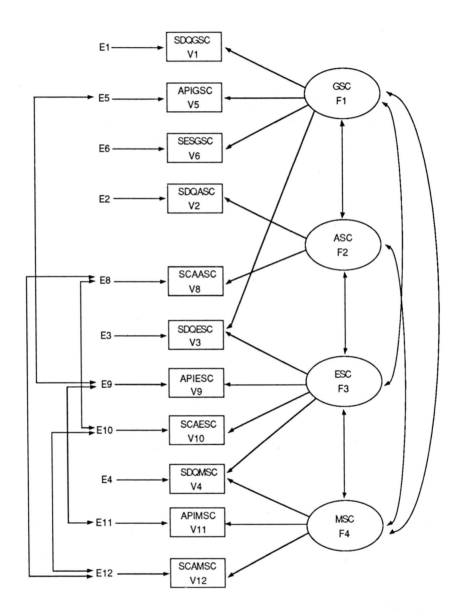

FIGURE 8.1. Baseline Models of Self-Concept for Adolescent Males and Females

Source: Adapted from Byrne & Shavelson (1987). Copyright (1987) by the American Educational Research Association. Reprinted by permission.

FEMALES

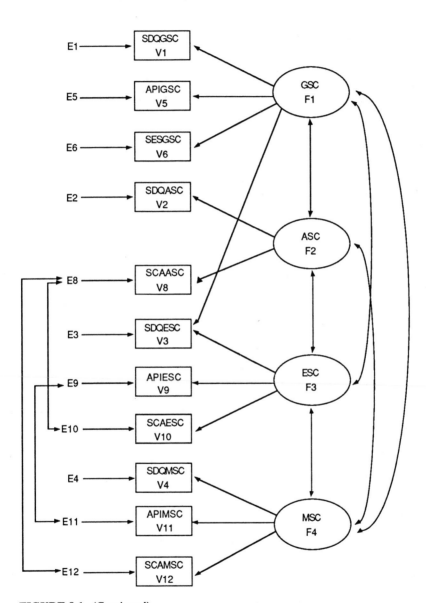

FIGURE 8.1. (Continued)

Shavelson (1987) study, and we'll embed them into our EQS input file. The standard deviations are also used, because cross-group comparisons are generally only valid when covariance matrices are generated and analyzed.

TESTING FOR INVARIANCE ACROSS GENDER

As noted earlier, when analyses focus on multigroup comparisons with constraints between the groups (i.e., particular parameters are constrained equal across groups), it is imperative that parameters for all groups be estimated simultaneously. For this to be possible, model specifications for each group must reside in the same file. This is accomplished by stacking the input file for each group, one after the other. In the present case, model specifications for males appear first, followed by those for females. We turn now to a review of this input file, which is presented in Table 8.1.

EQS Input File: The Measurement Model

Several unique features of the multigroup file need to be noted. First, the complete input file for males and for females is included; each terminates with the **/END** statement. In the present case, the male group is described first (**N=412**), followed by the female group (**N=420**). Second, in the **/SPECIFICATIONS** paragraph, you will see that robust statistics are not requested. This is because the S-Bχ^2 statistic is not yet available for multigroup analyses. Also included here is a statement that **GROUPS=2**; in multigroup files, the number of groups must **always** be specified. Third, although the data are in correlation matrix form, analyses **must** be based on the covariance matrix in all multigroup comparisons. Thus the standard deviations for each group have been included in the **/STANDARD DEVIATIONS** paragraph. Nonetheless, as noted in Chapter 3, unless **MA=COR** is specified, EQS assumes that the data are in covariance matrix form. Finally, you will note that the **/CONSTRAINTS** and **/LMTEST** paragraphs follow specification for the second (or last) group. The **/CONSTRAINTS** paragraph is used to specify which parameters are to be held equal across the groups, and the **/LMTEST** one is used to indicate that these constraints are to be tested statistically using the LM Test.

Let's go back now and review again the models under study.

Turning first to specifications for adolescent males, we see that there are two cross-loadings (V3,F1; V4,F3), in addition to five error covariances (E10,E8; E12,E8; E11,E9; E5,E9; E12,E10), over and above the initially hypothesized model. By way of contrast, specifications for adolescent females include only one crossloading (V3,F1), and three error covariances

TABLE 8.1. EQS Input: Testing for Equality of Factor Loadings in Self-Concept Model

```
/TITLE
 TESTING FOR INVARIANCE OF SELF-CONCEPT
 TEST FOR EQULITY OF FACTOR LOADINGS
 GROUP1=MALES
/SPECIFICATIONS
 CASE=412; VAR=15; MA=COR; ME=ML; FO='(15F4.3)'; GROUPS=2;
/MATRIX
1000
3451000
287 3771000
252 579 1141000
637 335 253 2551000
768 339 302 278 6001000
543 640 382 451 656 5661000
254 703 337 591 312 313 5871000
166 429 724 143 264 216 445 3641000
104 411 506 142 199 163 373 551 63010000
247 601 202 880 288 309 530 621 290 1991000
208 526 127 827 253 231 473 676 155 234 8081000
035 517 117 481 067 080 374 687 121 340 434 5241000
-020 410 158 272 003 062 297 507 215 492 261 294 7861000
040 378 060 609 076 074 295 525 077 172 560 649 746 5331000
/STANDARD DEVIATIONS
 13.856 13.383 10.017 15.977 9.442 4.999 9.999 5.943 11.099 5.929
 11.762 7.873 11.232 12.664 16.898
/LABELS
 V1=SDQGSC;    V2=SDQASC;    V3=SDQESC;    V4=SDQMSC;
 V5=APIGSC;    V6=SESGSC;    V7=APIASC;    V8=SCAASC;
 V9=APIESC;    V10=SCAESC;   V11=APIMSC;   V12=SCAMSC;
 V13=GPA;      V14=ENG;      V15=MATH;
 F1=GSC;       F2=ASC;       F3=ESC;       F4=MSC;
/EQUATIONS
 V1 = 30 F1 + E1;
 V5 = 15*F1 + E5;
 V6 = 15*F1 + E6;
    V2 = 30 F2 + E2;
    V8 = 15*F2 + E8;
       V3 = 30 F3 + 5*F1 + E3;
       V9 = 15*F3 + E9;
       V10 = 15*F3 + E10;
          V4 = 30 F4 + -5*F3 + E4;
          V11 = 15*F4 + E11;
          V12 = 15*F4 + E12;
/VARIANCES
 F1 TO F4 = .1*;
 E1 TO E6 = 40*; E8 TO E12 = 15*;
/COVARIANCES
 F1 TO F4 = .05*;
 E10,E8 = 6*; E12,E8 = 6*; E11,E9 = 6*; E5,E9 = 6*; E12,E10 = 6*;
/END
/TITLE
 TESTING FOR INVARIANCE OF SELF-CONCEPT
 GROUP2=FEMALES
/SPECIFICATIONS
 CASE=420; VAR=15; MA=COR; ME=ML; FO='(15F4.3)';
```

(Continued)

TABLE 8.1. (Continued)

```
/MATRIX
1000
 2931000
 278 3771000
 109 379-0681000
 656 300 211 1291000
 825 331 311 160 6771000
 519 569 329 321 595 5661000
 191 659 336 378 137 263 4951000
 146 400 677-042 185 211 397 4091000
 168 474 554 026 140 233 353 626 6571000
 123 406-026 857 186 185 388 408 071 0491000
 079 362-039 822 082 124 320 509-026 080 8061000
 014 487 165 394 027 096 345 675 115 344 316 4671000
 022 451 252 257 058 083 305 557 269 554 175 250 7791000
-056 272-006 550-033-001 216 439-059 073 475 662 732 4641000
/STANDARD DEVIATIONS
 14.524 11.014 9.479 16.347 8.853 5.019 8.656 4.873 10.701 5.319
 11.073 7.087 9.828 11.655 14.643
/LABELS
 V1=SDQGSC;   V2=SDQASC;   V3=SDQESC;   V4=SDQMSC;
 V5=APIGSC;   V6=SESGSC;   V7=APIASC;   V8=SCAASC;
 V9=APIESC;   V10=SCAESC;  V11=APIMSC;  V12=SCAMSC;
 V13=GPA;     V14=ENG;     V15=MATH;
 F1=GSC;      F2=ASC;      F3=ESC;      F4=MSC;
/EQUATIONS
 V1 = 30 F1 + E1;
 V5 = 15*F1 + E5;
 V6 = 15*F1 + E6;
    V2 = 30 F2 + E2;
    V8 = 15*F2 + E8;
       V3 = 30 F3 + 5*F1 + E3;
       V9 = 15*F3 + E9;
       V10 = 15*F3 + E10;
          V4 = 30 F4 + E4;
          V11 = 15*F4 + E11;
          V12 = 15*F4 + E12;
/VARIANCES
 F1 TO F4 = .1*;
 E1 TO E6 = 40*; E8 TO E12 = 15*;
/COVARIANCES
 F1 TO F4 = .05*;
 E10,E8 = 6*; E12,E8 = 6*; E11,E9 = 6*;
/CONSTRAINTS
 (1,V5,F1)=(2,V5,F1);
 (1,V6,F1)=(2,V6,F1);
 (1,V8,F2)=(2,V8,F2);
 (1,V3,F1)=(2,V3,F1);
 (1,V9,F3)=(2,V9,F3);
 (1,V10,F3)=(2,V10,F3);
 (1,V11,F4)=(2,V11,F4);
 (1,V12,F4)=(2,V12,F4);
/LMTEST
/END
```

(E10,E8; E12,E8; E11,E9). Thus, prior to testing for invariance, we already know that three of these parameters are different across the two groups. As such, these parameters are estimated freely for males, and are **not** constrained equal across males and females. With the exception of these three parameters, then, all remaining **estimated** parameters can be tested for their invariance across groups. This situation provides an excellent example of what is termed **partial measurement invariance** (see Byrne et al., 1989).

One important caveat in testing for invariance is that only estimated parameters can have equality constraints imposed upon them (i.e., fixed parameters are not eligible). Although we could certainly test for the invariance of all selected parameters, in this initial run we limit our testing to the factor-loading parameters for purposes of comparison with the original study. In examining the **/CONSTRAINTS** paragraph, you will see that one equality specification statement is required for each parameter being constrained equal across groups; the parameter relative to Group 1 is specified in the first parenthesis and the parameter relative to Group 2 in the second parenthesis. You will note also that (a) all constrained parameters are estimable, and (b) given the same loading pattern for males and females, the cross-loading of SDQESC on the general self-concept factor (V3,F1) is tested for its intergroup equivalency. Finally, unlike previous **/LMTEST** paragraphs that we have observed thus far, the one presented here involves no parameter specifications. This is because in testing for invariance, the purpose of the LM Test is to test the null hypothesis that each specified constraint is true in the population.

EQS Output File: The Measurement Model

Let's turn now to the results of this initial test for invariance, which are presented in Table 8.2. Shown first are the goodness-of-fit statistics relative to the entire model, which comprises the two baseline models with certain equality constraints between them.[4] As indicated by a CFI of .989, this multigroup model represents an excellent fit to the data.

The remainder of the table relates to the validity of the imposed equality constraints. You will see that the program first echoes the constraints specified and then presents results for both univariate and multivariate tests of hypotheses. Associated with each constraint is a LM χ^2. In EQS, one simply has to check the related probablity values to determine if any of the tests were statistically significant. In the present case, all probability values were greater than .05, thereby indicating that the hypothesized equality of the specified factor loadings held; these results replicated those from the LISREL

TABLE 8.2. Selected EQS Output: Testing for Equality of Factor Loadings in Self-Concept Model

```
STATISTICS FOR MULTIPLE POPULATION ANALYSIS

ALL EQUALITY CONSTRAINTS WERE CORRECTLY IMPOSED
```

GOODNESS OF FIT SUMMARY

```
INDEPENDENCE MODEL CHI-SQUARE =       6465.413 ON    110 DEGREES OF FREEDOM

INDEPENDENCE AIC =  6245.41260   INDEPENDENCE CAIC =  5615.79103
        MODEL AIC =    -1.60202         MODEL CAIC =  -419.44179

CHI-SQUARE =      144.398 BASED ON     73 DEGREES OF FREEDOM
PROBABILITY VALUE FOR THE CHI-SQUARE STATISTIC IS LESS THAN 0.001

BENTLER-BONETT NORMED     FIT INDEX=      0.978
BENTLER-BONETT NONNORMED FIT INDEX=      0.983
COMPARATIVE FIT INDEX              =      0.989
```

LAGRANGE MULTIPLIER TEST (FOR RELEASING CONSTRAINTS)

```
CONSTRAINTS TO BE RELEASED ARE:

              CONSTRAINTS FROM GROUP  2
              CONSTR:   1    (1,V5,F1)-(2,V5,F1)=0;
              CONSTR:   2    (1,V6,F1)-(2,V6,F1)=0;
              CONSTR:   3    (1,V8,F2)-(2,V8,F2)=0;
              CONSTR:   4    (1,V3,F1)-(2,V3,F1)=0;
              CONSTR:   5    (1,V9,F3)-(2,V9,F3)=0;
              CONSTR:   6    (1,V10,F3)-(2,V10,F3)=0;
              CONSTR:   7    (1,V11,F4)-(2,V11,F4)=0;
              CONSTR:   8    (1,V12,F4)-(2,V12,F4)=0;
```

UNIVARIATE TEST STATISTICS:

NO	CONSTRAINT	CHI-SQUARE	PROBABILITY
1	CONSTR: 1	1.708	0.191
2	CONSTR: 2	1.282	0.257
3	CONSTR: 3	0.284	0.594
4	CONSTR: 4	0.544	0.461
5	CONSTR: 5	0.364	0.546
6	CONSTR: 6	0.611	0.435
7	CONSTR: 7	0.711	0.399
8	CONSTR: 8	0.651	0.420

		CUMULATIVE MULTIVARIATE STATISTICS			UNIVARIATE INCREMENT	
STEP	PARAMETER	CHI-SQUARE	D.F.	PROBABILITY	CHI-SQUARE	PROBABILITY
1	CONSTR: 1	1.708	1	0.191	1.708	0.191
2	CONSTR: 7	2.407	2	0.300	0.699	0.403
3	CONSTR: 8	4.047	3	0.256	1.639	0.200
4	CONSTR: 6	4.690	4	0.321	0.644	0.422
5	CONSTR: 2	5.131	5	0.400	0.440	0.507
6	CONSTR: 4	5.467	6	0.486	0.336	0.562
7	CONSTR: 3	5.764	7	0.568	0.298	0.585
8	CONSTR: 5	5.962	8	0.651	0.198	0.657

analyses reported in the original paper (Byrne & Shavelson, 1987). Because this was so for the univariate tests, it also held for the multivariate tests.

Given these findings, we can now feel confident that all measures of self-concept are operating in the same way for both groups, and we proceed in testing for equality of the structural parameters. No doubt you are wondering what the procedure would have been if not all measurement parameters had been found equal across the groups. Therefore I will address this issue before continuing with our invariance testing. Essentially, such results would invoke the use of partial measurement invariance in testing for the equality of factor variances/covariances. However, the use of partial measurement invariance is contingent on the number of indicator variables used in measuring each latent construct. Given multiple indicators and at least one invariant measure (other than the one fixed to 1.00 for identification purposes), remaining noninvariant measures can be specified as unconstrained across groups; that is, they can be freely estimated (Byrne et al., 1989; Muthén & Christoffersson, 1981).

EQS Input File: The Structural Model

We turn now to the testing of equality constraints related to the factor variances and covariances.[5] EQS input related to these specifications is presented in Table 8.3. In keeping with the double label convention in EQS, the variances are easily identified by their paired identical numbers (e.g., F1,F1), and the covariances by their paired dissimilar numbers (e.g., F2,F1). The important point to note here is that the equality of these structural parameters is tested while concomitantly maintaining equality of measurement parameters across groups. Thus it is easy to see why the invariance-testing criteria become increasingly stringent as one progresses from tests of the measurement model to tests of the structural model.

EQS Output File: The Structural Model

Results for this second run are presented in Table 8.4. Although the goodness-of-fit statistics are still indicative of a well-fitting model, comparison with those of the previous run reveal an ever so slight decrement in fit (CFI = .989 vs. CFI = .983); the difference in χ^2 values, however, is statistically significant ($\Delta\chi^2_{(10)} = 49.31$, $p < .001$). These findings suggest that the specification of certain cross-group equivalencies of factor variances and covariances may be somewhat problematic. To glean further insight into this finding of fit decrement, let's turn now to the LM χ^2 test results bearing on the specified equality of the factor variances and covariances.

TABLE 8.3. Selected EQS Input: Testing for Equality of Factor Variances and Covariances in Self-Concept Model

```
/CONSTRAINTS
 (1,V5,F1)=(2,V5,F1);
 (1,V6,F1)=(2,V6,F1);
 (1,V8,F2)=(2,V8,F2);
 (1,V3,F1)=(2,V3,F1);
 (1,V9,F3)=(2,V9,F3);
 (1,V10,F3)=(2,V10,F3);
 (1,V11,F4)=(2,V11,F4);
 (1,V12,F4)=(2,V12,F4);
 (1,F1,F1)=(2,F1,F1);
 (1,F2,F2)=(2,F2,F2);
 (1,F3,F3)=(2,F3,F3);
 (1,F4,F4)=(2,F4,F4);
 (1,F2,F1)=(2,F2,F1);
 (1,F3,F1)=(2,F3,F1);
 (1,F4,F1)=(2,F4,F1);
 (1,F3,F2)=(2,F3,F2);
 (1,F4,F2)=(2,F4,F2);
 (1,F4,F3)=(2,F4,F3);
/LMTEST
/END
```

Reviewing the univariate statistics, we can see that four of the specified equality constraints did not hold (#11 [F3,F3]; #12 [F4,F4]; #16 [F3,F2]; #17 [F4,F2]). Likewise, turning to the multivariate LM χ^2 statistics, we see that although four constraints were statistically significant (#10 [F2,F2]; #16 [F3,F2]; #17 [F4,F2]; #18 [F4,F3]), they varied somewhat from the univariate results. To investigate these findings further, the model was respecified and reestimated with the latter four constraints released. Results are presented in Table 8.5.

As can be determined from a review of the goodness-of-fit statistics, the releasing of the three problematic cross-group constraints led to a significant improvement in model fit ($\Delta\chi^2_{(3)} = 38.22$, $p < .001$), and the CFI is once again .988, indicating an excellent fit to the data. If we turn now to the multivariate LM statistics, we see that, indeed, all equality constraints now hold; identical findings held for the univariate results (but are not presented here because of space considerations).

Now let's see how our EQS results compare with the LISREL ones reported by Byrne and Shavelson (1987).[6] Although EQS and LISREL both identified the noninvariance of four structural parameters, only three replicated across programs; these represent (a) the variance of academic self-concept (Constraint 10), and (b) the covariances between mathematics and academic self-concept (Constraint 17) and between mathematics and English

TABLE 8.4. Selected EQS Output: Testing for Equality of Factor Variances and Covariances in Self-Concept Model

GOODNESS OF FIT SUMMARY

INDEPENDENCE MODEL CHI-SQUARE =   6465.413 ON   110 DEGREES OF FREEDOM

INDEPENDENCE AIC = 6245.41260   INDEPENDENCE CAIC =   5615.79103
        MODEL AIC =   27.71172   MODEL CAIC =   -447.36637

CHI-SQUARE =   193.712 BASED ON   83 DEGREES OF FREEDOM
PROBABILITY VALUE FOR THE CHI-SQUARE STATISTIC IS LESS THAN 0.001

BENTLER-BONETT NORMED   FIT INDEX=   0.970
BENTLER-BONETT NONNORMED FIT INDEX=   0.977
COMPARATIVE FIT INDEX   =   0.983

LAGRANGE MULTIPLIER TEST (FOR RELEASING CONSTRAINTS)

CONSTRAINTS TO BE RELEASED ARE:

        CONSTRAINTS FROM GROUP   2

        CONSTR: 1   (1,V5,F1)-(2,V5,F1)=0;
        CONSTR: 2   (1,V6,F1)-(2,V6,F1)=0;
        CONSTR: 3   (1,V8,F2)-(2,V8,F2)=0;
        CONSTR: 4   (1,V3,F1)-(2,V3,F1)=0;
        CONSTR: 5   (1,V9,F3)-(2,V9,F3)=0;
        CONSTR: 6   (1,V10,F3)-(2,V10,F3)=0;
        CONSTR: 7   (1,V11,F4)-(2,V11,F4)=0;
        CONSTR: 8   (1,V12,F4)-(2,V12,F4)=0;
        CONSTR: 9   (1,F1,F1)-(2,F1,F1)=0;
        CONSTR: 10   (1,F2,F2)-(2,F2,F2)=0;
        CONSTR: 11   (1,F3,F3)-(2,F3,F3)=0;
        CONSTR: 12   (1,F4,F4)-(2,F4,F4)=0;
        CONSTR: 13   (1,F2,F1)-(2,F2,F1)=0;
        CONSTR: 14   (1,F3,F1)-(2,F3,F1)=0;
        CONSTR: 15   (1,F4,F1)-(2,F4,F1)=0;
        CONSTR: 16   (1,F3,F2)-(2,F3,F2)=0;
        CONSTR: 17   (1,F4,F2)-(2,F4,F2)=0;
        CONSTR: 18   (1,F4,F3)-(2,F4,F3)=0;

UNIVARIATE TEST STATISTICS:

NO	CONSTRAINT		CHI-SQUARE	PROBABILITY
1	CONSTR:	1	1.022	0.312
2	CONSTR:	2	2.915	0.088
3	CONSTR:	3	3.858	0.050
4	CONSTR:	4	0.450	0.502
5	CONSTR:	5	0.588	0.443
6	CONSTR:	6	0.246	0.620
7	CONSTR:	7	0.173	0.677
8	CONSTR:	8	0.138	0.710
9	CONSTR:	9	2.311	0.128
10	CONSTR:	10	2.077	0.150
11	CONSTR:	11	7.606	0.006
12	CONSTR:	12	7.743	0.005
13	CONSTR:	13	0.333	0.564
14	CONSTR:	14	0.339	0.561
15	CONSTR:	15	0.060	0.807
16	CONSTR:	16	8.454	0.004
17	CONSTR:	17	4.910	0.027
18	CONSTR:	18	3.724	0.054

(Continued)

TABLE 8.4. (Continued)

		CUMULATIVE MULTIVARIATE STATISTICS			UNIVARIATE INCREMENT	
STEP	PARAMETER	CHI-SQUARE	D.F.	PROBABILITY	CHI-SQUARE	PROBABILITY
1	CONSTR: 16	8.454	1	0.004	8.454	0.004
2	CONSTR: 17	22.370	2	0.000	13.917	0.000
3	CONSTR: 10	27.964	3	0.000	5.594	0.018
4	CONSTR: 18	37.176	4	0.000	9.211	0.002
5	CONSTR: 9	40.808	5	0.000	3.632	0.057
6	CONSTR: 11	42.759	6	0.000	1.951	0.162
7	CONSTR: 1	44.698	7	0.000	1.940	0.164
8	CONSTR: 13	45.724	8	0.000	1.025	0.311
9	CONSTR: 15	49.177	9	0.000	3.454	0.063
10	CONSTR: 8	50.181	10	0.000	1.004	0.316
11	CONSTR: 7	52.033	11	0.000	1.852	0.174
12	CONSTR: 2	52.511	12	0.000	0.478	0.489
13	CONSTR: 3	52.971	13	0.000	0.460	0.498
14	CONSTR: 4	53.341	14	0.000	0.370	0.543
15	CONSTR: 5	53.554	15	0.000	0.213	0.644
16	CONSTR: 12	53.620	16	0.000	0.066	0.797
17	CONSTR: 6	53.664	17	0.000	0.044	0.834
18	CONSTR: 14	53.664	18	0.000	0.001	0.979

self-concept (Constraint 18). Whereas Byrne and Shavelson reported the covariance between mathematics and general self-concepts to be noninvariant, the EQS results indicated its equivalence across males and females; in contrast, the present analysis found the relation between academic and English self-concepts to be noninvariant across gender.

The question to be addressed now is why these results should differ. There are two possible explanations. The first might lie with the fact that whereas EQS is able to test the validity of the equality constraints multivariately, LISREL does so univariately. A second explanation is possibly linked to the manner by which equality constraints are specified and tested using LISREL. Given findings of noninvariance at the matrix level (e.g., constraints involving all factor loadings or all factor loadings and all variances/covariances), one must next test, independently, each parameter in the offending matrix in an effort to identify the source of noninvariance; this information is determined by means of the χ^2-difference test ($\Delta\chi^2$). As each invariant parameter is uncovered, it is subsequently and cumulatively constrained equal across groups. The multiple-testing approach used with this procedure leaves it wide open to capitalization on chance factors and thus to the possibility of Type I errors.

TABLE 8.5. Selected EQS Output: Respecification of Equality Constraints in Self-Concept Model

GOODNESS OF FIT SUMMARY

INDEPENDENCE MODEL CHI-SQUARE =   6465.413 ON   110 DEGREES OF FREEDOM

INDEPENDENCE AIC =   6245.41260   INDEPENDENCE CAIC =   5615.79103
        MODEL AIC =   -2.51143   MODEL CAIC =   -454.69419

CHI-SQUARE =   155.489 BASED ON   79 DEGREES OF FREEDOM
PROBABILITY VALUE FOR THE CHI-SQUARE STATISTIC IS LESS THAN 0.001

BENTLER-BONETT NORMED   FIT INDEX=   0.976
BENTLER-BONETT NONNORMED FIT INDEX=   0.983
COMPARATIVE FIT INDEX   =   0.988

LAGRANGE MULTIPLIER TEST (FOR RELEASING CONSTRAINTS)

CONSTRAINTS TO BE RELEASED ARE:

    CONSTRAINTS FROM GROUP 2

        CONSTR: 1   (1,V5,F1)-(2,V5,F1)=0;
        CONSTR: 2   (1,V6,F1)-(2,V6,F1)=0;
        CONSTR: 3   (1,V8,F2)-(2,V8,F2)=0;
        CONSTR: 4   (1,V3,F1)-(2,V3,F1)=0;
        CONSTR: 5   (1,V9,F3)-(2,V9,F3)=0;
        CONSTR: 6   (1,V10,F3)-(2,V10,F3)=0;
        CONSTR: 7   (1,V11,F4)-(2,V11,F4)=0;
        CONSTR: 8   (1,V12,F4)-(2,V12,F4)=0;
        CONSTR: 9   (1,F1,F1)-(2,F1,F1)=0;
        CONSTR: 10   (1,F3,F3)-(2,F3,F3)=0;
        CONSTR: 11   (1,F4,F4)-(2,F4,F4)=0;
        CONSTR: 12   (1,F2,F1)-(2,F2,F1)=0;
        CONSTR: 13   (1,F3,F1)-(2,F3,F1)=0;
        CONSTR: 14   (1,F4,F1)-(2,F4,F1)=0;

			CUMULATIVE MULTIVARIATE STATISTICS			UNIVARIATE INCREMENT	
STEP	PARAMETER		CHI-SQUARE	D.F.	PROBABILITY	CHI-SQUARE	PROBABILITY
1	CONSTR:	9	3.360	1	0.067	3.360	0.067
2	CONSTR:	10	5.406	2	0.067	2.045	0.153
3	CONSTR:	1	7.280	3	0.063	1.874	0.171
4	CONSTR:	12	8.273	4	0.082	0.993	0.319
5	CONSTR:	14	11.732	5	0.039	3.459	0.063
6	CONSTR:	7	12.775	6	0.047	1.043	0.307
7	CONSTR:	8	14.760	7	0.039	1.985	0.159
8	CONSTR:	3	15.449	8	0.051	0.689	0.407
9	CONSTR:	2	16.038	9	0.066	0.589	0.443
10	CONSTR:	4	16.415	10	0.088	0.377	0.539
11	CONSTR:	5	16.865	11	0.112	0.449	0.503
12	CONSTR:	11	16.929	12	0.152	0.065	0.799
13	CONSTR:	6	16.988	13	0.200	0.059	0.808
14	CONSTR:	13	16.991	14	0.257	0.003	0.958

Applications Related to Other Disciplines

BUSINESS: Marcoulides, G. A., & Heck, R. H. (1993). Structural components of organizational culture and their effects on organizational performance. *Journal of Management and Business, 1,* 20-32.

KINESIOLOGY: Marsh, H. W. (in press). The multidimensional structure of physical fitness: Invariance over gender and age. *Research Quarterly of Exercise Science.*

MEDICINE: Johnson, S. B., Tomer, A., Cunningham, W. R., & Henretta, J. C. (1990). Adherence in childhood diabetes: Results of a confirmatory factor analysis. *Health Psychology, 9,* 493-501.

Notes

1. Although trivial inequalities related to particular errors of measurement were identified.

2. A variable's measurement loading on more than one factor.

3. Fit of the null model for males was $\chi^2_{(55)} = 3258.48$, and for females was $\chi^2_{(55)} = 3206.94$.

4. If we had created a multigroup model input file that included specifications for each baseline model but no equality constraints, we would see that the χ^2 value represented the sum of the two models estimated separately. Indeed, this model is required when using the LISREL program (see Byrne, 1989, pp. 134-135; Byrne & Shavelson, 1987).

5. Although testing for equivalent factor covariances would seem more meaningful than testing for equivalent variances within the context of the present data, we test for the equality of both for purposes of consistency with the original study. Byrne and Shavelson (1987), in turn, tested the entire matrix in keeping with the Jöreskog tradition in testing for factorial invariance.

6. Given that the testing of equality constraints related to error variances and covariances is now considered to be excessively stringent, these analyses were not conducted.

9

Application 7
Testing for Invariant Factorial Structure of a Measuring Instrument (First-Order CFA Model)

In contrast to the example provided in Chapter 8, the present application focuses on tests for invariance related to a single measuring instrument and involving three groups in lieu of only two. Specifically, we test for equivalency of the factorial measurement (i.e., scale items) of the Maslach Burnout Inventory (MBI; Maslach & Jackson, 1986) and its underlying latent structure (i.e., relations among dimensions of burnout) across elementary, intermediate, and secondary teachers.

Purposes of the original study, from which this example is taken (Byrne, 1993), were (a) to test for the factorial validity of the MBI separately for each of these teacher groups, (b) given findings of inadequate fit, to propose and test an alternative factorial structure, (c) to cross-validate this structure across independent samples for each teacher group, and (d) to test for the equivalence of item measurements and theoretical structure across the three teaching panels.[1] Only analyses related to the latter are central to the present chapter. We turn now to the model under study.

THE BASELINE MODEL

In my preliminary single-group analyses reported in Byrne (1993), I found that for each teacher group, Items 12 and 16 of the MBI were problematic; these items were subsequently deleted, and analyses based on a 20-item instrument. Additionally, the identification of substantially abnormal correlated errors between Items 1 and 2 and between Items 10 and 11 across teaching panels led to their specification as free parameters. A final model that reflected these modifications was fully cross-validated for independent samples of elementary, intermediate, and secondary teachers. Given findings of complete model invariance across calibration and validation groups, the cross-validation samples for each teaching level were subsequently combined for tests of invariance across panels.[2] The hypothesized model under test in the present example, then, is the revised 20-item MBI structure as schematically depicted in Figure 9.1.

As I noted in the original paper, just because the revised model was similarly specified for elementary, intermediate, and secondary teachers, this in no way guaranteed the equivalence of item measurements and underlying theoretical structure across teacher groups; these hypotheses must be tested statistically. For example, despite an identically specified factor loading or latent structural pattern, it is possible that with the imposition of equality constraints across groups the tenability of invariance does not hold. That is to say, the link between a particular item and its target factor differs, or relations among the underlying burnout dimensions differ, respectively. These are the questions addressed in the present application. Specifically, we test for the invariance of the model portrayed in Figure 9.1 across combined calibration/validation samples for elementary ($n = 1159$), intermediate ($n = 388$), and secondary ($n = 1384$) teachers.

THE MEASUREMENT MODEL

EQS Input File

For purposes of the present chapter, data are in the form of a raw matrix that resides as an external file. Specifications related to this multigroup test of the hypothesized model are presented in Table 9.1.

Once again, to maintain consistency with the original study, we test first for group invariance related to the measurement model. However, in contrast to the previous chapter, in which tests of only the factor loadings were of interest, here we test for equivalence of both the factor loadings and the two error covariances.[3] Although I noted in Chapter 8 that, in general, testing for the equality of error variances across groups is considered to be excessively

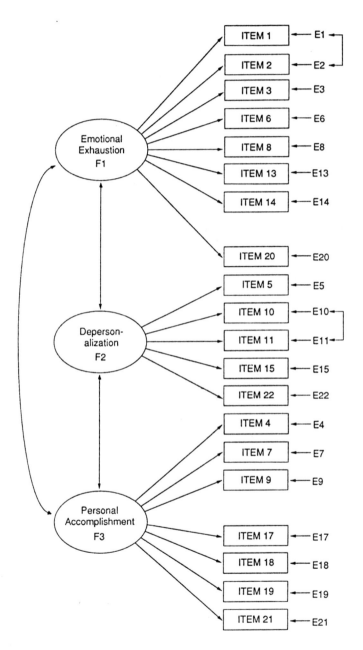

FIGURE 9.1. Baseline Model of Revised Maslach Burnout Inventory Structure for Elementary, Intermediate, and Secondary School Teachers

TABLE 9.1. EQS Input: Testing for Equality of Factor Measurements in Model of
Teacher Burnout

```
/TITLE
 TESTING FOR INVARIANCE OF MBI FACTOR MEASUREMENTS "MBI3GRPM"
 20-ITEM SCALE (#12, #16 DELETED); 2 ERROR CORRS (E1,E2;E10,E11)
 GROUP 1 = ELEMENTARY TEACHERS
/SPEC
 CASE=1159; VAR=22; ME=ML; MA=RAW; FO='(22F1.0)'; GROUPS=3;
 DATA='CVELM.DAT';
/LABELS
 V1=MBI1;        V2=MBI2;        V3=MBI3;        V4=MBI4;        V5=MBI5;
 V6=MBI6;        V7=MBI7;        V8=MBI8;        V9=MBI9;        V10=MBI10;
 V11=MBI11;      V12=MBI12;      V13=MBI13;      V14=MBI14;      V15=MBI15;
 V16=MBI16;      V17=MBI17;      V18=MBI18;      V19=MBI19;      V20=MBI20;
 V21=MBI21;      V22=MBI22;
 F1=EE;     F2=DP;     F3=PA;
/EQUATION
 V1   =    F1 + E1;
 V2   =   *F1 + E2;
 V3   =   *F1 + E3;
 V6   =   *F1 + E6;
 V8   =   *F1 + E8;
 V13  =   *F1 + E13;
 V14  =   *F1 + E14;
 V20  =   *F1 + E20;
                V5   =    F2 + E5;
                V10  =   *F2 + E10;
                V11  =   *F2 + E11;
                V15  =   *F2 + E15;
                V22  =   *F2 + E22;
                               V4   =    F3 + E4;
                               V7   =   *F3 + E7;
                               V9   =   *F3 + E9;
                               V17  =   *F3 + E17;
                               V18  =   *F3 + E18;
                               V19  =   *F3 + E19;
                               V21  =   *F3 + E21;
/VARIANCES
 F1 TO F3 = *;
 E1 TO E11 = *;
 E13 TO E15 = *;
 E17 TO E22 = *;
/COVARIANCES
 F1 TO F3 = *;
 E1,E2 = *;
 E10,E11 = *;
/END
/TITLE
 GROUP 2 = INTERMEDIATE TEACHERS
/SPEC
 CASE=388; VAR=22; ME=ML; MA=RAW; FO='(22F1.0)';
 DATA='CVINT.DAT';
/LABELS
 V1=MBI1;        V2=MBI2;        V3=MBI3;        V4=MBI4;        V5=MBI5;
 V6=MBI6;        V7=MBI7;        V8=MBI8;        V9=MBI9;        V10=MBI10;
 V11=MBI11;      V12=MBI12;      V13=MBI13;      V14=MBI14;      V15=MBI15;
 V16=MBI16;      V17=MBI17;      V18=MBI18;      V19=MBI19;      V20=MBI20;
 V21=MBI21;      V22=MBI22;
 F1=EE;     F2=DP;     F3=PA;
```

TABLE 9.1. (Continued)

```
/EQUATION
V1   =    F1 + E1;
V2   =   *F1 + E2;
V3   =   *F1 + E3;
V6   =   *F1 + E6;
V8   =   *F1 + E8;
V13  =   *F1 + E13;
V14  =   *F1 + E14;
V20  =   *F1 + E20;
              V5   =    F2 + E5;
              V10  =   *F2 + E10;
              V11  =   *F2 + E11;
              V15  =   *F2 + E15;
              V22  =   *F2 + E22;
                           V4   =    F3 + E4;
                           V7   =   *F3 + E7;
                           V9   =   *F3 + E9;
                           V17  =   *F3 + E17;
                           V18  =   *F3 + E18;
                           V19  =   *F3 + E19;
                           V21  =   *F3 + E21;
/VARIANCES
 F1 TO F3 = *;
 E1 TO E11 = *;
 E13 TO E15 = *;
 E17 TO E22 = *;
/COVARIANCES
 F1 TO F3 = *;
 E1,E2 = *;
 E10,E11 = *;
/END
/TITLE
 GROUP 3 = SECONDARY TEACHERS
/SPEC
 CASE=1384; VAR=22; ME=ML; MA=RAW; FO='(22F1.0)';
 DATA='CVSEC.DAT';
/LABELS
 V1=MBI1;      V2=MBI2;      V3=MBI3;       V4=MBI4;       V5=MBI5;
 V6=MBI6;      V7=MBI7;      V8=MBI8;       V9=MBI9;       V10=MBI10;
 V11=MBI11;    V12=MBI12;    V13=MBI13;     V14=MBI14;     V15=MBI15;
 V16=MBI16;    V17=MBI17;    V18=MBI18;     V19=MBI19;     V20=MBI20;
 V21=MBI21;    V22=MBI22;
 F1=EE;     F2=DP;    F3=PA;
/EQUATION
V1   =    F1 + E1;
V2   =   *F1 + E2;
V3   =   *F1 + E3;
V6   =   *F1 + E6;
V8   =   *F1 + E8;
V13  =   *F1 + E13;
V14  =   *F1 + E14;
V20  =   *F1 + E20;
              V5   =    F2 + E5;
              V10  =   *F2 + E10;
              V11  =   *F2 + E11;
              V15  =   *F2 + E15;
              V22  =   *F2 + E22;
```

(Continued)

TABLE 9.1. (Continued)

```
                              V4  =    F3 + E4;
                              V7  =   *F3 + E7;
                              V9  =   *F3 + E9;
                              V17 =   *F3 + E17;
                              V18 =   *F3 + E18;
                              V19 =   *F3 + E19;
                              V21 =   *F3 + E21;
/VARIANCES
 F1 TO F3 = *;
 E1 TO E11 = *;
 E13 TO E15 = *;
 E17 TO E22 = *;
/COVARIANCES
 F1 TO F3 = *;
 E1,E2 = *;
 E10,E11 = *;
/CONSTRAINTS
 (1,V2,F1)=(2,V2,F1)=(3,V2,F1);
 (1,V3,F1)=(2,V3,F1)=(3,V3,F1);
 (1,V6,F1)=(2,V6,F1)=(3,V6,F1);
 (1,V8,F1)=(2,V8,F1)=(3,V8,F1);
 (1,V13,F1)=(2,V13,F1)=(3,V13,F1);
 (1,V14,F1)=(2,V14,F1)=(3,V14,F1);
 (1,V20,F1)=(2,V20,F1)=(3,V20,F1);
 (1,V10,F2)=(2,V10,F2)=(3,V10,F2);
 (1,V11,F2)=(2,V11,F2)=(3,V11,F2);
 (1,V15,F2)=(2,V15,F2)=(3,V15,F2);
 (1,V22,F2)=(2,V22,F2)=(3,V22,F2);
 (1,V7,F3)=(2,V7,F3)=(3,V7,F3);
 (1,V9,F3)=(2,V9,F3)=(3,V9,F3);
 (1,V17,F3)=(2,V17,F3)=(3,V17,F3);
 (1,V18,F3)=(2,V18,F3)=(3,V18,F3);
 (1,V19,F3)=(2,V19,F3)=(3,V19,F3);
 (1,V21,F3)=(2,V21,F3)=(3,V21,F3);
 (1,E1,E2)=(2,E1,E2)=(3,E1,E2);
 (1,E10,E11)=(2,E10,E11)=(3,E10,E11);
/LMTEST
/END
```

stringent, I believe that testing related to the error covariances specified in the present context is well justified. I base this decision on the fact that both error covariances were found to be excessively large for each teacher group. Thus, from a psychometric perspective, it seems prudent to ascertain whether these parameters hold across teaching panels.

Consistent with the multigroup model setup presented in Chapter 8, you will note that specifications for each group have been stacked, with those for elementary teachers presented first, followed by those for intermediate and secondary teachers, respectively. Accordingly, the specification that **GROUPS=3** has been placed in the **/SPEC** paragraph. Turning to the **/CONSTRAINTS** paragraph, you will note that equality constraints related to each free factor loading (recall that cross-group constraints cannot be specified for fixed parameters) and the two error covariances are specified across the three groups, the initial number within each parenthesis representing the group.

EQS Output File

Results for this first test of the measurement model are presented in Table 9.2. As indicated by a CFI value of .92, the hypothesized constrained model represents a fairly good fit to the data.

In reviewing the echoed group constraints, you will note that EQS breaks each specification into two components. The logic here is that if Group 1 equals Group 2, and Group 1 equals Group 3, then axiomatically, Group 2 must equal Group 3. An examination of probability values associated with the LM univariate χ^2 test statistic reveals that for 6 of the 34 factor-loading constraints specified, the null hypothesis of intergroup equality must be rejected; the invariance of both error covariances held. The noninvariant factor loadings relate to the following MBI items:

- Item 10 (measuring DP) across elementary/intermediate teachers
- Item 11 (measuring DP) across elementary/intermediate teachers
- Item 11 (measuring DP) across elementary/secondary teachers
- Item 15 (measuring DP) across elementary/secondary teachers
- Item 17 (measuring PA) across elementary/secondary teachers
- Item 18 (measuring PA) across elementary/secondary teachers

However, given the propensity for univariate tests of equality constraints to capitalize on chance factors, it behooves us to consult the multivariate test statistics before drawing conclusions related to the invariance of the measurement model. Indeed, a review of these LM χ^2 statistics reveals only four of the six to be noninvariant across groups (Item 10 across elementary/intermediate teachers; Items 11, 17, and 18 across elementary/secondary teachers). As a follow-up to these findings, a second test of invariant measurements was conducted in which these four equality constraints were released. Results yielded a CFI value of .93 and indicated a measurement model that was fully invariant across the three teacher groups. Presented with these findings, we now proceed to test for the equality of the structural model.

THE STRUCTURAL MODEL

EQS Input File

Because only the factor covariances are of interest, we test for the equality of these parameters, while concomitantly constraining all invariant item

TABLE 9.2. Selected EQS Output: Testing for Equality of Factor Measurements in Model of Teacher Burnout

GOODNESS OF FIT SUMMARY

INDEPENDENCE MODEL CHI-SQUARE =   23810.882 ON   570 DEGREES   OF FREEDOM

INDEPENDENCE AIC = 22670.88159   INDEPENDENCE CAIC = 18690.51520
        MODEL AIC =   1238.30982   MODEL CAIC = -2483.68191

CHI-SQUARE =   2304.310 BASED ON   533 DEGREES OF FREEDOM
PROBABILITY VALUE FOR THE CHI-SQUARE STATISTIC IS LESS THAN 0.001

BENTLER-BONETT NORMED   FIT INDEX=   0.903
BENTLER-BONETT NONNORMED FIT INDEX=   0.918
COMPARATIVE FIT INDEX   =   0.924

LAGRANGE MULTIPLIER TEST (FOR RELEASING CONSTRAINTS)

CONSTRAINTS TO BE RELEASED ARE:

                CONSTRAINTS FROM GROUP   3
        CONSTR: 1 $(1,V2,F1)-(2,V2,F1)=0;$
        CONSTR: 2 $(1,V2,F1)-(3,V2,F1)=0;$
        CONSTR: 3 $(1,V3,F1)-(2,V3,F1)=0;$
        CONSTR: 4 $(1,V3,F1)-(3,V3,F1)=0;$
        CONSTR: 5 $(1,V6,F1)-(2,V6,F1)=0;$
        CONSTR: 6 $(1,V6,F1)-(3,V6,F1)=0;$
        CONSTR: 7 $(1,V8,F1)-(2,V8,F1)=0;$
        CONSTR: 8 $(1,V8,F1)-(3,V8,F1)=0;$
        CONSTR: 9 $(1,V13,F1)-(2,V13,F1)=0;$
        CONSTR: 10 $(1,V13,F1)-(3,V13,F1)=0;$
        CONSTR: 11 $(1,V14,F1)-(2,V14,F1)=0;$
        CONSTR: 12 $(1,V14,F1)-(3,V14,F1)=0;$
        CONSTR: 13 $(1,V20,F1)-(2,V20,F1)=0;$
        CONSTR: 14 $(1,V20,F1)-(3,V20,F1)=0;$
        CONSTR: 15 $(1,V10,F2)-(2,V10,F2)=0;$
        CONSTR: 16 $(1,V10,F2)-(3,V10,F2)=0;$
        CONSTR: 17 $(1,V11,F2)-(2,V11,F2)=0;$
        CONSTR: 18 $(1,V11,F2)-(3,V11,F2)=0;$
        CONSTR: 19 $(1,V15,F2)-(2,V15,F2)=0;$
        CONSTR: 20 $(1,V15,F2)-(3,V15,F2)=0;$
        CONSTR: 21 $(1,V22,F2)-(2,V22,F2)=0;$
        CONSTR: 22 $(1,V22,F2)-(3,V22,F2)=0;$
        CONSTR: 23 $(1,V7,F3)-(2,V7,F3)=0;$
        CONSTR: 24 $(1,V7,F3)-(3,V7,F3)=0;$
        CONSTR: 25 $(1,V9,F3)-(2,V9,F3)=0;$
        CONSTR: 26 $(1,V9,F3)-(3,V9,F3)=0;$
        CONSTR: 27 $(1,V17,F3)-(2,V17,F3)=0;$
        CONSTR: 28 $(1,V17,F3)-(3,V17,F3)=0;$
        CONSTR: 29 $(1,V18,F3)-(2,V18,F3)=0;$
        CONSTR: 30 $(1,V18,F3)-(3,V18,F3)=0;$
        CONSTR: 31 $(1,V19,F3)-(2,V19,F3)=0;$
        CONSTR: 32 $(1,V19,F3)-(3,V19,F3)=0;$
        CONSTR: 33 $(1,V21,F3)-(2,V21,F3)=0;$
        CONSTR: 34 $(1,V21,F3)-(3,V21,F3)=0;$
        CONSTR: 35 $(1,E1,E2)-(2,E1,E2)=0;$
        CONSTR: 36 $(1,E1,E2)-(3,E1,E2)=0;$
        CONSTR: 37 $(1,E10,E11)-(2,E10,E11)=0;$
        CONSTR: 38 $(1,E10,E11)-(3,E10,E11)=0;$

                UNIVARIATE TEST STATISTICS:

NO	CONSTRAINT	CHI-SQUARE	PROBABILITY
1	CONSTR: 1	0.279	0.597
2	CONSTR: 2	0.166	0.684

TABLE 9.2. (Continued)

3	CONSTR:	3	0.329	0.566
4	CONSTR:	4	0.005	0.943
5	CONSTR:	5	1.306	0.253
6	CONSTR:	6	0.353	0.552
7	CONSTR:	7	0.001	0.974
8	CONSTR:	8	0.193	0.661
9	CONSTR:	9	1.349	0.246
10	CONSTR:	10	0.557	0.455
11	CONSTR:	11	0.789	0.374
12	CONSTR:	12	0.452	0.501
13	CONSTR:	13	0.009	0.926
14	CONSTR:	14	0.683	0.408
15	CONSTR:	15	6.864	0.009
16	CONSTR:	16	2.580	0.108
17	CONSTR:	17	7.861	0.005
18	CONSTR:	18	8.070	0.005
19	CONSTR:	19	3.279	0.070
20	CONSTR:	20	4.232	0.040
21	CONSTR:	21	0.793	0.373
22	CONSTR:	22	1.641	0.200
23	CONSTR:	23	0.014	0.905
24	CONSTR:	24	3.885	0.049
25	CONSTR:	25	0.031	0.860
26	CONSTR:	26	2.451	0.117
27	CONSTR:	27	0.738	0.390
28	CONSTR:	28	8.688	0.003
29	CONSTR:	29	0.073	0.786
30	CONSTR:	30	4.077	0.043
31	CONSTR:	31	0.410	0.522
32	CONSTR:	32	2.275	0.131
33	CONSTR:	33	1.586	0.208
34	CONSTR:	34	0.105	0.745
35	CONSTR:	35	0.988	0.320
36	CONSTR:	36	0.281	0.596
37	CONSTR:	37	0.193	0.660
38	CONSTR:	38	0.073	0.788

		CUMULATIVE MULTIVARIATE STATISTICS			UNIVARIATE INCREMENT	
STEP	PARAMETER	CHI-SQUARE	D.F.	PROBABILITY	CHI-SQUARE	PROBABILITY
1	CONSTR: 28	8.688	1	0.003	8.688	0.003
2	CONSTR: 18	16.758	2	0.000	8.070	0.005
3	CONSTR: 30	24.058	3	0.000	7.299	0.007
4	CONSTR: 15	28.429	4	0.000	4.371	0.037
5	CONSTR: 20	31.556	5	0.000	3.127	0.077
6	CONSTR: 19	36.593	6	0.000	5.037	0.025
7	CONSTR: 17	39.879	7	0.000	3.286	0.070
8	CONSTR: 33	42.285	8	0.000	2.406	0.121
9	CONSTR: 22	44.147	9	0.000	1.862	0.172
10	CONSTR: 9	45.496	10	0.000	1.349	0.246
11	CONSTR: 38	46.777	11	0.000	1.281	0.258
12	CONSTR: 5	47.851	12	0.000	1.074	0.300
13	CONSTR: 35	48.863	13	0.000	1.012	0.314
14	CONSTR: 36	49.852	14	0.000	0.989	0.320
15	CONSTR: 16	50.565	15	0.000	0.714	0.398
16	CONSTR: 14	51.267	16	0.000	0.701	0.402
17	CONSTR: 24	51.902	17	0.000	0.635	0.425
18	CONSTR: 23	53.017	18	0.000	1.116	0.291

TABLE 9.2. (Continued)

19	CONSTR:	11	53.632	19	0.000	0.614	0.433
20	CONSTR:	25	54.239	20	0.000	0.607	0.436
21	CONSTR:	37	54.749	21	0.000	0.510	0.475
22	CONSTR:	21	55.243	22	0.000	0.494	0.482
23	CONSTR:	26	55.668	23	0.000	0.425	0.514
24	CONSTR:	3	56.064	24	0.000	0.395	0.529
25	CONSTR:	31	56.387	25	0.000	0.323	0.570
26	CONSTR:	27	56.787	26	0.000	0.400	0.527
27	CONSTR:	29	58.276	27	0.000	1.488	0.222
28	CONSTR:	32	59.097	28	0.001	0.822	0.365
29	CONSTR:	1	59.403	29	0.001	0.306	0.580
30	CONSTR:	34	59.688	30	0.001	0.285	0.594
31	CONSTR:	10	59.889	31	0.001	0.201	0.654
32	CONSTR:	7	59.984	32	0.002	0.095	0.758
33	CONSTR:	8	60.035	33	0.003	0.051	0.821
34	CONSTR:	12	60.123	34	0.004	0.088	0.767
35	CONSTR:	4	60.228	35	0.005	0.105	0.746
36	CONSTR:	6	60.345	36	0.007	0.117	0.732
37	CONSTR:	2	60.428	37	0.009	0.082	0.775
38	CONSTR:	13	60.445	38	0.012	0.018	0.894

measurements and the two error covariances across groups. The **/CON-STRAINTS** paragraph related to this input file is presented in Table 9.3.

EQS Output File

Results from this run yielded a CFI value of .93, as shown in Table 9.4. A review of the univariate LM χ^2 statistics revealed the relation between Emotional Exhaustion and Depersonalization to be significantly different across elementary and secondary teachers; the multivariate test for invariance yielded the same results.

For readers who may be interested in comparing these results with those derived from the LISREL analyses reported in the original article (Byrne, 1993), you will note that two additional noninvariant item loadings were detected via the present analyses. Whereas both the LISREL and EQS analyses identified MBI Items 17 and 18 as being nonequivalent across elementary and secondary teachers, the EQS results pinpointed two additional items: Item 10 was noninvariant across elementary and intermediate teachers, and Item 11 was noninvariant across elementary and secondary teachers; both belonged to the Depersonalization subscale. With respect to the invariance of structure, analyses from both programs were consistent in determining the relation between Depersonalization and Emotional Exhaustion as nonequivalent across elementary and secondary teachers.

The detection of two additionally nonequivalent items in the present example is undoubtedly explained by the differential statistical and procedural approaches used by the EQS and LISREL programs in testing for multi-

TABLE 9.3. Selected EQS Input: Testing for Equality of Maslach Burnout
            Inventory Structure

```
/CONSTRAINTS
  (1,V2,F1)=(2,V2,F1)=(3,V2,F1);
  (1,V3,F1)=(2,V3,F1)=(3,V3,F1);
  (1,V6,F1)=(2,V6,F1)=(3,V6,F1);
  (1,V8,F1)=(2,V8,F1)=(3,V8,F1);
  (1,V13,F1)=(2,V13,F1)=(3,V13,F1);
  (1,V14,F1)=(2,V14,F1)=(3,V14,F1);
  (1,V20,F1)=(2,V20,F1)=(3,V20,F1);
  (1,V10,F2)=(3,V10,F2);
  (1,V11,F2)=(2,V11,F2);
  (1,V15,F2)=(2,V15,F2)=(3,V15,F2);
  (1,V22,F2)=(2,V22,F2)=(3,V22,F2);
  (1,V7,F3)=(2,V7,F3)=(3,V7,F3);
  (1,V9,F3)=(2,V9,F3)=(3,V9,F3);
  (1,V17,F3)=(2,V17,F3);
  (1,V18,F3)=(2,V18,F3);
  (1,V19,F3)=(2,V19,F3)=(3,V19,F3);
  (1,V21,F3)=(2,V21,F3)=(3,V21,F3);
  (1,E1,E2)=(2,E1,E2)=(3,E1,E2);
  (1,E10,E11)=(2,E10,E11)=(3,E10,E11);
  (1,F2,F1)=(2,F2,F1)=(3,F2,F1);
  (1,F3,F1)=(2,F3,F1)=(3,F3,F1);
  (1,F3,F2)=(2,F3,F2)=(3,F3,F2);
/LMTEST
/END
```

group invariance. Statistically, the difference lies with the univariate versus multivariate approach in testing for the significance of specified group equality constraints. Whereas EQS uses the LM χ^2 test to provide both univariate and multivariate test statistics, LISREL uses a univariate approach based on the usual $\Delta\chi^2$ derived from the comparison of competing nested models.

Procedurally, the programs differ in two ways: The first pertains to the identification of the parameter(s), the second to the identification of the group(s) for which a specified constraint does not hold. That a block of parameters (e.g., all factor loadings) can be simultaneously tested for their invariance across groups holds for both computer programs. Differences arise, however, if the parameter block is found not to be group invariant. With EQS, as was evident in this chapter, equality constraints for the three groups were tested simultaneously, and test results made it easy to pinpoint both the nonequivalent parameters and the groups involved. On the other hand, to identify individual parameters contributing to noninvariance within the LISREL framework requires that the researcher respecify and reestimate a series of models that cumulatively incorporate all noninvariant parameters; each newly specified model must then be compared with some less restrictive model (for a more detailed discussion and demonstration of the procedure, see Byrne, 1989, 1993; Byrne et al., 1989; Byrne, Shavelson, & Marsh, 1992;

TABLE 9.4. Selected EQS Output: Testing for Equality of Maslach Burnout Inventory Structure

---

GOODNESS OF FIT SUMMARY

INDEPENDENCE MODEL CHI-SQUARE =   23810.882 ON   570 DEGREES OF FREEDOM

INDEPENDENCE AIC = 22670.88159   INDEPENDENCE CAIC = 18690.51520
        MODEL AIC = 1215.36140   MODEL CAIC = -2520.59653

CHI-SQUARE =   2285.361 BASED ON   535 DEGREES OF FREEDOM
PROBABILITY VALUE FOR THE CHI-SQUARE STATISTIC IS LESS THAN 0.001

BENTLER-BONETT NORMED   FIT INDEX=   0.904
BENTLER-BONETT NONNORMED FIT INDEX=   0.920
COMPARATIVE FIT INDEX   =   0.925

LAGRANGE MULTIPLIER TEST (FOR RELEASING CONSTRAINTS)
CONSTRAINTS TO BE RELEASED ARE:

    CONSTRAINTS FROM GROUP 3

        CONSTR: 1   (1,V2,F1)-(2,V2,F1)=0;
        CONSTR: 2   (1,V2,F1)-(3,V2,F1)=0;
        CONSTR: 3   (1,V3,F1)-(2,V3,F1)=0;
        CONSTR: 4   (1,V3,F1)-(3,V3,F1)=0;
        CONSTR: 5   (1,V6,F1)-(2,V6,F1)=0;
        CONSTR: 6   (1,V6,F1)-(3,V6,F1)=0;
        CONSTR: 7   (1,V8,F1)-(2,V8,F1)=0;
        CONSTR: 8   (1,V8,F1)-(3,V8,F1)=0;
        CONSTR: 9   (1,V13,F1)-(2,V13,F1)=0;
        CONSTR: 10   (1,V13,F1)-(3,V13,F1)=0;
        CONSTR: 11   (1,V14,F1)-(2,V14,F1)=0;
        CONSTR: 12   (1,V14,F1)-(3,V14,F1)=0;
        CONSTR: 13   (1,V20,F1)-(2,V20,F1)=0;
        CONSTR: 14   (1,V20,F1)-(3,V20,F1)=0;
        CONSTR: 15   (1,V10,F2)-(3,V10,F2)=0;
        CONSTR: 16   (1,V11,F2)-(2,V11,F2)=0;
        CONSTR: 17   (1,V15,F2)-(2,V15,F2)=0;
        CONSTR: 18   (1,V15,F2)-(3,V15,F2)=0;
        CONSTR: 19   (1,V22,F2)-(2,V22,F2)=0;
        CONSTR: 20   (1,V22,F2)-(3,V22,F2)=0;
        CONSTR: 21   (1,V7,F3)-(2,V7,F3)=0;
        CONSTR: 22   (1,V7,F3)-(3,V7,F3)=0;
        CONSTR: 23   (1,V9,F3)-(2,V9,F3)=0;
        CONSTR: 24   (1,V9,F3)-(3,V9,F3)=0;
        CONSTR: 25   (1,V17,F3)-(2,V17,F3)=0;
        CONSTR: 26   (1,V18,F3)-(2,V18,F3)=0;
        CONSTR: 27   (1,V19,F3)-(2,V19,F3)=0;
        CONSTR: 28   (1,V19,F3)-(3,V19,F3)=0;
        CONSTR: 29   (1,V21,F3)-(2,V21,F3)=0;
        CONSTR: 30   (1,V21,F3)-(3,V21,F3)=0;
        CONSTR: 31   (1,E1,E2)-(2,E1,E2)=0;
        CONSTR: 32   (1,E1,E2)-(3,E1,E2)=0;
        CONSTR: 33   (1,E10,E11)-(2,E10,E11)=0;
        CONSTR: 34   (1,E10,E11)-(3,E10,E11)=0;
        CONSTR: 35   (1,F2,F1)-(2,F2,F1)=0;
        CONSTR: 36   (1,F2,F1)-(3,F2,F1)=0;
        CONSTR: 37   (1,F3,F1)-(2,F3,F1)=0;
        CONSTR: 38   (1,F3,F1)-(3,F3,F1)=0;
        CONSTR: 39   (1,F3,F2)-(2,F3,F2)=0;
        CONSTR: 40   (1,F3,F2)-(3,F3,F2)=0;

TABLE 9.4. (Continued)

UNIVARIATE TEST STATISTICS:

NO	CONSTRAINT		CHI-SQUARE	PROBABILITY
1	CONSTR:	1	0.278	0.598
2	CONSTR:	2	0.098	0.754
3	CONSTR:	3	0.391	0.532
4	CONSTR:	4	0.015	0.902
5	CONSTR:	5	1.316	0.251
6	CONSTR:	6	0.267	0.606
7	CONSTR:	7	0.007	0.933
8	CONSTR:	8	0.016	0.901
9	CONSTR:	9	1.526	0.217
10	CONSTR:	10	0.775	0.379
11	CONSTR:	11	0.761	0.383
12	CONSTR:	12	0.268	0.605
13	CONSTR:	13	0.017	0.897
14	CONSTR:	14	0.954	0.329
15	CONSTR:	15	1.080	0.299
16	CONSTR:	16	1.948	0.163
17	CONSTR:	17	4.418	0.036
18	CONSTR:	18	1.917	0.166
19	CONSTR:	19	0.406	0.524
20	CONSTR:	20	0.683	0.409
21	CONSTR:	21	0.239	0.625
22	CONSTR:	22	1.300	0.254
23	CONSTR:	23	0.093	0.761
24	CONSTR:	24	0.545	0.460
25	CONSTR:	25	0.011	0.915
26	CONSTR:	26	0.262	0.609
27	CONSTR:	27	0.004	0.950
28	CONSTR:	28	0.096	0.756
29	CONSTR:	29	2.403	0.121
30	CONSTR:	30	0.684	0.408
31	CONSTR:	31	0.986	0.321
32	CONSTR:	32	0.336	0.562
33	CONSTR:	33	0.854	0.356
34	CONSTR:	34	0.107	0.744
35	CONSTR:	35	1.684	0.194
36	CONSTR:	36	6.622	0.010
37	CONSTR:	37	1.002	0.317
38	CONSTR:	38	0.016	0.901
39	CONSTR:	39	1.050	0.306
40	CONSTR:	40	2.872	0.090

	CUMULATIVE MULTIVARIATE STATISTICS					UNIVARIATE INCREMENT	
STEP	PARAMETER		CHI-SQUARE	D.F.	PROBABILITY	CHI-SQUARE	PROBABILITY
1	CONSTR:	36	6.622	1	0.010	6.622	0.010
2	CONSTR:	18	10.438	2	0.005	3.816	0.051
3	CONSTR:	17	17.306	3	0.001	6.868	0.009
4	CONSTR:	16	21.050	4	0.000	3.743	0.053
5	CONSTR:	29	23.574	5	0.000	2.524	0.112
6	CONSTR:	20	25.849	6	0.000	2.275	0.131
7	CONSTR:	15	27.373	7	0.000	1.524	0.217
8	CONSTR:	5	28.797	8	0.000	1.424	0.233
9	CONSTR:	9	29.911	9	0.000	1.114	0.291
10	CONSTR:	31	30.920	10	0.001	1.009	0.315

(Continued)

TABLE 9.4. (Continued)

11	CONSTR:	32	32.015	11	0.001	1.096	0.295
12	CONSTR:	11	32.778	12	0.001	0.763	0.382
13	CONSTR:	33	33.386	13	0.001	0.608	0.435
14	CONSTR:	34	34.155	14	0.002	0.769	0.381
15	CONSTR:	22	34.744	15	0.003	0.589	0.443
16	CONSTR:	21	35.851	16	0.003	1.107	0.293
17	CONSTR:	14	36.444	17	0.004	0.592	0.442
18	CONSTR:	23	36.979	18	0.005	0.535	0.465
19	CONSTR:	24	37.640	19	0.007	0.662	0.416
20	CONSTR:	1	38.068	20	0.009	0.427	0.513
21	CONSTR:	19	38.471	21	0.011	0.403	0.525
22	CONSTR:	35	38.766	22	0.015	0.295	0.587
23	CONSTR:	3	39.094	23	0.019	0.328	0.567
24	CONSTR:	27	39.321	24	0.025	0.227	0.634
25	CONSTR:	25	39.661	25	0.032	0.340	0.560
26	CONSTR:	26	40.293	26	0.037	0.632	0.427
27	CONSTR:	28	40.769	27	0.043	0.476	0.490
28	CONSTR:	37	41.064	28	0.053	0.295	0.587
29	CONSTR:	39	41.841	29	0.058	0.777	0.378
30	CONSTR:	10	41.994	30	0.072	0.153	0.695
31	CONSTR:	40	42.108	31	0.088	0.114	0.736
32	CONSTR:	38	42.443	32	0.103	0.335	0.563
33	CONSTR:	30	42.904	33	0.116	0.461	0.497
34	CONSTR:	7	42.989	34	0.139	0.085	0.770
35	CONSTR:	8	43.045	35	0.165	0.056	0.813
36	CONSTR:	12	43.118	36	0.193	0.073	0.787
37	CONSTR:	4	43.232	37	0.222	0.114	0.735
38	CONSTR:	6	43.380	38	0.253	0.148	0.701
39	CONSTR:	2	43.454	39	0.287	0.074	0.785
40	CONSTR:	13	43.477	40	0.326	0.022	0.881

Jöreskog & Sörbom, 1988). To determine the group associated with particular noninvariant parameters when the number of groups is greater than two, one must work with one pair of groups at a time, as is illustrated in the article related to the present example.

Applications Related to Other Disciplines

MEDICINE: Coulton, C. J., Hyduk, C. M., & Chow, J. C. (1989). An assessment of the Arthritis Impact Measurement Scales in 3 ethnic groups. *Journal of Rheumatology, 16,* 1110-1115.

Notes

1. For a detailed description of the MBI, readers are referred to Chapter 4 of the present volume.

2. For a more detailed account of analyses leading up to the 20-item model, readers are referred to the original article (Byrne, 1993).

3. Equality of the two error covariances was not tested in the original study.

10

Application 8
Testing for Invariant
Latent Mean Structures

Consistent with Bentler's (1980) observation over a decade ago, studies involving multigroup comparisons of latent mean structures are still few and far between (for a review, see Byrne et al., 1989). This situation is probably due to the many complexities associated with the implementation of these analyses using programs such as LISREL (up to and including version 6). Indeed, it was this very fact that prompted the writing of the above article. Nonetheless, to intimate that testing for invariant latent mean structures is easy and straightforward using EQS would be to oversimplify the case. Certainly, it is easier to grasp than the earlier LISREL versions, but both programs require that particular specification "tricks" be implemented.

The aim of this chapter is to introduce you to basic concepts associated with the analysis of latent mean structures, and to walk you through an application that tests for their invariance across two groups. Specifically, we test for differences in the latent means of general, academic, English, and mathematics self-concepts across high- and low-track secondary school students. The example presented here draws from two published papers: one focusing on methodological issues related to testing for invariant covariance and mean structures (Byrne et al., 1989) and one oriented towards substantive issues related to social comparison theory (Byrne, 1988c).

BASIC CONCEPTS UNDERLYING TESTS
OF LATENT MEAN STRUCTURES

In the usual univariate or multivariate analyses involving multigroup comparisons, one is interested in testing whether the **observed** means representing the various groups are statistically significantly different from each other. Because these values are directly calculable from the raw data, they are considered to be **observed** values. In contrast, the means of latent variables (i.e., latent constructs) are **unobservable**; that is, they are not directly observed. Rather, they derive their structure indirectly from their indicator variables, which in turn are directly observed and hence measurable. Testing for the invariance of mean structures, then, means that we intend to test for the equivalence of means related to each underlying construct or factor. Another way of saying the same thing, of course, is that we intend to test for differences in the latent means (of factors for each group).

For all the examples that we have considered thus far, the analyses have been based on **covariance structures**. In other words, only parameters representing regression coefficients, variances, and covariances have been of interest. Accordingly, the covariance structure of the (observed) indicator variables constitutes the crucial parametric information; a hypothesized model can thus be estimated and tested via the sample covariance matrix.

In the analysis of covariance structures, it is implicitly assumed that all observed variables are measured as deviations from their means; in other words, their means are equal to zero. As a consequence, the intercept terms generally associated with regression equations are not relevant to the analyses. However, when the observed means take on nonzero values, the intercept parameter must be considered, thereby necessitating a reparameterization of the hypothesized model. Such is the case when one is testing for the invariance of latent **mean structures**. An example taken from the EQS manual (Bentler, 1989, 1992a) should help to clarify both the concept and term of "mean structures." Consider first, the following regression equation:

$$y = \alpha + \beta x + \varepsilon$$

where α is an intercept parameter. Although the intercept can assist in defining the mean of y, it does not generally equal the mean. Now, if we take expectations of both sides of this equation and assume that the mean of ε is zero, the above expression yields:

$$\mu_y = \alpha + \beta \mu_x$$

where μ_y is the mean of y, and μ_x is the mean of x. As such, y and its mean can now be expressed in terms of the model parameters α, β, and μ_x. It is this decomposition of the mean of y, the dependent variable, that leads to the term

mean structures. More specifically, it serves to characterize a model in which the means of the dependent variables can be expressed, or "structured," in terms of structural coefficients and the means of the independent variables. The above equation serves to illustrate how the incorporation of a mean structure into a model necessarily includes the new parameters α and μ_x, the intercept and observed mean (of x), respectively. Thus it should now be easy to see how models with structured means merely extend the basic concepts associated with the analysis of covariance structures.

Recall that with each of our previous applications involving the analysis of covariance structures, variances of dependent variables were never parameters in the model. The same dictum holds true in the analysis of mean structures: dependent variable means cannot be parameters in the model. However, as will become clear in the next section, the intercepts of dependent variables actually **do** become parameters in the model—but only because they operate as the regression coefficients of a "constant" variable that EQS creates in order to carry out the analyses of mean structures; it functions as an independent variable within the context of the Bentler-Weeks schema.

In summary, any model involving mean structures may include the following parameters:

- regression coefficients
- variances and covariances of the independent variables
- intercepts of the dependent variables
- means of the independent variables

MODELING MEAN STRUCTURES IN EQS

The Single-Group Model

As you have probably already guessed, if we are going to accommodate two additional parameters into the model and yet retain the restriction that means and variances of dependent variables cannot be parameterized, we will have to restructure the model in some way. This is exactly what does take place in order for EQS to complete the analyses. Achievement of this task entails the utilization of two unique tricks: (a) creation of a constant variable that EQS designates as V999,[1] and (b) reconceptualization of the independent variables as dependent variables, in the Bentler-Weeks sense. To illustrate these points and better conceptualize how the covariance structure model transforms into a means structure model, let's examine a simple CFA model as presented in Figure 10.1.

Here we see the same set of variables and factors parameterized in two different configurations: in (a) as a covariance structure model and in (b) as

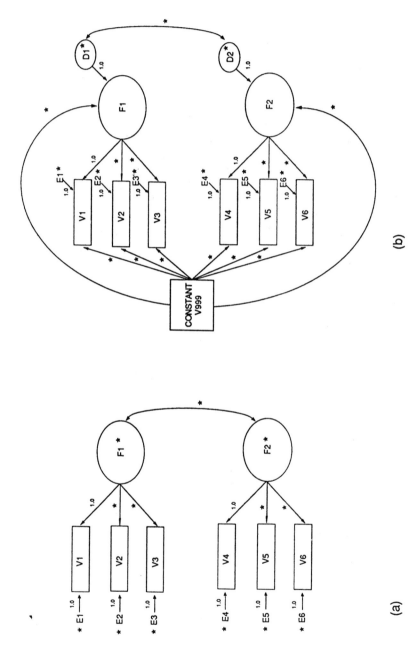

194

(a)

(b)

FIGURE 10.1. Sample Models of Covariance and Mean Structures: (a) Covariance Structure Model; (b) Mean Structure Model

a means structure model. Turning first to the covariance structure model, we see three measured variables each regressed on two factors; the factors are hypothesized to be correlated. Consistent with EQS notation, the asterisks represent parameters to be estimated; the first of each set of congeneric measures is fixed to 1.00 for purposes of statistical identification. In terms of the Bentler-Weeks conceptualization, this model has eight independent variables (two Fs, six Es) and six dependent variables (six Vs). As usual, variances can be estimated for only the independent variables. Finally, with 21 elements in the sample covariance matrix (6[6 + 1]/2) and 13 estimable parameters, this model is overidentified, with 8 overidentifying restrictions.

Turning next to the means structure model in Figure 10.1 (b), we see a schematic representation that is vastly different from its covariance structure counterpart in (a). Let's now examine these differences more closely. First, you will see the inclusion in the model of a constant that EQS labels as V999. The important aspect of this variable is that although it is an independent variable in the Bentler-Weeks sense, it does not have variance as a parameter in the model; rather, its variance remains fixed at zero.

Second, note that the six observed variables and the two factors are regressed onto the constant. Each coefficient associated with these regression one-way arrows represents an intercept, which in turn expresses a mean value. Regression of the two factors onto the constant yields intercepts that represent the latent factor means; regression of the measured variables onto the constant represents the variable intercepts. Whenever there are no indirect effects of the constant on the measured variables, each of these intercept values represents a direct effect and should equal the observed mean.[2] If, on the other hand, there are indirect effects in the model, as is the case in Figure 10.1 (b), the expected mean of a measured variable is represented by a total effect (direct effect + indirect effect). A brief example may serve to clarify these points. Suppose the intercept for Factor 1 (V999→F1) were fixed to zero. The expected mean value of V2 would then be determined solely by the direct effect of the constant (V999) on V2; this value would therefore have to equal the observed mean. By contrast, the expected mean value of V5 would be determined by both the direct effect of V999 on V5 and the indirect effect of V999→F2 on V5, these values in combination representing a total effect. Based on the tracing rule used in path analysis, the indirect effect on V5 would equal the product of paths V999→F2 and V5→F2. The decomposition of effects can be obtained as an option within the **/PRINT** paragraph of EQS.

As a consequence of their regression onto the constant V999, the two factors are now dependent variables and, as such, cannot have variances and covariances. Instead, the residual of a variable that is a **dependent** variable by sole virtue of its regression onto the constant manifests the variance and covariance information for that variable. Thus, as shown in Figure 10.1 (b), variances associated with D1 and D2 are estimated, as well as the covariance between them.

Bentler (1989, 1992a) has noted that in analyzing structured means models, there must always be fewer intercepts than there are measured variables. The intent of this caveat is to guard against possible underidentification related to the structured means portion of the model. To fully comprehend this advice, let's reexamine Figure 10.1 (b) more closely. We can see that it is actually composed of both a covariance structure, as depicted in Figure 10.1 (a), **and** a means structure. Now let's think about these two structures in terms of sample data. From all examples in the book thus far, we know that data for the covariance structure derive from the sample variance-covariance matrix. As noted above, in the test of the model this portion was overidentified, with eight overidentifying restrictions that provide degrees of freedom for fitting.

But what about the means structure portion of the model in terms of statistical identification? It was noted earlier that to analyze a structured means model, the user must input the observed mean value for each measured variable; these, then, provide the data and are fundamental to determining the status of statistical identification. Thus if the number of intercepts being estimated exceeds the amount of information coming into the structured means portion of the model as per the observed mean values, the model will be underidentified. Indeed, the model in Figure 10.1 (b) exemplifies this very situation. Here we have six measured variables and consequently six pieces of information (i.e., six observed mean values) from which to estimate the means-related parameters. However, as indicated by the asterisks, the number of intercepts to be estimated is eight (six variable intercepts, two factor intercepts), thereby rendering the model underidentified. Fortunately, in multisample models, as we shall see shortly, this type of situation can be resolved nicely with the imposition of equality constraints across groups.

The Multigroup Model

As with previous invariance examples, applications to structured means models involve testing simultaneously across two or more groups. Typically, the multigroup model is used here when one is interested in testing for differences in the means of particular latent constructs.

In essence, the basic configuration of and principles related to structured means models hold true for both single- and multigroup models. However, two important additional factors are unique to the latter. First, because the two (or more) groups under study are tested simultaneously, evaluation of the identification criterion is made across groups. As a consequence, although the structured means model may not be identified in one group, it can become so when analyzed across groups. This outcome occurs as a function of specified equality constraints across groups.

A second feature of the multigroup model is that it requires a new, additional concept of factor identification. Specifically, it imposes the restriction that factor intercepts for one group be fixed to zero; this group then operates as a reference group against which latent means for the other group(s) are compared. The reason for this reconceptualization is that when the intercepts of the measured variables are constrained equal across groups (as they typically should be),[3] the latent factor intercepts have an arbitrary origin. A standard way of fixing the origin, then, is to set the factor intercepts of one group to zero (Bentler, 1989, 1992a). As a consequence, factor intercepts are interpretable only in a relative sense.

Finally, another feature of the structured means multigroup model is its use in addressing missing data issues. For example, in a situation where missing data related to particular variables are substantially greater in one group than in another, the researcher may wish to test for latent mean differences in order to argue for (or against) the equality of the groups under study. Although a missing data application is not included here, a fully documented and illustrated example is provided in the manual (Bentler, 1989, 1992a).

THE HYPOTHESIZED MODEL

The application to be examined in this chapter bears on the equivalency of latent mean structures related to four self-concept dimensions (general, academic, English, mathematics) for high and low academically tracked high school students (Byrne, 1988c; Byrne et al., 1989). Specifically, the substantive focus of the initial study (Byrne, 1988c) was to test for latent mean differences in multidimensional self-concepts across these two ability groups. The originally hypothesized model replicated the one portrayed in Figure 3.1.[4]

The Baseline Models

As with our previous examples in Part 3, it is considered most appropriate to fit the postulated model to each group separately before testing for equality across groups. These baseline models, as reported by Byrne et al. (1989), are presented in Figure 10.2.

The baseline model for both the high and low academic tracks was derived from post hoc model fitting that included sensitivity analyses (see Byrne et al., 1989). These analyses led to final models that specified one differential cross-loading and four partially common error covariances. Whereas general self-concept cross-loaded onto the English SC subscale of the Self

198

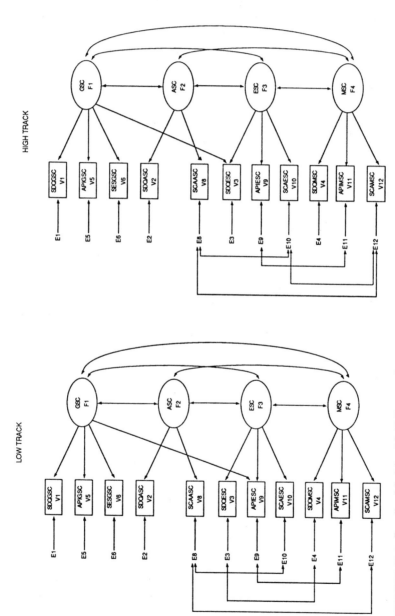

FIGURE 10.2. Baseline Models of Self-Concept Structure for High- and Low-Track High School Students

Source: Adapted from Byrne (1989). Copyright (1989) by Springer-Verlag. Reprinted by permission.

Decription Questionnaire (SDQ; Marsh & O'Neill, 1984) for high-track students (GSC→SDQESC), it cross-loaded onto the English SC subscale of the Affective Perception Inventory (API; Soares & Soares, 1979) for those in the low track (GSC→APIESC). As can be seen in Figure 10.2, three of the four error covariances were common across track. These baseline models, then, provided the fundamental structures that were tested for differences in latent factor means.

Structured Means Models

As an earlier example demonstrated, the covariance structures depicted in Figure 10.2 can be schematically transformed into a model representing mean structures. However, in lieu of visually describing a model for each group, we are presenting a single model accompanied by symbols indicative of the various constraints to be imposed. This hypothesized model is portrayed in Figure 10.3.

Before reviewing symbols in the model, let's first examine the basic structure so that you are assured of its equivalence to the covariance structure model depicted in Figure 10.2. Accordingly, there are four factors (F1-F4), each correlated with the other, as indicated by the curved arrows connecting the Ds. Recall that because the factors are now dependent variables as a consequence of their regression on the constant (V999), the associated residuals operate as their proxies in carrying their variances and covariances. Except for academic self-concept, which has only two observed measures regressed on it (V2, V8), three such measures are regressed on each of Factors 1, 3 and 4; the first loading of each congeneric set of measures is fixed at 1.0 for purposes of identification. Finally, associated with each observed measure is an error term (E).

Inclusion of various constraints in the model depicted in Figure 10.3 is meant only as an aid to a simultaneous portrayal of the model representing each group of students; it is not a conventional path diagram. An explanation of the symbols denoting these constraints is as follows:

* Denotes a parameter to be freely estimated in each group
*= Denotes a parameter that, althoughly freely estimated, is constrained equal across groups
*0 Denotes a parameter to be freely estimated in one group but fixed to zero in the other group

So now let's once again review Figure 10.3, but this time taking all paths and symbols into account. Interpretation of the model can be summarized as follows:

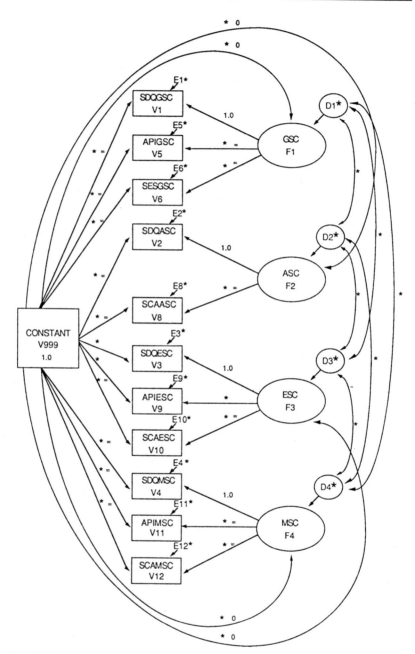

FIGURE 10.3. Multigroup Mean Structure Model of Self Concept for High- and Low-Track High School Students.

Note: Error covariances have been omitted for the sake of simplicity.

- Variances of the Ds are freely estimated in each group, as are the covariances among them.
- Variances of the Es are freely estimated in each group. Although not shown in the figure for purposes of clarity, error covariances specific to each group are freely estimated.[5]
- Except for factor loadings fixed to 1.00 and the loading of V9 (API-ESC) on F3 (ESC), all factor loadings are constrained equal across groups. Recall that V9 loaded on F1 (GSC) for low-track but not for high-track students. Given a differential loading pattern, this parameter is thus freely estimated in each group (see Byrne et al., 1989).[6]
- Except for the two intercepts related to V3 and V9 (the variables associated with the differential cross-loadings), all intercepts for the observed measures are constrained equal across groups.
- The four factor intercepts are freely estimated in one group (high track) and constrained equal to zero in the other group (low track); the latter is therefore regarded as the "reference" group.[7]
- As noted earlier, variance associated with the constant (V999) is not estimated, but rather remains fixed to 1.00.

Before we turn to the EQS input file related to this model, some explanation is needed with respect to the intercepts. First, recall that the number of estimated intercepts must be less than the number of measured variables. In a multigroup model, as noted earlier, this is controlled by the imposition of equality constraints across the groups. In the present case, a review of the structured means portion of the model in Figure 10.3 reveals that there are 22 measured variables (11 for each group); there are 17 intercepts to be estimated (9 equated across groups, 4 freely estimated in each group, and 4 freely estimated in one group, but fixed to zero in the other group), leaving 5 degrees of freedom.

The second point relates to the interpretation of intercepts. In the present application, we are primarily interested in the comparison of latent mean values and thus in values representing the factor intercepts only. Nonetheless, a brief explanation of effects related to the variable intercepts may be helpful. Recall that when there are no indirect effects, the variable intercepts should equal the actual observed means if the model is to be plausible. Relatedly, because the factor intercepts are fixed to zero for the low-track group (the reference group), there are consequently no indirect effects, and thus the expected means should approximate the observed sample means. For the high-track group, on the other hand, expected means for the measured variables will derive from the indirect effect of the constant on the related factor and its loading plus the direct effect of the constant on the variable itself. We turn now to the analysis of the model shown in Figure 10.3.

TESTING FOR INVARIANT
LATENT MEAN STRUCTURES

EQS Input File

The input file for the present application is set up for the microcomputer. Data are in correlational matrix form as presented in the Byrne et al. (1989) article and are inbedded within the file. Specifications for the mean structures model shown in Figure 10.3 are presented in Table 10.1.

By now, most of the information in the /SPEC paragraph will be readily discernible to you. However, one major difference here is the specification of ANAL=MOM. This keyword causes EQS to analyze the first moments (i.e., means), as well as the second moments (i.e., variances/covariances) of the sample data. Whenever this analysis specification is made, two other conditions hold: (a) the method of analysis must be maximum likelihood (ME=ML),[8] and (b) the constant variable V999 **must** be included in the /EQUATIONS paragraph of the input file. As noted, its variance will be fixed to zero. This is done automatically by the program, and you need not specify it. Finally, I wish to remind you that because the data are in correlational matrix form, the specification of MA=COR must be included; the mere input of standard deviations does not automatically result in the analyses' being based on the covariance matrix.

Many readers may be familiar with the LISREL approach to structured means models and its requirement that the analysis be based on what LISREL calls the **moment** matrix. However, this matrix should not be confused with the specification in EQS that ANALYSIS=MOMENT; the two are vastly different. Analysis of structured means using LISREL is based on a matrix of moments around zero (i.e., a moment matrix), rather than the covariance matrix (Jöreskog & Sörbom, 1988). In contrast, the same analysis using EQS is based on the first and second moments about the means (i.e., both the means and covariance structures are used). Consequently, the moment matrix, as in LISREL, is irrelevant to either model specification or the underlying statistical theory of EQS.

Because the data are in the form of a correlation matrix, the /MATRIX paragraph has been included. To enable the covariance matrix to be analyzed, the standard deviations are also added, along with the required observed means. Although encountered before, it is worth noting again that because there are 12 variables in the model, 12 standard deviations and 12 means must be specified; only 11, however, are actually used in the analysis.

We turn now to the /EQUATIONS paragraph. Here we see that, in addition to the usual factor loading specifications, the constant variable (V999) is also included; the latter represents the intercept from the constant to each

TABLE 10.1. EQS Input: Testing for Invariance of Latent Mean Structures in Self-Concept Model

```
/TITLE
 TESTING FOR INVARIANCE OF MEAN STRUCTURES ACROSS ABILITY
 "AGINV1"
 GROUP1=HIGH TRACK
/SPECIFICATIONS
 CASE=582; VAR=12; ME=ML; MA=COR; ANAL=MOM; FO='(12F4.3)';
 GROUPS=2;
/MATRIX
1000
 3301000
 267 3971000
 173 427-0111000
 658 323 212 2001000
 812 325 290 226 6681000
 556 624 338 325 618 5671000
 250 660 342 500 266 312 5391000
 151 412 723-040 188 201 408 3411000
 100 415 559-007 107 140 329 536 6941000
 180 455 041 892 272 275 405 516 066 0411000
 133 401 015 843 193 189 351 612-016 086 8241000
/STANDARD DEVIATIONS
 14.563 11.723 9.867 16.951 9.394 5.063 9.556 4.919 11.191 5.727
 11.606 7.986
/MEANS
 75.792 57.830 57.569 49.043 76.768 31.467 73.802 30.301 61.794
 28.933 47.223 26.223
/LABELS
V1=SDQGSC;   V2=SDQASC;   V3=SDQESC;   V4=SDQMSC;
V5=APIGSC;   V6=SESGSC;   V7=APIASC;   V8=SCAASC;
V9=APIESC;   V10=SCAESC;  V11=APIMSC;  V12=SCAMSC;
F1=GSC;      F2=ASC;      F3=ESC;      F4=MSC;
/EQUATIONS
V1 = 75*V999 + F1 + E1;
V5 = 76*V999 + .83*F1 + E5;
V6 = 31*V999 + 1.0*F1 + E6;
    V2 =  57*V999 + F2 + E2;
    V8 = 30*V999 + .98*F2 + E8;
        V3 =  57*V999 + F3 + .17*F1 + E3;
        V9 = 61*V999 + 1.2*F3 + E9;
        V10 = 28*V999 + 1.0*F3 + E10;
            V4 =  49*V999 + F4 + E4;
            V11 = 47*V999 + .98*F4 + E11;
            V12 = 26*V999 + .90*F4 + E12;
F1=10*V999 + D1;
    F2=10*V999 + D2;
        F3=10*V999 + D3;
            F4=10*V999 +D4;
/VARIANCES
E1, E12=2*; E2, E3, E8=3*; E4=1*; E5, E10=4*;
E6, E9, E11=1*;
D1 TO D4=3*;
/COVARIANCES
E10,E8=.2*; E12,E8=.1*; E11,E9=.06*; E12,E10=.07*;
D1 to D4 = .1*;
/END
/TITLE
 GROUP2=LOW TRACK
```

(Continued)

TABLE 10.1. (Continued)

```
/SPECIFICATIONS
 CASE=248; VAR=12; ME=ML; MA=COR; ANAL=MOM; FO='(12F4.3)';
/MATRIX
1000
3201000
307 2981000
244 355-0551000
614 237 214 2671000
755 261 276 255 5881000
456 571 392 345 547 4581000
270 580 265 226 219 270 5231000
143 430 623 030 181 108 476 3731000
231 377 433 004 265 245 424 509 4981000
250 388 063 779 245 234 409 345 232 0271000
234 348-012 719 199 214 362 442 075 077 7421000
/STANDARD DEVIATIONS
 13.442 12.391 9.468 13.416 9.028 4.875 8.830 4.480 10.701 4.858
 10.566 5.824
/MEANS
 75.936 49.415 55.036 41.569 76.758 31.157 70.165 24.746 57.794
 25.343 41.710 22.944
/LABELS
 V1=SDQGSC;   V2=SDQASC;   V3=SDQESC;   V4=SDQMSC;
 V5=APIGSC;   V6=SESGSC;   V7=APIASC;   V8=SCAASC;
 V9=APIESC;   V10=SCAESC;  V11=APIMSC;  V12=SCAMSC;
 F1=GSC;      F2=ASC;      F3=ESC;      F4=MSC;
/EQUATIONS
 V1 =   75*V999 + F1 + E1;
 V5 = 76*V999 + .78*F1 + E5;
 V6 = 31*V999 + .95*F1 + E6;
    V2 =   49*V999 + F2 + E2;
    V8 = 24*V999 + .82*F2 + E8;
       V3 =   55*V999 + F3 + E3;
       V9 = 57*V999 + 1.4*F3 + -.33*F1 + E9;
       V10 = 25*V999 + .87*F3 + E10;
          V4 =   41*V999 + F4 + E4;
          V11 = 41*V999 + .99*F4 + E11;
          V12 = 22*V999 + .93*F4 + E12;
 F1=0.0V999 + D1;
    F2=0.0V999 + D2;
       F3=0.0V999 + D3;
          F4=0.0V999 +D4;
/VARIANCES
 E1, E4, E6, E11=2*; E2, E12=3*; E3, E5, E8=5*; E9=1*; E10=6*;
 D1 TO D4=3*;
/COVARIANCES
 E10,E8=.21*; E12,E8=.15*; E11,E9=.16*; E3,E4=-.07*;
 D1 to D4 = .1*;
/CONSTRAINTS
 (1,V5,F1)=(2,V5,F1);
 (1,V6,F1)=(2,V6,F1);
 (1,V8,F2)=(2,V8,F2);
 (1,V10,F3)=(2,V10,F3);
 (1,V11,F4)=(2,V11,F4);
 (1,V12,F4)=(2,V12,F4);
 (1,V1,V999)=(2,V1,V999);
 (1,V5,V999)=(2,V5,V999);
 (1,V6,V999)=(2,V6,V999);
 (1,V2,V999)=(2,V2,V999);
```

TABLE 10.1. (Continued)

```
(1,V8,V999)=(2,V8,V999);
(1,V10,V999)=(2,V10,V999);
(1,V4,V999)=(2,V4,V999);
(1,V11,V999)=(2,V11,V999);
(1,V12,V999)=(2,V12,V999);
/LMTEST
/PRINT
 EFFECTS=YES;
/END
```

measured variable. The start value associated with each V999 is the actual observed mean value.[9] Note also that the intercepts associated with each factor are estimated here for Group 1 but not for Group 2; as can be seen in the /EQUATIONS paragraph for Group 2, these parameters are fixed to zero. Because specifications bearing on variances and covariances are all straightforward and probably require no further explanation, let's turn our attention now to the /CONSTRAINTS paragraph.

Looking first at specifications related to only the factor loadings, we see that just 6 of the 11 are accounted for. Of course, 4 are fixed to 1.00 for identification purposes; the missing loading belongs to V9, which was found to cross-load c.1to F1 for the low track only (see Figure 10.2). Because this variable was operating differentially across high- and low-track students, it is not constrained equal across groups (see Byrne et al., 1989). The remaining constraints relate to the measured variable intercepts; except for the one associated with V9, all are constrained equal across the two groups. In order to test statistically for validity of these constraints, the /LMTEST statement has been implemented. It should be noted that EQS will converge more rapidly if parameters that are constrained equal across groups have equal start values.

Finally, although not necessary for answering the question being asked of the present data, decomposition of the effects has been requested in the /PRINT paragraph.

EQS Output Files

The output for the above input file indicated that the start values were somewhat less than adequate; these values were subsequently revised and the job reexecuted. However, before turning to the revised output, it's worthwhile to examine the related error messages and the output information immediately preceding them. This portion of the output is presented in Table 10.2.

TABLE 10.2. Selected EQS Output: Initial Check for Viability of Start Values in Self-Concept Model

MATRIX CONTAINS SPECIAL VARIABLE V999, THE UNIT CONSTANT
COVARIANCE MATRIX IS IN UPPER TRIANGLE; MEANS ARE IN BOTTOM ROW OF MATRIX
COVARIANCE/MEAN MATRIX TO BE ANALYZED:

11 VARIABLES (SELECTED FROM   12 VARIABLES), BASED ON   582 CASES.

			SDQGSC V 1	SDQASC V 2	SDQESC V 3	SDQMSC V 4	APIGSC V 5
SDQGSC	V	1	212.081				
SDQASC	V	2	56.338	137.429			
SDQESC	V	3	38.366	45.921	97.358		
SDQMSC	V	4	42.706	84.852	-1.840	287.336	
APIGSC	V	5	90.018	35.571	19.650	31.848	88.247
SESGSC	V	6	59.871	19.290	14.487	19.396	31.771
SCAASC	V	8	17.909	38.059	16.599	41.691	12.292
APIESC	V	9	24.609	54.051	79.835	-7.588	19.764
SCAESC	V	10	8.340	27.862	31.588	-0.680	5.757
APIMSC	V	11	30.423	61.906	4.695	175.486	29.655
SCAMSC	V	12	15.468	37.542	1.182	114.117	14.479
V999	V999		75.792	57.830	57.569	49.043	76.768

			SESGSC V 6	SCAASC V 8	APIESC V 9	SCAESC V 10	APIMSC V 11
SESGSC	V	6	25.634				
SCAASC	V	8	7.770	24.197			
APIESC	V	9	11.389	18.772	125.238		
SCAESC	V	10	4.059	15.100	44.479	32.799	
APIMSC	V	11	16.159	29.458	8.572	2.725	134.699
SCAMSC	V	12	7.642	24.041	-1.430	3.933	76.373
V999	V999		31.467	30.301	61.794	28.933	47.223

			SCAMSC V 12	V999 V999
SCAMSC	V	12	63.776	
V999	V999		26.223	1.000

BENTLER-WEEKS STRUCTURAL REPRESENTATION:

```
    NUMBER OF DEPENDENT VARIABLES = 15
        DEPENDENT V'S :       1    2    3    4    5    6    8    9   10   11
        DEPENDENT V'S :      12
        DEPENDENT F'S :       1    2    3    4
    NUMBER OF INDEPENDENT VARIABLES = 16
        INDEPENDENT V'S :    999
        INDEPENDENT E'S :      1    2    3    4    5    6    8    9   10   11
        INDEPENDENT E'S :     12
        INDEPENDENT D'S :      1    2    3    4
```

IN ITERATION #   1,MATRIX W_CFUNCT MAY NOT BE POSITIVE DEFINITE

YOU HAVE BAD START VALUES TO BEGIN WITH.
IF ABOVE MESSAGE APPEARS ON EVERY ITERATION, PLEASE PROVIDE BETTER START
VALUES AND RE-RUN THE JOB.
.
.
.
.

IN ITERATION #   5,MATRIX W_CFUNCT MAY NOT BE POSITIVE DEFINITE

PARAMETER ESTIMATES APPEAR IN ORDER,
NO SPECIAL PROBLEMS WERE ENCOUNTERED DURING OPTIMIZATION.

The first statement issued in the output is a notation that the sample matrix to follow contains the constant variable V999. As you will see in examining the matrix, the subsequent statement points out that observed mean values (for V999) are entered on the bottom row of the matrix; the rest of the matrix contains the sample variances and covariances. Shown here is the matrix relative to the high-track students (Group 1) only; this information is then presented later in the output for the low-track students (Group 2).

Turning to the **Bentler-Weeks representation** of the model, we see that there are 12 dependent observed measures and 4 dependent factors. Given the deletion of one observed measure (APIASC), however, EQS automatically adjusts the total number of dependent variables to 15 rather than 16. This same adjustment holds true for the total number of independent variables, which is 16 rather than 17. This representation of the data is totally consistent with the model presented in Figure 10.3.

Next we see the warning message that **"IN ITERATION #1, ..."**, followed by the suggestion that the start values are bad. The program then warns that if this message appears on every iteration, you should revise the start values and rerun the job. In the present case, the message was printed several times over relative to Iterations 1 through 5 (these repeated messages are excluded here to conserve space). Given that the message appeared for only the first five iterations, and given that a final message reported that **"no special problems were encountered during optimization"**, there was no real need to respecify the start values. Nonetheless, this output provides me with the opportunity to show you the type of error message that can appear should the problem occur. One solution to getting better start values is simply to replace the original start values with those representing the parameter estimates from the same output. This procedure was followed here and the model reestimated. Let's turn now to Table 10.3, where selected portions of the output resulting from this second run of the initially hypothesized model are presented.

As reflected by the iterative summary, the solution converged quite smoothly, and the goodness-of-fit statistics show the model to be an excellent fit to the multigroup data, as indicated by a CFI of .978. In reviewing the LM χ^2 multivariate statistics,[10] however, we can see that four constraints in the model are misspecified (#11, #5, #3, #4); three relate to the nonequivalence of factor loadings across groups (#3, #4, #5) and one to the nonequivalence of a variable intercept (#11). The model was subsequently reestimated, with these four constraints deleted from the model specifications. Results of this respecified model are presented in Table 10.4.

As might be expected, given a model that was already well fitting, removal of the above restrictions yielded but a modest improvement in goodness of fit (CFI = .986). Although not shown in Table 10.4, all remaining

TABLE 10.3. Selected EQS Output: Testing for Invariant Factor Loadings and
Intercepts in Self-Concept Model

STATISTICS FOR MULTIPLE POPULATION ANALYSIS
ALL EQUALITY CONSTRAINTS WERE CORRECTLY IMPOSED

GOODNESS OF FIT SUMMARY

INDEPENDENCE MODEL CHI-SQUARE =   6214.454 ON   110 DEGREES OF FREEDOM

INDEPENDENCE AIC = 5994.45410   INDEPENDENCE CAIC = 5365.09727
        MODEL AIC =   60.10856   MODEL CAIC = -380.44122

CHI-SQUARE =   214.109 BASED ON   77 DEGREES OF FREEDOM
PROBABILITY VALUE FOR THE CHI-SQUARE STATISTIC IS LESS THAN 0.001

BENTLER-BONETT NORMED   FIT INDEX=   0.966
BENTLER-BONETT NONNORMED FIT INDEX=   0.968
COMPARATIVE FIT INDEX   =   0.978

ITERATIVE SUMMARY

	PARAMETER		
	ABS CHANGE	ALPHA	FUNCTION
ITERATION			
1	1.368102	1.00000	0.26508
2	0.414822	1.00000	0.25905
3	0.164374	1.00000	0.25865
4	0.060740	1.00000	0.25860
5	0.028439	1.00000	0.25859
6	0.012127	1.00000	0.25858
7	0.005390	1.00000	0.25859
8	0.002367	1.00000	0.25859
9	0.001045	1.00000	0.25858
10	0.000459	1.00000	0.25859

LAGRANGE MULTIPLIER TEST (FOR RELEASING CONSTRAINTS)
CONSTRAINTS TO BE RELEASED ARE:

    CONSTRAINTS FROM GROUP   2

        CONSTR: 1   (1,V5,F1)-(2,V5,F1)=0;
        CONSTR: 2   (1,V6,F1)-(2,V6,F1)=0;
        CONSTR: 3   (1,V8,F2)-(2,V8,F2)=0;
        CONSTR: 4   (1,V10,F3)-(2,V10,F3)=0;
        CONSTR: 5   (1,V11,F4)-(2,V11,F4)=0;
        CONSTR: 6   (1,V12,F4)-(2,V12,F4)=0;
        CONSTR: 7   (1,V1,V999)-(2,V1,V999)=0;
        CONSTR: 8   (1,V5,V999)-(2,V5,V999)=0;
        CONSTR: 9   (1,V6,V999)-(2,V6,V999)=0;
        CONSTR: 10   (1,V2,V999)-(2,V2,V999)=0;
        CONSTR: 11   (1,V8,V999)-(2,V8,V999)=0;
        CONSTR: 12   (1,V10,V999)-(2,V10,V999)=0;
        CONSTR: 13   (1,V4,V999)-(2,V4,V999)=0;
        CONSTR: 14   (1,V11,V999)-(2,V11,V999)=0;
        CONSTR: 15   (1,V12,V999)-(2,V12,V999)=0;

	CUMULATIVE MULTIVARIATE STATISTICS				UNIVARIATE INCREMENT	
STEP	PARAMETER	CHI-SQUARE	D.F.	PROBABILITY	CHI-SQUARE	PROBABILITY
1	CONSTR: 11	33.937	1	0.000	33.937	0.000
2	CONSTR: 5	42.375	2	0.000	8.439	0.004
3	CONSTR: 3	47.188	3	0.000	4.813	0.028
4	CONSTR: 4	53.543	4	0.000	6.355	0.012
5	CONSTR: 9	55.674	5	0.000	2.130	0.144
6	CONSTR: 14	56.595	6	0.000	0.921	0.337
7	CONSTR: 6	57.148	7	0.000	0.553	0.457
8	CONSTR: 2	57.242	8	0.000	0.094	0.759
9	CONSTR: 13	57.308	9	0.000	0.067	0.796
10	CONSTR: 1	57.339	10	0.000	0.031	0.860

TABLE 10.4. Selected EQS Output: Goodness-of-Fit Statistics, Parameter
Estimates, and Total Effects for Self-Concept Model

GOODNESS OF FIT SUMMARY

INDEPENDENCE MODEL CHI-SQUARE =   6214.454 ON   110 DEGREES OF FREEDOM

INDEPENDENCE AIC = 5994.45410   INDEPENDENCE CAIC = 5365.09727
         MODEL AIC =   12.46980   MODEL CAIC = -405.19427

CHI-SQUARE =   158.470 BASED ON   73 DEGREES OF FREEDOM
PROBABILITY VALUE FOR THE CHI-SQUARE STATISTIC IS LESS THAN 0.001

BENTLER-BONETT NORMED   FIT INDEX=   0.974
BENTLER-BONETT NONNORMED FIT INDEX=   0.979
COMPARATIVE FIT INDEX   =   0.986

Group 1 (High Track)

MEASUREMENT EQUATIONS WITH STANDARD ERRORS AND TEST STATISTICS

SDQGSC =V1 =   1.000 F1   + 75.687*V999 + 1.000 E1
                                      .814
                                    92.956

SDQASC =V2 =   1.000 F2   + 49.481*V999 + 1.000 E2
                                      .785
                                    62.995

SDQESC =V3 =   .118*F1   + 1.000 F3   + 51.589*V999   + 1.000 E3
                   .023   .725
                  5.106   71.194

SDQMSC =V4 =   1.000 F4   + 41.484*V999 + 1.000 E4
                                      .811
                                    51.122

APIGSC =V5 =   .533*F1   + 76.679*V999 + 1.000 E5
                   .022   .474
                  24.112   161.929

SESGSC =V6 =   .356*F1   + 31.334*V999 + 1.000 E6
                   .012   .292
                  30.817   107.447

SCAASC =V8 =   .411*F2   + 26.869*V999 + 1.000 E8
                   .021   .401
                  19.738   66.927

APIESC =V9 =   1.391*F3   + 53.486*V999 + 1.000 E9
                   .068   .903
                  20.533   59.219

SCAESC =V10 =   .603*F3   + 25.348*V999 + 1.000 E10
                   .031   .309
                  19.167   81.912

APIMSC =V11 =   .674*F4   + 42.028*V999 + 1.000 E11
                   .014   .574
                  46.765   73.246

SCAMSC =V12 =   .424*F4   + 22.997*V999 + 1.000 E12
                   .010   .351
                  41.863   65.490

CONSTRUCT EQUATIONS WITH STANDARD ERRORS AND TEST STATISTICS

  GSC   =F1 =   .246*V999 + 1.000 D1
                   .980
                   .251

(Continued)

TABLE 10.4. (Continued)

```
ASC   =F2  =     8.349*V999  +   1.000 D2
                  .924
                 9.037
ESC   =F3  =     5.951*V999  +   1.000 D3
                  .721
                 8.258
MSC   =F4  =     7.620*V999  +   1.000 D4
                 1.060
                 7.189
```

DECOMPOSITION OF EFFECTS WITH NONSTANDARDIZED VALUES
PARAMETER TOTAL EFFECTS

```
SDQGSC  =V1  =    1.000 F1   + 75.933*V999  +  1.000 E1   +  1.000 D1
SDQASC  =V2  =    1.000 F2   + 57.830*V999  +  1.000 E2   +  1.000 D2
SDQESC  =V3  =     .118*F1   +  1.000 F3    + 57.569*V999 +  1.000 E3
                   .118 D1   +  1.000 D3
SDQMSC  =V4  =    1.000 F4   + 49.104*V999  +  1.000 E4   +  1.000 D4
APIGSC  =V5  =     .533*F1   + 76.810*V999  +  1.000 E5   +   .533 D1
SESGSC  =V6  =     .356*F1   + 31.422*V999  +  1.000 E6   +   .356 D1
SCAASC  =V8  =     .411*F2   + 30.303*V999  +  1.000 E8   +   .411 D2
APIESC  =V9  =    1.391*F3   + 61.765*V999  +  1.000 E9   +  1.391 D3
SCAESC  =V10 =     .603*F3   + 28.934*V999  +  1.000 E10  +   .603 D3
APIMSC  =V11 =     .674*F4   + 47.162*V999  +  1.000 E11  +   .674 D4
SCAMSC  =V12 =     .424*F4   + 26.228*V999  +  1.000 E12  +   .424 D4
  GSC   =F1  =     .246*V999  +  1.000 D1
  ASC   =F2  =    8.349*V999  +  1.000 D2
  ESC   =F3  =    5.951*V999  +  1.000 D3
  MSC   =F4  =    7.620*V999  +  1.000 D4
```

Group 2 (Low track)
MEASUREMENT EQUATIONS WITH STANDARD ERRORS AND TEST STATISTICS

```
SDQGSC  =V1  =    1.000 F1   + 75.687*V999  +  1.000 E1
                               .814
                             92.956
SDQASC  =V2  =    1.000 F2   + 49.481*V999  +  1.000 E2
                               .785
                             62.995
SDQESC  =V3  =    1.000 F3   + 55.097*V999  +  1.000 E3
                               .596
                             92.392
SDQMSC  =V4  =    1.000 F4   + 41.484*V999  +  1.000 E4
                               .811
                             51.122
APIGSC  =V5  =     .533*F1   + 76.679*V999  +  1.000 E5
                   .022         .474
                 24.112      161.929
SESGSC  =V6  =     .356*F1   + 31.334*V999  +  1.000 E6
                   .012         .292
                 30.817      107.447
```

TABLE 10.4. (Continued)

```
SCAASC  =V8  =     .303*F2    + 24.763*V999  +  1.000 E8
                   .033          .278
                  9.262        88.974

APIESC  =V9  =    -.269*F1    +  1.591*F3    + 57.960*V999  +  1.000 E9
                   .072          .186            .652
                 -3.716         8.549         88.907

SCAESC  =V10 =     .450*F3    + 25.348*V999  +  1.000 E10
                   .049          .309
                  9.137        81.912

APIMSC  =V11 =     .800*F4    + 42.028*V999  +  1.000 E11
                   .041          .574
                 19.635        73.246

SCAMSC  =V12 =     .424*F4    + 22.997*V999  +  1.000 E12
                   .010          .351
                 41.863        65.490
```

CONSTRUCT EQUATIONS WITH STANDARD ERRORS AND TEST STATISTICS

```
GSC   =F1  =    1.000 D1

ASC   =F2  =    1.000 D2

ESC   =F3  =    1.000 D3

MSC   =F4  =    1.000 D4
```

DECOMPOSITION OF EFFECTS WITH NONSTANDARDIZED VALUES

PARAMETER TOTAL EFFECTS

```
SDQGSC  =V1  =    1.000 F1    + 75.687*V999  +  1.000 E1   +  1.000 D1
SDQASC  =V2  =    1.000 F2    + 49.481*V999  +  1.000 E2   +  1.000 D2
SDQESC  =V3  =    1.000 F3    + 55.097*V999  +  1.000 E3   +  1.000 D3
SDQMSC  =V4  =    1.000 F4    + 41.484*V999  +  1.000 E4   +  1.000 D4
APIGSC  =V5  =     .533*F1    + 76.679*V999  +  1.000 E5   +   .533 D1
SESGSC  =V6  =     .356*F1    + 31.334*V999  +  1.000 E6   +   .356 D1
SCAASC  =V8  =     .303*F2    + 24.763*V999  +  1.000 E8   +   .303 D2
APIESC  =V9  =    -.269*F1    +  1.591*F3    + 57.960*V999  +  1.000 E9
                  -.269 D1    +  1.591 D3
SCAESC  =V10 =     .450*F3    + 25.348*V999  +  1.000 E10  +   .450 D3
APIMSC  =V11 =     .800*F4    + 42.028*V999  +  1.000 E11  +   .800 D4
SCAMSC  =V12 =     .424*F4    + 22.997*V999  +  1.000 E12  +   .424 D4
 GSC    =F1  =    1.000 D1
 ASC    =F2  =    1.000 D2
 ESC    =F3  =    1.000 D3

 MSC    =F4  =    1.000 D4
```

equality constraints were found to be tenable. We can therefore feel confident in interpreting the estimates associated with the current solution. In the interest of space, however, only results related to the factor loadings, intercepts, and total effects are reported.

In reviewing the measurement equations, we see that all estimates related to the factor loadings (including the one cross-loading for each group) and variable intercepts are significant for both the high- and low-track groups.

To answer the primary question of whether the latent construct means for the two groups are significantly different, however, we must turn to the construct equations. The parameters of interest in answering this question are the factor intercepts that represent the latent mean values. Because the low-track group was designated the reference group and, as such, had their parameters fixed to zero, we concentrate solely on estimates for the high track. Indeed, although the factor intercepts for the more specific facets of academic, English, and mathematics self-concepts were significant, this was not the case for general self-concept. From these findings, we can conclude that latent mean structures related to these more specific and school-related self-concept dimensions are not equivalent for low- and high-track high school students; there appears to be little difference between the groups with respect to a more global perception of self. Importantly, these findings are consistent with those reported by Byrne (Byrne, 1988c; Byrne et al., 1989), despite the completely different approaches taken by the EQS and LISREL programs in analyzing the data.

Finally, for sake of completeness, the unstandardized values for parameter total effects in the model are shown in Table 10.4. It is important to note, however, that because low-track students served as the reference group, these effects, for them, are actually direct effects. For both groups, the V999 coefficients represent the reproduced means of the measured variables; they should replicate the actual observed values. Nonetheless, in comparing these coefficients with the observed mean values, we find several instances where there is a slight discrepancy between the two values. First, whereas the model overpredicted the mean of V1 (SDQGSC), V4 (SDQMSC), and V5 (APIGSC) for the high track (Group 1), it underpredicted these values for the low track (Group 2); conversely, the mean of V11 (APIMSC) was underpredicted for the high track, but overpredicted for the low track. Second, the model overpredicted the means of V6 (SESGSC) and V9 (APIESC) for Group 2. All remaining V999 coefficients replicated the observed mean values to at least the first decimal place.

As noted earlier, the decomposition of effects is not directly relevant to the present application, and thus I have not elaborated on this portion of the output. My intent in including this brief section in Table 10.4 was to give you at least a flavor of the information provided in the EQS output. For a more detailed treatment of the topic, readers are referred to the EQS manual (Bentler, 1989, 1992a).

Applications Related to Other Disciplines

EDUCATION: Kinnunen, U., & Leskinen, E. (1989). Teacher stress during the school year: Covariance and mean structure analyses. *Journal of Occupational Psychology, 62,* 111-122.

MEDICINE: Aiken, L. S., Stein, J. A., & Bentler, P. M. (in press). Structural equation analyses of clinical sub-population differences and comparative treatment outcomes: Characterizing the daily lives of drug addicts. *Journal of Consulting and Clinical Psychology.*

Notes

1. The rationale here is that relative to the measured variables in the input file, the constant will always be considered last.

2. Direct effects represent the impact of one variable on another, with no mediation by any other variable; indirect effects operate through at least one intervening variable (Bollen, 1989).

3. Of course, partial measurement invariance may be specified (see Byrne et al., 1989), as will be demonstrated in the example presented in this chapter.

4. Consistent with earlier tests of this model (see Chapters 3 and 8), the Academic self-concept subscale of the Affective Perception Inventory was deleted as one measure of this construct.

5. Because specification of equality constraints related to the Es and Ds is considered to be excessively stringent, these constraints were not imposed.

6. Although V3 (SDQESC) cross-loaded on F1 (GSC) for the high track, thereby making this subscale score differentially valid across groups, this parameter is already unconstrained by virtue of its fixed value of 1.00.

7. Determination of which group to serve as the reference group is purely arbitrary.

8. Only the normal theory maximum likelihood method is currently available in EQS for structured means models.

9. Because structured means models are extremely sensitive to the start values provided, the input of the actual mean values helps in the convergence of the model.

10. In the interest of space, the univariate statistics have been deleted.

11

Application 9
Testing for Invariant
Causal Structure

Subsequent to and probably consequent to Bentler's seminal articles describing, in nonmathematical language, the underlying theory, analytic strategy, and many advantages of structural equation modeling (SEM) for nonexperimental research (Bentler, 1978, 1980), there have been a growing number of SEM applications reported in the social science literature. In the wake of these (largely) substantive studies, there has been a similarly expanding literature in which quantitative researchers have decried the proliferating abuse of the SEM methodology. Of particular concern has been the post hoc fitting of misspecified models, with little or no regard for capitalization on chance factors or for generalizability to the population (e.g., Anderson & Gerbing, 1988; Breckler, 1990; Cliff, 1983; Cudeck & Browne, 1983; MacCallum, 1986; MacCallum, Roznowski, & Necowitz, 1992; Sörbom, 1989). One approach to addressing these concerns has been to urge researchers to cross-validate their modified models over independent samples. Nonetheless, MacCallum et al. (1992) recently reported that such advice is rarely followed in practice.

In the present chapter, then, invariance testing is conducted within the context of cross-validation. Although there are different approaches to cross-validation in the analysis of covariance structures, depending on the focus of one's study (see Anderson & Gerbing, 1988; Browne & Cudeck, 1989; Cudeck & Browne, 1983), the application described here is straightforward in addressing the question of whether a model that has been respecified in one sample replicates over a second independent sample from the same population (for an alternate approach, see Byrne & Baron, in press-a). The example comes from the same study briefly described in Chapter 7 (Byrne, in press). The intent of this study was (a) to validate a causal structure involving the impact of organizational and personality factors on three facets of burnout for elementary, intermediate, and secondary teachers, (b) to cross-validate this model across a second independent sample within each teaching panel, and (c) to test for the invariance of common structural paths across teaching panels. In this chapter, we focus on (b) in testing for model replication across calibration and validation samples of elementary teachers. (For an in-depth examination of invariance-testing procedures within and between the three teacher groups, see Byrne, in press.)

It is perhaps important to note that although the present example of cross-validation is based on a full structural equation model, the practice is in no way limited to such applications. Indeed, cross-validation is equally as important for CFA models, and examples of such applications can be found across a variety of disciplines. For those relevant to psychology, see Byrne (1992, 1993), Byrne & Baron (1993), and Byrne et al. (1993, in press); to education, see Benson and Bandalos (1992); and to medicine, see Francis, Fletcher, and Rourke (1988). We turn now to the model under study.

THE HYPOTHESIZED MODEL

The original study comprised a sample of 1203 elementary school teachers. For purposes of cross-validation, this sample was randomly split into two; Sample A ($n = 602$) was used as the calibration group and Sample B ($n = 601$) as the validation group. Specifically, the originally hypothesized model was tested and modified based on data from the calibration group (as was demonstrated in Chapter 7). The final best fitting model for this sample is presented schematically in Figure 11.1.

Testing of the initially hypothesized model revealed a modest amount of misspecification. In particular, the LM χ^2 statistics suggested the addition of three structural paths to the model, and the Wald Test identified five that could be deleted from the model with no deterioration of fit. This final model of burnout structure for elementary teachers yielded a Satorra-Bentler $\chi^2_{(443)}$ of 1097.10 and a CFI of .93. Thus our present task is to determine if this model replicates over Sample B, the validation group of elementary teachers.

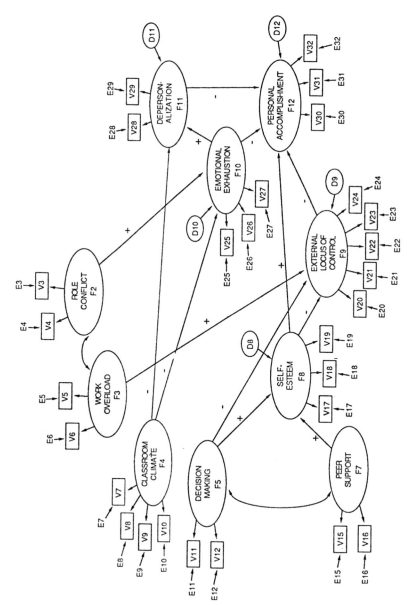

FIGURE 11.1. Final Model of Burnout for Calibration Sample of Elementary School Teachers

216

TESTING FOR INVARIANCE
ACROSS CALIBRATION/VALIDATION SAMPLES

EQS Input File

Because specification of data files in a multigroup model differs slightly when the EQS job is excuted in a mainframe rather than a microcomputer system, I again considered it worthwhile to include at least one example of the former in this section; the present application, then, is structured for the mainframe. The input file is presented in Table 11.1.

Turning first to the job language, you will observe two differences here from the previous mainframe example; both relate to the fact that the estimation of multigroup models, as might be expected, requires substantially more time and space. To accommodate the first requirement, **TIME=10** has been added to the first line; this allows for 10 minutes of CPU time, which should be ample for most multigroup job runs. With reference to the second requirement, two requests for space have been added to the second line. The first, **RG=6M,** indicates that up to 6 megabytes of space have been requested on the main computer system; the second, **PARM=500000,** means that 500,000 bytes of space have been requested within the EQS program.

A third consideration with the mainframe multigroup file is that the external data file for the **first group only** is placed in the JCL setup, as was the case for a single-group application (see Chapter 4). As a consequence of this specification, no data file is specified under the **/SPEC** paragraph (for Group 1). Note, however, that for each subsequent group, the external data file **is** specified in the **/SPEC** paragraph.

Because the primary purpose of a cross-validation SEM application is to determine if the final model that was derived from exploratory work based on one sample can replicate across a second sample, model specification for the latter will be identical to that of the first group. In the interest of space, then, the related paragraphs have been deleted for the validation sample (Group 2) in Table 11.1. Close scrutiny of the specified constraints will reveal that all freely estimated factor loadings and structural paths have been constrained equal across calibration and validation samples; these include the three factor cross-loadings.

EQS Output File

Results from this test of invariance are presented in Table 11.2. We note, first of all, that goodness of fit for this highly restrictive model is quite satisfactory (CFI = .92), thereby providing favorable evidence in support of replication. Turning to the univariate LM χ^2 statistics and related probability values associated with each equality constraint, however, we see that all

TABLE 11.1. EQS Input: Validating Final Elementary School Teacher Burnout
Model Across Random Samples

```
//IAVPBMB JOB TIME=10
//    EXEC    EQS,RG=6M,PARM=500000
//DATA  DD    DSN=IAVPBMB.ELEMIND1.DATA,DISP=SHR
/TITLE
VALIDATION OF FINAL MODEL ACROSS CALIBRN/VALIDN SAMPLES "BURNECV1.EQS"
GROUP 1 = CALIBRATION
/SPEC
CASE=602; VAR=32; GROUPS=2; ME=ML; MA=RAW; UN=9; FO='(19F4.2/13F4.2)';
DEL= 34, 168, 601;
/LABELS
V1=ROLEA1;    V2=ROLEA2;    V3=ROLEC1;    V4=ROLEC2;    V5=WORK1;
V6=WORK2;     V7=CLIMATE1;  V8=CLIMATE2;  V9=CLIMATE3;  V10=CLIMATE4;
V11=DEC1;     V12=DEC2;     V13=SSUP1;    V14=SSUP2;    V15=PSUP1;
V16=PSUP2;    V17=SELF1;    V18=SELF2;    V19=SELF3;    V20=XLOC1;
V21=XLOC2;    V22=XLOC3;    V23=XLOC4;    V24=XLOC5;    V25=EE1;
V26=EE2;      V27=EE3;      V28=DP1;      V29=DP2;      V30=PA1;
V31=PA2;      V32=PA3;
F1=ROLEA; F2=ROLEC; F4=CLIMATE; F3=WORK; F5=DEC; F6=SSUP; F7=PSUP;
F8=SELF; F9=XLOC; F10=EE; F11=DP; F12=PA;
/EQU
V1= .9*F1+ -.4*F5+E1;
V2= F1+ -.5*F5+E2;
  V3= .9*F2+ -.2*F6+E3;
  V4= F2+E4;
    V5= .9*F3+E5;
    V6= F3+E6;
      V7= .6*F4+E7;
      V8= .6*F4+E8;
      V9= .6*F4+E9;
      V10= F4+E10;
        V11= F5+E11;
        V12= 1.*F5+E12;
          V13= F6+E13;
          V14= 1.*F6+E14;
            V15= F7+E15;
            V16= 1.*F7+E16;
              V17= F8+E17;
              V18= .8*F8+E18;
              V19= .8*F8+E19;
                V20= F9+E20;
                V21= .8*F9+E21;
                V22= .8*F9+E22;
                V23= .8*F9+E23;
                V24= .8*F9+E24;
                  V25= F10+E25;
                  V26= 1.*F10+E26;
                  V27= .9*F10+E27;
                    V28= F11+E28;
                    V29= .9*F11+E29;
                      V30= F12+E30;
                      V31= .8*F12+E31;
                      V32= .9*F12+E32;
F8= .4*F5+.4*F7+D8;
F9= -.3*F5+ .2*F3+ -.2*F8+ D9;
F10= .6*F2+ -.3*F4+D10;
F11= .5*F10+ -.2*F4+D11;
F12= .5*F8+ -.5*F10+ -.5*F11+D12;
```

TABLE 11.1. (Continued)

```
/VAR
 F1 TO F2= .3*;
 F3= .6*; F5= .6*; F6= .8*; F7= .5*;
 E1 TO E32= .2*;
 D8 TO D12= .1*;
/COV
 F1 TO F3= .3*;
 F5 TO F7= .5*;
/END
/TITLE
 GROUP 2 = VALIDATION
/SPEC
 CASE=601; VAR=32; ME=ML; MA=RAW; UN=9; FO='(19F4.2/13F4.2)';
 DATA=ELEMIND2.DATA;
 .
 .
 .
 .
 .
 .
/CONSTRAINTS
 (1,V1,F1)=(2,V1,F1);
 (1,V1,F5)=(2,V1,F5);
 (1,V2,F5)=(2,V2,F5);
 (1,V3,F2)=(2,V3,F2);
 (1,V3,F6)=(2,V3,F6);
 (1,V5,F3)=(2,V5,F3);
 (1,V7,F4)=(2,V7,F4);
 (1,V8,F4)=(2,V8,F4);
 (1,V9,F4)=(2,V9,F4);
 (1,V12,F5)=(2,V12,F5);
 (1,V14,F6)=(2,V14,F6);
 (1,V16,F7)=(2,V16,F7);
 (1,V18,F8)=(2,V18,F8);
 (1,V19,F8)=(2,V19,F8);
 (1,V21,F9)=(2,V21,F9);
 (1,V22,F9)=(2,V22,F9);
 (1,V23,F9)=(2,V23,F9);
 (1,V24,F9)=(2,V24,F9);
 (1,V26,F10)=(2,V26,F10);
 (1,V27,F10)=(2,V27,F10);
 (1,V29,F11)=(2,V29,F11);
 (1,V31,F12)=(2,V31,F12);
 (1,V32,F12)=(2,V32,F12);
 (1,F11,F4)=(2,F11,F4);
 (1,F10,F4)=(2,F10,F4);
 (1,F11,F10)=(2,F11,F10);
 (1,F9,F5)=(2,F9,F5);
 (1,F8,F5)=(2,F8,F5);
 (1,F9,F8)=(2,F9,F8);
 (1,F12,F8)=(2,F12,F8);
 (1,F12,F11)=(2,F12,F11);
 (1,F10,F2)=(2,F10,F2);
 (1,F9,F3)=(2,F9,F3);
 (1,F12,F10)=(2,F12,F10);
 (1,F8,F7)=(2,F8,F7);
/LMTEST
/END
```

TABLE 11.2. Selected EQS Output: Validating Final Elementary School Teacher Burnout Model Across Random Samples

GOODNESS OF FIT SUMMARY

INDEPENDENCE MODEL CHI-SQUARE =   21255.090 ON   992 DEGREES OF FREEDOM

INDEPENDENCE AIC = 19271.08984   INDEPENDENCE CAIC = 13229.73362
        MODEL AIC =   755.87607   MODEL CAIC = -4853.08469

CHI-SQUARE =   2597.876 BASED ON   921 DEGREES OF FREEDOM
PROBABILITY VALUE FOR THE CHI-SQUARE STATISTIC IS LESS THAN 0.001

BENTLER-BONETT NORMED   FIT INDEX=   0.878
BENTLER-BONETT NONNORMED FIT INDEX=   0.911
COMPARATIVE FIT INDEX   =   0.917

LAGRANGE MULTIPLIER TEST (FOR RELEASING CONSTRAINTS)

CONSTRAINTS TO BE RELEASED ARE:

        CONSTRAINTS FROM GROUP   2

        CONSTR: 1   (1,V1,F1)-(2,V1,F1)=0;
        CONSTR: 2   (1,V1,F5)-(2,V1,F5)=0;
        CONSTR: 3   (1,V2,F5)-(2,V2,F5)=0;
        CONSTR: 4   (1,V3,F2)-(2,V3,F2)=0;
        CONSTR: 5   (1,V3,F6)-(2,V3,F6)=0;
        CONSTR: 6   (1,V5,F3)-(2,V5,F3)=0;
        CONSTR: 7   (1,V7,F4)-(2,V7,F4)=0;
        CONSTR: 8   (1,V8,F4)-(2,V8,F4)=0;
        CONSTR: 9   (1,V9,F4)-(2,V9,F4)=0;
        CONSTR: 10   (1,V12,F5)-(2,V12,F5)=0;
        CONSTR: 11   (1,V14,F6)-(2,V14,F6)=0;
        CONSTR: 12   (1,V16,F7)-(2,V16,F7)=0;
        CONSTR: 13   (1,V18,F8)-(2,V18,F8)=0;
        CONSTR: 14   (1,V19,F8)-(2,V19,F8)=0;
        CONSTR: 15   (1,V21,F9)-(2,V21,F9)=0;
        CONSTR: 16   (1,V22,F9)-(2,V22,F9)=0;
        CONSTR: 17   (1,V23,F9)-(2,V23,F9)=0;
        CONSTR: 18   (1,V24,F9)-(2,V24,F9)=0;
        CONSTR: 19   (1,V26,F10)-(2,V26,F10)=0;
        CONSTR: 20   (1,V27,F10)-(2,V27,F10)=0;
        CONSTR: 21   (1,V29,F11)-(2,V29,F11)=0;
        CONSTR: 22   (1,V31,F12)-(2,V31,F12)=0;
        CONSTR: 23   (1,V32,F12)-(2,V32,F12)=0;
        CONSTR: 24   (1,F11,F4)-(2,F11,F4)=0;
        CONSTR: 25   (1,F10,F4)-(2,F10,F4)=0;
        CONSTR: 26   (1,F11,F10)-(2,F11,F10)=0;
        CONSTR: 27   (1,F9,F5)-(2,F9,F5)=0;
        CONSTR: 28   (1,F8,F5)-(2,F8,F5)=0;
        CONSTR: 29   (1,F9,F8)-(2,F9,F8)=0;
        CONSTR: 30   (1,F12,F8)-(2,F12,F8)=0;
        CONSTR: 31   (1,F12,F11)-(2,F12,F11)=0;
        CONSTR: 32   (1,F10,F2)-(2,F10,F2)=0;
        CONSTR: 33   (1,F9,F3)-(2,F9,F3)=0;
        CONSTR: 34   (1,F12,F10)-(2,F12,F10)=0;
        CONSTR: 35   (1,F8,F7)-(2,F8,F7)=0;

        UNIVARIATE TEST STATISTICS:

NO	CONSTRAINT		CHI-SQUARE	PROBABILITY
1	CONSTR:	1	0.049	0.825
2	CONSTR:	2	0.383	0.536
3	CONSTR:	3	0.378	0.539

TABLE 11.2. (Continued)

4	CONSTR:	4	0.261	0.609
5	CONSTR:	5	0.219	0.640
6	CONSTR:	6	1.149	0.284
7	CONSTR:	7	0.052	0.820
8	CONSTR:	8	1.627	0.202
9	CONSTR:	9	1.244	0.265
10	CONSTR:	10	3.134	0.077
11	CONSTR:	11	1.454	0.228
12	CONSTR:	12	1.019	0.313
13	CONSTR:	13	0.102	0.750
14	CONSTR:	14	3.118	0.077
15	CONSTR:	15	0.178	0.673
16	CONSTR:	16	0.012	0.911
17	CONSTR:	17	1.898	0.168
18	CONSTR:	18	0.071	0.790
19	CONSTR:	19	1.073	0.300
20	CONSTR:	20	3.158	0.076
21	CONSTR:	21	0.015	0.903
22	CONSTR:	22	4.511	0.034
23	CONSTR:	23	1.276	0.259
24	CONSTR:	24	1.068	0.301
25	CONSTR:	25	0.122	0.726
26	CONSTR:	26	0.084	0.772
27	CONSTR:	27	0.006	0.937
28	CONSTR:	28	1.844	0.174
29	CONSTR:	29	0.361	0.548
30	CONSTR:	30	0.738	0.390
31	CONSTR:	31	2.578	0.108
32	CONSTR:	32	0.257	0.612
33	CONSTR:	33	5.481	0.019
34	CONSTR:	34	1.372	0.241
35	CONSTR:	35	2.369	0.124

	CUMULATIVE MULTIVARIATE STATISTICS				UNIVARIATE INCREMENT	
STEP	PARAMETER	CHI-SQUARE	D.F.	PROBABILITY	CHI-SQUARE	PROBABILITY
1	CONSTR: 33	5.481	1	0.019	5.481	0.019
2	CONSTR: 22	9.985	2	0.007	4.505	0.034
3	CONSTR: 20	13.193	3	0.004	3.207	0.073
4	CONSTR: 10	16.310	4	0.003	3.118	0.077
5	CONSTR: 14	19.311	5	0.002	3.001	0.083
6	CONSTR: 13	21.355	6	0.002	2.044	0.153
7	CONSTR: 31	23.139	7	0.002	1.783	0.182
8	CONSTR: 8	24.733	8	0.002	1.595	0.207
9	CONSTR: 17	26.282	9	0.002	1.549	0.213
10	CONSTR: 11	27.757	10	0.002	1.475	0.225
11	CONSTR: 3	29.053	11	0.002	1.296	0.255
12	CONSTR: 12	29.838	12	0.003	0.785	0.376
13	CONSTR: 24	30.535	13	0.004	0.698	0.404
14	CONSTR: 9	31.302	14	0.005	0.767	0.381
15	CONSTR: 35	31.853	15	0.007	0.551	0.458
16	CONSTR: 32	32.397	16	0.009	0.544	0.461
17	CONSTR: 5	32.834	17	0.012	0.436	0.509
18	CONSTR: 23	33.225	18	0.016	0.391	0.532
19	CONSTR: 29	33.494	19	0.021	0.269	0.604

(Continued)

TABLE 11.2. (Continued)

20	CONSTR:	30	33.770	20	0.028	0.276	0.599
21	CONSTR:	15	34.046	21	0.036	0.276	0.600
22	CONSTR:	6	34.269	22	0.046	0.223	0.637
23	CONSTR:	16	34.434	23	0.059	0.165	0.685
24	CONSTR:	4	34.582	24	0.075	0.149	0.700
25	CONSTR:	18	34.692	25	0.094	0.110	0.741
26	CONSTR:	27	34.822	26	0.116	0.129	0.719
27	CONSTR:	21	34.914	27	0.141	0.092	0.761
28	CONSTR:	1	34.964	28	0.171	0.051	0.822
29	CONSTR:	2	35.011	29	0.204	0.046	0.830
30	CONSTR:	25	35.056	30	0.241	0.046	0.831
31	CONSTR:	7	35.070	31	0.281	0.013	0.908
32	CONSTR:	19	35.081	32	0.324	0.011	0.915
33	CONSTR:	34	35.092	33	0.369	0.011	0.917
34	CONSTR:	26	35.098	34	0.416	0.006	0.939
35	CONSTR:	28	35.098	35	0.464	0.000	0.983

except two constraints (#22, #33) were tenable across the two groups. These results were consistent across univariate and multivariate analyses in reflecting the noninvariance of one factor loading (V31,F12) and one structural path (F9,F3) across calibration/validation groups.

To follow up on these two problematic parameters, a second job was executed in which the related equality constraints were released. Results for this run are presented in Table 11.3.

Not unexpectedly, goodness of fit for this model remained unchanged (CFI = .92). Moreover, a review of both the univariate and multivariate LM statistics substantiates the tenability of all equality constraints. In fact, however, the initial test of invariance conducted here represented an excessively rigid test of cross-validation. Indeed, Bollen (1989, p. 360) has indicated that if a researcher's multigroup focus is directed more towards the equality of structural than measurement parameters, then testing for the invariance of the former may precede the latter. Results of this approach, wherein only the structural paths were constrained equal across groups, yielded findings of total equivalency across the two teaching panels (CFI = .93), with LM χ^2 probability values ranging from .73 to .99 ($M = .94$).

In light of the recent work of MacCallum et al. (1992), in which they demonstrate the difficulty in replicating models over repeated samples, I would argue that the present model replicated satisfactorily over the two independent samples of elementary teachers. Thus I consider it appropriate to combine these two samples for any subsequent comparisons across teaching panels.

TABLE 11.3. Selected EQS Output: Respecification of Equality Constraints for
Teacher Burnout Model

GOODNESS OF FIT SUMMARY

INDEPENDENCE MODEL CHI-SQUARE =   21255.090 ON   992 DEGREES OF FREEDOM

INDEPENDENCE AIC = 19271.08984   INDEPENDENCE CAIC = 13229.73362
     MODEL AIC =   750.60039   MODEL CAIC = -4846.18022

CHI-SQUARE =   2588.600 BASED ON   919 DEGREES OF FREEDOM
PROBABILITY VALUE FOR THE CHI-SQUARE STATISTIC IS LESS THAN 0.001

BENTLER-BONETT NORMED   FIT INDEX=   0.878
BENTLER-BONETT NONNORMED FIT INDEX=   0.911
COMPARATIVE FIT INDEX   =   0.918

LAGRANGE MULTIPLIER TEST (FOR RELEASING CONSTRAINTS)

CONSTRAINTS TO BE RELEASED ARE:

         CONSTRAINTS FROM GROUP 2

    CONSTR: 1   (1,V1,F1)-(2,V1,F1)=0;
    CONSTR: 2   (1,V1,F5)-(2,V1,F5)=0;
    CONSTR: 3   (1,V2,F5)-(2,V2,F5)=0;
    CONSTR: 4   (1,V3,F2)-(2,V3,F2)=0;
    CONSTR: 5   (1,V3,F6)-(2,V3,F6)=0;
    CONSTR: 6   (1,V5,F3)-(2,V5,F3)=0;
    CONSTR: 7   (1,V7,F4)-(2,V7,F4)=0;
    CONSTR: 8   (1,V8,F4)-(2,V8,F4)=0;
    CONSTR: 9   (1,V9,F4)-(2,V9,F4)=0;
    CONSTR: 10   (1,V12,F5)-(2,V12,F5)=0;
    CONSTR: 11   (1,V14,F6)-(2,V14,F6)=0;
    CONSTR: 12   (1,V16,F7)-(2,V16,F7)=0;
    CONSTR: 13   (1,V18,F8)-(2,V18,F8)=0;
    CONSTR: 14   (1,V19,F8)-(2,V19,F8)=0;
    CONSTR: 15   (1,V21,F9)-(2,V21,F9)=0;
    CONSTR: 16   (1,V22,F9)-(2,V22,F9)=0;
    CONSTR: 17   (1,V23,F9)-(2,V23,F9)=0;
    CONSTR: 18   (1,V24,F9)-(2,V24,F9)=0;
    CONSTR: 19   (1,V26,F10)-(2,V26,F10)=0;
    CONSTR: 20   (1,V27,F10)-(2,V27,F10)=0;
    CONSTR: 21   (1,V29,F11)-(2,V29,F11)=0;
    CONSTR: 22   (1,V32,F12)-(2,V32,F12)=0;
    CONSTR: 23   (1,F11,F4)-(2,F11,F4)=0;
    CONSTR: 24   (1,F10,F4)-(2,F10,F4)=0;
    CONSTR: 25   (1,F11,F10)-(2,F11,F10)=0;
    CONSTR: 26   (1,F9,F5)-(2,F9,F5)=0;
    CONSTR: 27   (1,F8,F5)-(2,F8,F5)=0;
    CONSTR: 28   (1,F9,F8)-(2,F9,F8)=0;
    CONSTR: 29   (1,F12,F8)-(2,F12,F8)=0;
    CONSTR: 30   (1,F12,F11)-(2,F12,F11)=0;
    CONSTR: 31   (1,F10,F2)-(2,F10,F2)=0;
    CONSTR: 32   (1,F12,F10)-(2,F12,F10)=0;
    CONSTR: 33   (1,F8,F7)-(2,F8,F7)=0;

         UNIVARIATE TEST STATISTICS:

NO	CONSTRAINT	CHI-SQUARE	PROBABILITY
1	CONSTR: 1	0.040	0.842
2	CONSTR: 2	0.392	0.531
3	CONSTR: 3	0.359	0.549
4	CONSTR: 4	0.219	0.640

(Continued)

TABLE 11.3. (Continued)

5	CONSTR:	5	0.202	0.653
6	CONSTR:	6	0.222	0.638
7	CONSTR:	7	0.053	0.818
8	CONSTR:	8	1.624	0.203
9	CONSTR:	9	1.261	0.261
10	CONSTR:	10	2.517	0.113
11	CONSTR:	11	1.441	0.230
12	CONSTR:	12	0.995	0.318
13	CONSTR:	13	0.127	0.721
14	CONSTR:	14	3.231	0.072
15	CONSTR:	15	0.057	0.810
16	CONSTR:	16	0.049	0.825
17	CONSTR:	17	1.273	0.259
18	CONSTR:	18	0.433	0.510
19	CONSTR:	19	1.022	0.312
20	CONSTR:	20	3.238	0.072
21	CONSTR:	21	0.044	0.834
22	CONSTR:	22	0.117	0.732
23	CONSTR:	23	1.027	0.311
24	CONSTR:	24	0.127	0.722
25	CONSTR:	25	0.058	0.810
26	CONSTR:	26	1.492	0.222
27	CONSTR:	27	1.758	0.185
28	CONSTR:	28	2.153	0.142
29	CONSTR:	29	0.247	0.619
30	CONSTR:	30	1.508	0.220
31	CONSTR:	31	0.240	0.624
32	CONSTR:	32	0.531	0.466
33	CONSTR:	33	2.316	0.128

	CUMULATIVE MULTIVARIATE STATISTICS				UNIVARIATE INCREMENT	
STEP	PARAMETER	CHI-SQUARE	D.F.	PROBABILITY	CHI-SQUARE	PROBABILITY
1	CONSTR: 20	3.238	1	0.072	3.238	0.072
2	CONSTR: 14	6.468	2	0.039	3.231	0.072
3	CONSTR: 10	8.918	3	0.030	2.450	0.118
4	CONSTR: 13	11.226	4	0.024	2.307	0.129
5	CONSTR: 26	12.939	5	0.024	1.713	0.191
6	CONSTR: 30	14.595	6	0.024	1.656	0.198
7	CONSTR: 8	16.194	7	0.023	1.600	0.206
8	CONSTR: 17	17.680	8	0.024	1.486	0.223
9	CONSTR: 11	19.123	9	0.024	1.443	0.230
10	CONSTR: 3	20.528	10	0.025	1.405	0.236
11	CONSTR: 12	21.297	11	0.030	0.770	0.380
12	CONSTR: 28	22.059	12	0.037	0.762	0.383
13	CONSTR: 23	22.755	13	0.045	0.695	0.404
14	CONSTR: 9	23.530	14	0.052	0.775	0.379
15	CONSTR: 33	24.137	15	0.063	0.607	0.436
16	CONSTR: 31	24.655	16	0.076	0.517	0.472
17	CONSTR: 5	25.149	17	0.091	0.494	0.482
18	CONSTR: 22	25.560	18	0.110	0.411	0.521
19	CONSTR: 15	25.829	19	0.135	0.269	0.604
20	CONSTR: 6	26.051	20	0.164	0.222	0.638
21	CONSTR: 16	26.210	21	0.199	0.159	0.690
22	CONSTR: 18	26.387	22	0.235	0.176	0.675
23	CONSTR: 4	26.508	23	0.277	0.122	0.727
24	CONSTR: 29	26.621	24	0.322	0.112	0.737

TABLE 11.3. (Continued)

25	CONSTR:	21	26.721	25	0.370	0.100	0.751
26	CONSTR:	2	26.781	26	0.421	0.059	0.807
27	CONSTR:	24	26.831	27	0.473	0.051	0.822
28	CONSTR:	1	26.872	28	0.525	0.041	0.840
29	CONSTR:	7	26.885	29	0.578	0.014	0.907
30	CONSTR:	19	26.898	30	0.629	0.013	0.909
31	CONSTR:	25	26.902	31	0.677	0.004	0.951
32	CONSTR:	32	26.905	32	0.722	0.003	0.958
33	CONSTR:	27	26.905	33	0.764	0.000	0.983

Applications Related to Other Disciplines

BUSINESS: Durvasula, S., Andrews, J. C., Lysonski, S., & Netemeyer, R. G. (1993). Assessing the cross-national applicability of consumer behavior models: A model of attitudes toward advertising in general. *Journal of Consumer Research, 19,* 626-636.

EDUCATION: Ethington, C. A., & Wolfle, L. M. (1986). A structural model of mathematics achievement for men and women. *American Educational Research Journal, 23,* 65-75.

MEDICINE: Ellison, P. H., Greisen, G., Foster, M., Petersen, M. B., & Friis-Hansen, B. (1991). The relation between perinatal conditions and developmental outcome in low birthweight infants: Comparison of two cohorts. *Acta Paediatrica Scandinavica, 80,* 28-35.

PART FOUR

Window Treatments: A Look at EQS/Windows (Version 4)

CHAPTER 12: INTRODUCTION TO EQS/WINDOWS

CHAPTER 13: APPLICATION 10
Preliminary Data-Screening Analyses

CHAPTER 14: APPLICATION 11
Building an EQS Model File—Instantly!

12

Introduction to EQS/Windows

Although EQS to date has generally been considered to be the most user friendly of all structural equation programs, the recent release of EQS/Windows (Version 4; Bentler & Wu, 1993)[1] makes it a leader in the move to demystify the use of software packages in the application of structural equation modeling. This program operates within the environment of Microsoft Windows and can perform many statistical, graphical, and data handling procedures that previously required the use of other statistical packages such as BMDP, SPSS, or SAS. Using EQS/Windows, you can prepare a raw data set, identify and impute missing values, visually inspect the data, identify and delete outliers, and plot and print graphs.

In addition to these invaluable data summary features, the revised program has expanded its modeling procedures to include the analysis of categorical data.[2] Furthermore, you can even build an entire input file through an interactive response mechanism. Improvements have also been made to the LM and Wald Tests.

These final three chapters are devoted to the new EQS/Windows version. The present chapter serves as a brief introduction to the basic approach of working with EQS within the Windows environment. In Chapter 13, I review features that will be helpful to you in your preanalysis of data. Finally, in Chapter 14, I walk you through the automatic building of an EQS input file. Although the number of examples presented in Chapters 13 and 14 must necessarily be limited for practical reasons, I hope to give you at least a taste of the wonderful things that await you when you use this extremely avantgarde version of the program. For details related to graphics, data management, interactive file building, and the general "Windows" approach to using EQS, readers are referred to the *User's Guide* (Bentler & Wu, 1993); for details concerning aspects of structural equation modeling with EQS, the manual should be consulted (Bentler, 1989, 1992a).

RUNNING EQS/WINDOWS

As with other Windows applications, all that is needed to run EQS/Windows is to simply double click on the EQS icon which looks like this:

Once you do this, you will see two windows, one superimposed upon the other as shown in Figure 12.1. At the top, you will see the Main Window, which displays a **menu bar** and a series of icons. The menu bar provides for the retrieval of data files and for various procedures related to editing, data management, analyses, and so on. The **icons** represent particular plotting options; these will be reviewed in more detail in Chapter 13. The bottom window displays the heading **OUTPUT.LOG**. As the first step to running EQS, you are asked to open a data file. Because EQS is data analysis oriented, this action must be taken before any aspects of the program can be initiated.

OPENING A DATA FILE

The Retrieval Process

To open a file, you now click on **FILE** in the Main Window menu bar. You will then be presented with a series of choices; click on **OPEN**. A dialog box, partially shown in Figure 12.2, will appear. What you will see initially is shown in the upper dialog box of Figure 12.2. Under **FILE NAME,** in the upper left-hand corner, you will see a series of files all ending with the extension **.ESS**; these represent EQS data system files, which I shall explain shortly. By default, this dialog box always opens with the **.ESS** file list.

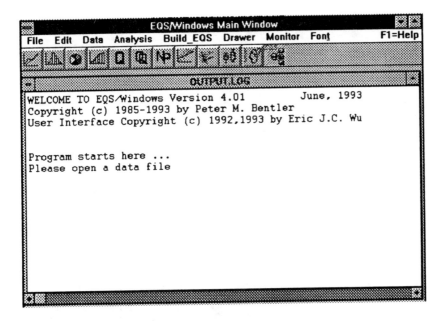

FIGURE 12.1. Main and **OUTPUT.LOG** Windows

Consistent with this default, note that the selection bar, appearing below the list of files and under the heading **LIST FILES OF TYPE:**, indicates **EQS SYSTEM DATA (.ESS)**. If you were to press the down arrow (↓), you would see that listed under this heading are other types of files which may, alternatively, be selected. An example appears in the lower dialog box in Figure 12.2. Here we see that the selection bar indicates **RAW DATA FILES**; listed above is a series of raw data files. To open a data file, then, you must first indicate its file type by clicking on the appropriate selection bar; presented with all files belonging to the same type, you next click on the file you want. EQS will highlight the file and move it to the box immediately below **FILE NAME**. To finish the retrieval process, you now click on the **OK** button.

Types of Data Files

In EQS/Windows, file type is always indicated by a dotted extension (.). Although it is possible to have files of many different types, those most commonly used are as follows:

- **FILENAME.DAT**—raw data files containing variable scores only
- **FILENAME.EQS**—EQS structural equation model input files

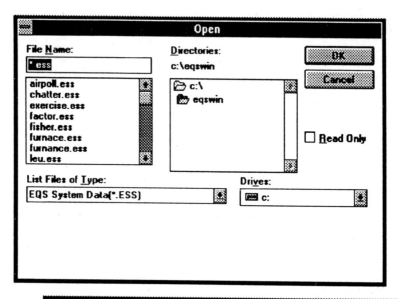

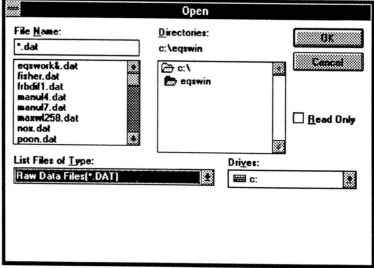

FIGURE 12.2. OPEN FILE Dialog Boxes

- **FILENAME.ESS**—EQS raw or covariance data system files. In addition to the data, these files contain information related to the number of variables and cases, and missing data codes

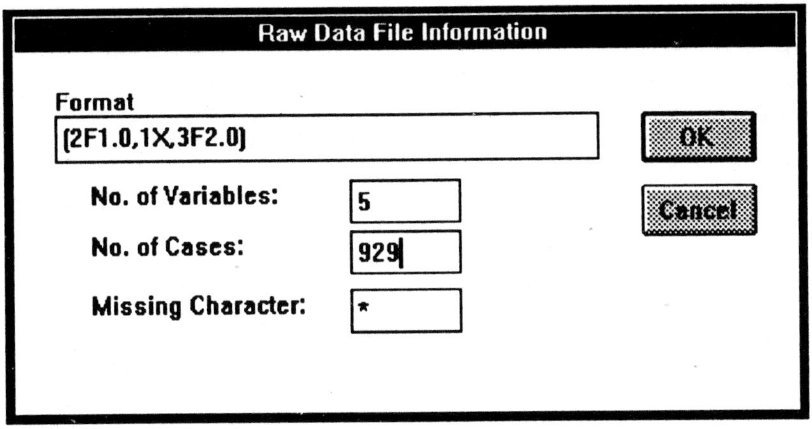

```
┌─────────────────────────────────────────────────────────────┐
│                  Raw Data File Information                    │
├─────────────────────────────────────────────────────────────┤
│  Format                                                       │
│  ┌────────────────────────────────────────┐    ┌──────────┐  │
│  │ (2F1.0,1X,3F2.0)                        │    │    OK    │  │
│  └────────────────────────────────────────┘    └──────────┘  │
│                                                               │
│      No. of Variables:    ┌──────────┐          ┌──────────┐  │
│                           │ 5        │          │  Cancel  │  │
│      No. of Cases:        ├──────────┤          └──────────┘  │
│                           │ 929      │                        │
│      Missing Character:   ├──────────┤                        │
│                           │ *        │                        │
│                           └──────────┘                        │
│                                                               │
└─────────────────────────────────────────────────────────────┘
```

FIGURE 12.3. RAW DATA FILE INFORMATION Dialog Box for SCAA Data

Defining an EQS Data System File

As noted at the beginning of this chapter, to activate any operation in EQS/Windows you must first open a data file. If this is a raw data file, EQS will prompt you for further information, after which the data are presented in a designated .ESS file. Throughout the process of working on this file, it remains as a system file. To give you an idea how this works, let's now go through the steps involved in retrieving a raw data file. The name of the file is **SCAA.DAT**. This data set contains numerical codes for two categorical variables (Grade, Sex) and scores for three continuous variables (GSC, ASC, AA); the number of subjects is 929.

Up to this point we would have done the following:

- double-clicked on the EQS icon
- clicked on **FILE** from the Main Window menu bar
- clicked on **OPEN** from the **FILE** menu
- used the key to move down the list of **FILE TYPES**
- clicked on **RAW DATA FILES (DAT)**
- double clicked **SCAA.DAT** from the list of raw data files
- clicked the **OK** button

Once you click on the **OK** button, you will be presented with a dialog box carrying the heading **RAW DATA FILE INFORMATION**. At this point, you merely provide the information requested. In Figure 12.3 you will see the completed information box based on the above data set. Note that, in

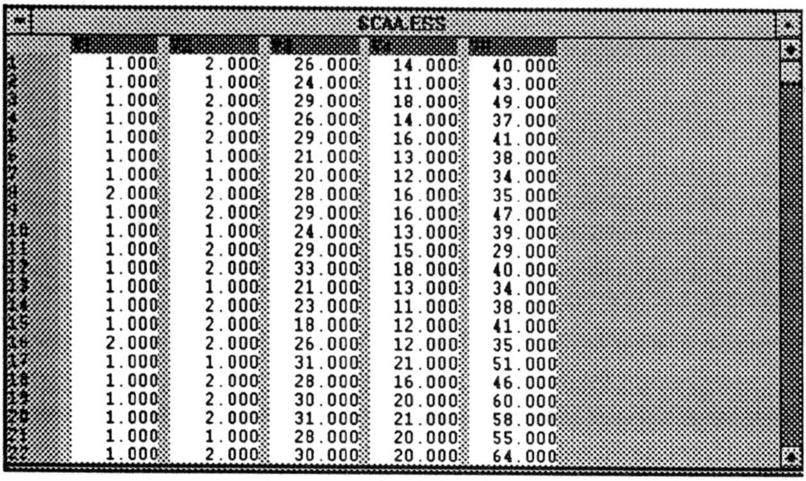

SCAA.ESS

1	1.000	2.000	26.000	14.000	40.000
2	1.000	1.000	24.000	11.000	43.000
3	1.000	2.000	29.000	18.000	49.000
4	1.000	2.000	26.000	14.000	37.000
5	1.000	2.000	29.000	16.000	41.000
6	1.000	1.000	21.000	13.000	38.000
7	1.000	1.000	20.000	12.000	34.000
8	2.000	2.000	28.000	16.000	35.000
9	1.000	2.000	29.000	16.000	47.000
10	1.000	1.000	24.000	13.000	39.000
11	1.000	2.000	29.000	15.000	29.000
12	1.000	2.000	33.000	18.000	40.000
13	1.000	1.000	21.000	13.000	34.000
14	1.000	2.000	23.000	11.000	38.000
15	1.000	2.000	18.000	12.000	41.000
16	2.000	2.000	26.000	12.000	35.000
17	1.000	1.000	31.000	21.000	51.000
18	1.000	2.000	28.000	16.000	46.000
19	1.000	2.000	30.000	20.000	60.000
20	1.000	2.000	31.000	21.000	58.000
21	1.000	1.000	28.000	20.000	55.000
22	1.000	2.000	30.000	20.000	64.000

FIGURE 12.4. DATA EDITOR Displaying Unlabeled SCAA Variables

contrast to the DOS version of EQS, the format statement for EQS/Windows does not require that quotation marks enclose the parenthesized statement. (For more details regarding format statements, see the *User's Guide*.)

After all information has been added to the dialog box, we click on the **OK** button (or press **ENTER**). Our **SCAA** data are now displayed in spreadsheet form on the **DATA EDITOR,** as shown in Figure 12.4. Note that the heading in the window is **SCAA.ESS**. This is because EQS now has all the information it needs on the raw data in order to create a workable system data file. In fact, this **.ESS** file is actually a copy of the raw data so that the original file remains intact.

Consistent with EQS notation, you will note that the variables are labeled as V1, V2, . . . V5. Typically, you would want to replace these labels with the actual variable names. To do this, simply click on **DATA** in the Main Window menu bar; from this menu, click on **INFORMATION,** and the dialog box shown in Figure 12.5 will appear. Following the directions as indicated, the double clicking of any variable will then move the V label to a separate box where you can replace it with the actual variable name. Once you have done this, you click on the **OK** button, and the variable will return to its former position. As you can see in Figure 12.5, only the first two variables have thus far been altered. Once all variable names have been replaced and you have clicked on the **OK** button, the data spread sheet will reappear, though with the new variable labels, as shown in Figure 12.6.

Before moving on to various analytic or plotting procedures, it's a good idea to first save the data system file so that the next time you open the data

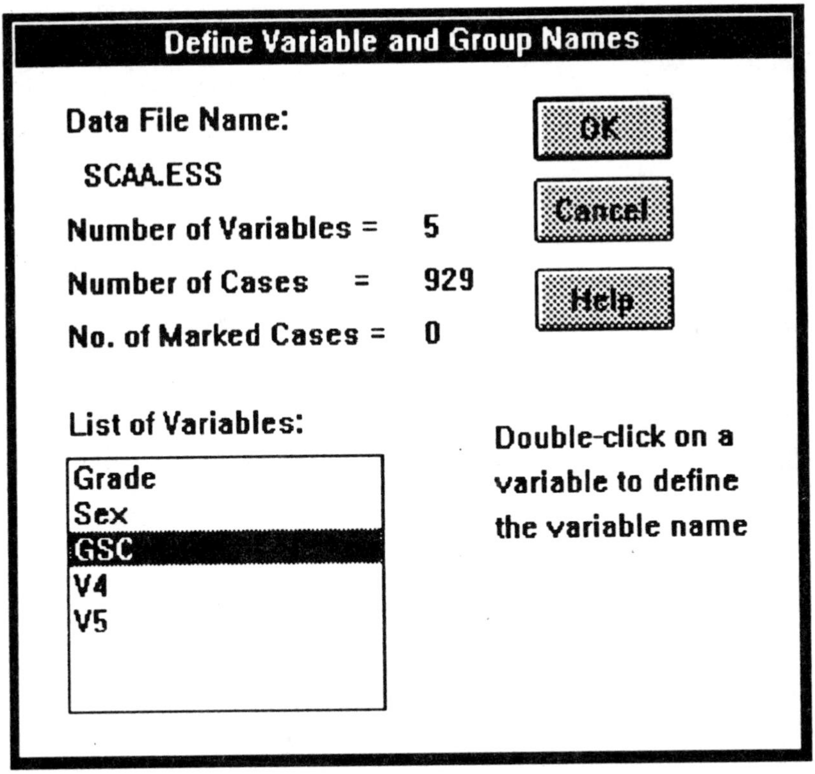

FIGURE 12.5. DATA INFORMATION Dialog Box for SCAA Data

file you will not need to reenter information such as I have just illustrated here because the **.ess** file will already exist. Thus, in lieu of opening the raw data file, you will open the system data file. To save the **.ESS** file, you click on **FILE** and then click on **SAVE AS** from its menu. This provides you with the **SAVE AS** dialog box as shown in Figure 12.7. You will note that the system file name appears in the upper left-hand corner. All you need to do now is to click on the **OK** button. You will subsequently be prompted with another dialog box asking if you wish to retain all cases and variables. Presuming that your answer is affirmative, you once again click on the **OK** button, at which point you will be returned to the data spread sheet.

It is important to reemphasize that in order to conduct any operations in EQS/Windows, you **must** have opened a data file. Thus, with the data editor activated, you would now go on to perform various data analytic or file-building procedures. If you wished to end your EQS session, however, you would click on **FILE** and then click on **Close**. At this point, you would be

1.000	2.000	26.000	14.000	40.000
1.000	1.000	24.000	11.000	43.000
1.000	2.000	29.000	18.000	49.000
1.000	2.000	26.000	14.000	37.000
1.000	2.000	29.000	16.000	41.000
1.000	1.000	21.000	13.000	38.000
1.000	1.000	20.000	12.000	34.000
2.000	2.000	28.000	16.000	35.000
1.000	2.000	29.000	16.000	47.000
1.000	1.000	24.000	13.000	39.000
1.000	2.000	29.000	15.000	29.000
1.000	2.000	33.000	18.000	40.000
1.000	1.000	21.000	13.000	34.000
1.000	2.000	23.000	11.000	38.000
1.000	2.000	18.000	12.000	41.000
2.000	2.000	26.000	12.000	35.000
1.000	1.000	31.000	21.000	51.000
1.000	2.000	28.000	16.000	46.000
1.000	2.000	30.000	20.000	60.000
1.000	2.000	31.000	21.000	58.000
1.000	1.000	28.000	20.000	55.000
1.000	2.000	30.000	20.000	64.000

FIGURE 12.6. DATA EDITOR Displaying Labeled SCAA Variables

returned to the **Main** and **OUTPUT.LOG** windows (see Figure 12.1). To exit from EQS/Windows, simply click on the small square in the upper left corner of the Main Window bar, and click on **CLOSE** from its menu.

Now that you have a general idea of how EQS/Windows functions, let's move on to Chapter 13, where we explore some of its plotting and data analytic capabilities.

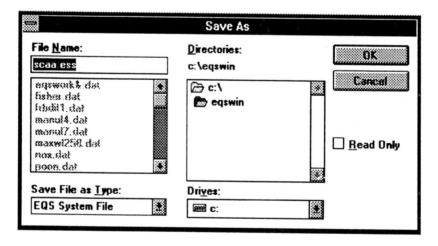

FIGURE 12.7. SAVE AS Dialog Box for SCAA Data

Notes

1. Version 4 is also available in DOS.

2. At the present time, a maximum of 20 categorical variables can be handled by EQS/Windows Version 4. This limit is expected to be increased in later versions of the program.

13

Application 10
Preliminary Data-Screening Analyses

ACTIVATING A PROGRAM FUNCTION

As emphasized in Chapter 12, before we can activate any program function in EQS/Windows, we must first open a data file. For our purposes here, we shall open the **SCAA.ESS** file that was formulated in the last chapter. Once it is opened, we can then proceed in activating any of several available EQS functions as listed on the menu or icon bars of the Main Window (see Figure 12.1). To select a particular function, simply click on the related menu item or icon. Let's begin by working through a few of the plotting functions.

PLOTTING DATA

Each plotting function is represented by one of the 11 icons shown in Figure 13.1. Plot selection is made by clicking on the appropriate icon. The last icon serves only as an identifying one and has no functional meaning.

FIGURE 13.1. Plot Function Icons

The function represented by each of these icons, from left to right, is as follows:[1]

- Line Plot
- Histogram
- Pie Chart
- Cumulative Histogram
- Quantile Plot
- Quantile-Quantile Plot
- Normal Probability Plot
- Scatter Plot (including Matrix Plot)
- 3D Spin Plot
- Box Plot
- Missing Data Plot (with Imputation Functions)

We turn now to examples of plotting functions as they pertain first to categorical variables and then to continuous variables.

Categorical Data

Although a study's major focus may be on scores derived from continuous variables, researchers are often interested in obtaining frequency counts related to the number of subjects falling into a particular category: demographic variables such as gender, income level, and educational level are typical examples of such categories. The histogram (or bar chart) is the plotting tool used to graphically display this type of information. Let's see how it works with our **SCAA.ESS** data.

With the pointer on the second icon, simply click, and the the **HISTO-GRAM** dialog box shown in Figure 13.2 will appear. In this example, we are going to request a histogram related to one variable only—Grade. We do so by placing the pointer on **GRADE** and then clicking, which results in the program's highlighting of the selected variable, as shown in Figure 13.2. The duplicate variable list adjacent to the first one is used only when the data are to be displayed by group; because we have not chosen this option here, the lettering is purposely faded.

Clicking on the **PLOT** button will initiate the histogram portrayed in Figure 13.3; each vertical bar represents one grade, where 1 = Grade 9, 2 = Grade 10, 3 = Grade 11, and 4 = Grade 12. At the side of the histogram window you will note three small boxes, each displaying a symbol. These features allow you to customize your plot. The symbol on top represents the **Setup Tool,** which you can use to alter both the type of plot frame and the

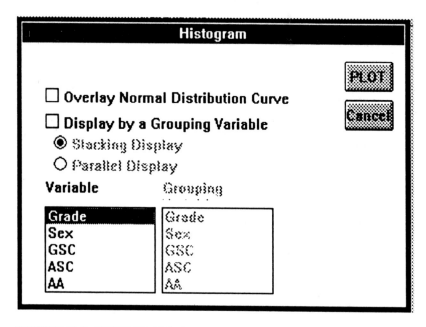

FIGURE 13.2. HISTOGRAM Dialog Box

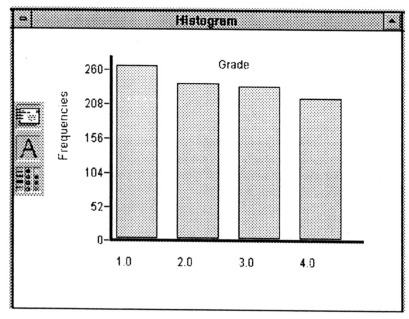

FIGURE 13.3. Histogram Based on Grade

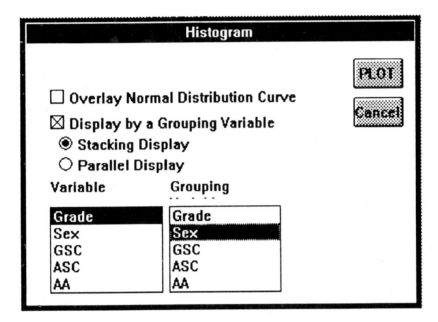

FIGURE 13.4. HISTOGRAM Dialog Box Indicating Grouping by Sex

background color. The middle symbol (A) is the **Text Tool**; it enables you to alter or add text to the plot window. Finally, the lower symbol represents the **Color Tool**, which permits you to modify either the color or the type of plot symbols used; the latter tool applies only to scattergrams. Each of these tools is activated by clicking on the appropriate symbol.

Let's go back now and look again at the variable of Grade, but this time as it pertains to males and females. The grouping variable of Sex is invoked by first clicking on **DISPLAY BY GROUPING VARIABLE** in the **HISTOGRAM** dialog box, which is shown in Figure 13.4. This time you will note that both variable lists are of the same light intensity; we click on both **GRADE** and **SEX** in the appropriate column.

This histogram, grouped by Sex, is shown in Figure 13.5. The one printed at the top represents the stacked display, the default option; the bottom one represents the parallel display. In both graphs, males are represented by the light-colored bars.

The pie chart is another way of graphically displaying categorical data. To obtain this graph, click on the third icon. In contrast to the histogram, the pie graph indicates the proportion represented by each category. For the variable Grade, the pie chart is presented in Figure 13.6.

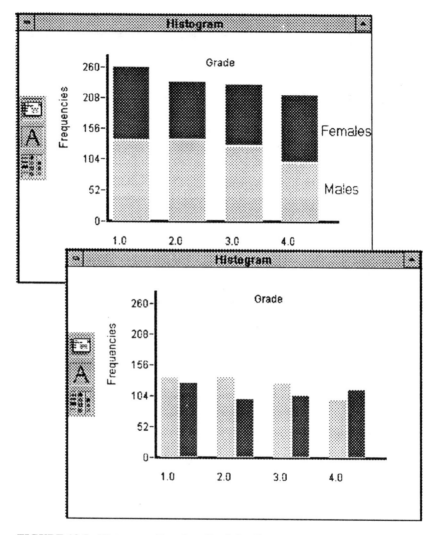

FIGURE 13.5. Histograms Based on Grade by Sex

Continuous Data

EQS offers a number of different plots for evaluating continuous data. To complete our review of histograms and pie charts, however, let's begin by examining these first. When the histogram and pie chart are based on continuous data, you are presented with display options. The first allows you to group the scores such that meaningful interpretation is maximized. If, on

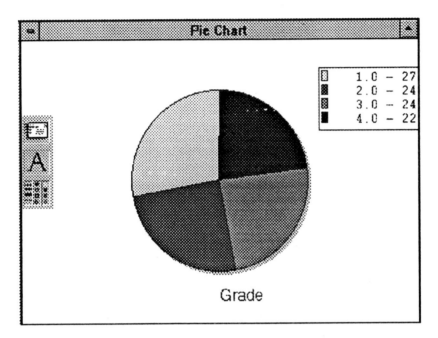

FIGURE 13.6. Pie Chart Based on Grade

the other hand, you just want to take a quick look at the distribution of a variable, the second option fulfills this need. Given that the sample size is greater than 15, and given that there are more than 15 unique scores, the program will automatically divide the range into 15 equal intervals and will count and display the frequency for each. This same automatic grouping mechanism operates for the pie chart as well. One additional option available for the histogram is that it be displayed with the normal curve superimposed. Portrayed in Figures 13.7 and 13.8, respectively, is a histogram with normal curve overlay and a pie chart based on the continuous variable of ASC.

Another useful graphing mechanism for continuous data is the normal probability plot; its symbol appears in the seventh icon. In this plot, the distribution of the observed variable (represented along the x axis) is compared against the expected normal distribution (represented along the y axis). The y axis is derived by first ranking the observed variables in ascending order and then computing the expected normal value from the rank of each observed variable. If the data are normally distributed, the normal probability plot should approximate a straight line that follows a 45-degree angle.

A normal probability plot based on the ASC variable is displayed in Figure 13.9. Although the data are fairly close to representing a normal distri-

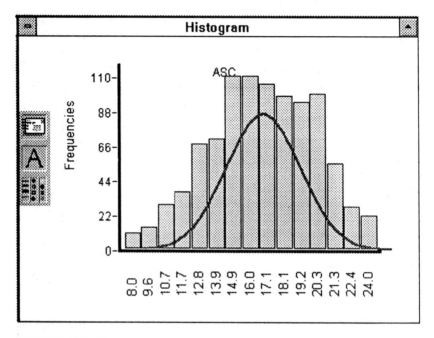

FIGURE 13.7. Histogram Based on ASC

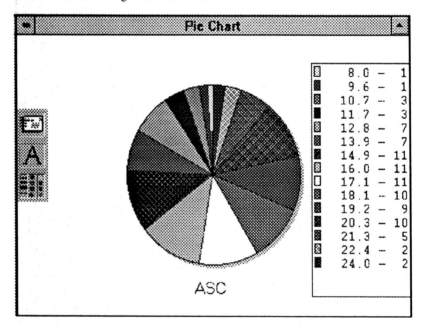

FIGURE 13.8. Pie Chart Based on ASC

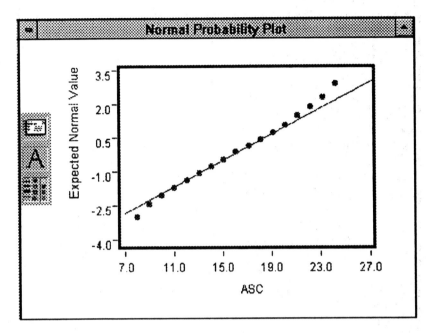

FIGURE 13.9. Normal Probability Plot Based on ASC

bution, there is some evidence of nonnormality at the low- and high-scoring ends.

In Figure 13.10, we have an example of a box plot, which is invoked by clicking the tenth icon. This type of plot, sometimes called the **box-and-whisker plot,** is useful for examining the distribution of the data and for detecting outliers. The lines emanating out from the rectangle are the "whiskers," and the rectangle itself is the "box." The box contains scores falling between the 25th percentile (or 1st quartile) and 75th percentile (or 3rd quartile). In other words, it represents 50% of scores falling at the median plus and minus one semi-interquartile range. The dotted line within the box represents the median and the dashed line the mean. From the plot in Figure 13.10, we see that the middle 50% of ASC scores fall between approximately 16 and 20, with a median value of approximately 17.5.

The bottom whisker begins at the lowest score point and extends to the 25th percentile; the upper whisker begins at the 75th percentile and extends to the highest score point. In other words, they represent the lowest and highest 25% of scores, respectively. Dots appearing on either side of the whiskers represent outliers. In Figure 13.10, then, we see that the lowest and highest ASC scores are approximately 8.5 and 24.5, respectively. From this plot we can see that there is a slightly greater spread of scores at the low end

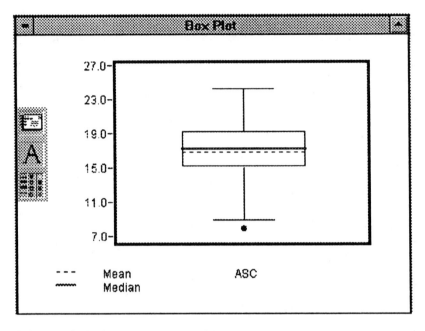

FIGURE 13.10. Box Plot Based on ASC

of the scale than at the high end, indicating a minor negative skew to the data. These findings are consistent with the normal probability scatter plot presented in Figure 13.9. Finally, the box plot indicates that there is one outlier case with a score of approximately 8.0.

Now let's see what EQS can do with scatter plots. Such graphs are used to plot the joint distribution of two continuous variables. In addition to displaying a visual representation of the bivariate relation, this is an excellent mechanism for detecting outliers in the data. For one example, let's look at the regression of AA on ASC. To initiate this plot, you first click on the scatter plot icon (#8), which subsequently produces the dialog box shown in Figure 13.11. Clicking on **ASC** for the y axis and **AA** for the x axis results in the scatter plot shown in Figure 13.12.

Within this plot frame you will notice three lines. The middle one represents the bivariate regression line, and the other two enclose the related 95% confidence intervals. Displayed in the lower left corner of the window is the regression equation and its R^2 value. As noted above, this scatter plot also makes it easy to detect outliers, a task to which we return later in this chapter.

To conclude our look at EQS scatter plots here,[2] we turn to the extremely effective matrix plot. By selecting more than one variable on the y axis (e.g.,

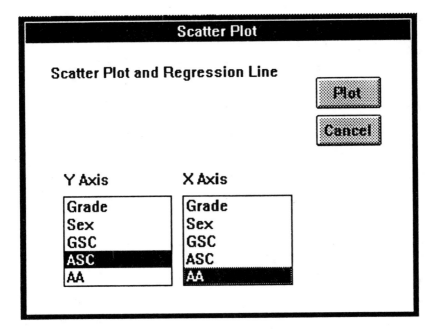

FIGURE 13.11. Dialog Box for Scatter Plot

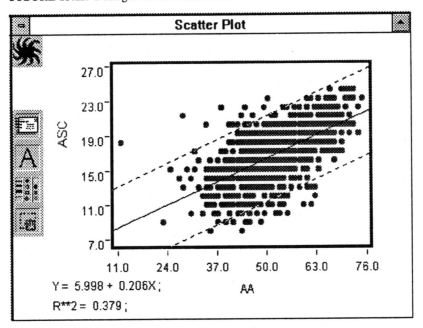

FIGURE 13.12. Scatter Plot Based on ASC with AA

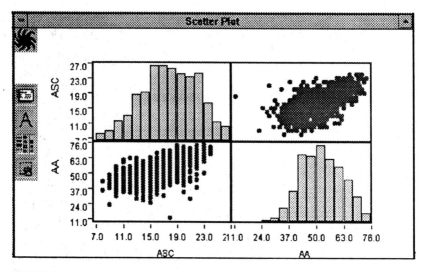

FIGURE 13.13. Matrix of Scatter Plots for ASC and AA

ASC, AA) and the same variables on the *x* axis, we produce the matrix plot in Figure 13.13. When the same variable is plotted against itself, EQS pro-

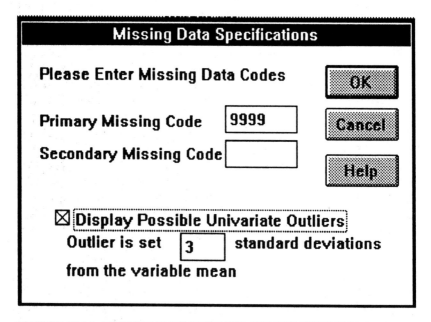

FIGURE 13.14. MISSING DATA/OUTLIER SPECIFICATION Dialog Box

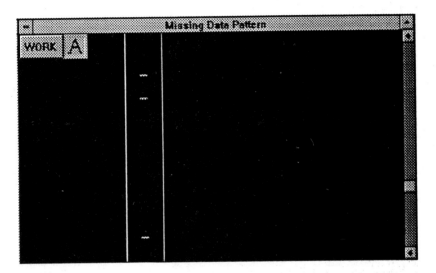

FIGURE 13.15. Pattern of Outliers for SCAA Data

duces this plot as a histogram rather than as a straight line. (Recall the automatic grouping of continuous variables noted above.)

DETECTING OUTLIERS AND MISSING DATA

Of course, no preliminary analysis should be considered complete without first checking for the presence of outliers and missing data. Indeed, EQS is unique in both the amount and type of information that it can provide you in this regard. However, because the SCAA data set has no missing data, here we examine information bearing on the detection of outliers only.[3] To initiate information related to either missing data or outliers, you click on the "Missing" icon (#11); the related dialog box, as shown at left in Figure 13.14, will then appear.

Because our focus in this example is to detect outliers, we click on the **DISPLAY OUTLIER** box. By default, cases for each variable having scores greater than three standard deviations from the mean are selected.[4] Clicking on the **OK** button will produce a pattern of the outlying cases; a small segment of the one based on the SCAA data is shown in Figure 13.15.

On a color screen, EQS produces this pattern with missing data shown in yellow, and outliers shown in green; the above figure reflects three outliers. An outstanding feature of the EQS/Windows program is that it enables you to obtain more precise information by simply clicking on a particular outlier marking. Doing so for the SCAA data resulted in Figure 13.16, which

EQS/Windows
Variable AA , Case 732,
value= 23.000
OK

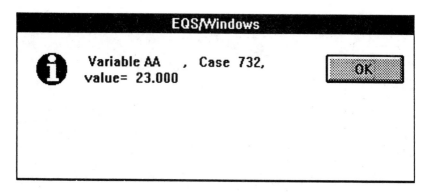

FIGURE 13.16. Score Information From Outlier Plot

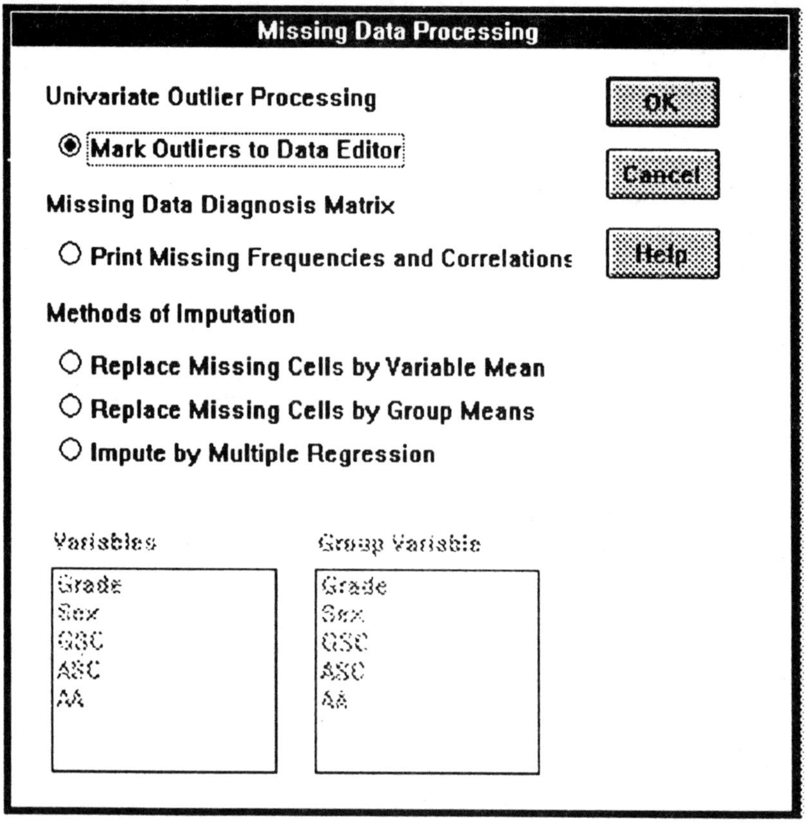

Missing Data Processing
Univariate Outlier Processing
Mark Outliers to Data Editor
Missing Data Diagnosis Matrix
Print Missing Frequencies and Correlations
Methods of Imputation
Replace Missing Cells by Variable Mean
Replace Missing Cells by Group Means
Impute by Multiple Regression
Variables
Group Variable
Grade
Sex
GSC
ASC
AA
Grade
Sex
GSC
ASC
AA
OK
Cancel
Help

FIGURE 13.17. MISSING DATA/OUTLIER PROCESSING Dialog Box

725	3.000	2.000	20.000	15.000	37.000
726	3.000	2.000	22.000	13.000	44.000
727	3.000	2.000	29.000	19.000	48.000
728	3.000	1.000	30.000	20.000	59.000
729	3.000	2.000	30.000	14.000	51.000
730	2.000	1.000	25.000	18.000	54.000
731	3.000	1.000	33.000	17.000	44.000
732					
733	3.000	1.000	30.000	20.000	67.000
734	3.000	2.000	26.000	14.000	49.000
735	3.000	1.000	23.000	15.000	38.000
736	3.000	2.000	30.000	17.000	49.000
737	3.000	1.000	25.000	17.000	62.000
738	4.000	1.000	17.000	16.000	45.000
739	3.000	1.000	22.000	17.000	56.000
740	3.000	2.000	25.000	14.000	51.000
741	3.000	2.000	20.000	13.000	40.000
742	3.000	1.000	31.000	18.000	65.000
743	3.000	1.000	25.000	17.000	51.000
744	3.000	1.000	29.000	17.000	52.000
745	3.000	2.000	24.000	16.000	49.000
746	3.000	1.000	23.000	15.000	52.000

FIGURE 13.18. Data Editor With Case 732 Highlighted

identifies Case 732 as having a score value of 23.00 on the AA variable. A check with the descriptive statistics for this variable (shown later in Table 13.1) reveals this score to exceed 3 standard deviations below the mean.

Returning again to Figure 13.15, we see a **WORK** button in the upper left-hand corner of the window. Clicking on this box initiates the dialog box shown at left in Figure 13.17. This box provides you with a number of options for isolating outliers and resolving the presence of missing data.

Limiting my review to outlier processing, I'll focus here on the first option only: that outliers will be marked in the data editor. More specifically, when you select this option and then click on the **OK** button, the data editor reappears with all outliers highlighted, as shown in Figure 13.18.

In addition to the above important features, EQS/Windows is unique in both its display and its identification of outliers and in permitting you to temporarily dispose of a particular outlier without first altering the data set. The temporary removal of an outlier is accomplished by using the art of "brushing." This technique allows you to first "capture" a specific data point by surrounding it with a rectangle defined by a broken line; this rectangle is termed a **brush**. You can then drag this rectangle to some other point within the window. To see how these features work, please turn back to Figure 13.12, where the scatter plot based on SCAA data is displayed. Note first of all the data point shown in the upper left part of the window. For illustration purposes here, we'll let this point serve as our target outlier.

Information related to this case is easily obtained simply by clicking anywhere on the data point. EQS then identifies the case number along with

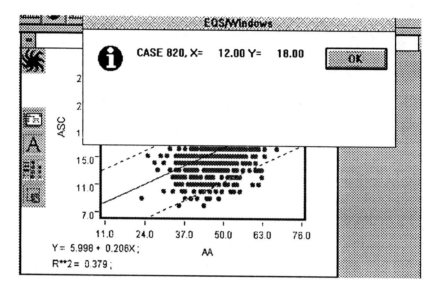

FIGURE 13.19. Information on Scatter Plot Outlier

scores on both the dependent and independent variables, as illustrated here in Figure 13.19.

We now wish to delete this outlier; to do so, the data point must first be "brushed," as shown in Figure 13.20. This was done by clicking on the upper left side of the data point and then dragging diagonally across the point to form a rectangle around it. On a color screen, this marked point would now be yellow, rather than red as are the other data points. To dispose of this outlier, we now drag the entire rectangle and deposit it in the **black hole,** which is the symbol in the upper left corner of the screen somewhat resembling a tarantula. To make this deposit, simply release the mouse button. By turning to Figure 13.21, you will see that once the outlier is deposited, the black hole reflects the presence of "captured" undesirables by exhibiting a dot in its center; this dot will be yellow on a color screen. Once an outlier is deposited in the black hole, the regression equation, R^2, and 95% confidence intervals are automatically recomputed. By comparing these values in Figures 13.20 and 13.21, you will see that the R^2, for example, increased from 0.379 to 0.389. You can repeatedly put more than one data point in the black hole and then assess the change in regression statistics. To recover deposited data points, simply double click on the black hole.

Because you may want to exclude these identified outliers from future analyses, you may want to mark these cases in the data editor. This can easily be done by activating the **Moving Tool,** which is the bottom icon resembling

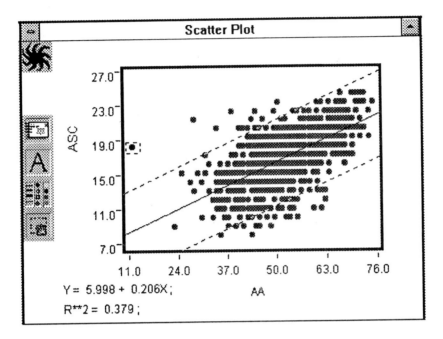

FIGURE 13.20. Scatter Plot With Outlier Brushed

a hand to the left of the window. Because the black hole is the link between the scatter plot and the data editor, there must be outliers in the black hole before the moving tool can be invoked. This is done by clicking on the icon, which will produce the dialog box shown in Figure 13.22. As you can see, you can either **APPEND** or **REPLACE** all marked cases. An important point here is that, for each scatter plot, the **REPLACE** option must be used the first time you mark cases to the data editor; this option clears the memory that stores the case information.

CONDUCTING BASIC STATISTICAL ANALYSES

Let's turn now to a few basic statistical procedures that are always helpful in the initial previewing of data. Although EQS/Windows can provide information related to basic descriptive statistics, frequency counts, t tests, cross-tabulations, one- and two-way analyses of variance, correlation/covariance matrices, regression, and exploratory factor analysis, only examples of the first two procedures are provided here. Each of these tools is available to you via the **ANALYSIS** box displayed in the EQS Main Window menu bar.

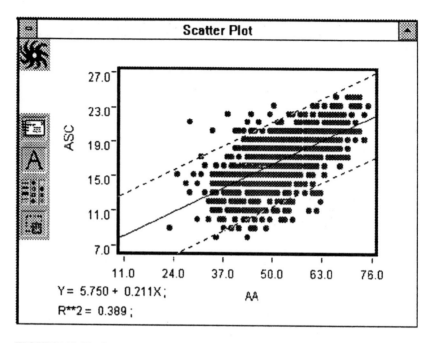

FIGURE 13.21. Scatter Plot With Outlier in the Black Hole

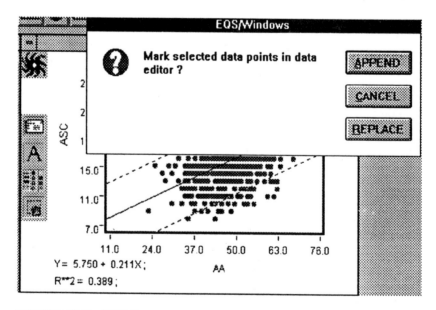

FIGURE 13.22. MARK DATA EDITOR Dialog Box

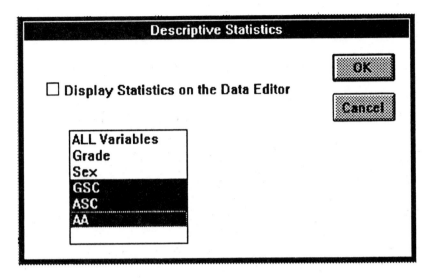

FIGURE 13.23. DESCRIPTIVE STATISTICS Dialog Box

Descriptive Statistics

To initiate any statistical procedure, click on the **ANALYSIS** box; **DE-SCRIPTIVE STATISTICS** is selected by clicking on the appropriate bar. These actions will yield the **DESCRIPTIVE STATISTICS** dialog box displayed in Figure 13.23. As indicated by the highlighted bars in this figure, I have chosen to have information related to only three variables: GSC, ASC, and AA (default is **ALL VARIABLES**). Once you have selected the variables of interest and clicked the **OK** button, you will get a message advising you that the descriptive statistics are done. The information provided from this analysis is presented in Table 13.1.

TABLE 13.1. Selected EQS Output: Descriptive Statistics for GSC, ASC, AA

Regroup Cumulative Histogram on variable ASC

ID	Code	Low Range	High Range	Counts
1	8.0	7.00	9.07	10
2	9.6	9.07	10.13	14
3	10.7	10.13	11.20	28
4	11.7	11.20	12.27	36
5	12.8	12.27	13.33	66
6	13.9	13.33	14.40	69
7	14.9	14.40	15.47	108
8	16.0	15.47	16.53	108
9	17.1	16.53	17.60	103
10	18.1	17.60	18.67	96

(Continued)

TABLE 13.1. (Continued)

11	19.2	18.67	19.73	92
12	20.3	19.73	20.80	97
13	21.3	20.80	21.87	54
14	22.4	21.87	22.93	27
15	24.0	22.93	25.00	21

DESCRIPTIVE STATISTICS

3 Variables are selected from file C:\EQSWIN\SCAA.ESS

Number of cases in data file are   929
Number of cases used in this analysis are ..   929

Variable ID	NAME	MEAN	SUM	SUM of SQUARE	Standard Deviation
3	GSC	25.938	24096.000	641246.000	4.185
4	ASC	16.709	15523.000	268483.000	3.132
5	AA	51.885	48201.000	2581787.000	9.336

ID	Median	One Quartile	Three Quartile	Minimum	Maximum	Range
3	26.000	24.000	29.000	10.000	33.000	23.000
4	17.000	15.000	19.000	8.000	24.000	16.000
5	52.000	45.000	59.000	12.000	74.000	62.000

ID	SKEWNESS	KURTOSIS
3	-0.709	0.308
4	-0.159	-0.477
5	-0.146	-0.230

Frequency Counts

Frequency distributions on variables can be summarized and displayed in table form. To obtain this information, again click on **ANALYSIS** in the Main Window and then select **FREQUENCY** from the menu. Once again, I have elected to obtain frequency information related to three rather than all variables, as indicated in the FREQUENCY TABLE dialog box shown in Figure 13.24. Clicking on the box above the VARIABLE menu would cause the descriptive statistics shown in Table 13.1 to be also included in this output. The frequency table related only to ASC is printed in Table 13.2.

Notes

1. Readers are referred to the *User's Guide* for a full description of each plotting function.

2. Although other scatter plots are available, space limitations preclude their presentation here.

3. Nonetheless, readers are urged to study carefully all options related to the presence of missing data.

4. The user has the option to change these default values.

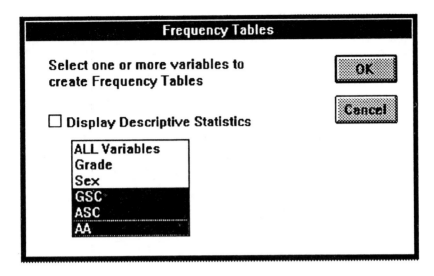

FIGURE 13.24. FREQUENCY TABLES Dialog Box

TABLE 13.2. Selected EQS Output: Frequency Distribution for ASC

FREQUENCY TABLES

3 Variables are selected from file C:\EQSWIN\SCAA.ESS

Number of cases in data file are   929

```
* * * * * * * * * * * * * *
*        ASC    *
* * * * * * * * * * * * * *
```

CATEGORY		P E R C E N T	
VALUE	COUNT	CELL	CUMULATIVE
8.00	2	0.22	0.22
9.00	8	0.86	1.08
10.00	14	1.51	2.58
11.00	28	3.01	5.60
12.00	36	3.88	9.47
13.00	66	7.10	16.58
14.00	69	7.43	24.00
15.00	108	11.63	35.63
16.00	108	11.63	47.26
17.00	103	11.09	58.34
18.00	96	10.33	68.68
19.00	92	9.90	78.58
20.00	97	10.44	89.02
21.00	54	5.81	94.83
22.00	27	2.91	97.74
23.00	16	1.72	99.46
24.00	5	0.54	100.00
TOTAL COUNT	929	TOTAL PERCENT	100.00

14

Application 11
Building an EQS Model File—Instantly!

N ow that we have worked our way through several different EQS applications, let's see how the extremely innovative **BUILD EQS** feature of EQS/
Windows enables us to create a model file in a just matter of minutes. In this
final chapter I not only walk you through the interactive process but also
introduce you to three additional program options that are truly unique in the
world of SEM computing! All three features provide for extensions to the
LM Test. The **BLOCK** option allows you to eliminate backward paths from
the LM Test, and the **LAG** option, to define the time lag involved; the **RE-
TEST** option causes model modifications suggested in the previous run (as
per the LM Test) to be automatically included in the new model file created
by **RETEST**. Details related to each of these features are provided later in
the chapter.

THE HYPOTHESIZED MODEL

The model under study was formulated for the purpose of testing hypotheses bearing on the issue of causal predominance between general self-concept,
academic self-concept, and academic achievement. It is a longitudinal model
involving the measurement of these constructs at two points in time (October,
May) during the same academic year for high school adolescents. The example presented here, however, represents only a portion of the original study
(Byrne, 1986).[1] A schematic portrayal of the hypothesized model is shown
in Figure 14.1.

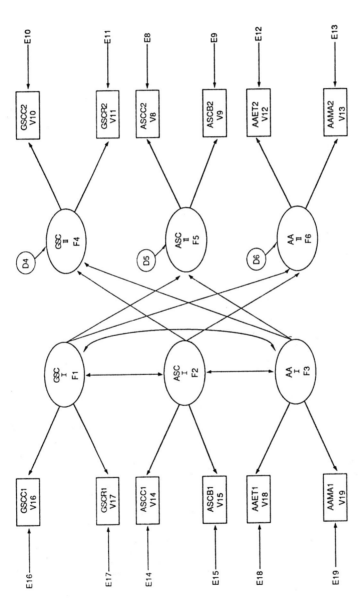

TIME 1   TIME 2

FIGURE 14.1. Hypothesized Model for Testing Causal Predominance among General Self-Concept, Academic Self-Concept, and Academic Achievement

Source: Adapted from Byrne (1986). Copyright 1986. Canadian Psychological Association. Reprinted by permission.

As can be seen in Figure 14.1, each latent construct is measured by the same two observed variables at each of two time points. In broad terms, the hypotheses of this study addressed the issue of whether self-concept "causes" academic achievement, or whether the process operates in reverse, such that academic achievement "causes" self-concept. For our purposes here, only one of the original four hypotheses is tested: that academic achievement is causally predominant over academic self-concept.

BUILDING THE EQS INPUT FILE

As emphasized and demonstrated in Chapters 12 and 13, the first step in using any EQS/Windows function is to open a data file. In this case I have brought a file called **NOX.ESS** to the data editor, so now we are ready to build an EQS input file.

TITLE/SPECIFICATION

To begin the process, we click on the **BUILD EQS** selection in the Main Window menu bar. By so doing, you are presented with a drop-down menu offering several selections. However, whenever you are initiating the building of a new file, you will always want to click on the first one, which is **TITLE/SPECIFICATION**. This action will generate the dialog box shown in Figure 14.2.

As you will note in the figure, I have inserted the title **SC/AA Causal Predominance**. The next question to be answered is whether you wish to invoke the **EASY BUILD** feature. Because I want to show you how this automatic file-building option works, we'll leave the button designated as **YES,** which is default. Alternatively, if we clicked on **NO,** we would then proceed in building an EQS file as previously demonstrated in Chapters 3 through 11. Selection of the **EASY BUILD** facility means that we will now be presented with a series of questions; our responses will serve to build the hypothesized model in the form of an .EQS file that is used as input to the computational part of the EQS program. So now let's move on by clicking the **OK** button, which then triggers the **SPECIFICATIONS** dialog box appearing in Figure 14.3.

In reviewing this window, you will see very quickly that it contains all information needed in the **/SPECIFICATIONS** paragraph of an EQS file. By default, most of this information has already been provided. From the **NOX.ESS** file, the program has automatically specified that there are 19 variables and 929 cases. Although only 12 of these variables will actually be

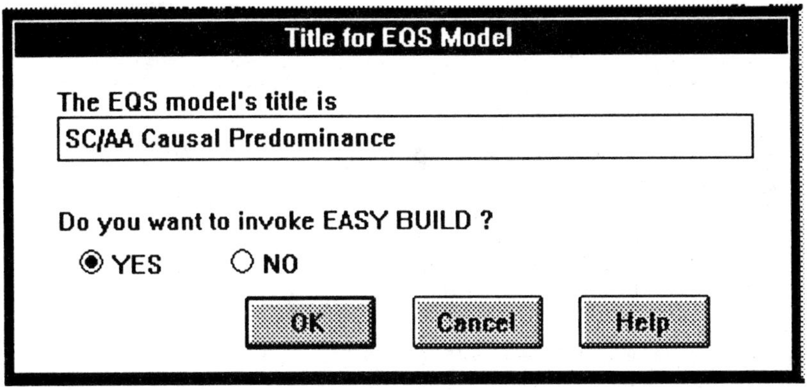

FIGURE 14.2. BUILD EQS Title Dialog Box

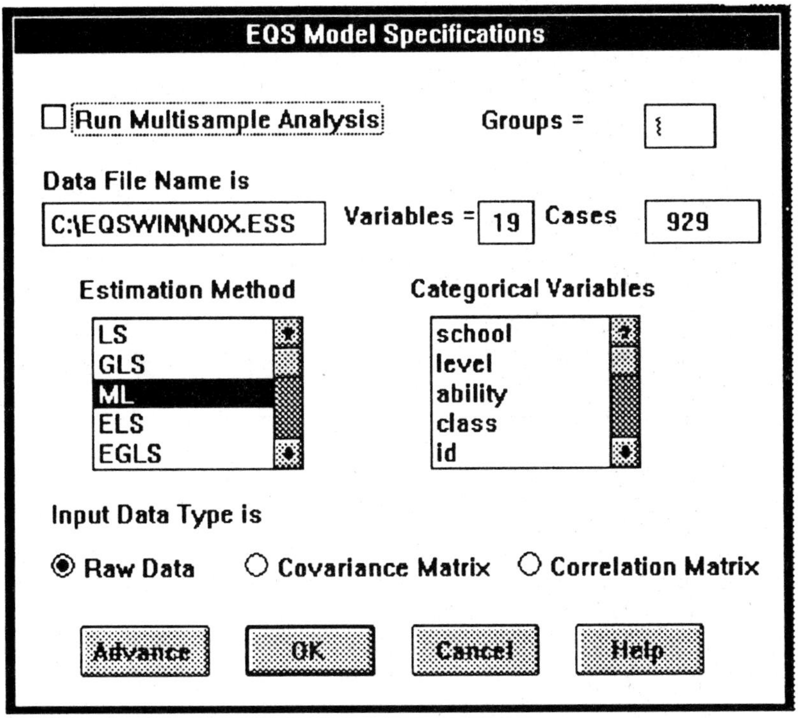

FIGURE 14.3. BUILD MODEL SPECIFICATIONS Dialog Box

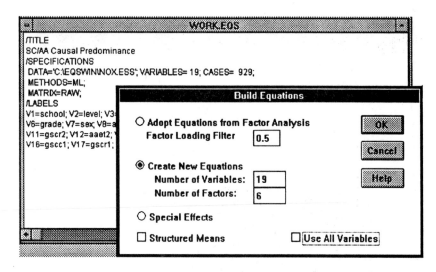

FIGURE 14.4. Partial Work File and **BUILD EQUATIONS** Dialog Box (1)

used in building the hypothesized model, as is customary, this information is provided to the program in the **/EQUATIONS** paragraph. Note additionally that the **BUILD EQS** function has presumed that analyses will be based on **raw data** for **one group** using **maximum likelihood** estimation procedures. Of course, the user is free to change these default options as he or she wishes. Finally, I would like to draw your attention to the column of variable names under the heading **CATEGORICAL VARIABLES**. If you wished to have the program treat particular variables as categorical, you would indicate it by clicking on the related bars; analyses would then be based on the appropriate polychoric and/or polyserial correlations. Because all information is correct for our needs here, we again click on **OK,** which will generate the **BUILD EQUATIONS** dialog box shown in Figure 14.4.

Building Equations

Partially shown in Figure 14.4, behind the dialog box, is the **NOX.ESS** file, which EQS uses in building the input file. As you can readily ascertain, all information derived from both the **NOX.ESS** file and the **TITLE/SPECIFICATIONS** dialog box is thus far included in this model file. A review of Figure 14.1 will assure you that in creating our **/EQUATIONS** paragraph, we are using 12 (of 19) variables to measure six factors. Relatedly, note that the box in the bottom right corner has been left blank because we are **not** using all variables. As you will see, other options are also available, although

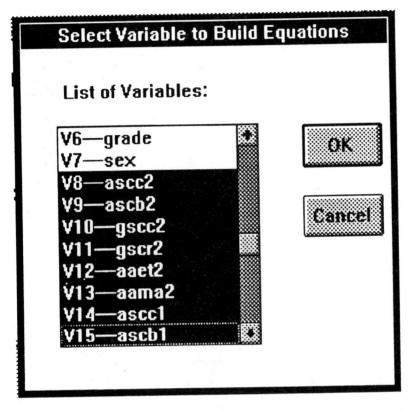

FIGURE 14.5. BUILD VARIABLE SELECTION Dialog Box

they are not pertinent to our analyses at this time. We therefore click on the **OK** button, after which we are presented with the dialog box shown in Figure 14.5.

This **SELECT VARIABLE** dialog box follows from our previous denotation that only some of the 19 variables will be used in building the model. We now need to specify which variables are to be included in the analysis. Selection is made by simply clicking on the appropriate variables; these will be highlighted automatically as shown in Figure 14.5. Once this task is completed, we again click on the **OK** button; the **CREATE NEW EQUATIONS** dialog box will then appear as shown in Figure 14.6.

This dialog box has a table-like entry field with the number of variables (Vs) and factors (Fs) used in both rows and columns. The row variables represent those that are dependent in the model, and the column variables represent those that are independent. Because each row corresponds to a depen-

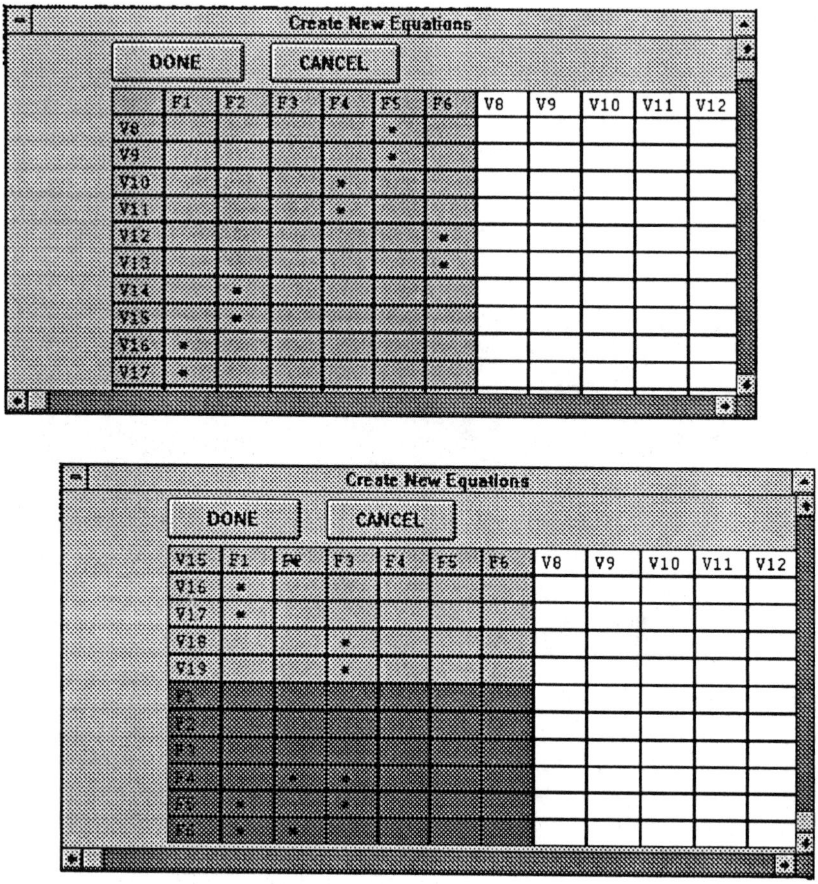

FIGURE 14.6. BUILD EQUATIONS Dialog Box (2)

dent variable in the path diagram (i.e., has one or more arrows pointing at it), each represents a possible equation in the model; likewise, each column represents one possible predictor of that variable. Note that Variables 1 through 7 (School through Sex; see Figure 14.4) are not included in the dialog box because they are not of interest in building the hypothesized model.

Before proceeding with our /EQUATIONS paragraph, it is important to point out that the dialog box intentionally omits residual independent variables; these are created automatically by the program when the actual equations are formulated. As a consequence, there are no E or D variables listed in the columns.

Now, with Figure 14.1 handy for easy reference, let's move on to create our equations. This task is accomplished by simply clicking each cell that is to be a free parameter in the model; as you click, an asterisk (*) will automatically appear in the target cell;[2] unmarked factor loadings will be fixed to zero by the program. In reviewing the placement of asterisks in the dialog box (shown in two sections in Figure 14.6), you will see that it corresponds to the hypothesized model portrayed in Figure 14.1. The pattern of asterisks appearing on the lighter grey portion of the box represents the factor loadings for V8 through V19; asterisks shown against the darker grey background represent construct equations that describe the impact of general self-concept, academic self-concept, and academic achievement at Time 1 (F1, F2, F3, respectively) on the same three variables at Time 2 (F3, F4, F5, respectively). In practice, of course, you would not see the **EQUATIONS** dialog box split into two as displayed here; rather, you would be presented with only the initial portion of the box, as shown in the upper section of Figure 14.6. The remaining V and F variables could then be brought up on screen by pressing on the down arrow (↓) at the bottom of the far right border.

Before we move on to the next task, it is perhaps worth noting that should you make a mistake when inserting the asterisks, it is easily corrected by simply reclicking on the same cell; this action will delete the asterisk. Because our equations are now complete, we can now click on the **DONE** button. The **CREATE VARIANCES/COVARIANCES** dialog box will then appear as shown in Figure 14.7.

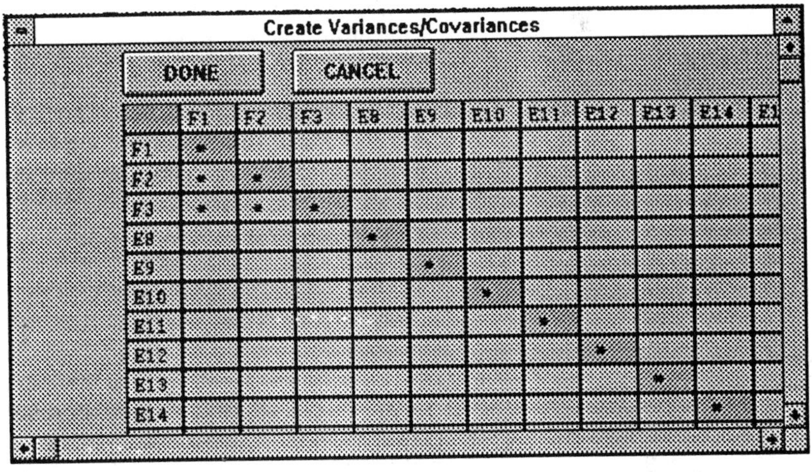

FIGURE 14.7. **BUILD VARIANCES/COVARIANCES** Dialog Box

Building Variances/Covariances

When this dialog box first appeared, the diagonal cells for all independent factors (F1-F3) as well as those for the implied residual variables (E8-E19; D4-D6) were marked with an asterisk, indicating that they were to be free parameters in the model; these cells, of course, represented their variances. However, it will be clear to you that these specifications will need to be altered because, as indicated in Figure 14.1, the independent factors at Time 1 (F1, F2, F3) are intercorrelated; these covariances therefore needed to be added to the dialog box. Finally, you may be wondering why I left the asterisks for Factors 1, 2, and 3 unchanged when both factor loadings for each were also specified as free (see Figure 14.6). (Recall that for purposes of identification, either one in a congeneric set of factor loadings is fixed to 1.0 or the variance of the factor is fixed to 1.0, but not both.) As indicated in Figure 14.1, I intend to fix the first of each pair of factor loadings to 1.0. This can be accomplished by editing the file before running the analyses.[3] Now that specifications related to the variances and covariances are complete, we press the **DONE** button.

Building in the LM Test

As we have witnessed from the assessment of previous models studied in this book, the LM Test is critical to the pinpointing of misfit in misspecified models. Thus we want to include the **/LMTEST** paragraph here as well. Additionally, because our model is of a longitudinal nature, it behooves us to also build in specifications that (a) prevent the designation of malfitting parameters resulting from backward paths and (b) target malfitting parameters within and across specific time points. Both of these options are specified within the **/LMTEST** paragraph.

Because the LM Test is itself optional, its related dialog box does not appear automatically after you have completed specifications regarding model variances and covariances. To initiate the **LMTEST** dialog box, you must click on **BUILD EQS** from the Main Window and then, from the drop-down window, click on **LMTEST**. The related box is shown in Figure 14.8.

When this dialog box first appeared, several options were available. For purposes of the present application, I have selected only the **PEE** option, which, as you will recall, relates to correlations among the Es.[4] Because we wish to incorporate the **BUILD BLOCK AND LAG** feature indicated in the lower right portion of the dialog box, we click on that option and then click on **OK**. The dialog box shown in Figure 14.9 will thus appear next.

Because longitudinal models typically comprise variables that can be ordered in time, only paths leading from Time 1 to Time 2 are appropriate; backward paths from Time 2 to Time 1 cannot be permitted because they

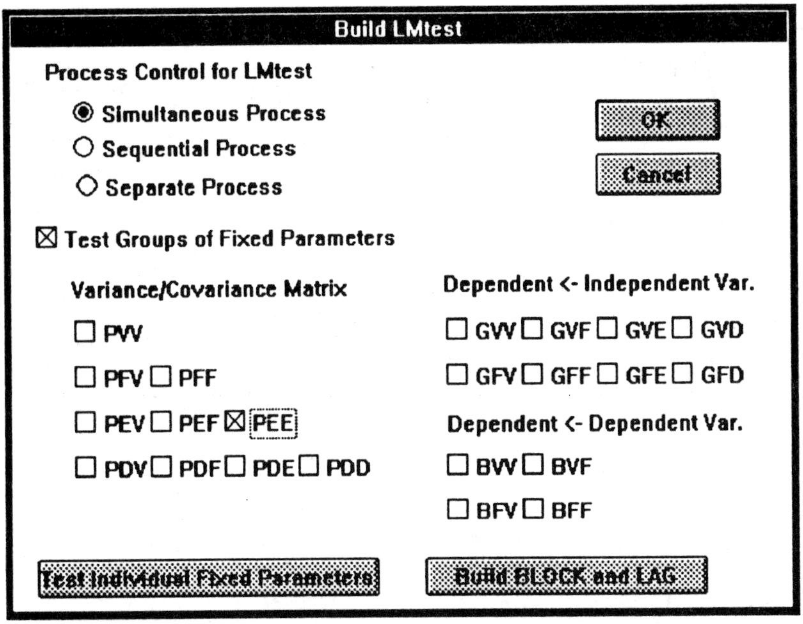

FIGURE 14.8. BUILD LMTEST Dialog Box

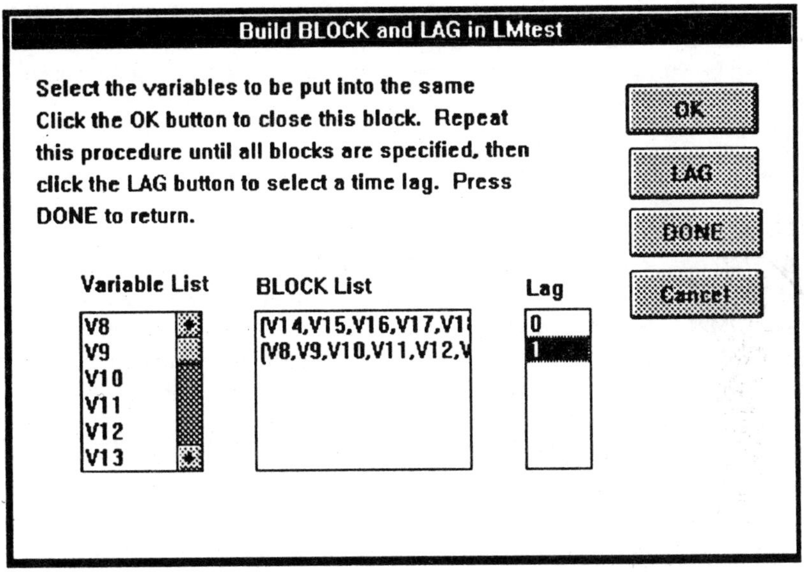

FIGURE 14.9. BUILD BLOCK AND LAG IN LMTEST Dialog Box

would result in nonsense parameters. The **BLOCK** feature of the LM Test is designed to assure that such backward paths do not occur. In the present application, however, all possible structural paths have been specified, thereby obviating the possibility of alternate paths. Nonetheless, correlated errors across time, as a consequence of test-retest effects, are highly likely. Thus we need to block each set of variables within each time frame.

Essentially, specification of the **BLOCK** command (a) allows you to group variables into blocks, (b) partitions the matrices specified in **SET**[5] into smaller matrices for purposes of analyses, and then (c) specifies the direction of possible paths. Only V and F variables can be listed as blocks. Nonetheless, EQS will search for Es and Ds and group them appropriately in accordance with their corresponding V- and F-type variables. Turning to the **BLOCK** dialog box in Figure 14.9, you will see (only partially) that the variables have been grouped into two blocks, each consistent with one of two time points. This was done by first selecting from the **VARIABLE LIST** all variables comprising the first block (V14-V19) and then clicking on **OK**; the program then automatically grouped and placed the variables in the **BLOCK List,** as shown in Figure 14.9. The process was then repeated for the second block.

Once the blocks are defined, and if you wish to incorporate the **LAG** option, you then click on the **LAG** button. By default, the program inserted 0 and 1 in the **LAG LIST**. (Possible values are b-1, where b = number of blocks.) **LAG=0** means that only variables within the same block will be selected; **LAG=1,** that only paths or covariances across adjacent paths will be evaluated.[6] Because only effects across two time points are of interest here, we select "1" as shown in Figure 14.9. After completing these specifications, we click on **DONE**.[7]

Building in the RETEST Option

Unique to the Windows version of EQS is the possibility of linking the **RETEST** option to the **LMTEST.** Recall from Application 2 (Chapter 4) that **RETEST** makes possible the insertion of final estimated values from the **/EQUATION, /VARIANCE,** and **/COVARIANCE** paragraphs of a completed EQS run into a new file that can be submitted, with only minor modifications, for a subsequent EQS run. To invoke **RETEST,** you first click on **BUILD EQS** from the Main Window and then select the **RETEST** option. The **BUILD PRINT OPTIONS** dialog box will appear, as shown in Figure 14.10.

The linkage of **RETEST** to **LMTEST** further extends its time-saving capabilities. Specifically, by selecting the **LMTEST** option, as shown here in the dialog box, **RETEST** takes parameters that are significant in the multivariate LM Test and adds them automatically to the equations, variances,

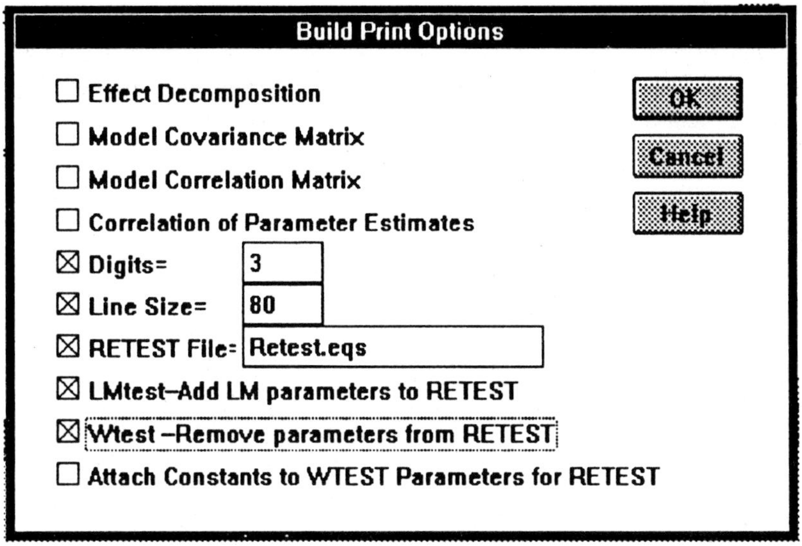

Build Print Options

☐ Effect Decomposition
☐ Model Covariance Matrix
☐ Model Correlation Matrix
☐ Correlation of Parameter Estimates
☒ Digits=   3
☒ Line Size=   80
☒ RETEST File= Retest.eqs
☒ LMtest–Add LM parameters to RETEST
☒ Wtest –Remove parameters from RETEST
☐ Attach Constants to WTEST Parameters for RETEST

OK
Cancel
Help

FIGURE 14.10. BUILD PRINT OPTIONS Dialog Box

and covariances as needed. These newly added parameters are easily identified because, unlike the model parameters from the original run that will have
optimal estimates associated with them, the **LMTEST** parameters will have
only an asterisk next to them. Of course, it goes without saying that you
should scrutinize these parameters closely, accepting only those that make
sense to the model under study. All other information in the dialog box was
provided by the program automatically. We now click on the **OK** button.

Once an input file is completed using the **BUILD EQS** option, the
WORK.EQS file is available to you to edit as you see fit. With respect to
the present file, as mentioned earlier, I altered the factor-loading specifications such that the first of each pair of loadings for a particular factor was
fixed to 1.0. At this point, then, the input file is complete and we are ready
to test our hypothesized model. Let's now examine the findings.

TESTING THE HYPOTHESIZED MODEL

Running EQS/Windows

To run an EQS job using EQS/Windows, you once again return to the
BUILD EQS window, this time selecting **RUN EQS/386** from the drop-
down menu. You will then be presented with a **SAVE AS** dialog box that asks
whether you wish to retain the filename of **WORK.EQS** or to replace it with

another one of your choice. If you wish to replace it (for practical reasons, it is always wise to do so), simply type in the new name and then click **OK**. At this point, you will see a series of screens indicating that EQS is running the job. These are the same screens that you see when running the DOS version of the program (which can be done without using Windows).

EQS/Windows Output File

When the job has been completed, you will see the **OPEN** dialog box as shown in Figure 14.11; it parallels the one presented in Chapter 12 (Figure 12.2) that illustrated the listing of files grouped according to their type. In Figure 12.2, we saw examples of data system (***.ESS**.) and external data (***.DAT**) files. In Figure 14.11, we see a listing of output (***.OUT**) files. The current job is highlighted and appears in the rectangle at the top of, but separated from the remaining output files; as you will note, I have changed the **WORK.EQS** file to correspond with the input filename (i.e., **SCCAUSEI.OUT**).

To retrieve the output file, we click on the **OK** button in the **OPEN** dialog box; the top portion of the file is shown in Figure 14.12. So that you may have a more complete picture of the model input file, this portion of the output is presented separately in Table 14.1.

A couple of points related to this file are perhaps worthy of note. First, under the **/SPECIFICATIONS** paragraph, you will see **DATA='C:\EQS WIN\NOX.ESS'**; (line 4). This statement indicates that the data are located in a file called **NOX.ESS,** which is in the **EQSWIN** directory and resides on the **C** disk drive. (During the EQS run, the program actually uses a file called **EQSWORK&.DAT,** which is a copy of the **NOX.ESS** file with all extraneous information deleted.)[8] The second point to note is that the disturbance term for Factor 6 (D6, line 46) has been fixed to a value of .001; this specification was based on previous knowledge of the data and the hypothesized model. Finally, you will note in line 63 that the Wald Test, as well as the LM Test, have been included in the **/PRINT** paragraph. These options modify the new retest file based on these test results.

Pertinent results from this initial EQS run are presented in Table 14.2. Before discussing the fit of the hypothesized model, I wish first to draw your attention to the **Iterative Summary** and the warning messages that follow. The fact that the program reached the default limit of 30 iterations indicates clearly that it had difficulty in the minimization process; hence the user is warned that the estimates may not be optimal. Whenever this situation is encountered, it is nearly always a consequence of poor start values. Provided with values closer to the estimates, convergence is usually attained fairly

Open
File Name:
sccausei.out
frbdif1f.out
nox.out
sccausei.out
work.out
Directories:
c:\eqswin
c:\
eqswin
OK
Cancel
Read Only
List Files of Type:
Output Files(*.OUT)
Drives:
c:

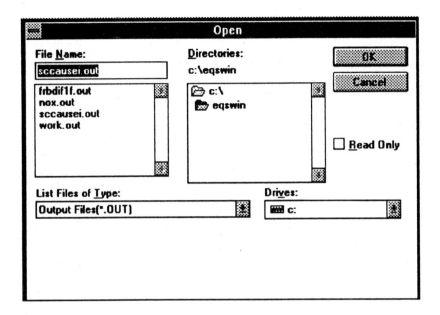

FIGURE 14.11. OPEN FILE Dialog Box

rapidly. Because our initial model included the **RETEST** option, we can certainly accommodate this modification very easily.

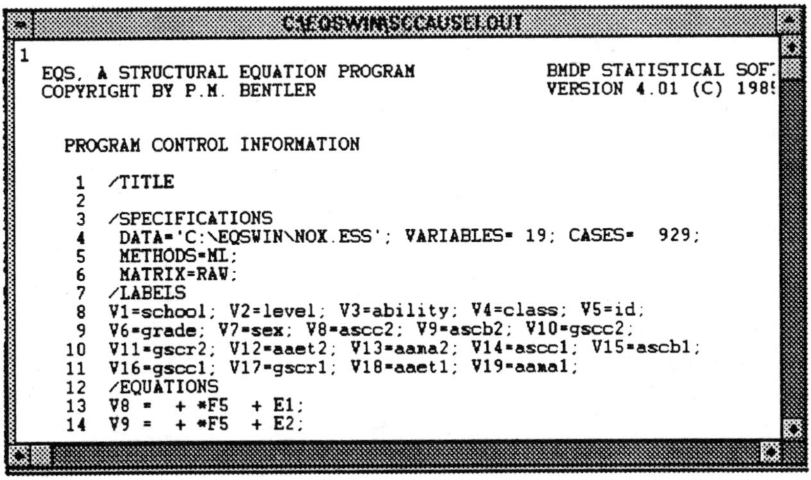

C:\EQSWIN\SCCAUSEI.OUT
1
EQS, A STRUCTURAL EQUATION PROGRAM BMDP STATISTICAL SOF
COPYRIGHT BY P.M. BENTLER VERSION 4.01 (C) 198
PROGRAM CONTROL INFORMATION
1 /TITLE
2
3 /SPECIFICATIONS
4 DATA='C:\EQSWIN\NOX.ESS'; VARIABLES= 19; CASES= 929;
5 METHODS=ML;
6 MATRIX=RAW;
7 /LABELS
8 V1=school; V2=level; V3=ability; V4=class; V5=id;
9 V6=grade; V7=sex; V8=ascc2; V9=ascb2; V10=gscc2;
10 V11=gscr2; V12=aaet2; V13=aama2; V14=ascc1; V15=ascb1;
11 V16=gscc1; V17=gscr1; V18=aaet1; V19=aama1;
12 /EQUATIONS
13 V8 = + *F5 + E1;
14 V9 = + *F5 + E2;

FIGURE 14.12. EQS Output File for Hypothesized Model

TABLE 14.1. EQS Input File: Initially Hypothesized Model of Self-Concept

```
 1   /TITLE
 2    SC/AA Causal Predominance
 3   /SPECIFICATIONS
 4    DATA='C:\EQSWIN\NOX.ESS'; VARIABLES= 19; CASES=  929;
 5    METHODS=ML;
 6    MATRIX=RAW;
 7   /LABELS
 8   V1=school; V2=level; V3=ability; V4=class; V5=id;
 9   V6=grade; V7=sex; V8=ascc2; V9=ascb2; V10=gscc2;
10   V11=gscr2; V12=aaet2; V13=aama2; V14=ascc1; V15=ascb1;
11   V16=gscc1; V17=gscr1; V18=aaet1; V19=aama1;
12   /EQUATIONS
13   V8  = +    F5  + E8;
14   V9  = +   *F5  + E9;
15   V10 = +    F4  + E10;
16   V11 = +   *F4  + E11;
17   V12 = +    F6  + E12;
18   V13 = +   *F6  + E13;
19   V14 = +    F2  + E14;
20   V15 = +   *F2  + E15;
21   V16 = +    F1  + E16;
22   V17 = +   *F1  + E17;
23   V18 = +    F3  + E18;
24   V19 = +   *F3  + E19;
25   F4  = +   *F2  + *F3  + D4;
26   F5  = +   *F1  + *F3  + D5;
27   F6  = +   *F1  + *F2  + D6;
28   /VARIANCES
29   F1  = *;
30   F2  = *;
31   F3  = *;
32   E8  = *;
33   E9  = *;
34   E10 = *;
35   E11 = *;
36   E12 = *;
37   E13 = *;
38   E14 = *;
39   E15 = *;
40   E16 = *;
41   E17 = *;
42   E18 = *;
43   E19 = *;
44   D4  = *;
45   D5  = *;
46   D6  = .001;
47   /COVARIANCES
48   F2,F1 = *;
49   F3,F2 = *;
50   F3,F1 = *;
51   /LMTEST
52   PROCESS=SIMULTANEOUS;
53   SET=PEE;
57   BLOCK=(V14,V15,V16,V17,V18,V19) (V8,V9,V10,V11,V12,V13);
58   LAG=1;
59   /PRINT
60   digit=3;
61   linesize =80;
62   RETEST='Retest.eqs';
63   lmtest=yes; wtest=yes;
64   /END
```

TABLE 14.2. Selected EQS Output: Initially Hypothesized Model of Self-Concept

GOODNESS OF FIT SUMMARY

INDEPENDENCE MODEL CHI-SQUARE =   7099.447 ON   66 DEGREES OF FREEDOM

INDEPENDENCE AIC =   6967.44740   INDEPENDENCE CAIC =   6582.39623
       MODEL AIC =   1618.50793   MODEL CAIC =   1350.13893

CHI-SQUARE =   1710.508 BASED ON   46 DEGREES OF FREEDOM
PROBABILITY VALUE FOR THE CHI-SQUARE STATISTIC IS LESS THAN 0.001
THE NORMAL THEORY RLS CHI-SQUARE FOR THIS ML SOLUTION IS   1488.948.

BENTLER-BONETT NORMED   FIT INDEX=   0.759
BENTLER-BONETT NONNORMED FIT INDEX=   0.660
COMPARATIVE FIT INDEX   =   0.763

ITERATIVE SUMMARY

ITERATION	PARAMETER ABS CHANGE	ALPHA	FUNCTION
1	8.107393	1.00000	21.59447
2	14.101622	0.50000	15.41556
3	8.212750	0.50000	14.98472
4	14.279476	0.50000	14.66997
5	60.322456	0.50000	12.96261
6	31.636658	0.25000	11.13567
7	22.123241	0.50000	9.64074
8	15.135922	1.00000	6.62535
9	7.856266	1.00000	5.08282
10	3.746217	1.00000	3.90081
11	3.469952	1.00000	2.57638
12	1.120544	1.00000	1.92047
13	0.462353	1.00000	1.86317
14	0.280536	1.00000	1.85064
15	0.174350	1.00000	1.84583
16	0.135097	1.00000	1.84444
17	0.093595	1.00000	1.84384
18	0.076929	1.00000	1.84356
19	0.057236	1.00000	1.84341
20	0.045493	1.00000	1.84333
21	0.034363	1.00000	1.84328
22	0.026986	1.00000	1.84326
23	0.020508	1.00000	1.84324
24	0.016116	1.00000	1.84323
25	0.012209	1.00000	1.84323
26	0.009626	1.00000	1.84322
27	0.007267	1.00000	1.84322
28	0.005752	1.00000	1.84322
29	0.004325	1.00000	1.84322
30	0.003438	1.00000	1.84322

****
****
 ** NOTE: DO NOT TRUST THIS OUTPUT. ITERATIVE PROCESS HAS NOT CONVERGED.
MAXIMUM NUMBER OF ITERATIONS WAS REACHED. **
 **
        **
 ** 30 ITERATIONS HAVE BEEN COMPLETED AND THE PROGRAM STOPPED. CHECK
PARAMETER IDENTIFICATION.
        **
 ** IF IDENTIFIED, USE THE UPDATED PARAMETERS TO START AGAIN.
        **
 **

(Continued)

TABLE 14.2. (Continued)

ULTIVARIATE LAGRANGE MULTIPLIER TEST BY SIMULTANEOUS PROCESS IN STAGE 1

PARAMETER SETS (SUBMATRICES) ACTIVE AT THIS STAGE ARE:

PEE

		CUMULATIVE MULTIVARIATE STATISTICS			UNIVARIATE INCREMENT	
STEP	PARAMETER	CHI-SQUARE	D.F.	PROBABILITY	CHI-SQUARE	PROBABILITY
1	E18,E12	571.689	1	0.000	571.689	0.000
2	E15,E9	901.718	2	0.000	330.028	0.000
3	E14,E8	987.955	3	0.000	86.238	0.000
4	E16,E10	1072.030	4	0.000	84.075	0.000
5	E19,E13	1134.607	5	0.000	62.577	0.000
6	E17,E11	1158.609	6	0.000	24.002	0.000
7	E16,E9	1177.916	7	0.000	19.307	0.000
8	E15,E8	1194.108	8	0.000	16.193	0.000
9	E19,E11	1210.268	9	0.000	16.160	0.000
10	E19,E10	1229.115	10	0.000	18.846	0.000
11	E18,E13	1243.532	11	0.000	14.418	0.000
12	E18,E8	1258.811	12	0.000	15.279	0.000
13	E15,E12	1270.152	13	0.000	11.341	0.001
14	E14,E10	1279.731	14	0.000	9.579	0.002
15	E16,E12	1287.798	15	0.000	8.068	0.005
16	E14,E12	1293.962	16	0.000	6.163	0.013
17	E15,E11	1300.055	17	0.000	6.094	0.014
18	E15,E10	1308.210	18	0.000	8.155	0.004

Turning now to the goodness-of-fit statistics, we see that with a CFI of .76, the model is most certainly misspecified. For clues related to possible areas of misfit, let's review the LM Test multivariate statistics (see Table 14.2). Interestingly, the first five parameters all represent error covariances across time, and all account for a substantial degree of misfit in the model. That error terms associated with these five measures should correlate over time is perfectly reasonable because they are likely indicators of memory carryover effects.

Given both the convergence warning and findings of poor fit, the model was respecified to include start values derived from the **RETEST** file and the five error covariances noted above. Before we examine these results, however, let's take a quick look at this **RETEST** file as shown in Table 14.3.

As mentioned earlier, when the **LMTEST** option is included in **RE-TEST**, the misspecified parameters are automatically added to the file. In reviewing this file, these parameters are easy to spot because they do not have any start values associated with them; all other originally specified parameters do. As you will note also, the misspecified parameters are not ranked according to their LM χ^2 values. Rather, they are ordered according to the first E variable, which is E10. In modifying the input file to include

TABLE 14.3. EQS Retest Output: Initially Hypothesized Model of Self-Concept

```
!
! Following lists are generated from RETEST
!
/EQUATION
    V8  =  1.000 F5   +   1.000 E8;
    V9  =  4.671*F5   +   1.000 E9;
    V10 =  1.000 F4   +   1.000 E10;
    V11 =  1.193*F4   +   1.000 E11;
    V12 =  1.000 F6   +   1.000 E12;
    V13 =  1.581*F6   +   1.000 E13;
    V14 =  1.000 F2   +   1.000 E14;
    V15 =  3.771*F2   +   1.000 E15;
    V16 =  1.000 F1   +   1.000 E16;
    V17 =  1.070*F1   +   1.000 E17;
    V18 =  1.000 F3   +   1.000 E18;
    V19 =  2.059*F3   +   1.000 E19;
    F4  =  3.841*F2   +   -.512*F3   +   1.000 D4;
    F5  =   .143*F1   +    .140*F3   +   1.000 D5;
    F6  = -1.718*F1   +   8.893*F2   +   1.000 D6;
/VARIANCES
      F1=  10.756*;
      F2=   1.100*;
      F3=  22.570*;
      E8=   2.316*;
      E9=   8.881*;
     E10=   7.279*;
     E11=   9.967*;
     E12=  77.827*;
     E13=  34.696*;
     E14=   2.279*;
     E15=   9.753*;
     E16=   8.767*;
     E17=   9.417*;
     E18=  48.278*;
     E19=  19.662*;
      D4=   5.129*;
      D5=    .065*;
      D6=    .001 ;
/COVARIANCES
      F2,F1  =   2.692*;
      F3,F1  =   3.259*;
      F3,F2  =   4.170*;
     E10,E8  =      *;
     E12,E8  =      *;
     E13,E9  =      *;
     E14,E8  =      *;
    E14,E10  =      *;
    E14,E12  =      *;
     E15,E8  =      *;
     E15,E9  =      *;
    E16,E10  =      *;
    E16,E11  =      *;
    E16,E12  =      *;
    E16,E14  =      *;
    E17,E10  =      *;
     E18,E8  =      *;
    E18,E12  =      *;
    E18,E13  =      *;
    E18,E14  =      *;
    E18,E15  =      *;
     E19,E9  =      *;
    E19,E11  =      *;
    E19,E13  =      *;
      D6,D4  =      *;
/END
```

TABLE 14.4. Selected EQS Output: Reestimated Model of Self-Concept

GOODNESS OF FIT SUMMARY

INDEPENDENCE MODEL CHI-SQUARE =   7099.447 ON   66 DEGREES OF FREEDOM

INDEPENDENCE AIC =   6967.44740   INDEPENDENCE CAIC =   6582.39623
        MODEL AIC =   260.53880   MODEL CAIC =   21.34034

CHI-SQUARE =   342.539 BASED ON   41 DEGREES OF FREEDOM
PROBABILITY VALUE FOR THE CHI-SQUARE STATISTIC IS LESS THAN 0.001
THE NORMAL THEORY RLS CHI-SQUARE FOR THIS ML SOLUTION IS   334.118.
BENTLER-BONETT NORMED   FIT INDEX=   0.952
BENTLER-BONETT NONNORMED FIT INDEX=   0.931
COMPARATIVE FIT INDEX   =   0.957

ITERATIVE SUMMARY

ITERATION	PARAMETER ABS CHANGE	ALPHA	FUNCTION
1	3.245426	1.00000	0.58575
2	0.368888	1.00000	0.38001
3	0.228082	1.00000	0.37267
4	0.119114	1.00000	0.36952
5	0.045406	1.00000	0.36918
6	0.027439	1.00000	0.36913
7	0.007872	1.00000	0.36912
8	0.005017	1.00000	0.36912
9	0.001524	1.00000	0.36912
10	0.000871	1.00000	0.36912

CONSTRUCT EQUATIONS WITH STANDARD ERRORS AND TEST STATISTICS

F4   =F4 =   5.017*F2   + -.851*F3   + 1.000 D4
                .502   .105
              10.000   -8.100

F5   =F5 =   .116*F1   + .152*F3   + 1.000 D5
                .012   .014
               9.308   10.952

F6   =F6 =   -1.129*F1   + 7.693*F2   + 1.000 D6
                .132   .619
              -8.526   12.433

these start values and the five error covariances, it was of course necessary to first delete all additional parameters provided by the LM Test. Pertinent results from the respecified model are presented in Table 14.4.

Note first of all that with the addition of start values, the solution converged in only 10 iterations. With respect to goodness of fit, we can see that the specification of error covariances over the two time points certainly led to a highly significant difference in overall fit ($\Delta\chi^2_{(5)} = 1367.97$) and a very substantial CFI value of .96. Finally, it should be noted that estimated values for the path coefficients of interest are all statistically significant.

Given these findings, then, we can now proceed in testing for causal predominance. Specifically, we test the hypothesis that academic achievement is causally predominant over academic self-concept (i.e., AA causes ASC, rather than the reverse). This is accomplished by first estimating a model in which the competing paths are constrained equal and then comparing the fit of this model with one in which the same paths are specified as free. The difference in χ^2 values between the two models provides the basis for statistical significance, and the size of the parameter estimates determines which of the paths is causally dominant.

A review of Figure 14.1 will confirm that the testing of this hypothesis involved the comparison of paths F6,F2 with F5,F3. The difference in χ^2 between the two estimated models was highly significant ($\Delta\chi^2_{(1)} = 213.43$). Because the estimated path leading from academic self-concept to academic achievement was higher than the one leading from academic achievement to academic self-concept (7.69 vs. 0.15, respectively), we conclude that in contrast to the stated hypothesis, academic self-concept is causally predominant over academic achievement.

Applications Related to Other Disciplines

BUSINESS: Thorendou, P. (1993). A test of reciprocal causality for absenteeism. *Journal of Organizational Behavior, 14,* 269-290.

EDUCATION: Reynolds, A. J., & Walberg, H. J. (1991). A structural model of science achievement. *Journal of Educational Psychology, 83,* 97-107.

MEDICINE: Newcomb, M. D., & Bentler, P. M. (1987). The impact of late adolescent substance use on young adult health status and utilization of health services: A structural equation model over four years. *Social Science and Medicine, 24,* 71-82.

Notes

1. It is important to note that analyses for the original study were based on the LISREL IV program (Jöreskog & Sörbom, 1978); as a result, some of the techniques used at that time are now obsolete and have been replaced by a more sophisticated approach.

2. If you have a large block of cells in which you wish to insert asterisks, an easier way to mark them is to use the point-and-drag mouse option, which is fully described in the EQS/ Windows *User's Guide.*

3. Another way of accomplishing this is to double-click on selected asterisks in the **EQUATIONS** (or **VARIANCES/COVARIANCES**) dialog box; each asterisk is then replaced by a "1."

4. Some readers might wonder why I did not target misspecified factor-loading parameters by clicking on the GVF button. In principle, this would be unwise because there are only two indicators per factor, and the incorporation of cross-loadings would probably lead to an empirically underidentified model (see Bentler & Chou, 1987). Nonetheless, had I selected **GVF,** EQS would have automatically fixed LM χ^2s to 0.0 for parameters that could not be freed.

5. Recall that **SET** is the standard command of **LMTEST** that specifies which submatrices of parameter matrices are eligible for evaluation.

6. It is easy to see that with models involving several time waves, the **LAG** option can be used very effectively.

7. For a more detailed description of the LM Test in general, and the **BLOCK** and **LAG** functions in particular, readers are referred to both the EQS manual and the EQS/Windows *User's Guide*.

8. In the initial version of EQS/Windows, there were two lines of text pertaining to the data; the first one identified the original data source (**NOX.ESS**), the second one the working data file (**EQSWORK.EQS**).

References

Akaike, H. (1987). Factor analysis and AIC. *Psychometrika, 52,* 317-332.

Anderson, J. C., & Gerbing, D. W. (1988). Structural equation modeling in practice: A review and recommended two-step approach. *Psychological Bulletin, 103,* 411-423.

Bacharach, S. B., Bauer, S. C., & Conley, S. (1986). Organizational analysis of stress: The case of elementary and secondary schools. *Work and Occupations, 13,* 7-32.

Bagozzi, R. P. (1991). Structural equation models in marketing research. In W. D. Neal (Ed.), *First annual advanced research techniques forum* (pp. 335-379). Chicago: American Marketing Association.

Bagozzi, R. P., & Yi, Y. (1990). Assessing method variance in multitrait-multimethod matrices: The case of self-reported affect and perceptions at work. *Journal of Applied Psychology, 75,* 547-560.

Beck, A. T., Ward, C. H., Mendelson, M., Mock, J., & Erbaugh, J. (1961). An inventory for measuring depression. *Archives of General Psychiatry, 4,* 561-571.

Benson, J., & Bandalos, D. L. (1992). Second-order confirmatory factor analysis of the Reactions to Tests Scale with cross-validation. *Multivariate Behavioral Research, 27,* 459-487.

Bentler, P. M. (1978). The independence of theory, methodology, and empirical data: Causal modeling as an approach to construct validity. In D. B. Kandel (Ed.), *Longitudinal research on drug use: Empirical findings and methodological issues* (pp. 267-302). New York: John Wiley.

Bentler, P. M. (1980). Multivariate analysis with latent variables: Causal modeling. *Annual Review of Psychology, 31,* 419-456.

Bentler, P. M. (1983). Some contributions to efficient statistics for structural models: Specification and estimation of moment structures. *Psychometrika, 48,* 493-517.

Bentler, P. M. (1988). Causal modeling via structural equation systems. In J. R. Nesselroade & R. B. Cattell (Eds.), *Handbook of multivariate experimental psychology* (2nd ed., pp. 317-335). New York: Plenum.

Bentler, P. M. (1989). *EQS: Structural equations program manual.* Los Angeles: BMDP Statistical Software.

Bentler, P. M. (1990a). Comparative fit indexes in structural models. *Psychological Bulletin, 107,* 238-246.

Bentler, P. M. (1990b). Fit indexes, Lagrange Multipliers, constraint changes, and incomplete data in structural models. *Multivariate Behavioral Research, 25,* 163-172.

Bentler, P. M. (1992a). *EQS: Structural equations program manual.* Los Angeles: BMDP Statistical Software.

Bentler, P. M. (1992b). On the fit of models to covariances and methodology to the *Bulletin. Psychological Bulletin, 112,* 400-404.

Bentler, P. M., & Bonett, D. G. (1980). Significance tests and goodness of fit in the analysis of covariance structures. *Psychological Bulletin, 88,* 588-606.

Bentler, P. M., & Bonett, D. G. (1987). This week's citation classic. *Current Contents* [Institute for Scientific Information], *9,* 16.

Bentler, P. M., & Chou, C. P. (1987). Practical issues in structural modeling. *Sociological Methods & Research, 16,* 78-117.

Bentler, P. M., & Dijkstra, T. (1985). Efficient estimation via linearization in structural models. In P. R. Krishnaiah (Ed.), *Multivariate analysis VI* (pp. 9-42). Amsterdam: North-Holland.

Bentler, P. M., & Stein, J. A. (1992). Structural equation models in medical research. *Statistical Methods in Medical Research, 1,* 159-181.

Bentler, P. M., & Weeks, D. G. (1979). Interrelations among models for the analysis of moment structures. *Multivariate Behavioral Research, 14,* 169-185.

Bentler, P. M., & Weeks, D. G. (1980). Linear structural equations with latent variables. *Psychometrika, 45,* 289-308.

Bentler, P. M., & Wu, E.J.C. (1993). *EQS/Windows User's Guide: Version 4.* Los Angeles: BMDP Statistical Software.

Berkane, M., & Bentler, P. M. (1988). Estimation of contamination parameters and identification of outliers in multivariate data. *Sociological Methods & Research, 17,* 55-64.

Bollen, K. A. (1989). *Structural equations with latent variables.* New York: John Wiley.

Bourque, P., & Beaudette, D. (1982). Étude psychometrique du questionnaire de depression de Beck aupres d'un echantillon d'étudiants universitaires francophones. *Revue Canadienne des Sciences du Comportement, 14,* 211-221.

Bozdogan, H. (1987). Model selection and Akaike's information criteria (AIC): The general theory and its analytical extensions. *Psychometrika, 52,* 345-370.

Breckler, S. J. (1990). Applications of covariance structure modeling in psychology: Cause for concern? *Psychological Bulletin, 107,* 260-273.

Browne, M. W., & Cudeck, R. (1989). Single sample cross-validation indices for covariance structures. *Multivariate Behavioral Research, 24,* 445-455.

Byrne, B. M. (1986). Self-concept/academic achievement relations: An investigation of dimensionality, stability, and causality. *Canadian Journal of Behavioural Science, 18,* 173-186.

Byrne, B. M. (1988a). Measuring adolescent self-concept: Factorial validity and equivalency of the SDQ III across gender. *Multivariate Behavioral Research, 24,* 361-375.

Byrne, B. M. (1988b). The Self Description Questionnaire III: Testing for equivalent factorial validity across ability. *Educational and Psychological Measurement, 48,* 397-406.

Byrne, B. M. (1988c). Adolescent self-concept, ability grouping, and social comparison: Reexamining academic track differences in high school. *Youth and Society, 20,* 46-67.

Byrne, B. M. (1989). *A primer of LISREL: Basic applications and programming for confirmatory factor analytic models.* New York: Springer Verlag.

Byrne, B. M. (1991). The Maslach Inventory: Validating factorial structure and invariance across intermediate, secondary, and university educators. *Multivariate Behavioral Research, 26,* 583-605.

Byrne, B. M. (July, 1992). *The Maslach Inventory: Testing for invariant factorial structure across gender for elementary and secondary teachers.* Paper presented at the International

Congress of Psychology, Brussels. (ERIC Document Reproduction Service Microfiche No. TM019164)

Byrne, B. M. (in press). Burnout: Testing for the validity, replication, and invariance of causal structure across elementary, intermediate, and secondary teachers. *American Educational Research Journal*.

Byrne, B. M. (1993). The Maslach Inventory: Testing for factorial validity and invariance across elementary, intermediate, and secondary teachers. *Journal of Organizational and Occupational Psychology, 66*, 197-212.

Byrne, B. M., & Baron, P. (1993). The Beck Depression Inventory: Testing and cross-validating a hierarchical factor structure for nonclinical adolescents. *Measurement and Evaluation in Counseling and Development, 26*, 164-178.

Byrne, B. M., & Baron, P. (in press). Measuring adolescent depression: Tests of equivalent factorial structure for English and French versions of the Beck Depression Inventory. *Applied Psychology: An International Review*.

Byrne, B. M., Baron, P., & Campbell, T. L. (1993). Measuring adolescent depression: Factorial validity and invariance of the Beck Depression Inventory across gender. *Journal of Research on Adolescence, 3*, 127-143.

Byrne, B. M., Baron, P., & Campbell, T. L. (in press). The Beck Depression Inventory (French Version): Testing for gender-invariant factorial structure for nonclinical adolescents. *Journal of Adolescent Research*.

Byrne, B. M., & Goffin, R. D. (1993). Modeling MTMM data from additive and multiplicative covariance structures: An audit of construct validity concordance. *Multivariate Behavioral Research, 28*, 67-96.

Byrne, B. M., & Schneider, B. H. (1988). Perceived Competence Scale for Children: Testing for factorial validity and invariance across age and ability. *Applied Measurement in Education, 1*, 171-187.

Byrne, B. M., & Shavelson, R. J. (1986). On the structure of adolescent self-concept. *Journal of Educational Psychology, 78*, 474-481.

Byrne, B. M., & Shavelson, R. J. (1987). Adolescent self-concept: Testing the assumption of equivalent structure across gender. *American Educational Research Journal, 24*, 365-385.

Byrne, B. M., Shavelson, R. J., & Marsh, H. W. (1992). Multigroup comparisons in self-concept research: Reexamining the assumption of equivalent structure and measurement. In T. M. Brinthaupt & R. P. Lipka (Eds.), *The self: Definitional and methodological issues* (pp. 172-203). Albany: State University of New York Press.

Byrne, B. M., Shavelson, R. J., & Muthén, B. (1989). Testing for the equivalence of factor covariance and mean structures: The issue of partial measurement invariance. *Psychological Bulletin, 105*, 456-466.

Campbell, D. T., & Fiske, D. W. (1959). Convergent and discriminant validation by the multitrait-multimethod matrix. *Psychological Bulletin, 56*, 81-105.

Chou, C.-P., Bentler, P. M., & Satorra, A. (1991). Scaled test statistics and robust standard errors for nonnormal data in covariance structure analysis. *British Journal of Mathematical and Statistical Psychology, 44*, 347-357.

Cliff, N. (1983). Some cautions concerning the application of causal modeling methods. *Multivariate Behavioral Research, 18*, 115-126.

Comrey, A. L. (1992). *A first course in factor analysis*. Hillsdale, NJ: Lawrence Erlbaum.

Cudeck, R. (1989). Analysis of correlation matrices using covariance structure models. *Psychological Bulletin, 105*, 317-327.

Cudeck, R., & Browne, M. W. (1983). Cross-validation of covariance structures. *Multivariate Behavioral Research, 18*, 147-167.

Dijkstra, T. K. (1992). On statistical inference with parameter estimates on the boundary of parameter space. *British Journal of Mathematical and Statistical Psychology, 45*, 289-309.

Dillon, W. R., Kumar, A., & Mulani, N. (1987). Offending estimates in covariance structure analysis: Comments on the causes of, and solution to Heywood cases. *Psychological Bulletin, 101*, 126-135.

Fornell, C. (1982). *A second generation of multivariate analysis Vol. 1. Methods.* New York: Praeger.

Francis, D. J., Fletcher, J. M., & Rourke, B. P. (1988). Discriminant validity of lateral sensorimotor tests in children. *Journal of Clinicial and Experimental Neuropsychology, 10*, 779-799.

Gerbing, D. W., & Anderson, J. C. (1984). On the meaning of within-factor correlated measurement errors. *Journal of Consumer Research, 11*, 572-580.

Gerbing, D. W., & Anderson, J. C. (1987). Improper solutions in the analysis of covariance structures: Their interpretability and a comparison of alternate respecifications. *Psychometrika, 52*, 99-111.

Gerbing, D. W., & Anderson, J. C. (1993). Monte Carlo evaluations of goodness-of-fit indices for structural equation models. In K. A. Bollen & J. S. Long (Eds.), *Testing structural equation models* (pp. 40-65). Newbury Park, CA: Sage.

Gorsuch, R. L. (1983). *Factor analysis.* Hillsdale, NJ: Lawrence Erlbaum.

Hayduk, L. A. (1987). *Structural equation modeling with LISREL: Essentials and advances.* Baltimore, MD: Johns Hopkins University Press.

Hu, L.-T., Bentler, P. M., & Kano, Y. (1992). Can test statistics in covariance structure analysis be trusted? *Psychological Bulletin, 112*, 351-362.

Jöreskog, K. G. (1971). Simultaneous factor analysis in several populations. *Psychometrika, 36*, 409-426.

Jöreskog, K. G., (1993). Testing structural equation models. In K. A. Bollen & J. S. Long (Eds.), *Testing structural equation models* (pp. 294-316). Newbury Park, CA: Sage.

Jöreskog, K. G., & Sörbom, D. (1978). *LISREL IV's user's guide.* Chicago: National Educational Resources.

Jöreskog, K. G., & Sörbom, D. (1988). *LISREL 7: A guide to the program and applications.* Chicago: SPSS Inc.

Jöreskog, K. G., & Sörbom, D. (1993). *New features in LISREL 8.* Chicago: Scientific Software.

Kenny, D. A. (1979). *Correlation and causality.* New York: John Wiley.

Kerlinger, F. N. (1984). *Liberalism and conservatism: The nature and structure of social attitudes.* Hillsdale, NJ: Lawrence Erlbaum.

Leiter, M. P. (1991). Coping patterns as predictors of burnout: The function of control and escapist coping patterns. *Journal of Organizational Behavior, 12*, 123-144.

Loehlin, J. C. (1992). *Latent variable models: An introduction to factor, path, & structural analyses.* Hillsdale, NJ: Lawrence Erlbaum.

Long, J. S. (1983a). *Confirmatory factor analysis.* Newbury Park, CA: Sage.

Long, J. S. (1983b). *Covariance structure models: An introduction to LISREL.* Newbury Park, CA: Sage.

MacCallum, R. C. (1986). Specification searches in covariance structure modeling. *Psychological Bulletin, 100*, 107-120.

MacCallum, R. C., Roznowski, M., & Necowitz, L. B. (1992). Model modifications in covariance structure analysis: The problem of capitalization on chance. *Psychological Bulletin, 111*, 490-504.

Mardia, K. V. (1970). Measures of multivariate skewness and kurtosis with applications. *Biometrika, 57*, 519-530.

Mardia, K. V. (1974). Applications of some measures of multivariate skewness and kurtosis in testing normality and robustness studies. *Sankhva, B36*, 115-128.

Marsh, H. W., Balla, J. R., & McDonald, R. P. (1988). Goodness-of-fit indexes in confirmatory factor analysis: The effect of sample size. *Psychological Bulletin, 103*, 391-410.

Marsh, H. W., & O'Neill, R. (1984). Self Description Questionnaire III: The construct validity of multidimensional self-concept ratings by late adolescents. *Journal of Educational Measurement, 21*, 153-174.

Maslach, C., & Jackson, S. E. (1981). *Maslach Burnout Inventory manual*. Palo Alto, CA: Consulting Psychologists Press.

Maslach, C., & Jackson, S. E. (1986). *Maslach Burnout Inventory manual* (2nd ed.). Palo Alto, CA: Consulting Psychologists Press. .

McDonald, R. P., & Marsh, H. W. (1990). Choosing a multivariate model: Noncentrality and goodness of fit. *Psychological Bulletin, 107*, 247-255.

Mulaik, S. A. (1972). *The foundations of factor analysis*. New York: McGraw-Hill.

Muthén, B., & Christoffersson, A. (1981). Simultaneous factor analysis of dichotomous variables in several groups. *Psychometrika, 46*, 407-419.

Muthén, B., Kaplan, D., & Hollis, M. (1987). Structural equation modeling for data that are not missing completely at random. *Psychometrika, 51*, 431-462.

Newcomb, M. D., Huba, G. T., & Bentler, P. M. (1986). Determinants of sexual and dating behaviors among adolescents. *Journal of Personality and Social Psychology, 50*, 428-438.

Pettegrew, L. S., & Wolf, G. E. (1982). Validating measures of teacher stress. *American Educational Research Journal, 19*, 373-396.

Rindskopf, D. (1984). Structural equation models: Empirical identification, Heywood cases, and related problems. *Sociological Methods and Research, 13*, 109-119.

Rindskopf, D., & Rose, T. (1988). Some theory and applications of confirmatory second-order factor analysis. *Multivariate Behavioral Research, 23*, 51-67.

Saris, W., & Stronkhorst, H. (1984). *Causal modelling: nonexperimental research: An introduction to the LISREL approach*. Amsterdam: Sociometric Research Foundation.

Satorra, A., & Bentler, P. M. (1988a). Scaling corrections for chi square statistics in covariance structure analysis. *American Statistical Association 1988 Proceedings of the Business and Economic Sections* (pp. 308-313). Alexandria, VA: American Statistical Association.

Satorra, A., & Bentler, P. M. (1988b). *Scaling corrections for statistics in covariance structure analysis*. (UCLA Statistics Series 2). Los Angeles: University of California at Los Angeles, Department of Psychology.

Schmitt, N., & Stults, D. M. (1986). Methodology review: Analysis of multitrait-multimethod matrices. *Applied Psychological Measurement, 10*, 1-22.

Shavelson, R. J., Hubner, J. J., & Stanton, G. C. (1976). Self-concept: Validation of construct interpretations. *Review of Educational Research, 46*, 407-441.

Soares, A. T., & Soares, L. M. (1979). *The Affective Perception Inventory: Advanced Level*. Trumbell, CT: ALSO.

Sörbom, D. (1989). Model modification. *Psychometrika, 54*, 371-384.

Tanaka, J. S. (1993). Multifaceted conceptions of fit in structural equation models. In J. A. Bollen & J. S. Long (Eds.), *Testing structural equation models* (pp. 10-39). Newbury Park, CA: Sage.

Tanaka, J. S., & Huba, G. J. (1984). Confirmatory hierarchical factor analyses of psychological distress measures. *Journal of Personality and Social Psychology, 46,* 621-635.

Wald, A. (1943). Tests of statistical hypotheses concerning several parameters when the number of observations is large. *Transactions of the American Mathematical Society, 54,* 426-482.

Widaman, K. F. (1985). Hierarchically tested covariance structure models for multitrait-multi-method data. *Applied Psychological Measurement, 9,* 1-26.

Wothke, W. (1993). Nonpositive definite matrices in structural modeling. In K. A. Bollen & J. S. Long (Eds.), *Testing structural equation models* (pp. 256-293). Newbury Park, CA: Sage.

Index

About the Author

BARBARA M. BYRNE is Associate Professor in the School of Psychology at the University of Ottawa, where she has taught since 1987. Subsequent to obtaining her Ph.D. in 1982 she worked as a Research Associate at the Child Study Centre, University of Ottawa; held a 1-year term appointment in the Department of Psychology at Carleton University; held a 2-year post-doctoral fellowship at the UCLA Graduate School of Education, where she worked with Richard J. Shavelson and consulted with Bengt Muthén; and recently spent a 6-month sabbatical as a visiting scholar in the Department of Psychology at UCLA where she worked with Peter M. Bentler. She has published more than 40 journal articles and five book chapters, most of which have involved applications of structural equation modeling; she is also the author of *A Primer of LISREL: Basic Applications and Programming for Confirmatory Factor Analytic Models*, an introductory book to the LISREL program. Her research interests focus on structural equation modeling, particularly as it relates to construct validation issues bearing on the structure and measurement of self-concept, burnout, and depression.